THE

MOUNT VERNON PAPERS.

BY

EDWARD EVERETT.

NEW YORK:
D. APPLETON AND COMPANY,
443 & 445 BROADWAY.
LONDON: 16 LITTLE BRITAIN.
M.DCCC.LX.

PREFACE.

The following correspondence sufficiently explains the origin of the "Mount Vernon Papers," and will serve as an appropriate introduction to the present volume.

LEDGER OFFICE, NEW YORK, *September* 2, 1858.

DEAR SIR :—I have a proposition of a somewhat peculiar nature to make to you : For the purchase of the Mount Vernon property you have done more than any other man, or, I might say, than all other men. To your eloquent appeal in its behalf is pre-eminently due the credit of the progress already made in that noble work, and the favor with which the subject is universally received by our people from one extremity of the land to the other. The heart of the public has naturally warmed towards you, on account of your well-timed and well-directed efforts to rescue the tomb of the Father of our country from neglect and dilapidation.

Knowing that you have been no less distinguished in literature than in official life, it has occurred to me that it might be as agreeable to you to aid the patriotic and benevolent enterprise which you have undertaken, by contributions to the columns of a weekly paper of unprecedented circulation, as by a public address. I have accordingly to propose that, if you will furnish to the NEW YORK LEDGER one original article a week, for one year, I will, immediately on receiving your assent to this proposition, place at your disposal, for the benefit of the Mount Vernon Association, my check for the sum of Ten Thousand Dollars.

I am aware, sir, that you are not in the habit of contributing to the columns of any periodical, and that you are fortunately so situated, financially, that no pecuniary reward offered to you for your own personal benefit, would induce you to deviate from your usual course; but your disinterested devotion to, and the deep interest you have taken in, the noble work to which I have referred, leads me to hope that, for the sake of aiding it, you may accept my proposition.

Very respectfully,

ROBERT BONNER,

Proprietor of the New York Ledger.

HON. EDWARD EVERETT.

BOSTON, 6 *November*, 1858.

DEAR SIR—Your letter of the 2d of September was placed in my hands on the 14th of that month. In consideration of your check for ten thousand dollars to be placed at my disposal for the benefit of the Mount Vernon Association, on the receipt of my letter accepting the offer, you propose to me to furnish an original article weekly for the "NEW YORK LEDGER" for one year.

This liberal offer has received my thoughtful consideration. I have been and am strongly tempted, on the one hand, to make this noble addition to the Mount Vernon Fund. On the other hand, among other grounds of hesitation, I have been afraid that I could not do justice to your liberality, without giving up more time to the preparation of the articles, than is consistent with other engagements and duties.

You are right in supposing that no pecuniary benefit accruing to myself would induce me to undertake the task; although the "financial situation" to which you allude is far less brilliant than you may have been led to think by exaggerated newspaper reports. I feel, however, that it is my duty not to forego this opportunity of adding so large a sum, at once, to the Mount Vernon fund, and I accept the offer. I will begin to furnish the articles, as soon as the immediate demands upon my time to fulfil some previous engagements, shall cease,—in the course of this month at furthest, —and I will continue them as far as possible weekly, making up at the end of the year for any omission in the regular supply.

They will, I hope, be received by you and the Public, with the indulgence usually extended to gratuitous labors in a meritorious cause.

I shall venture to call the articles thus furnished by me "The Mount Vernon Papers," scarcely daring to assume that honored name, which however may perhaps be permitted, as appropriately indicating the object for which they are prepared, and so excusing their imperfections.

I remain, Dear Sir, respectfully yours,

EDWARD EVERETT.

ROBERT BONNER, ESQ.

These papers are reprinted in the present form, with no other change than a few verbal corrections.

D. APPLETON & CO.

NEW YORK, *April*, 1860.

CONTENTS.

NUMBER ONE.

Reason for assuming the name of "Mount Vernon Papers"—Intended character of the subjects treated—Objects of the Ladies' Mount Vernon Association—Present state of Mount Vernon described in the introduction to Mr. Everett's address as delivered at New York—This description not made by way of reproach to the present proprietor—Necessity created by the crowd of visitors and the vandalism of some of them of selling the property—The purchase could only be made by private speculators—By Congress or the Legislature of Virginia—Or a patriotic association duly authorized to hold and manage the property, and the last mode in some respects the best—A feat of Ledgerdemain proposed in aid of the purchase. 1

NUMBER TWO.

CHRISTMAS.

Christmas day simultaneously celebrated in the Catholic and Protestant church—Not recognized by the Puritans, and why—Had degenerated into a disorderly Festival—Lord of Misrule—Extravagant revels in the sixteenth century—Mince pie and plum porridge—Baron of beef—Superstitions in the West of England relative to cattle—Anecdotes of the reformation of the calendar—Lord Chesterfield and Lord Macclesfield—Milton's beautiful ode to the nativity—Sir Walter Scott—Mr. Irving's charming description of the manner in which Christmas is celebrated in England at the present day. 11

NUMBER THREE.

THE HOUSE OF FRANKLIN.

Demolition of the house of Franklin in Boston—Why necessary—Crooked and narrow Streets of Boston and their origin—Great inconvenience from this cause and necessity of widening the Streets—Union Street widened and the house at the corner of Union and Hanover Streets, in which Franklin lived, necessarily removed—Description of the house and of its changes—Reasons against removing it to another place—All the original portions of it preserved. . . 21

NUMBER FOUR.

A SAFE ANSWER.

Reuben Mitchell's education—Becomes a partner in business with his master—Marries his daughter—Succeeds to the inheritance and business of his Father-in-law—Invests the profits of his business in real estate—Gradually purchases a large number of farms, many of which are unproductive—The number of his farms known only to himself—Curiosity of friends and the community on that subject—It becomes a topic of public remark—Measures adopted to solve the mystery—And the result. 32

NUMBER FIVE.

THE COMET.

Visit to the Observatory at Cambridge on the 6th of October—Description of the evening—Position of the Comet and its appearance through the Comet-seeker—Drawings by Mr. George P. Bond and Mr. Fette—Appearance of the Comet through the great refractor—Professor Lovering's experiments with the Polariscope—The Cluster in the Constellation Hercules—Remarks of Professor Nichol—The Penny Cyclopædia—History of Donati's Comet—Its period—Its rapid development—Progress of Astronomy in the United States—Remark of Gibbon—Comets no longer subjects of alarm—Beautiful reflections of Addison—Apostrophe to the Comet. 42

NUMBER SIX.

AN INCURSION INTO THE EMPIRE STATE.

PART I.

Extra clothing prepared for the journey and the result—Sandwiches as compared with a hasty dinner at an inn—Sixty cents saved and proposed investment for it—Six hours comfortably spent at Albany—Sleeping cars and the excellence of their arrangements—Unexpected obstacle to the enjoyment of their full benefit—Arrival at Canandaigua—The great land purchase of Gorham and Phelps. . 53

NUMBER SEVEN.

AN INCURSION INTO THE EMPIRE STATE.

PART II.

Unpromising weather at Canandaigua—History of the settlement—Oliver Phelps—Anecdote of Judge Gorham—Visit to Rochester—Reserved seats—Astonishing progress of the settlement—Return to Auburn—Change in the weather—From Auburn to Syracuse and detention there—Sleeping cars from Syracuse to Albany—Wakeful fellow-passengers—Collision at Albany—Kind-hearted Conductors—Return home. 62

NUMBER EIGHT.

THE PARABLE AGAINST PERSECUTION.

First published by Lord Kames in 1774 as having been communicated to him by Dr. Franklin—Soon discovered in Jeremy Taylor's Liberty of Prophesying—Next found in the dedication to the Senate of Hamburg of the Latin translation by George Genz of a Rabbinical work—Afterwards traced to the "Flower-Garden" of the celebrated Persian poet Saadi—Some account of Saadi—Possibly still to be found in some Jewish writer—Defence of Dr. Franklin against the charge of plagiarism—Quoted by Sydney Smith before the Mayor and Corporation of Bristol in 1829—The parable given entire from Dr. Franklin's works. . . 72

NUMBER NINE.

WASHINGTON'S DIARY.—ROBERTSON'S MINIATURES OF GENERAL AND MRS. WASHINGTON.

A portion of General Washington's Diary the property of Mr. J. Carson Brevoort—Recently printed for private circulation—Illness of Washington in the summer of 1789—Tour in the East partly to recruit his health—A considerable portion of the Diary relates to this tour—Washington consults his friends as to the expediency of the tour—Their opinion—Anecdote of Henry IV. of France, and his ministers Villeroi, Sully, and Jeannin—Robertson's miniature of Gen. Washington forms the vignette to this edition of the Diary—Account of Robertson—And his likenesses of General and Mrs. Washington—Colonel Trumbull's opinion—Photographic copies—Pine's portrait of Washington in Mr. Brevoort's possession—Gen. Washington's letter about it—An original letter of the Duke of Wellington in reply to a request to sit for his portrait to Mr. Inman. 81

NUMBER TEN.

WASHINGTON'S DIARY.

PART II.

Commencement of his tour to the Eastern States in 1789—First day's journey to Rye—Description of the road—The three different visits of Washington to this part of the country—Second day's journey to Fairfield and description of the road—Third day's journey to New Haven through Stratford and Milford—Description of New Haven—Sunday passed at New Haven—Fourth day's journey to Hartford through Wallingford and Middletown and incidents by the way—Fifth day's journey to Springfield and description of that place—Sixth day's journey to Spencer—Express received at Brookfield from Governor Hancock—Seventh day's journey to Worcester and arrangements for entering Boston—Eighth day's journey to Weston—Arrival at Boston on the ninth travelling day from New York. 89

NUMBER ELEVEN.

LOUIS NAPOLEON.—THREE PHASES IN HIS LIFE.

The Downfall of Napoleon the First—His escape from Elba in 1815—His second fall and retirement of his family at Rome—Louis Napoleon a boy at his father's table

—after a lapse of twenty-one years on trial for his life at Paris—His appearance and demeanor—His imprisonment at Ham—The revolution of February, 1848, and downfall of Louis Philippe—Re-appearance of Louis Napoleon as deputy, Prince, President, and Emperor—General character of his administration—Unscrupulous violence of the party press under Louis Philippe—His government overturned by leaders who aspired only to supplant his ministers—The Press of the United States. 98

NUMBER TWELVE.

WASHINGTON'S DIARY.

Washington's entrance into Boston involved, to some extent, a question of State rights —Major Russell's account inexact—General Washington's own account—Gov. Hancock abandons his ground and calls first on the President—Termination of the affair—Oratorio—Dinner at Fanueil Hall—The President requested to sit for his portrait—Postponement of the music at the Oratorio—Duck Manufactory described—Card Manufactory—Visit to the French vessels of War—Departure from Boston and continuation of the journey—Letter to Mr. Taft at Uxbridge. 106

NUMBER THIRTEEN.

ABBOTSFORD VISITED AND REVISITED.

PART I.

Invitation to Abbotsford—Arrival at Melrose—Ruins of Melrose hastily visited—Walk to Abbotsford—And reception there—Church at Selkirk—Walk to the Mushroom Park—Dogs in company, who accidentally start a hare—The house and grounds—Ornaments of the rooms—Reading of the Heart of Mid Lothian—Visit to Melrose—Manner of passing the time at Abbotsford—Charles Scott—Departure for Selkirk, but the London Mail Coach being full, return to Abbotsford—Sir Walter's fondness for animals, dogs and cats—Piper at dinner. . . 115

NUMBER FOURTEEN.

THE FOURTH OF MARCH, 1789.

Commencement of the present United States Government in New York seventy years ago this day—Sketch of the History of the promulgation and ratification of the Constitution—Delay in organizing the new Congress—Arrival of Washington at New York and his inauguration—Question as to the titles to be given to the President and Vice President—Amusing anecdote—Causes of the prevailing apathy—The general languor of the country a circumstance favorable to a peaceful revolution—No such revolution possible in highly prosperous times—Much owing to the disinterested patriotism of the revolutionary and constitutional leaders and especially Washington—Closing reflection. 124

NUMBER FIFTEEN.

ABBOTSFORD VISITED AND REVISITED.

PART II.

The family of Sir Walter Scott in 1818—His mode of life and study—Playful names given his daughters—A visitor recognized by the print of his horse's shoe before he was seen—Gratitude more affecting than ingratitude—German studies—Jesting anecdotes at table—A walk of a mile on your own land—Natural features of Abbotsford—Departure—Personal appearance of Sir Walter—Conversation—Opinions as to the authorship of the Waverley novels—Pecuniary embarrassments—Sad changes in the family—Visit to Abbotsford in 1844—Border Scenery—Otterburn, Jedborough—Remains of Dryburgh Abbey—Tomb of Sir Walter Scott—Melrose Abbey—Changes at Abbotsford—The Poems and Novels of Sir Walter Scott. 135

NUMBER SIXTEEN.

THE COURT OF FRANCE IN 1818.

Impressions of the French revolution derived from Burke—Presentation at court in France in 1818—Court dress and diplomatic uniform—Mr. Gallatin and the ambassadors' reception—Appearance of Louis XVIII.—Duchess d'Angoulême—Duke d'Angoulême—The Count d'Artois, afterwards Charles X.—The Duke de Berri and the Duchess—Fortitude of the Duchess when her husband was assassinated, and her heroic conduct in 1832—Concealed at Nantes behind the back of a fireplace for fifteen hours—The King and Count d'Artois as described by Burke—The fortunes of the Duchess de Berri. 145

NUMBER SEVENTEEN.

LORD ERSKINE'S TESTIMONY TO WASHINGTON.

Lord Erskine said by Lord Campbell to have saved the liberties of his country—His testimony to Washington—Sketch of his life—The Earl of Buchan—Narrow circumstances of the family—Enters the navy—Original anecdote of his surveying the coast of Florida—Passes from the navy to the army—Commences the study of the law—Brilliant début in the Greenwich Hospital case—His own account of the manner in which he came to be retained in that case—Extract from the pamphlet sent by him to General Washington—His tribute to Washington on the blank leaf. 155

NUMBER EIGHTEEN.

THE FINANCIAL DISTRESS OF THE YEAR 1857.

PART I.

An inquiry into the causes of the distress of the year 1857 proposed—Difficulty of the investigation—The facts of the case stated—And the extent of the distress briefly described—The general paralysis of business and credit—What could have produced it, in the absence of all the usual causes of public distress?—Its probable cause to be found in DEBT—An estimate of the personal debt of the people of the United States—Its annual interest ninety millions of dollars—The business debt is vastly greater—The Corporate debt—The Bank debt and the elements of which it is composed—Banks create no additional capital—By sudden contraction of credit in times of pressure produce or increase the panic. 163

NUMBER NINETEEN.

THE FINANCIAL DISTRESS OF THE YEAR 1857.

PART II.

The view taken in the preceding paper best explains the periodical recurrence of a financial crisis—Origin of the term Panic—Its connection with seasons of pressure and distress—The only remedy is to keep out of debt—The abuses of credit the chief cause of great commercial revulsions—Long credits deprecated by distinguished financial authorities—The agency of banks in the dangerous extension of credit—Doubtful utility of a paper currency—Individual prudence must furnish the main protection—The soundness of these views confirmed by the manner in which the country is returning to a state of prosperity. . . . 173

NUMBER TWENTY.

TRAVELLING IN FORMER TIMES.

First visit to New York by packet from Newport in 1810—Exodus from Dorchester to Connecticut River in 1635, in fourteen days—Madam Knight's journey to New York in 1704—Extracts—Franklin's voyage to New York in 1723—Abandons vegetable diet by the way—Franklin's reasons in 1754 for recommending Philadelphia as the seat of a provincial Union—Anecdote of General Adair and General Root—Rapid journey of Cardinal Wolsey from Richmond to Bruges and back—Washington's first journey to the Eastern States in 1756—Travelling by stage coach fifty years ago—"Waking up the wrong passenger"—Indifferent accommodations both for passengers and baggage—Anecdote of a German traveller—This mode of travelling sometimes very pleasant. . . . 188

NUMBER TWENTY-ONE.

TRAVEL IN EUROPE.

No Railroads or Steamers in Europe in 1818—Fulton's first passage to Albany—Stage-coaches, posting, and vetturino in Europe—Travelling on foot and on horseback—The ancient Roman roads almost wholly lost—Visit to the Continent in 1818—Guide books—Hon. T. H. Perkins and tribute to him by John Quincy Adams—Stone Henge—Wilton House—Old Sarum—Salisbury Cathedral—Passage from Southampton to Havre—Freedom from care at sea—Transition from England to France and points of contrast—French custom-house—Anecdote of a dyspeptic Bostonian. 193

NUMBER TWENTY-TWO.

HAVRE AND ROUEN.

The importance of Havre owing to its position at the mouth of the Seine and the American trade—St. Pierre—Conflict of races in Normandy—Lillebonne—The council-hall of William the Conqueror swept away by a cotton spinner—Detention at Rouen—Ugo Foscolo—Thomas Moore—Béranger—Society at Paris in 1817-1818—Importance of Rouen—The Cathedral—Heart of Richard Cœur de Lion—Church of Saint Ouen—William the Conqueror could not write his name—Deserted at his death—Place de la Pucelle, where Joan of Arc was burned—Reflections on her fate—Her statue by the Princess Marie, daughter of Louis Philippe—Voltaire, Schiller—Corneille—Regrets that he had not chosen the Maid of Orleans for a heroine—Overturn of the diligence. . . 203

NUMBER TWENTY-THREE.

WILL THERE BE A WAR IN EUROPE

The vast importance of this question—Comparative strength of the parties in a military point of view—The leaders described, the Austrian Emperor Francis Joseph, the King of Sardinia Victor Emmanuel II., the Emperor of the French—The German Confederation in its relations to the contest—Hungary and the possibility of a new revolution—The general spirit of disaffection in Italy and the strength which it lends to Sardinia as the champion of Italian nationality—Qualified in practice by the hostile feelings of the Italian States toward each other. 213

NUMBER TWENTY-FOUR.

ANOTHER VOLUME OF WASHINGTON'S DIARY.

Another portion of Washington's Diary in the possession of J. K. Marshall, Esq.—Description of the manuscript and its contents—Circumspection of Washington in receiving foreigners—General appropriation bill for 1790—Tour on Long Island—Presents to foreign ministers on taking leave—Chasms in the Diary—The President starts on a Southern tour—In great danger in crossing from the Eastern shore of Maryland to Annapolis—Reception there—Continues his journey to Georgetown—Conference with the proprietors of the lands on which the city of Washington was to be erected—They agree to a cession of lands for public purposes—District of Columbia; Alexandria retroceded to Virginia—Description of the city of Washington. 221

NUMBER TWENTY-FIVE.

WASHINGTON'S SOUTHERN TOUR.

Washington's Southern tour in 1791 less known than his Eastern tour in 1789—Departure from Mount Vernon 7th of April—Accident in crossing the ferry at Colchester—Fredericksburgh—Richmond—Locks in the James River Canal—State of public opinion in Virginia on the assumption of the State debts and the Excise law—Petersburgh and the President's account of it—Innocent artifice to escape an escort—Halifax, N. Carolina—No stabling at Allen's—Arrival at Newbern and description of that place—Its present condition and appearance—Arrival at Wilmington and account of that place—The mode of taking the first census described by Washington—Present condition of Wilmington—Recent visit of the writer to North Carolina—Its general prosperity—Raleigh—Chapel Hill. . . 230

NUMBER TWENTY-SIX.

WASHINGTON'S SOUTHERN TOUR CONCLUDED.

Departure from Wilmington—The Swash crossed—Arrival at Georgetown, S. C.—Capt. Alston's plantation—Description of Georgetown—Arrival at Charleston and reception and festivities there—Description of Charleston—No mention of cotton among the exports—Journey resumed on the 9th of May—Mrs. Gen. Green—Arrival at Savannah—Military operations in 1779—Savannah described—Road through Waynesborough to Augusta—Reception at Augusta—Description of that place—Return to the North by the way of Columbia, Camden, Charlotte, Salisbury, and Salem. 240

NUMBER TWENTY-SEVEN.

ADAMS' EXPRESS AND THE EXPRESS SYSTEM OF THE UNITED STATES.

Scene at Embarcation at New York for Charleston—Quantity of packages put on board by Adams' Express—The Expressage not to be confounded with commercial transportation—Miscellaneous nature of articles transported by Express—Connection of the Express with the periodical press—Want of all facilities for the conveyance of small parcels in former times—Sketch of the Origin and progress of the Express System—Wm. F. Harnden—Alvin Adams—His associates—And successors—Present state of Adams' Express and extent of its operations—Importance of the Express system compared with commercial exchanges—Comparison of the Express with the Post-office—Origin and functions of the Post-office—Growing importance of the Express. 248

NUMBER TWENTY-EIGHT.

AT PARIS, IN 1818.

The fête of St. Louis—His name in the United States—The festivities of the day contrasted with those usual in this country—A Mat de Cocagne described—Preparations for departure—Gen. Lyman—Relations with Coray, the celebrated modern Greek scholar and patriot—Brief account of his life and services—Transmits to this country the Address to the People of the United States of the Messenian Senate at Calamata—Its effects here—Contributions for the relief of the Greeks distributed by Dr. Howe—Death and autobiography of Coray. . . 258

NUMBER TWENTY-NINE.

THE ILLUSTRIOUS DEAD OF 1859—PRESCOTT, BOND, HALLAM, VON HUMBOLDT.

The value of their example to young men—Traits of Mr. Prescott's character, which are within the reach of imitation by others—William Cranch Bond the Astronomer—Remarkable variety and union of qualities, scientific and practical—His amiable temper and disposition—His enthusiasm for Astronomy—Liberal appreciation of others—Visit of Jenny Lind to the Cambridge Observatory—Succeeded in the Observatory at Cambridge by his son George P. Bond—Scientific reputation of Mr. Bond, Jnr. 268

NUMBER THIRTY.

THE ILLUSTRIOUS DEAD OF 1859—PRESCOTT, BOND, HALLAM, VON HUMBOLDT.

Simultaneous death of Hallam and Prescott—Hallam the first standard writer of history in England after Hume, Gibbon, and Robertson—Compared with those writers—Brief account of the History of Europe in the middle ages—Of the Constitutional history of England—Of the introduction to the Literature of Europe for the fifteenth, sixteenth, and seventeenth centuries—Personal History—Loss of his two sons—Henry counsels his father not to accept the title of Baronet—Receives the honorary degree of Doctor of Laws from Harvard College—Letter of acknowledgment. 276

NUMBER THIRTY-ONE.

THE ILLUSTRIOUS DEAD OF 1859—PRESCOTT, BOND, HALLAM, VON HUMBOLDT.

The year 1769 famous for the birth of great men—The memory of Humboldt associated with America—His unsuccessful plans before coming to this continent—His great reputation founded on his American works—His place at the head of the men of science of the day—Great age to which his literary labors were protracted—Accustomed to sleep but four hours in the twenty-four—His social disposition—Acquaintance of the writer with Mr. von Humboldt in 1818—His liberal appreciation of others—Sits to Mr. Wight of Boston for his portrait—Remarks on the assertion that he was an Atheist. 284

NUMBER THIRTY-TWO.

ITALIAN NATIONALITY.

Reasons of State and Public opinion mingled in the present struggle—Growth of liberal views in Italy—How far the feelings of the masses will affect the result of the contest—The different views of the different parties—Elements of nationality possessed by the Italians—A compact geographical position—A fusion of the original races—One language—A common faith—In all these respects their claim to an independent nationality equal to that of any of the great powers of Europe—To what is the want of it owing?—By no means to the degeneracy of the population. 293

NUMBER THIRTY-THREE.

ITALIAN NATIONALITY.

It has failed to exist for want of a comprehensive patriotic sentiment—Difficulties in the way of the formation of such a sentiment arising from the multiplication of local governments—Benefits and evils of this multiplication—Probable consequences of the present struggle—Will not result in a republican confederacy—Nor probably in the immediate establishment of an Italian monarchy—But may prepare the way for such an event in future—Lessons to be drawn from Italian history—All other circumstances favorable to an Independent nationality unavailing without a comprehensive patriotism. 302

NUMBER THIRTY-FOUR.

THE LIGHT-HOUSE.

The greatest dangers of the sea are in nearing the land—To obviate some of these light-houses have been erected—The Colossus of Rhodes—The Pharos of Alexandria—Great improvements in modern times—Fresnel—Feelings in contemplating a light-house—The Fitzmaurice light—Number of light-houses in England, France, and the United States—Dangers sometimes of their multiplication—Anecdote of a narrow escape—Minot's Ledge described—Destruction of the iron screw-pile light-house in April, 1851—The violence of the gale described—A new light-house of solid masonry in progress of erection under Capt. Alexander—Progress of the work—An eclipsing light a beautiful object—Via Crucis, via Lucis. 310

NUMBER THIRTY-FIVE.

PRINCE METTERNICH.

Should he be classed with the Illustrious dead of 1859 ?—His success civil not military—Not cruel nor bloodthirsty—His government mild for an absolute despotism—Is Lombardy an exception ?—Anecdote of Silvio Pellico and the other conductors of the Conciliatore—Metternich's first service at the Congress of Rastadt—The four coalitions—His conduct as the Austrian minister in France—Anecdote from Capefigue of doubtful authenticity—Was he the projector of the marriage of Napoleon I. with Marie Louise ?—Rules Austria in peace for thirty-three years—Sinks at last in 1848—His exile, return, and the close of his career as a private man. 318

NUMBER THIRTY-SIX.

SEVEN CRITICAL OCCASIONS AND INCIDENTS IN THE LIFE OF WASHINGTON.

Instances of an overruling Providence in the lives of distinguished men, and signally in the life of Washington—His brother Lawrence an officer in the expedition under Admiral Vernon against Carthagena—Plan for placing George in the British

Navy, and a midshipman's warrant procured—His mother opposes the plan, and it is abandoned—Accompanies his brother to Barbadoes at the age of nineteen and takes the small-pox—Terrific nature of that disease before the discovery of Vaccination—Appears in the American Army in 1775 and afterwards—Great dangers to which Washington was exposed on his mission to Venango—Hazards of an excursion at that time in the districts occupied by the Indians—Their cruelties—Narrow escape of Washington on the return—Concluding reflection. . 327

NUMBER THIRTY-SEVEN.

SEVEN CRITICAL OCCASIONS AND INCIDENTS IN THE LIFE OF WASHINGTON.

Braddock's expedition in 1755—Washington a volunteer aid—Falls ill on the way and sent back to the reserve—Joins the army the day before the engagement—Beautiful scene of war on the morning of the battle—Surprise and total defeat of General Braddock's army—Gallant conduct of Colonel Washington throughout the engagement—Great danger to which he was exposed—Interview with an Indian Chieftain on the Kanawha in 1770—Prediction in 1755 of his future career—Reflection by Mr. Sparks—Washington's visit to New York in 1756, where he is the guest of Beverley Robinson—Makes the acquaintance of Mary Philipse—She marries Captain Orme and adheres with her family to the royal cause. 335

NUMBER THIRTY-EIGHT.

SEVERAL CRITICAL OCCASIONS AND INCIDENTS IN THE LIFE OF WASHINGTON.

Washington desires in early life a commission in the Royal Army—Exclusion of Colonists from promotion in the Royal establishments—His taste for military life—His distinguished services in the seven years' war attract no notice "at home"—At its close, having no hope of advancement, he retires from military life—After an interval of seventeen years, re-appears commander-in-chief of the armies of United America—At the battle of Princeton, Washington, in his own opinion, ran the greatest risk of his life, being between the fire of both parties—Colonel Trumbull's picture—Reputation acquired by Washington abroad by the surprise of the Hessians and the battle at Princeton—Testimony of the historian Botta. 343

NUMBER THIRTY-NINE.

FONTAINEBLEAU, BURGUNDY, AUTUN, TALLEYRAND.

Leave Paris en route for Italy—Passports—Couriers—Fontainebleau and its historical recollections—Appearance of a wine-growing region—The Côte d'or—Autun, its antiquity and architectural remains—Epigram about the two Bishops of Autun—Character of Talleyrand—His emigration to America, and intention to become a citizen of the United States—Anecdote of Benedict Arnold—Talleyrand's course in this country—His friendship for General Hamilton—Curious anecdote of Aaron Burr, related by Talleyrand—Miniature of General Hamilton—Talleyrand's character as a statesman—The Duke of Magenta born at Autun—Another anecdote of Benedict Arnold. 352

NUMBER FORTY.

LYONS.

Hotel de l'Europe at Lyons—The hill of Fourvières—Description of the Panorama seen from its top—Distant view of Mont Blanc—Pilgrimages to the shrine of our Lady of Fourvières—Resort of beggars and almsgiving on the part of the Pilgrims—Anecdote of a professed Scottish beggar—The bronze tablets containing the speech of the Emperor Claudius—Martyrdom of Saint Irenæus and Blandina—The Persecutions of the early Christians as recorded in ecclesiastical history compared with the cruelties practised at Lyons in the French revolution.—Wholesale massacre in the Brotteaux—Escape and career of Jacquard, the inventor of the celebrated loom that bears his name—saying of Napoleon I. about him—His epitaph. 361

NUMBER FORTY-ONE.

FROM LYONS TO GENEVA.

Silk fabrics of Lyons—First glimpse of mountain scenery—Nantua—Bellegarde—Ingenious smuggling—Pert du Rhone—Cæsar's description of the defile—Ancient Switzerland compared to Michigan and Wisconsin—First appearance of the Helvetii or ancient Swiss in history—Emigration of the entire people into France—Overtaken and defeated with great loss by Cæsar, and the survivors compelled to return to Switzerland—A muster-roll in Greek characters discovered in their camp which gives their numbers—Cæsar's great career begins with the conquest of the Helvetii—beautiful prospects on the way from Fort l'Ecluse to Geneva. 370

NUMBER FORTY-TWO.

EXCURSION FROM GENEVA TO CHAMOUNI, MONT BLANC.

The various attractions in Geneva—The influence of Calvin—The road to Chamouni up the valley of the Arve—Remarkable scene beyond Bonneville—Nant d'Arpennaz—First view of Mont Blanc—Goitres, whether considered a beauty by the peasantry—Lac de Chède—Servoz—The Upper Arve—Entrance into the valley of Chamouni—The glaciers—Description of a glacier—Their motion—Investigation of the cause by Professor Agassiz—The valley of Chamouni first made known to the travelling world by Pococke and Windham in 1741—Alpine scenery less frequently described by the poets than might have been expected. 379

NUMBER FORTY-THREE.

THE MONTANVERT, THE SEA OF ICE, AND THE GREEN GARDEN.

Excursion to the Jardin Vert—Ascent to the Montanvert—Prospect from it—Solitary cabin—Beautiful midnight scene—Crossing the Mer de Glace, crevasses—Dangerous pass along the face of the mountain—Reach the Jardin—Sublimity of the scene—Return to the Montanvert—Descent to the lower end of the Mer de

Glace and the source of the Arveiron—Geological significance of the recent inquiries into the formation and movement of the Glaciers—Importance of these bodies in the economy of nature. 389

NUMBER FORTY-FOUR.

GENEVA, FERNEY, LAUSANNE.

Rousseau's house—His manuscripts—Partial insanity the best apology for his conduct—Voltaire's Chateau at Ferney—Description of his room and list of portraits in it—Other memorials—Contrast of Ferney as it was during Voltaire's life-time and its present appearance—His life and works an entire failure—Coppet and Madame de Staël—Gouverneur Morris—Lausanne—Gibbon's house—its appearance in 1818—Summer-house in the garden, where he was accustomed to study—Last lines of the Decline and Fall written there—Hume's striking remark in 1767, on the stability and duration of the English language, in consequence of its prevalence in America. 397

NUMBER FORTY-FIVE.

FROM LAUSANNE TO FREYBURG.

General Laharpe, the instructor of the Emperor Alexander—Origin of the Holy Alliance—Schools at Lausanne and the neighborhood—Scenery—Road to Vevay—Vineyards—Church of St. Martin at Vevay—General Ludlow's monument—Fate of the regicides—Scenery at Vevay—Clarens—Chillon—Its dungeons—Burke's judgment of Rousseau's writings—Moudon—Payerne—Bertha's saddle—Freyburg—Local description—The ancient Linden—Strange bas-relief at the cathedral—Point of junction of the French and German languages—Suspension bridge. 407

NUMBER FORTY-SIX.

BERNE.

From Freyburg to Berne—Change of costume—Appearance of the city—Lofty parapet wall and extraordinary leap from it—Alpine scenery—The Bear the heraldic emblem of Berne, and living bears kept at the public expense—The University—Manufactures of Berne, the Messrs. Schenck—Visit to the establishments of M. Von Fellenberg at Hofwyl—Anecdote of the director Reubel—High School—Industry School—The celebrated assistant teacher Wehrli—Agricultural School—M. Von Fellenberg's establishments, formerly an object of great attention in Europe. 416

NUMBER FORTY-SEVEN.

THE NINETEENTH OF APRIL, 1775.

Materials for the Romance of our history scattered through the country—Events of the 19th April, 1775—Alarm given from Boston to the neighboring towns—Escape of Adams and Hancock from Lexington to Woburn—A salmon left behind and sent for—Second retreat to the woods—Capture of a prisoner by Sylvanus Wood on the 19th of April—After thirty years Wood applies for and obtains a pension—Visits Washington and is introduced to General Jackson—Proposed National monument at Lexington commemorative of the 19th of April. 425

NUMBER FORTY-EIGHT.

FROM BERNE TO SACHSELN.

The Aar and its valley—Thun, its environs and lake—Unterseen—The Lauterbrunnen and Staubbach—A glimpse of the Swiss peasantry—Curious misprint in Goldsmith's Traveller—The Lake of Brienz—The Giesbach—The musical schoolmaster and his family—The pass of the Brünig—Entrance into Unterwalden—Lungern and its lake—Partially drained—Sachseln—St. Nicholas von der Flüe—Legends concerning him. 435

NUMBER FORTY-NINE.

STANZ, LUCERNE, TELL.

Sarnen, proposed drainage of the lake—The Landenberg—Schiller's Wilhelm Tell and birthday—Commotion in Unterwalden in 1818—Type of Swiss houses—Arnold von Winkelried—Resistance to the French in 1798—Atrocities described by Alison—The attack on Stanzstade commanded by General Foy—His character—Lake of the Four Cantons—Lucerne—General Pfyffer's model of Switzerland—Thorwaldsen's lion—Küssnacht one of Gessler's strongholds—Is the history of Tell authentic?—The story of the Apple said to be found in the Danish sagas—Does this prove Tell a myth?—The hollow way. 444

NUMBER FIFTY.

GOLDAU, ALOYS REDING, GRUTLI, THE TELLENSPRUNG.

The lake of Zug—The destruction of Goldau—Mr. Buckminster's description of it—Account of it by Dr. Zay of Arth, an eye-witness—Schwytz—Its early history—Events of 1798—Character and conduct of Aloys Reding—Brunnen—Passage to Altorf—Grutli—The three founders of Swiss Independence—The Tellensprung—Enthusiasm of Sir James Mackintosh—The Legends of the Apple-shooting. 453

NUMBER FIFTY-ONE.

ALTORF, THE VALLEY OF THE REUSS, THE VALAIS.

The Canton of Uri—The traditions of Tell—Valley of the Reuss—Wildness of the scene—The Devil's bridge—The army of Suwarrow in 1799—Andermatt—Head waters of the Ticino—Short Alpine summer—Passage of the Furca—Glacier of the Rhone—The Valais—the Brieg—The Simplon road—Farewell to Switzerland. 462

NUMBER FIFTY-TWO.

DANIEL BOON.

The " West " suggestive of important subjects of thought—Progress of settlement in South and North America—Conditions of life on the gradually receding frontier—Sergeant Plympton's fate in 1677—Daniel Boon the great Pioneer—His life by Mr. W. H. Bogart—Account of his family, parentage, and birth—Removal to North Carolina and settlement on the Yadkin—Marries Rebecca Bryan—Mission of the Anglo-Saxon race in America—Boon with five companions starts in quest of Kentucky in 1769—First sight of—Captured by the Indians—Escape—Meets his brother Squire—Squire Boon's return to the settlement for supplies—They both go back to North Carolina, and Daniel determines on a permanent removal to Kentucky. 471

NUMBER FIFTY-THREE,

AND THE LAST OF THE SERIES.

THE NEW YORK LEDGER.

Description of the Ledger establishment—Common printing—The power press—The Electrotype process—Press work—Distribution of the paper—Eighty thousand by mail—Ross & Tousey's news agency—" Ledger day " described—Immense amount of Printing annually done in the " Ledger " office—Convention for international copyright—Mode in which the establishment has been built up and general character and objects—The " Unknown Public "—Conclusion of the Mount Vernon Papers. 480

THE
MOUNT VERNON PAPERS.

NUMBER ONE.

Reason for assuming the name of "Mount Vernon Papers"—Intended character of the subjects treated—Objects of the Ladies' Mount Vernon Association—Present state of Mount Vernon described in the introduction to Mr. Everett's address as delivered at New York—This description not made by way of reproach to the present proprietor—Necessity created by the crowd of visitors and the vandalism of some of them of selling the property—The purchase could only be made by private speculators—By Congress or the Legislature of Virginia—Or a patriotic association duly authorized to hold and manage the property, and the last mode in some respects the best—A feat of Ledgerdemain proposed in aid of the purchase.

I HAVE already stated in my letter of the 6th of November to the Editor and Proprietor of the "LEDGER," that I have ventured to call these articles the "Mount Vernon Papers," as a name appropriately indicating the object for which they are prepared, and in that way suggesting an excuse for their imperfections. As they will generally be written under the pressure of other engagements and duties, the considerate reader will not expect to find in them that elaboration and finish, which he has a right to demand in compositions prepared at the leisure of their authors. I can only endeavor to do the best in my power, under the well known circumstances of the case, and candid persons will judge them accordingly.

But though called the "Mount Vernon Papers," it is not

intended that these articles should be exclusively or even chiefly taken up in discussing the subject of the purchase of Mount Vernon, or the topics connected or associated with it. They will indeed furnish an appropriate channel, for whatever information of an interesting character I may be able to offer the public on that subject. It was one of the chief inducements for undertaking their preparation, that they would afford me an opportunity for the attempt to interest a very large circle of readers, in an enterprise which I have so much at heart. I shall accordingly submit to them, from time to time, an account of the progress and prospects of the work, as far as they fall under my observation. Besides this, the country abounds with recollections and traditions of Washington connected with his civil and military career; with localities rendered interesting by his battles, his visits, or his sojourn; and with individuals still living who saw him, and of whom a few were personally known to him. There are many original portraits of him in existence, of which a few remain to be described; numerous autographic letters as yet unpublished; and personal relics of every description. Many of these traditions and objects of interest are constantly brought to my notice, in visiting different parts of the country, for the purpose of repeating my address on the character of Washington, and, if I do not mistake, will furnish interesting materials for a few of these papers. It is intended, however, that they shall, upon the whole, be of a miscellaneous character, and exhibit as much variety in the subjects treated, as can be expected from the productions of one pen.

A general statement of the object, in aid of which they are to be prepared, would seem to be a proper commencement of the series, and this I shall venture to give in a few paragraphs, which formed the introduction to my address as delivered (for the one hundred and first time) on the 12th of November, 1858, in New York, at the request of the managers of the Ladies' Mount Vernon Association.

"It is with unaffected diffidence that I present myself for a third time before a New York audience, to repeat the address which you expect from me this evening. I do it at the urgent request of those whose wish is a command, and who are devoting themselves with such admirable zeal and energy to one of the most praiseworthy enterprises that can appeal to the patriotic heart. The women of the country, and nowhere more earnestly than in the City and State of New York, have undertaken the noble work, neglected by Congress, not performed by Virginia, of rescuing the dwelling-place and the last resting-place of Washington from those chances and vicissitudes, and in this case I must add those desecrations, to which, as private property, they are necessarily exposed, and of placing them under the protection and guardianship of a permanent institution co-extensive with the Republic.

"For such, I am happy to say, and not less comprehensive, is the character of the Ladies' Mount Vernon Association of the Union. It was called into existence by the persevering and self-sacrificing efforts of a devoted daughter of South Carolina. It has, as was most fitting, received a charter of incorporation from the ancient Commonwealth, which boasts the incommunicable honor of having given birth to the Father of his Country. It is organized in branches established or to be established in every member of the Confederacy; and it has enlisted the energetic co-operation of some of the most excellent and patriotic women of your own and every other State in the Union. Much has already been done, but much remains to be accomplished. A formal agreement for the purchase of Mount Vernon was entered into last spring with its proprietor, by the government of the Association, and a considerable sum of money—eighteen thousand dollars—was paid down to ratify the bargain. The means are on hand to meet the payment of the next instalment; but an ample fund is of course wanting, to consummate the purchase; to restore the mansion and the grounds from their present state of melancholy neglect and decay, as far as possible, to their original condition, and to make adequate provision for their permanent conservation and care. Such, in a general statement, are the objects to be accomplished and the present state of the enterprise.

"No one, I am sure, who has visited the venerable spot; who has looked upon the weather-beaten building and its uninviting approaches; upon the falling columns and corroded pavement of the portico; the ruinous offices; the unfloored summer-house; the conservatory, of which a portion remains as it was left by the fire of 1832; the

——'spot where once a garden smiled;
And still where many a garden flower grows wild;'

the grounds relapsing into the roughness of nature; and above all, the raw incompleteness, the irreverent exposure, and the premature and untidy decay that reign about the tomb, but must bid God-speed to the efforts of these noble women and their worthy sisters, in every part of the land, who have determined that this public scandal, this burning shame, shall cease. No man of sensibility, who has contemplated the dismal spectacle of Mount Vernon in its present condition, but must wish success, and must feel it his duty to give his own co-operation to the effort that is now making, to redeem and enclose the hallowed and beautiful spot, (for a lovelier eminence does not, in all the land, look down upon a nobler river;) to bring it back, as far as may be, to its original order and comeliness; to clothe its neglected slopes with the familiar but never-wearying charm of grass and trees; to re-open the overgrown paths, once pressed by feet which consecrated the soil on which they trod; to renew the departed beauty of the garden and the conservatory which still contains plants that received the fostering care of Washington; to revive upon the denuded hill-sides the prostrate honors of the forest, and to watch over the preservation of some veterans of the soil, planted by the strong hand which grasped and guided the helm of State in the fiercest storms of policy or war; to replace the mansion in that condition of neatness and simple beauty, in which it so admirably reflected the well-compacted and harmoniously adjusted character of its great Inmate; there to form a collection of all the personal relics and memorials of him, which can be recovered from every part of the country; and above all, beneath the shadow of majestic trees, within the sound of flowing waters, and under the shelter of monumental walls, to enshrine the sacred ashes of the First of Men, in a mausoleum worthy of its deposit.

"To provide the means of effecting these objects, the women of America have determined to make their direct appeal to the heart of the country. They do not believe that it is the wish of the people that a state of things so unworthy and discreditable should continue to exist. It is in humble co-operation with them in the effort to put an end to it, that I appear before you this evening; not surely to argue the meritorious character of the undertaking, for that would be an insult alike to your understandings and your patriotic feelings, but to aid you in calling up the revered image of Washington, and to give some new distinctness to your recollections of those illustrious traits of character and those inestimable services which have given him the first place in the hearts of his countrymen, and have made the spot where he lived and where his ashes repose, dear and sacred to the end of time."

The foregoing allusions to the present condition of Mount Vernon are not made in the spirit of reproach to the present proprietor. It can rarely be proper to make the conduct of private citizens, and the manner in which they manage their affairs, the subject of public comment. So long as they keep within the bounds of morality and the law, belong to the same sect and party with ourselves, vote for the same candidates, use the same dictionary, read the same newspaper, and take off their hats to the ground when we pass, (for if they fail in any of these things, there is nothing too bad to say or print of them,) they ought not to be interfered with. I am not aware of any thing which ought to deprive the proprietor of Mount Vernon of the benefit of this principle, certainly not as far as I am concerned, indebted as I am to him and his amiable family for a most friendly and hospitable reception.

It could never, I think, have been a productive property, nor one capable of being kept in high condition, without a considerable annual outlay. It descended to the present proprietor, if I am not misinformed,—for I do not derive the impression from him,—in a neglected state. Supposing it true that he has shown himself not duly sensible to the interesting character of the spot, it does not, I think, lie with his fellow-citizens to reproach him. It will be time enough to do so, when, either by the acts of their public representatives, or any more informal demonstration, they shall themselves have manifested a sincere and effective interest in the care and preservation of Mount Vernon. While it remains a fact that nothing has been done by the leaders of public opinion in or out of Congress, or by any general popular movement, for its protection, it is unfair to reproach Mr. Washington for a supposed neglect of it. Considered merely as a patrimonial farm, he surely has a right to take care of it or neglect it at his pleasure. Considered in its great national and patriotic associations, it will be time enough for the Public to rebuke him when the Public has done its own duty.

But leaving reproaches aside, which seldom do much good to masses of men or to individuals, and are in general liberally dealt out by those who have little else to deal in, all persons must admit, that the state of things at present existing at Mount Vernon ought to cease. Nominally private property, and belonging to a private individual, the Public in effect lays claim to it, takes possession of it, occupies it, or at least overruns it. Visitors of every kind and in vast numbers, tourists and pilgrims, of our own and foreign lands, led by every motive from idle curiosity to patriotic feeling, resort to Mount Vernon in the pleasant season of the year, and more or less at all seasons. They wander over the grounds and through the house, the greater part of them, no doubt, conducting themselves with the decorum which belongs to the place, and the civility which belongs to all places. But in addition to the civil and well-bred, there are enough of an opposite description to inflict serious injury on the grounds and the house, and to cause the greatest annoyance to its inmates. Their retirement is invaded in the most unseemly and distressing manner; articles easily removed must be closely watched, to prevent their being carried off; whatever can be broken or cut is liable to be mutilated and defaced within doors, and the shrubbery in the walks and grounds is appropriated without scruple. Three or four of the pales have been wrenched from the balustrade of the front staircase, and carried away. An attempt was made last year to break the glass case which contains the key of the Bastile, given by Lafayette to Washington, and to purloin this remarkable relic. Most of the small projecting portions of the wrought marble mantel-piece presented to General Washington by Samuel Vaughan, Esq., of London, and forming the ornament of the fire-place in the dining-room, have been ruthlessly broken off; and in one case, at least, young magnolias planted in the grounds have been cut down by tourists, who were, as may be supposed, particular as to the quality of their walking-sticks. Were the fortune of the proprietor such as would enable him to restore a place like Mount Vernon from the effects of half a century of neglect, and to bring it into a state of ornamental culture, it is plain that it could not be kept in that condition without the additional expense (if there were no other difficulty) of a number of watchmen and guards.

It is quite natural that the People should wish to visit Mount Vernon, but if they insist on doing it in numbers that put to flight all ideas of private property, to say nothing of the seclusion which makes the charm of rural life, they ought to be willing to acquire a right to do so. They ought to possess themselves legally of the property, and not insist upon using it illegally. They not only ought not to reproach Mr. Washington with letting it go to decay, while they are themselves tearing it to pieces, but they ought not to permit him to be burdened with a nominal possession, unaccompanied by any genuine enjoyment of his property, while they are exercising upon it themselves some of the most absolute acts of ownership

I know of but three ways in which the end can be attained. An individual or company might purchase Mount Vernon, in order to throw it open as a place of public resort and recreation, and thus make it the subject of pecuniary speculation. Offers to this effect, tempting in their amount, have been made to the present proprietor, and are regarded by his friends as a justification for demanding a price for the estate, so much beyond its value for any ordinary private purpose. They urge that a gentleman of moderate means, actually coerced by the Public in the way described, into selling his property, has made sacrifice enough to patriotic feeling, in refusing the lucrative offers of private individuals, who might put the estate to an unworthy use; and that a farther pecuniary sacrifice ought not, in justice to his family, to be expected of him, in the price for which he is willing to cede it to a patriotic association. However this may be, all must approve the motives and feelings which have induced Mr. Washington (while virtually compelled to part with the estate) to refuse to sell it for the purposes alluded to.

Excluding then the alienation of Mount Vernon for the purposes of speculation, there is no way in which the Public can turn its present tumultuary, violent, and illegal occupation of it (the character of which is not essentially altered by the consent of the owner, a consent only in name, and really extorted by the duress of circumstances) into a legal and honest possession, but by the fair purchase of the property. This could be, or could have been, effected either by Congress or the State of Virginia. There are strong reasons in favor of either course, and practical difficulties in the way of both, which this is not the place to discuss. Proposals have occasionally been made both in Congress and the legislature of Virginia for this purpose, but without success.

Such a purchase therefore being out of the question, the only remaining mode by which the Public can honestly become possessed of it, is that which has actually been resorted to, and is now in progress of execution, and that is, the purchase of the estate by a voluntary association coextensive with the Union ;—endowed with requisite powers to hold and manage the property by a charter of incorporation from the State of Virginia, (and every one, I think, must admit that the legislature of the native State of Washington, and the State in which the property is situated, is the authority from which a charter could most appropriately be derived ;) composed of members and soliciting contributions from every part of the country. It is true that this mode of raising the funds to consummate the purchase is extremely laborious ;—that, in fact, is the only great difficulty attending it. The country is willing,—desirous to effect the object. The five hundred thousand dollars, required to fulfil all the designs of the association above alluded to, could be raised in a day, by the cheerful cooperation of the people of the United States, each one giving his proportionate mite; but to arrange the machinery, by which so large an amount can be collected throughout a country so vast as ours, is a matter of difficulty and labor.

It is really, however, as it seems to me, the best way to accomplish the object. It produces a more direct participation of the People in the result, than if it were accomplished by a legislative appropriation; and the zeal and energy with which the ladies of the association, alike those forming part of its central government, and those who, as local managers, have united with them, authorize a confident expectation of complete success, and that at no distant day. It is indeed very important that what is done should be done promptly, for Mr. Washington has engaged, in case the purchase money is paid in February next, to remit the interest due upon it for the current year.

I venture, in conclusion, to make a proposal, suggested by the munificence of the proprietor of the LEDGER, in paying the generous sum of Ten thousand dollars to the Mount Vernon Fund, for the preparation of these papers;—would that it were in my power to make them more worthy of his liberality! More than Three Hundred Thousand copies of this journal are circulated among the masses of the People, throughout the length and the breadth of the land. A large proportion of the copies are ordered by clubs, and are read in families, and I am told that it is not an extravagant calculation, that they are read by One Million of the People of the United States, each one of whom venerates the character of Washington, and would gladly co-operate in rescuing his dwelling and his tomb from neglect and decay. If this is a sound calculation, the contribution of half a dollar each by the readers of the LEDGER would at once accomplish the object!

I have hitherto taken no part in collecting funds for the purchase of Mount Vernon, in any other way, than by the repetition of my address on the character of Washington. But I shall be happy to aid the readers of the LEDGER to give effect to the above suggestion, by receiving any sum sent to me by mail or otherwise for that purpose, returning a receipt to the Donor, countersigned by the Treasurer of the Auxiliary Mount Vernon Fund.*

* The result of this suggestion will be stated in the Appendix to the present volume.

NUMBER TWO.

CHRISTMAS.

Christmas day simultaneously celebrated in the Catholic and Protestant church—Not recognized by the Puritans, and why—Had degenerated into a disorderly Festival—Lord of Misrule—Extravagant revels in the sixteenth century—Mince pie and plum porridge—Baron of beef—Superstitions in the West of England relative to cattle—Anecdotes of the reformation of the calendar—Lord Chesterfield and Lord Macclesfield—Milton's beautiful ode to the nativity—Sir Walter Scott—Mr. Irving's charming description of the manner in which Christmas is celebrated in England at the present day.

We have reached the season of the year when,—with a little variation as to the precise day, growing out of the difference between the old and new style,—Christians of almost every name commemorate the birthday of their common Master. On Christmas day, beginning at Jerusalem in the church of the sepulchre of our Lord, the Christmas anthem has travelled with the star that stood above his cradle, from region to region, from communion to communion, and from tongue to tongue, till it has compassed the land and the sea, and returned to melt away upon the sides of Mount Zion. By the feeble remnants of the ancient Syrian and Armenian churches, creeping to their furtive matins amidst the unbelieving hosts of Islam, in the mountains of Kurdistan and Erzeroum; within the venerable cloisters, which have braved the storms of barbarism and war for fifteen centuries on the reverend peaks of Mount Sinai; in the gorgeous cathedrals of Moscow and Vienna, of Madrid and Paris, and still imperial Rome; at the simpler altars of the Protestant church in western Europe and America; in the remote missions of our own continent, of the Pacific islands, and of the furthest East, on Saturday last, for the Catholic and Protestant churches, the song of the angels which hailed the birth of our Lord was repeated by the myriads of his followers all round the globe.

The twenty-fifth of December is celebrated with an approach to unanimity, by the Christian world, as the anniversary of the birthday of our Saviour. Our Puritan fathers are almost the only great body of Christian believers who did not observe it as a holiday, or set it apart for special religious services. Not finding the day of our Saviour's birth specified in the sacred text, they considered this festival as resting upon no firmer foundation that the other feasts and fasts and saints' days, which they regarded in the aggregate as a human invention. It is not the province of these papers to discuss theological questions, but it is highly probable that if Christmas and Easter had been the only days of this kind set apart for observance, their traditionary character would have been respected even by our scrupulous Puritan ancestors. As it was, their objection was perhaps rather to the mode in which Christmas was kept in their time, and still more to the manner in which it was kept at an earlier period, than to the observance of the day in itself. Milton's inimitable Christmas hymn shows us that there was at least one of those who paid little respect to the traditions of the Romish or the Anglican church, who felt in all its significance that

"This is the month, and this the happy morn."

Among the reasons which led the Puritans to oppose the observance of Christmas was no doubt the fact, that it had almost lost the character of a religious festival, even of a cheerful and joyous character, and had degenerated into a day of grotesque and not seldom licentious revelry. The period from Christmas to Twelfth Night resembled the Roman

Saturnalia so closely, before the Reformation, and to some extent after it, that it has been usually supposed to have been celebrated in imitation of that season. For these twelve days society was turned topsy-turvy; servant and master changed places, and all gave themselves up to antic games, coarse revelling, and licensed dissipation. An old Puritan writer on this subject (Prynne) says:—

> "Our Bacchannial Christmasses and New Years Tides with those Saturnalia and feasts of Janus, we shall find such near affinity between them, both in regard of time (they being both in the end of December and on the first of January,) and in their manner of solemnizing, (both of them being spent in revelling, epicurism, wantonness, idleness, dancing, drinking, stage plays, masques and carnal pomp and jollity,) that we must needs conclude the one to be the very ape or issue of the other. Hence Polydore Virgil affirms, in express terms, that our Christmas *Lords of Misrule* (which custom, saith he, is chiefly observed in England,) together with dancing, masques, mummeries, stage-plays, and such other Christmas disorder now in use with Christians, were derived from these Roman Saturnalia and other Bacchanalian festivals, which (concludes he) should cause all pious Christians eternally to abominate them."

It cannot be denied that many of the sports not only of Christmas but of other church festivals were of a character at once so coarse and absurd, as to justify in no small degree the hostility of the Puritans. Among the pageants of Christmas was the "Lord of Misrule," a mock dignitary invested, while the holidays lasted, with a sort of dictatorial power. The nature of his office may be inferred from his name. His authority was recognized in all the great houses, beginning with the royal residence. "In the feast of Christmas, (says the chronicler Stowe,) there was in the king's house, or wherever he lodged, a Lord of Misrule or Master of Merry Disports, and the like had ye in the house of every nobleman of honor or good worship, were he spiritual or temporal."

It is related of the great Sir Thomas More that "he was by his father's procurement, received into the house of the right reverend, wise, and learned prelate, Cardinal Morton, where (though he was young of years,) yet would he at *Christmas tide* suddenly sometimes *step in among the players*, and never studying for the matter, *make a part of his own there presently* among them, which made the lookers on more sport than all the players beside. In whose wit and towardness the Cardinal much delighting, would often say of him unto the nobles that divers times dined with him, 'This child here waiting at the table, whoever shall live to see it, will prove a marvelous man.'"

A quaint author, writing in 1585, gives a minute and scarcely credible account of the extravagance to which these strange Christmas revellings were sometimes carried. Although the account is rather long, we think the reader will not be displeased with the extract of a considerable portion of it:—

"First all the wild heads of the parish, conventing together, choose them a grand captain of mischief, whom they ennoble with the title of *Lord of Misrule*, and him they crown with great solemnity and adopt for their king. This king appointed chooseth forth twenty, forty, three score, or a hundred lusty fellows like himself, to wait upon his lordly majesty and to guard his noble person. Then every one of these his men he investeth with his liveries of green, yellow, or some other light wanton color, and as though that were not gaudy enough, they bedeck themselves with scarfs, ribbons and laces, hanged all over with gold rings, precious stones, and other jewels. This done they tie about either leg twenty or forty bells, with rich handkerchiefs in their hands, and sometimes laid across over their shoulders or necks, borrowed for the most part of their pretty Mopsies and loving Bessies. Thus things set in order, they have their hobby horses, dragons, and other antics, together with their pipers and thundering drummers, to strike up the devil's dance withal; then march these heathen company toward the church and church yard, their pipers piping, drummers thundering, their stumps dancing, their bells jingling, handkerchiefs swinging about their heads like madmen, their hobby horses and other monsters skirmishing amongst the throng; and in this sort they go to a church, (*though the minister be at prayer or preaching*,) dancing or swinging their handkerchiefs over their heads, in the church, like devils incarnate, with such a confused noise that no man can hear his own voice. Then the foolish people they look, they stare, they laugh, they fear, and mount upon forms and pews, to see these goodly pageants, solemnized in this sort. Then after this about the church they go, again and again, and so forth into the church yard, &c.

The hobby horse was cut out of stiff pasteboard, representing a pony with his housings, and attached to the reveller in such a way as to conceal as much as possible his biped character, and to form of the whole a very tolerable representation of horse and rider. This whimsical imitation may still be seen among the sports of Carnival at Rome and Naples.

After all allowance is made for exaggeration in the preceding description, it furnishes a pretty good apology for the dislike which the Puritans entertained for Christmas. Whether we shall feel equal sympathy with them in reference to one of the few incidents of a Christmas festival which have descended to the present day, is not so certain. Mince-pie and plum-porridge were an established part of the traditionary cheer, and probably did their share in rendering the celebration of the day popular. This was enough to disaffect the earnest reformers towards these tempting delicacies. Butler, in describing the objects of his ridicule, in Hudibras, says they

"Quarrel with minced pies, and disparage
Their best and dearest friend, plum-porridge."

It was in allusion probably to this passage in Hudibras, that Dr. Johnson in his life of Butler remarks, "that *we* have never been witnesses of the animosities excited by the use of mince-pies and plum-porridge; nor seen with what abhorrence those, who would eat them at all other times of the year, would shrink from them in December. An old Puritan, who was alive in my childhood, being, at one of the feasts of the church, invited by a neighbor to partake his cheer, told him, that if he would treat him at an ale-house with beer brewed for all times and seasons, he should accept his kindness, but would have none of his superstitious meats and drinks."

It is not easy, at this time of day, to write gravely about mince-pies; but regarding them as the Puritans did as a portion of the dainties devoted (as they viewed matters) to the cause of idolatry, they could not indulge in them without violating the spirit of the earliest law of the primitive church, which commanded abstinence from "meats offered to idols." At any rate, the ridicule is not all on one side. There was no more absurdity in rejecting than in adhering to this gastronomic article of faith. An ingenious writer in the "World," judicially commenting with mock gravity on the degeneracy of the age, observes,

> "How greatly ought we to regret the neglect of minced pies, which, besides the ideas of merry-making inseparable from them, were always considered as the test of schismatics! How zealously were they swallowed by the Orthodox, to the utter confusion of all fanatical recusants! If any country gentleman should be so unfortunate in this age (1755) as to lie under a suspicion of heresy, where will he find so easy a method of acquitting himself, as by the ordeal of Plum-porridge?"

Various other choice viands were appropriated to this season, some traces of which still remain in the old countries. A "*baron* of beef" is still served up at Christmas and other great festivities; this being the name of the two *sir*-loins roasted and brought to table undivided, a baron being of twice the dignity of a knight. A boar's head gaily dressed was a standing luxury at Christmas. As far back as 1170, according to the ancient chronicles, King Henry the Second, on occasion of the coronation of his son, during his own lifetime, served him at the table as a waiter, bringing up the boar's head, with trumpets before it, according to the manner. "Never was a monarch so served before," exclaimed the King to his Son. The latter instead of a dutiful response to his father's compliment, said in a low voice to the Archbishop of

York, who stood near him, that "it was no great condescension in the Son of an earl to wait on the Son of a King." Dugdale in his account of the middle temple, in describing the ceremonies of Christmas day says: "Service in the church ended, the gentlemen presently repair into the hall to breakfast with brawn, mustard, and malmsey." At dinner "at the first course, is served in a fair and large boar's head upon a silver platter, with minstrelsy." Among the earliest books published in England, was a collection of carols prepared to be sung as an accompaniment to the grand *entrée* of the boar's head; and Warton in his history of English poetry says that one of these carols, though with many innovations, was in his time retained at Queen's College, Oxford.

In some of the ancient Christmas superstitions there was a pathetic meaning which we can pardon if we cannot sympathize with it. A notion prevailed down to the close of the last century in the western parts of Devonshire, that at twelve o'clock at night on Christmas eve, the oxen in their stalls are always found on their knees as in an attitude of devotion; and (which is still more singular) since the adoption of the new style, they still continue to do this only on the eve of *old* Christmas day. "An honest countryman, living on the edge of St. Stephen's down near Launceston, Cornwwall, informed me" (I quote the words of Mr. Brand in "his Popular Antiquities," the learned work from which most of the materials of this desultory article are derived,) "that he once, with some others, made a trial of the truth of the above, and watching several oxen in their stalls at the above time, at twelve o'clock at night, they observed the two oldest oxen only fall upon their knees, and as he expressed it in the idiom of the country, make 'a cruel moan like Christian creatures.'"

This change from the old style to the new took place in England, as is well known, about the middle of the last century. The act of parliament, by which the alteration was effected, was carried through the house of Lords, principally under the influence of the celebrated Lord Chesterfield, and the Earl of Macclesfield, the son of the unfortunate Lord Chancellor of that name. Lord Macclesfield was eminent as a man of Science, President of the Royal Society, and thoroughly acquainted with the grounds, on which the reformation of the calendar had become necessary. He was however an indifferent speaker. Lord Chesterfield, on the other hand, had but an *amateur* acquaintance with the scientific bearings of the subject, but was an eloquent and persuasive orator. He was accordingly able to present the subject to the house of Lords in a very favorable light. Lord Macclesfield, on the contrary, (as we learn from Lord Chesterfield himself,) "who had the greatest share in forming the bill, and was one of the greatest mathematicians and astronomers in Europe, spoke afterwards with infinite knowledge and all the clearness that so intricate a matter could admit of; but as his words, his periods, and his utterance were not near so good as mine [Lord Chesterfield's] the preference was most unanimously, though most unjustly, given to me."

The reformation of the calendar was for the time an extremely unpopular measure. Its scientific grounds were not understood by the masses, and the fact that it emanated from the Pope was no recommendation to the Protestant world. The son of Lord Macclesfield standing as a candidate for parliament, in a contested election for Oxfordshire, some time afterward, the mob insultingly called out to him, "Give us back, you rascal, those eleven days which your father stole from us."

This pleasing specimen of electioneering candor and fairness to political opponents shows that we do not possess a monopoly of those articles, as the tone of our newspapers in the course of a warm canvass, might otherwise lead us to suppose.

But to return to Christmas.

Milton's devout imagination does not confine to animated

nature an instinctive sense of the blessed influence of the Nativity :—

> "———Peaceful was the night,
> Wherein the Prince of light
> His reign of peace upon the earth began;
> The winds with wonder whist
> Smoothly the waters kist,
> Whispering new joys to the wild ocean;
> Who now hath quite forgot to rave,
> While birds of calm sit brooding on the charmed wave."

Although the ancient superstitions (of which I have alluded to a very small part,) connected with Christmas and the fantastic revels with which it was celebrated, are now almost forgotten, it is still observed in the "old country," as we learn from Sir Walter Scott and our own Geoffrey Crayon, with no little cordiality and fervor. The church is decorated with evergreens and the hall adorned with misletoe. It is a holyday for the children and a season of good-fellowship for young and old. The scattered members of the family are re-assembled; the dependents of the house are gathered with patriarchal hospitality under the roof of its head, and while genial festivity prevails within doors, bountiful supplies of clothing and food are sent to the neighboring poor. The beautiful description of Christmas in the introduction to the Sixth Canto of Marmion, will immediately recur to the reader, though it contains the customary lament of the present day over the good old times which are passed and gone :—

> "England was merry England, when
> Old Christmas brought his sports again.
> 'Twas Christmas broached the mightiest ale;
> 'Twas Christmas told the merriest tale;
> A Christmas gambol oft could cheer
> The poor man's heart through half the year.

In the later editions of Marmion, an extract is given from

one of Ben Jonson's masques, which contains a kind of summary view of the Christmas sports as practised in his day.

But nothing has been better said or sung on the subject of Christmas than the delightful sketch of Mr. Irving. The various associations that give interest to the festival are alluded to with delicacy and truth. The religious significance of the event, the family-gatherings, the winter season with its indoor fireside enjoyments, its now obsolete sports remembered with a sigh at their exclusion from modern life, together with a warm picture of the kindliness and cheery festivity which are still kept up at Christmas, are touched in language as melodious as a carol of olden times. Having described the simple music of the "Waits," still to be heard in some parts of England, he draws to a close with one of those matchless strains of Shakespeare which pour life and poetry into the humblest recesses of nature.

"How delightfully the imagination, when wrought upon by these moral influences, turns every thing to melody and beauty! The very crowing of the cock, heard sometimes in the profound repose of the country, 'telling the night-watches to his feathery dames,' was thought by the common people to announce the approach of this sacred festival:—

"Some say that ever, 'gainst that season comes
Wherein our Saviour's birth is celebrated,
This bird of dawning singeth all night long,
And then they say no spirit dares stir abroad;
The nights are wholesome—then no planets strike,
No fairy takes, no witch hath power to charm,
So hallowed and so gracious is that time."

May this "hallowed and gracious time" diffuse its innocent cheer through every family circle, and scatter its bounties largely among the children of want!

NUMBER THREE.

THE HOUSE OF FRANKLIN.

Demolition of the house of Franklin in Boston—Why necessary—Crooked and narrow Streets of Boston and their origin—Great inconvenience from this cause and necessity of widening the Streets—Union Street widened and the house at the corner of Union and Hanover Streets, in which Franklin lived, necessarily removed—Description of the house and of its changes—Reasons against removing it to another place—All the original portions of it preserved.

On the morning of the 10th of November, 1858, His Honor Frederic W. Lincoln, Jr., the present active and intelligent Mayor of Boston, called upon me in his gig, and proposed to me to go down and see the house of Franklin, at the corner of Union and Hanover streets. He was led to do this, from the fact that the house and its impending fate had been the subject of repeated conferences between both the present and the last Mayor and myself. On our way His Honor suggested to me, that he had called upon me at a very early hour, in order that we might arrive perhaps "in season, to witness the first stroke of the sledge-hammer in demolishing the house."

Demolishing the house of Franklin! in the City of Boston, the house of her most illustrious native Son; in the middle of the nineteenth century, the house of the Philosopher, Statesman, and Patriot, who shone among the brightest lights of the eighteenth! What! shall the municipal government of the "American Athens" demolish the house of their own Franklin, while an enraged foreign conqueror could spare the house of the Bœotian Pindar, when every other edifice in Thebes was levelled with the dust?—a circumstance which, by the way, must have materially impaired the value of the one building left standing, as a piece of real estate. Shall the inhabitants of the "Literary Emporium," in time of peace, withhold from the dwelling of their own most distinguished fellow-citizen that protection, which Milton did not scruple to demand for his humble abode in time of civil war, from

"Captain, or Co-lo-nel, or knight at arms?"

Tell it not in New York; publish it not in the streets of Philadelphia; unless you publish and tell at the same time, (as you will be sure to do, from the amiable instinct which leads us to proclaim just what our neighbors do not want to hear,) that they also have demolished the houses of Franklin and Washington.

But is it absolutely necessary that the house of Franklin, at the corner of Union and Hanover streets in Boston, should be demolished?

To answer this question, we must go back to the origin of the ancient and venerable Metropolis of New England; somewhat as good Mr. Thomas Prince commences his New England chronology with the creation of Adam; fortifying the date before the flood, which he assigns to that important event, by the authority of Funccius, Bucholzer, Frankenberger, and other writers equally well-known and popular. Boston was not originally laid out like Philadelphia in squares, nor like Washington on a system of rectangles traversed obliquely by avenues. None of the streets follow a straight line for any considerable distance, and their ordinate of curvature has escaped Professor Pierce, in his entertaining work on "curves and functions." It is such, however, as to make it one of the most important functions of the City Government to straighten them. If the homely truth must be told, it is said that the streets in the ancient City of Boston were originally laid out by the cows, going to pasture in what is now Beacon street and Park street, and returning at night from those distant regions. While the greater part of the peninsula lay in a state of nature, and the population consisted of a few thousands, not to say a few hundreds, no inconvenience attended this primitive engineering; which was certainly more in conformity to the age of Adam, with which our ancient Chronologer begins his work, than to that of the "Colossus of Roads," who has prefixed a *Mac* to the family name.

This system of engineering could hardly fail to produce crooked and narrow streets, of which the effects are seen and felt to the present day, especially by that most dissatisfied and querulous class of mankind, the tax-payers. Nor are they the only class who suffer. In consequence of the crookedness of the streets, none but a native Bostonian, who has passed regularly through the primary and grammar schools, can find his way about the town without a guide. A stranger who comes for a few days, especially a Philadelphian, if he attempts to make his calls alone, generally brings up at the end of an hour or two on the steps of the Tremont from which he started, without having found one of the places for which he set out. A few years since, the choice of Mayor was decided by this circumstance. One of the candidates, having only lived five or six years in the City, could not, it was averred, find his way about the town, without the directory. His opponent was a native who could thread his way round the greater part of the City without a guide, and so carried the day. He has never once lost his way, and has just been re-elected.

The narrowness of the streets is a more serious evil. It was of little consequence, while the population was small, commerce inconsiderable, vehicles of all kinds few, and trucks short; but with a crowded population and an active commerce, a truck twenty-five feet in length is something of a circumstance in a street fifteen or twenty feet wide. It is said the ferret will turn round in a hole no bigger than himself; but that a truck twenty-five feet long, heavily loaded, and drawn by two or three horses *tandem*, could turn round in a street of twenty feet wide would be incredible, if it were not constantly seen in Boston. It is however felt to be a serious inconvenience, and it having been found that the trucks, however dangerous to the citizens, cannot be curtailed, with any safety to the municipal powers that attempt it, the alternative policy of widening the streets has as far as possible been adopted.

And here it may be proper, as we are writing for the information of many of those benighted persons, who live at a distance from what is called by the "Autocrat," (who rules us from the breakfast table with such mild and absolute sway,) "the hub of the Solar system," viz.: "Boston State House," to give a more particular description of The Truck, which, in its full development, is a Boston institution. Things bearing the name exist in other places, but they resemble a Boston truck, as a tadpole resembles a full-grown Batrachian; as a pig-nut resembles a shell-bark; as the sloe resembles the green-gage; as the crab-apple resembles the Newtown pippin; as the button pear, which takes hold of your gums and teeth, like a dentist's forceps, resembles a *glou morceau;* as the dog rose resembles the Queen of May; as the bitter almond resembles the Heath peach; in short, as a great many things resemble—that is, do not resemble—a great many other things, to which they bear a generic affinity, but no likeness.

The Boston truck is constructed of two long parallel shafts, hewn from the best of oak, winter felled, well seasoned, and free from faults. These shafts are twenty-five feet long, ten inches wide, and five inches thick; strengthened underneath with somewhat shorter pieces of the same width.

The upper ends of the shafts are cut curving and shaped round, to fit the sides of the wheel-horse. They are then framed together by two transverse pieces; the well compacted structure is placed upon a low axle, supported by wheels, which are three feet in diameter; and thus the truck is complete. It has no carriage-body of any kind; if there is a thing in the universe which a truckman disdains, it is the whole range of enclosed or covered vehicles from a hand-cart up to a Conestoga wagon. The truck has no head-board, no tail-board, no side-boards; but is open into free space on every side; a small movable block only at the lower end, being held by iron pins nearer or further from the horses, as the size of the load requires. A number of horses, in proportion to the load to be drawn, generally two or three, sometimes six or eight, are harnessed *tandem* to the truck; of mastodontic dimensions, high-fed, sleek, and docile. The truckman is in keeping with his truck and his horses; regularly six feet two in his shoes; stout in proportion; temperate, intelligent, patient; to drive a loaded truck in safety through Boston streets when business is brisk, requiring almost as much courage, self-possession, and alertness, as to take a three-decker through the Needles in a gale. The truckmen, consequently, several hundreds in number, form a very important body—the reserved power of the community. All else may go wrong—the upper ten, the lower ten thousand may fail; but if the readers of "the Ledger" and the truckmen stand firm, all comes out right at last. They quell riots, scatter mobs, compose a considerable part of the volunteer cavalry, work with a will at fires, make and unmake aldermen, and powerfully affect even the choice of Mayors.

As to the load of a truck, it has no precise limits. Neither Legendre or Bowditch has given a formula for the amount of goods that can be conveyed on a truck. The mode of loading is a problem in the Equilibrium of forces; the operation of unloading a study in Dynamics. The truck, for the latter purpose, ranges along the street till the axle is on a line with the door of the warehouse; the leaders are unhitched from the end of one of the shafts, so as to leave half the street open, and a word of command is uttered by the truckman, which the wheel horse understands as well as a common Christian understands his mother tongue, and which in English means, " Quick time, backward wheel, march!" instantly the truck, with its load, revolves as upon a pivot, through the arc of a quadrant; the tail of the truck is thus brought round, and runs far back into the warehouse; the chocking block is removed, and then the load—hogsheads of tobacco, sugar, oil, or molasses—tierces of rice—pipes of wine and bales of cotton, go down the inclined plane of the truck with a run, like a *bore* at the Sand Heads, or a spring tide in the Bay of Fundy. At this precise stage of the operation, it is prudent for all persons not immediately engaged in it, leisurely customers, genteel loafers, and outsiders generally, who may happen to be in the warehouse, to stand a little on one side; some difficult cases in surgery may be prevented by their doing so. When, however, by any chance, a package containing *bona fide* fragile and valuable articles (not a box of old brass andirons labelled " Glass, this side up, with care," but a Louis Quatorze clock or an alabaster copy of Canova's Hebe) is confided to a faithful truckman, he carries it as gently as he would a sick child. In a few moments the load is discharged; the leaders again hitched on; another impressive word of command uttered, which means, " Quick time, right or left wheel, (as the case may be,) forward, march;" sometimes a cheery, but good-natured crack of the whip is heard, which never touches the noble animals, (for a true-hearted truckman would about as soon beat his wife as his horse;) and the empty truck bounds over the ringing pavement in search of another load, like a *ricochet* shot.

The immediate object of the institution of trucks is of course to convey merchandise; the final cause (teleologically speaking) is to compel the widening of the streets. This subject accordingly occupies much of the time and attention of the municipal government of Boston. In all representative governments, whether of the City, the State, or the Union, in order to avoid uncomfortable jealousies that one part or region is preferred to another, it is requisite, when you undertake a public work in one place, to do the same thing in twenty others at the same time. On this principle, it is necessary to carry on the work of widening and improving the thoroughfares (which, while it is in progress, of course shuts them up altogether) in half a dozen different places at once; reducing the city for the time very much to the state of Paris in a season of barricades. Improvements of this kind are generally as much for the benefit of the abuttors as of the public at large, and accordingly in New York and some other cities, the owners of the property benefited are charged with a part of the expense. In Boston the public treasury (to the disgust of the above-mentioned taxpayers) remunerates the owner handsomely for having his property made more valuable.

In the progress of improvements of this description, one of the important streets leading directly from the centre of the city of Boston to a region containing the terminations of four railroads, and two bridges, took its turn to be widened. This has already been done in a considerable portion of the street, and the operation will soon extend to its entire length. It so happened that at the corner of this street and Hanover street, there stood an ancient building, of a very ordinary appearance, upon the spot to which the father of Benjamin Franklin removed from Milk street, shortly after Benjamin was born, and there carried on the trade of a soap-boiler, reluctantly assisted for some time by the ambitious boy, already aspiring to higher things. "At ten years old," says Benjamin Franklin, "I was taken [from school] to help my father in his business, which was that of a tallow chandler and soap boiler; a business to which he was not bred, but had assumed on his arrival in New England, because he found that his dyeing trade, being in little request, would not maintain his family. Accordingly I was employed in cutting wicks for the candles, filling the moulds for cast candles, attending the shop, going of errands, &c. I disliked the trade, and had a strong inclination to go to sea."

The house in which, as is commonly understood, this humble trade was carried on by Josiah Franklin, and in which Benjamin discontentedly assisted him for two years, now stood in the way of widening Union street. It presented a front on Hanover street of about fifteen feet, and Union street was to be widened to just that extent; in other words, it became necessary that the house in which Benjamin Franklin is supposed to have passed his childhood should come away.

Watching the progress of this improvement (for such unquestionably it was) from day to day, as I came into Boston from the country, in the summer of 1857, I was not a little concerned at what seemed to be the impending fate of the house of Franklin. That it must give way was certain, but the thought occurred to me, that it might be removed to the neighboring square, and there be restored by approximation at least to its original condition and appearance. On this subject I had several confidential communications with the then worthy Mayor of Boston, the Hon. A. H. Rice, lately chosen a representative in Congress. The year, however, passed away, and "the Franklin House" stood its ground. I brought the subject to the notice of our new Mayor the present year (1858), and to that of the intelligent and energetic chairman of the Committee of public buildings, Mr. Alderman Whiteman, respectfully urging them to consider the possibility of removing and so saving the Franklin House, an object in which they fully sympathized with me.

It was found, however, on examination, that this was impossible; and even if possible, of doubtful expediency.

In the first place, it is not certain, but the contrary is probable, that the house lately demolished is the one in which Franklin passed his boyhood, though built upon the spot occupied by the former dwelling, and, according to the economical practices of that day, as far as they were available, of materials taken from it. In the next place, the house just removed had undergone several successive modernizations. It had been so often built upon, altered and renovated, as to have lost all appearance of an ancient building both without and within. Its identity in fact was open to doubt, nearly as much as that of the ship Paralus in antiquity, which had been so often and so thoroughly repaired, that not a stick of the ancient timber remained; with the difference, however, that the ancient form and appearance of the Paralus were scrupulously kept up; while the old Franklin house had been transformed into a modern shop. It reminded me a little of the question, which was a good deal agitated in the metaphysical circles of the younger classes at Harvard, in my college days, whether, after a pen-knife had had first a new blade, and then a new handle, it was the same knife, or a different one. When this question was complicated by the additional hypothesis, that the original handle and blade had been successively picked up and put together by the "fortunate finder," it may be easily conceived to present points, with which the sophomoric mind would find it somewhat difficult to grapple.

I will not undertake to say, that if what has in successive periods been taken from the Franklin house had been preserved and put together, it would have made a duplicate house, but certainly there was nothing remaining of the ancient structure, but a portion of the old wall, much built upon by modern additions, and the main timbers and joists. The carpenter who had executed the last modernization, added his testimony to the same effect, in corroboration of what was plainly enough seen in the state of the building. A new story had, at that time, been added to a part of the building, the ancient partitions removed, the original windows taken out, much of the walls cut away to admit other windows of larger size and in modern taste, and all the wood-work, excepting timbers and joists as aforesaid, made new. What more than any thing else identified the building in its association with Franklin and his father,—the ancient soap kettle and the fire place in which it was incased,—were on this occasion removed from the cellar, which was probably in Franklin's time much less of an underground place than it has since become, by the gradual elevation of the level of the streets. Nothing of the original structure seemed left, but the bricks in the lower portions of the walls, the timbers and joists of the lower and perhaps the second floor, a door leading down into the cellar, half a window, and the hearth-stone of the fireplace, in what is now a completely subterranean cellar, but which was no doubt originally a basement room.

Had it been worth while to attempt the removal of a building of so questionable a character, it could not have been effected without further serious changes. The long side, parallel to that which faces Union street, was not of brick like the three other sides, but of slight frame-work. To put the building into a condition to be removed, this fourth side must have been built up of brick, with an entire renewal of the interior frame. This would have gone far to destroy what little remained of the identity of the house. The removal, for the sake of preserving it, of a structure of doubtful origin, already so greatly changed, and which required, as a preparation to be removed, changes still more essential, seemed an illusory operation, and the project was abandoned.

In this way the demolition of Franklin's house was inevitable. That it must disappear from the spot which it occupied was clear. The street must be widened. If the living Franklin, grown up to the height of his world-wide renown, had stood upon the spot, he must have stepped aside or been run down by the Charlestown Omnibus; and poor Richard,—as thrifty as poor,—was not the man who would have allowed a sentimental feeling about a ruinous old house to prevent the widening of a great thoroughfare. As little would he have countenanced the deceptive operation of transferring the building we have described to another spot, and that after another renovation under the pretence of removing, for the sake of preserving, a precious relic of antiquity.

Every thing removable and coeval with Benjamin will be preserved. The gilt globe which hung for a century and a half at the corner of the house, and was supposed to symbolize a round cake of soap, bearing the name of Josiah Franklin and the date of 1698, has been preserved by Gen'l E. L. Stone, the late proprietor of the house, and will doubtless find its way to some appropriate public institution. The handle and piston of the old pump, the door, the window, and the hearth-stone above referred to, are safe, with all that is valuable of the ancient frame. Little has been demolished that could be saved, and nothing that was worth saving.

But though it was not possible nor desirable to preserve the house of Franklin, as it is generally regarded,—the house certainly which stood on the spot where he passed his boyhood,—Boston has not been indifferent to the memorials contained within her precincts of the illustrious mechanic, philosopher, statesman, patriot, and philanthropist. But of these we must speak on some future occasion.

NUMBER FOUR.

A SAFE ANSWER.

Reuben Mitchell's education—Becomes a partner in business with his master—Marries his daughter—Succeeds to the inheritance and business of his Father-in-law—Invests the profits of his business in real estate—Gradually purchases a large number of farms, many of which are unproductive—The number of his farms known only to himself—Curiosity of friends and the community on that subject—It becomes a topic of public remark—Measures adopted to solve the mystery—And the result.

Reuben Mitchell belonged to an old Quaker family in the south-eastern part of Massachusetts, and had been brought up in the straitest peculiarities of the sect. His dress was in all respects in the modest Quaker style, and his speech retained the once universal solemnity of the second person. His calm and quiet temper was in unison with the gentle austerities of the sect; and the last thought of Reuben Mitchell's heart was to adopt the innovations in language, dress, and manner, which began to be attempted in his childhood, by some of the youthful members of the once persecuted but now respected brotherhood.

Reuben was brought up as a merchant, under a prosperous relative, who first in the whale fishery and then in general business had amassed a considerable property. First as apprentice and then as clerk, he went through the severe routine of the old school. Early hours and the performance of a great deal of manual and even menial labor, were then expected of all young men devoted to a business life, although belonging to what are called respectable families. Reuben submitted to these hardships, if hardships they are, with cheerfulness. In fact, they were formerly considered as a matter of course, and no more to be complained of than the order of the seasons.

With these feelings and habits Reuben Mitchell passed through his business novitiate, and was soon admitted a junior partner in the house by his late master, on the footing, as he could bring no money capital into the concern, of doing nearly all the work and receiving scarce any of the profits of the establishment. This arrangement, however, was not unusual, nor deemed oppressive. The gains which it yielded Reuben were small, but they satisfied his modest wants, and small as they were, he saved something.

In due time Reuben's business connection with his late master led to one of a gentler character. Hannah Folger was her father's only child; three or four years younger than Reuben; gay and sprightly after the type of Friends; dark hair; a smiling eye; a dimpled cheek; an air and manner, which, among the world's people, might have been thought to possess a dash of coquetry, but in Hannah serving only to create a pleasing contrast with the quiet garb and antiquated speech of the sect.

It was almost a matter of course that a tender feeling should spring up between Reuben and Hannah. We intend no disparagement by using the phrase, "matter of course." We have no doubt there is as much of the romance of Love among Friends, as among the world's people; but it was all but impossible, that, with the continual opportunities which presented themselves for friendly intercourse, something tenderer than friendship should not spring up between them. They had grown up together; Reuben had boarded while an apprentice in her father's family; he was now her father's partner, and possessed his entire confidence; and it is altogether probable that, in his quiet way, and as far as Friends may be supposed capable of entering into such calculations, he had for a long time intended that Reuben and Hannah should one day enter into a closer partnership.

In due time this event took place, and, as we have said, pretty much as a matter of course; and without involving for any of the parties a great change in the even tenor of their lives. They had always lived beneath the same roof, and moved in the same circle of friends. Their simple mode of life admitted of but little variety; their quiet tempers desired none. Her thoughts were given to the duties and cares of an increasing household; his to the demands of a growing business. They sympathized and co-operated with each other, as far as the relative sphere of the sexes admitted, lived in harmony and prosperity, and were remarked in the circle of their acquaintance, as an exemplary, respected, and happy couple.

At length the father died, and Reuben and Hannah succeeded to the inheritance,—a substantial, one might say large, property,—and the chief control of an extensive business. This event, however, changed little or nothing in their mode of life; nothing in their household arrangements and habits. It enlarged their means of active usefulness and charity. Ruben was enabled to contribute more liberally to the public objects favored by the yearly meeting; and Hannah's private charities, never stinted, became more frequent and ample; but the change was modestly and unostentatiously made. In a year, also, a sleek pair of horses and a four-wheeled carriage superseded the more quiet one-horse chaise, whch had hitherto served their purposes.

The most considerable change that took place in Reuben's habits, was one which, as he conducted it, attracted but little public attention at the outset, though it eventually became a matter of notoriety and remark. Though brought up to a life of active commerce, and succeeding at Mr. Folger's death to the entire control of an extensive and profitable establishment, Reuben was wholly free from the ambition of enlarging his operations, or rendering his commercial house more important and influential. He did not contract, but he did not extend the sphere of his operations. He built no new ships, and engaged in no large speculations. On the contrary, he invested his profits and the increasing surplus of his capital in real estate, and that not always of a very productive character. In a word, he was very much in the habit, when he had two or three thousand dollars to invest, of buying one of the numerous farms which are constantly on sale in this part of the country.

Reuben had retained the possession of a little estate of some sixty or seventy acres, where he was born and passed the years of his boyhood. The old house, the old trees, the old well, the still older rocks, had a charm for him. His very first accumulations were laid out in purchasing a small adjoining property. As his means increased, he successively made the acquisition of two or three other small farms. Land at that time, and in that neighborhood, was inexpensive. Railroads were unknown, and ten miles from a large town there were few farms that could not be bought for twenty-five dollars an acre, some for much less. In this way, at the cost of a few thousand dollars, Reuben had, in a very few years, become the owner of six or eight farms.

It was a period of unusual vicissitude in the commercial world. The Orders in Council and the French decrees swept the ocean of American commerce, and brought many a proud fortune to the ground. Reuben was prudent and was fortunate; he escaped without serious loss, but was confirmed in his preference of solid investments, and his aversion to expanding his commercial operations. His business continued to yield him ample returns, but he still invested the surplus in real estate. As the grass was springing up between the paving stones of the trading cities, it was not to be wondered at, that he should prefer good farms in the country, to stores and warehouses in the large towns, and so Reuben annually bought more farms.

In these purchases he had an eye of course principally to his own interest; but he also acted not seldom from other motives. He occasionally bought a farm to oblige a neighbor or friend. When the squire of his native village died, lieaving five children and considerable debts, Reuben did what no one else was willing, and few were able to do, and bought the farm for a fair price, though he was the only purchaser in the neighborhood. When Obadiah the miller died, and left a lonely widow whose only daughter and child was married in the West, Reuben bought the little homestead to accommodate her. There were few things he wanted less than a grist mill, but he took it to oblige the widow. In short, it got to be remarked, that, for one reason or another, Reuben Mitchell was constantly buying farms; and by the time he was forty years old, he owned more farms than any Friend in the Yearly Meeting.

Now these farms were seldom productive. A rural tenantry is hardly known among us; the land is not sufficiently fertile for great staple crops, which admit the payment of a high rent. Some of Reuben's farms were wholly unoccupied, a good many were let at the halves, but the landlord's half was generally very small; on some of the farms, especially those purchased from charitable and friendly motives, the former proprietor was allowed to live, not seldom on a nominal rent. This was the case with the clergyman's widow. Her husband had left her in straitened circumstances; but Reuben, though not brought up greatly to respect a professional clergy, considered all widows and orphans as belonging to the one church universal of Christian brotherhood. So he bought the widow's farm for a handsome price, but insisted on her still occupying it at a moderate rent, which was never asked for and never paid.

Thus Reuben Mitchell became the proprietor of a great

many farms, a circumstance which, as most of them must have been unprofitable, began to excite a good deal of attention among friends and neighbors, and finally led to no little wonderment and remark. "Dost thee know why friend Reuben purchased Jonah Littlefield's farm?" "What can be friend Reuben's reason for investing so much property in real estate, which brings him no return?" These were questions which were a good deal mooted; they were often raised by Friends on 'change; they were started in private circles, at the Yearly Meeting. But Reuben was habitually silent as to his own affairs. He never invited conversation on these topics, and as he avoided the subject himself, no one undertook to interrogate him. In fact, it is one of the traditions of Friends, to devote yourself principally to your own business. Some pretty fortunes have been made in New Bedford and Nantucket in this way. The credit of Friends who mind their own business is generally A No. 1; whereas Benaiah Busibody, who was always attending to the business of others, never could get his long paper done at the Rock-bottom Bank, without heavy collateral. When, in the panic, Benaiah had to ask an extension, it was found, on examination of his affairs, that his liabilities amounted to fifty thousand dollars, and that his assets consisted of the furniture of his counting-room, which, however, was not paid for. Benaiah laid the principal blame to the Rock-bottom Bank, which he declared was in the hands of a parcel of old fogies, who confined themselves to using their capital, for the purpose of discounting good business paper, whereas the real province of a bank, in Benaiah's opinion, was, to employ the deposits and circulation (no capital being necessary) in loans to the directors, to enable them to speculate in railroad bonds, fancy stocks, (so called because no man of sense fancies them,) and moonshine generally. It may be proper to state here, that the Editor and Proprietor of the New York Ledger keeps his account at the Rock-bottom Bank.

But human nature is human nature; though clothed in drab broadcloth or veiled in starched muslin. Notwithstanding the general habit to which I have alluded, which prevents Friends from prying too closely into their neighbors' concerns, some leading questions about the number of his farms were occasionally put to Reuben by his brethren; and more than once an adventurous sister, disguising a burning curiosity under an air of quiet sympathizing pleasantry, would hint to Hannah with a smile, that she did not believe even *she* could tell the number of Reuben's farms. Hannah, if she knew, never did tell.

Meantime the number went on steadily increasing. Reuben kept up his business establishment, which became more and more lucrative; but he firmly resisted all inducements to extend it on borrowed capital, and as resolutely set his face against speculations of every other kind. He would have nothing to do with the Bubbleville Factory or the Grand Trunk Railroad, which was intended to run round the skirts of Blue Hill, and connect the Old Colony, Providence, and Worcester lines. In a word, he did nothing but buy more farms.

This course of conduct at last became the subject of serious concernment, and Friends began to speak rather plainly about it. Most doubted the wisdom of these acquisitions; some thought it downright folly to purchase unprofitable farms. Some of the world's people suspected sinister designs. Why should a man like Reuben Mitchell wish to monopolize all the land in the country? It was certainly an unusual thing for a Quaker. It was foreign to the genius of our political institutions, and contrary to the first principles of republican government. It was a first and a dangerous step towards a landed aristocracy. The *Columbian Semi-weekly Mosquito & Hemisphere* came out with a stinging Leader, in which, under a feigned name, Reuben was evidently aimed at.

At length, as Reuben all the while went on buying more

farms, this subject began to be pretty loudly talked about at Quarterly Meeting and Yearly Meeting; and a proposition was seriously made in a private circle at which the public business was arranged, " to deal with Reuben on the subject." This was overruled by the older brethren, who admitted, however, that they felt some concern on the subject. One of them at length, who had for years been a business friend and a near neighbor of Reuben, suggested as a wise course, that some judicious friend should go to Reuben, and in a discreet and prudent manner, converse with him, and in fact interrogate him on the subject. This counsel found great favor with the brethren, and the Friend who proposed it,—Nahum by name,—was unanimously requested to assume the office.

Friend Nahum accordingly contrived as soon as possible, to fall in with Reuben. He felt, however, even in exchanging salutations, that he had undertaken a somewhat difficult task. He dwelt rather longer on the topic of the weather, than is customary among Friends, and prolonged his remarks on the prospects of the whaling season and the price of oil to a tedious extent. At length, clearing his throat, he approached the difficult topic: " Friends were conversing,—Friends had often wondered,—several Friends from a distance had inquired of him,—how it was that friend Reuben spent so much money in buying farms; and the question was often raised how many farms friend Reuben really owned;—and 'Thee is aware, friend Reuben,' continued Nahum, in the softest tone, 'that I have no knowledge on the subject, and I have thought I would just inquire of thee, what I shall say to Friends, who ask me how many farms friend Reuben Mitchell really owns.' "

Reuben listened to these remarks with calmness. Though it was the first time he had been directly questioned on the subject, he was aware that the number of his farms had been a matter of some curiosity, and had even been mooted at the formal gatherings of Friends. Considering it a business of his own, which concerned nobody else, he did not feel much disposed to gratify this curiosity. It was one of his maxims, that the best way to have your secret kept is not to tell it. Accordingly when Friend Nahum ceased, Reuben remained silent for a short time, reflecting on the proper reply. He was not at all embarrassed, but hesitated a little what to say. As men a little at a loss are apt to do, he looked up to the ceiling for a moment; looked out of the window for a moment; twirled his fingers; moved his lips silently without any definite object; and counted the fingers of his left hand with the forefinger of his right. These movements were almost unconsciously made; but Friend Nahum's imagination was excited; and he attached a great significance to Reuben's manner and motions. He thought that, by way of preparing an accurate answer, Reuben was counting up the number of his farms on his fingers.

In this he was altogether mistaken. Reuben in a moment or two roused himself from his *reverie* and said, "The number of the farms is indeed considerable; not so great perhaps as some Friends suppose; but larger than may be thought by others. .Friends thee says, are desirous of knowing the number, and thee has done wisely, Friend Nahum, not to attempt to give it at a venture. It is important Friends should not be misinformed. If thee states the number too high, thee gives an exaggerated idea of my means, and perhaps causes the tax-gatherer to raise my assessment. If thee states too few, Friends will not believe thee; and in either case thee errest from the truth."

These guarded remarks raised Nahum's curiosity to the highest pitch. He rejoiced at the same time at what he considered the certain success of his efforts to solve the great mystery. He eagerly assented to Reuben's reflections. He warmly and earnestly responded to his remark, that it was very important to avoid any mistake. He was fully confirmed in his idea that Reuben's momentary hesitation in replying arose from a wish to reckon up the exact number; and to prevent any lapse of memory, he took out his memorandum-book and pencil, and wrote the words "Fourth month, third day, number of Friend Reuben's farms,"—and then paused with a look of intense expectation, to write down the figures from Reuben's lips.

Reuben still hesitated a moment;—Nahum, with a most insinuating smile, renewed the question, "What shall I tell Friends who inquire how many farms thee has?" And Reuben replied, "In order to make the number neither too large nor too small, it will be safest for thee, when Friends next inquire, to tell them thee does not know."

NUMBER FIVE.

THE COMET.

Visit to the Observatory at Cambridge on the 6th of October—Description of the evening—Position of the Comet and its appearance through the Comet-seeker—Drawings by Mr. George P. Bond and Mr. Fette—Appearance of the Comet through the great refractor—Professor Lovering's experiments with the Polariscope—The Cluster in the Constellation Hercules—Remarks of Professor Nichol—The Penny Cyclopædia—History of Donati's Comet—Its period—Its rapid development—Progress of Astronomy in the United States—Remark of Gibbon—Comets no longer subjects of alarm—Beautiful reflections of Addison—Apostrophe to the Comet.

On the 6th of October last I visited the Observatory at Cambridge, accompanied by the accomplished and efficient Vice Regent of the Ladies' Mount Vernon Association for the State of New York, Mary Morris Hamilton (granddaughter of Alexander Hamilton), then on a visit in this neighborhood. I had asked permission the day before of the venerable Director of the Observatory, William C. Bond, to make this visit. Even with this precaution, it was not without hesitation that I allowed myself, for a half hour, to divert to the gratification of a curiosity, however natural and laudable, any of the precious moments which, when employed by the skilful observer in the use of a powerful telescope, are so important to science. No one ought to visit a first-class Observatory, without remembering that, while he is gratifying his taste by contemplating the heavens through an instrument like the great Equatorial at Cambridge, he is wasting the time of men of the highest eminence, and misapplying (to all scientific intents) one of the most powerful refractors in the world. But the temptation to behold this most extraordinary celestial phenomenon, the like of which has been seen but once before in my day, and in all human probability will not be seen again in this generation, was so strong as to overcome all scruples of delicacy.

It was a serene October evening, admirably adapted for observation. The sun set without a cloud, and the heavens, if less magnificent than when hung with the gorgeous drapery which sometimes decks the evening sky, were of course far better prepared for the inspection of the wonderful visitant. Venus was the evening star. The air was still, and free from that tremulousness which so often disturbs observations near the horizon. The light of the moon, new that day, was too faint to interfere with that of the portentous stranger, which, in his headlong course toward the sun, had left Arcturus five degrees behind, and was rushing to his perihelion, at the rate of a hundred and thirty millions of miles an hour.

The appearance of the heavens as the sun went down, and a fainter twilight diffused itself over the sky, was most impressive;—the gradual fading into obscurity of the terrestrial landscape,—at last the vanishing of all the details of village, field, and lake, under the broad and shadowy wings of night, leaving nothing visible but the larger dark masses,—spreading tree, church, and distant line of hills. Then came the apparition, one by one, of the heavenly luminaries; the thin sharp edge of the new moon,—Hesperus dropping diamonds and pearls from his imperial brow,—the magnificent stars of the higher magnitudes in this region, whose uncouth Arabic names Mizar, Alioth, Mirach, give so strange an aspect to the chart of the heavens, emerging from the gloom—and then, as the night advanced, in glittering succession those of inferior size, down to the smallest that can be discerned by the naked eye, till at length the whole concave was lighted up with its sparkling glories. It was an evening to make one feel the solemn significance of that glorious sonnet of Blanco White:

> Mysterious night! when our first parent knew
> Thee from report divine, and heard thy name,
> Did he not tremble for this goodly frame,
> This glorious canopy of light and blue?
> Yet 'neath a curtain of translucent dew,
> Bathed in the rays of the great setting flame,
> Hesperus with the host of Heaven came,
> And lo! creation widened in man's view!
> Who could have thought such darkness lay concealed
> Within thy beams, O Sun! or who could find,
> Whilst fly, and leaf and insect stood revealed,
> That to such countless orbs thou mad'st us blind.
> Why do we then shun death with anxious strife;
> *If light can thus deceive, why may not life?*

The great telescope, when we went into the Observatory, was in the occupation of Mr. George P. Bond, the son and assistant of the Director, who has already acquired a brilliant reputation as an observer, and unites to it that of a skilful geometer. He was, at this time, with the aid of Mr. H. G. Fette, preparing the materials for those magnificent drawings, which have been engraved on steel with extreme beauty, to illustrate Mr. Bond's article on the comet, in the second and third numbers of the "Mathematical Monthly." We willingly employed the time till we could look through the large instrument, in gazing at the comet with the naked eye, or through a glass of ordinary power. Seen in either way it was an object never to be forgotten. The nucleus was nearly equal to its neighbor Arcturus in brightness, and the curving tail shot upward through about fifty degrees, a length of forty-five millions of miles, or half the distance of the earth from the sun. In addition to the principal tail of the comet, on the evening of the 6th, a fainter pencil of rays streamed upward from the head, nearly on a line from the sun, to a height of fifty degrees, passing directly between the exterior stars of the "Northern Crown." This strange appendage was hardly visible to the naked eye, except of the practised observer.

The appearance of the comet through the comet-seeker was extremely beautiful, especially in consequence of the brightness of the stars seen through the tail, and that too very near the nucleus. In fact, to persons not accustomed to look through powerful glasses, and consequently not making due allowance for their effect, in diminishing the field of view, the comet-seeker exhibits the object, as far as general effect goes, more impressively than the great refractor.

At length the drawings for that evening were completed, and we were invited in our turns to the observing-chair, itself an admirable piece of mechanism, the contrivance of Mr. Bond, Senior. It would be impossible within the limits of a paper like this, were I otherwise qualified for the task, to do any justice to the appearances which presented themselves through the great magnifier, in the surface of the comet and in the region surrounding it. They are not only minutely and graphically described in the Memoir of Mr. George P. Bond above referred to; but they are illustrated by two admirable engravings on steel, from drawings executed from sketches taken by the aid of the great refractor, one by Mr. George P. Bond, and the other by Mr. Fette. Both are beautiful; but the former appears to me the most admirably executed work of the kind I have ever seen; not only far beyond any European drawing or engraving of this comet, which has yet reached us, but superior to any foreign drawings and engravings of any celestial phenomena; those, for instance, in Sir John Herschel's splendid work, "The Result of Astronomical Observations at the Cape of Good Hope." The drawings and engravings in that fine volume, though executed at the expense of a munificent patron (the Duke of Northumberland), and by the most skilful English artists, are inferior to the drawings of Messrs. Bond and Fette, engraved by J. W. Watts at Boston for the Mathematical Monthly.

But though it would be impossible, in this place, to give an adequate description of the apparent condition of the surface of the comet, as seen through the great telescope, some idea of it may be formed from the observation, that it was in a state of intense action and violent movement. An active evolution of the particles of matter, of which the comet is composed, was evidently in progress; not one of steady radiation but of reciprocating effervescence;—a superficial condition, which distinguishes the comet from all the other celestial luminaries.

Feeling too sensibly the value of the privilege we were enjoying, to monopolize it for any length of time, we soon gave up our seats at the glass to one or two other visitors; among them to Professor Lovering, who made some curious observations with Savart's Polariscope, which enabled him to pronounce, with confidence, that the comet is a body shining principally at least with reflected light.

After all the persons present had had an opportunity of looking at the comet through the great refractor, desirous that my companion, who had never had an opportunity of looking through a telescope of the greatest power (as, indeed, few persons have), should enjoy such an opportunity at this time, I requested Mr. Bond to point the glass to the cluster in Hercules, wihch I have ever regarded, as, upon the whole, the most interesting of the stellar phenomena. With the naked eye you see nothing; with a glass of moderate force you see a nebulous speck; under a very high power, you behold a group literally of thousands of stars. When you reflect, that each of these stars is a sun like our own, and as far as we can reason analogically, the centre of a solar system like that to which we belong, the most vigorous imagination sinks under the stupendous number and magnitude of the Universes comprehended in the cluster of Hercules. It is in reference to this cluster, of which he gives a striking engraved illustration, that Dr. Nichol, in his "Architecture of the Heavens," makes the following impressive remarks:

"Confirming by emphatic analogies his conceptions of the character of our Stellar System, Herschel discovered that beyond it, among the spaces to which its own stars do not reach, other gorgeous clusters are resting, separated from each other and from ours by gulfs, with which the distances between the different suns around us are no more comparable, then our small units on earth are with them. One of these stupendous systems [the cluster in Hercules] is fully represented in plate number I. as it might appear to the most powerful of our instruments. Even to a good telescope it is only like a speck; but what mind shall imagine the glories, the varieties of being that speck must contain! Such, our earliest glance of this new perspective: system on system of majesty unspeakable floating through that fathomless ocean: ours, with splendors that seemed illimitable, only an unit amid unnumbered throngs, we can think of it in comparison with creation, but as we were wont to think of one of its own stars."

The "Penny Cyclopædia," of which the scientific articles appear, for the most part, to be executed by very able hands, dismisses the Constellation Hercules with this remark: "This Constellation is situated between Draco, Boötes, Lyra, and Orphiuchus; but as there is no star in it larger than of the third magnitude, *there is nothing very remarkable about it.*" NOTHING VERY REMARKABLE ABOUT IT! only a mighty group, not of suns alone, but of the solar systems which depend upon them. Nothing but ten thousand Universes, invisible to the naked eye, but revealed, in the depths of the heavens, by a powerful glass, within the limits of this Constellation! Nothing very remarkable!

But to return to the comet. On the 2d of June, 1858, it was seen as a faint nebulosity by Professor Donati at Florence, in Italy, near the star Lambda, in the Constellation of the Lion. Its distance from the sun was then about two hundred millions of miles;—that from the earth still greater. Donati at first doubted whether this comet was not the same as that discovered in this country in May, by Mr. H. P. Tuttle of the Cambridge Observatory. Such, of course, was not the case, but as soon as the disappearance of the moon admitted good observations, it was detected nearly at the same time by three Astronomers in the United States, each observer being ignorant of Donati's discovery. It was seen by Mr. H. P. Tuttle at Cambridge on the evening of the 28th of June, and an accurate determination of its place made the same night at the Observatory in that place. On the 29th it was discovered by H. M. Parkhurst, Esq., at Perth Amboy, in New Jersey, and on the 1st of July by Miss Mitchell of Nantucket,—the lady who had the good fortune to gain the Comet Medal of the King of Denmark, for the first discovery of a telescopic comet in 1847, and the only lady to whom that medal was ever given.

Some difficulty was at first experienced in fixing upon the probable path of the comet, but by the middle of August its future course and the great increase of brightness which would take place as it approached the sun had been ascertained with certainty. It was still, however, invisible to the naked eye, and distinguishable from other telescopic comets only by the slowness of its motion and the vivid light of its nucleus. Traces of a tail were seen on the 20th of August, and on the 29th it appeared to the naked eye as a hazy star. For a few weeks it was seen both in the morning and evening sky, which led some to the opinion that there were two comets. It was at this time also supposed by some persons to be identical with the comet of 1264 and of 1556. It has since been ascertained that it is moving in an orbit (according to the mean of six calculations) of 2,156 years, consequently that if ever seen before by man, it was in the year 298 before our era,—two years before the capture of Athens by Demetrius Poliorcetes, and just a quarter of a century after the death of Alexander the Great.

On the 6th of September the curvature of the train was noticed for the first time, which afterward acquired such expansion, and constituted one of the most remarkable features of the comet. The streamers detached from the principal train first appeared on the 25th September, and increased in number and length; and a succession of most extraordinary, and some of them never before observed phenomena in the nucleus, in its immediate surroundings, and in the train, furnished matter of observation the most intensely interesting and curious, till the comet had passed its perihelion. It was brightest on the 5th of October, the day before I saw it.—Mr. George Bond, in drawing to a close the admirable Memoir to which I have already alluded, and from which such portions of this paper as were not matters of personal observation have been taken, says:

"The Comet of Donati, although surpassed by many others in size, has not often been equalled in the intensity of the light of the nucleus.—It would be difficult to instance any one of its predecessors, which has combined so many attractive features."

There is no branch of science in which the United States have made more rapid and substantial progress than in Astronomy. Our observatories, observers, and geometers, now take rank with those of Europe. Gibbon, after his magnificent enumeration of the seven appearances of the comet of 1680, given in his Decline and Fall of the Roman Empire, adds, "at the eighth period, in the year two thousand two hundred and fifty-five, the calculations of Bernouilli, Newton, and Halley, may perhaps be verified by the astronomers of some future capital in the Siberian or American wilderness." It is a somewhat singular circumstance, that, at a date nearly four hundred years in advance of that assumed by Gibbon, the two largest refracting telescopes in the world are found, the one in Russia, and the other in America; and in either country a degree of astronomical skill equal to the highest operations of the science.

I had a good deal more, when I commenced this paper, which I wished to say on the subject of the Observatory at Cambridge, and the labors and discoveries of its director and his assistants. I could not, however, do justice to the topic in the space which remains to me in this number, and I must reserve it for a future opportunity.

We have reason to be grateful that, in the progress of science, the superstitious alarms, once excited by the appearance of comets, have wholly ceased to be felt by well-informed persons. On one occasion when a comet was approaching its perihelion, it was said that the directors of the Bank of England requested the municipal authority to station fire-engines in Threadneedle street. It is now supposed by astronomers that the earth might pass through the tail of a comet, and that fact not be perceived by its inhabitants. The comet is the body which would suffer by the collision. That of Lexell so called was wholly deflected from its orbit in 1767, by coming within the attraction of Jupiter, which does not appear to have been in the least affected by the approach of the comet. But even if a collision were likely to prove disastrous to our planet, we have no more reason to apprehend that precise derangement in the order of the universe, as established by Creative wisdom and goodness, than we have to apprehend any other imaginable catastrophe.

The following thoughts by Addison, in the Guardian, on the comet of 1680, are so just and so beautifully expressed, that I am persuaded they will be acceptable to the reader:

"I seldom see any thing that raises wonder in me, which does not give my thoughts a turn that makes my heart the better for it. As I was lying in my bed, and ruminating on what I had seen, I could not forbear reflecting on the insignificancy of human art, when set in comparison with the designs of Providence. In the pursuit of this thought I considered a comet, or in the language of the vulgar, a blazing star, as a sky-rocket discharged by a hand that is almighty. Many of my readers saw that in the year 1680, and if they are not mathematicians, will be amazed to hear that it travelled in a much greater degree of swiftness than a cannon ball, and drew after it a tail of fire that was four score millions of miles in length. What an amazing thought is it to consider this stupendous body traversing the immensity of the creation with such a rapidity, and at the same time wheeling about in that line which the Almighty has prescribed for it? That it should move in such an inconceivable fury and combustion, and at the same time with such an exact regularity? How spacious must the universe be that gives such bodies as these their full play, without suffering the least disorder or confusion by it? What a glorious show are those Beings entertained with, that can look into this great theatre of nature, and see myriads of such tremendous objects wandering through those immeasurable depths of Ether, and running their appointed courses? Our eyes may hereafter be strong enough to command this magnificent prospect, and our understandings able to find out the several uses of these great parts of the universe. In the mean time they are very proper objects for our imaginations to contemplate, that we may form more exalted notions of infinite wisdom and power, and learn to think humbly of ourselves, and of all the little works of human invention."

Return, then, mysterious traveller, to the depths of the heavens, never again to be seen by the eyes of men now living! Thou hast run thy race with glory; millions of eyes have gazed upon thee with wonder; but they shall never look upon thee again. Since thy last appearance in these lower skies, empires, languages, and races of men have passed away; —the Macedonian, the Alexandrian, the Augustan, the Parthian, the Byzantine, the Saracenic, the Ottoman dynasties sunk or sinking into the gulf of ages. Since thy last appearance, old continents have relapsed into ignorance, and new worlds have come out from behind the veil of waters. The Magian fires are quenched on the hill-tops of Asia; the Chaldean seer is blind; the Egyptian hierogrammatist has lost his cunning; the oracles are dumb. Wisdom now dwells in furthest Thule, or in newly-discovered worlds beyond the sea. Haply when, wheeling up again from the celestial abysses, thou art once more seen by the dwellers on earth, the languages we speak shall also be forgotten, and science shall have fled to the uttermost corners of the earth. But even there His Hand, that now marks out thy wondrous circuit, shall still guide thy course; and then as now Hesper will smile at thy approach, and Arcturus with his sons rejoice at thy coming.

NUMBER SIX.

AN INCURSION INTO THE EMPIRE STATE.

PART I.

Extra clothing prepared for the journey and the result—Sandwiches as compared with a hasty dinner at an inn—Sixty cents saved and proposed investment for it—Six hours comfortably spent at Albany—Sleeping cars and the excellence of their arrangements.—Unexpected obstacle to the enjoyment of their full benefit—Arrival at Canandaigua—The great land purchase of Gorham and Phelps.

Being under engagement to repeat my Address on the Character of Washington, at two or three places, in the western part of the State of New York, circumstances had prevented my keeping the appointment till the middle of December. I must confess that I looked forward to the expedition with some anxiety. A journey of a thousand miles into the lake region, at this season of the year, to be made in six days, on three of which a discourse of two hours' length was to be pronounced, is, to a person who has reached the age of ,—but no matter about that,—a pretty serious affair. On taking counsel with a judicious friend upon the subject, he advised me, above all things, to take on me and with me, an extra supply of warm clothing, and, if I had occasion, as I certainly should, to travel in the night, to be sure to get a berth in one of the sleeping-cars. I promised to follow his advice on both points.

With respect to the first, I was already well provided with an ample supply of the accustomed articles of clothing, external and internal, of the warmest materials and closest tissues.

But following my friend's advice, and looking forward to the exposure of the journey, I laid in an extra supply, better adapted to a voyage of Arctic exploration, than to a trip into the State of New York. It consisted of a supplementary pair of overalls, made of pilot cloth, and well lined with thick cotton, a dreadnought cloak also lined and wadded, a sea-otter tippet, the gift of a kind friend, which Dr. Hayes might have envied, a pair of very warm gauntlets, lined with vicuña, and a voluminous Bay State shawl. These preparations for the wintry journey had not been made without fitting domestic advisement.

At length the appointed day arrived, and clad in all these habiliments, which had the effect of duplicating my "apparent diameter" to the naked eye, I took my seat in the car for Albany. A few moments only elapsed, before I perceived that the atmosphere was far from being of that boreal severity, which I had taken for granted, when, in the chill of the early morning, I had hurried on my ample stock of garments, ordinary and extraordinary. On the contrary it was, for the middle of December, a moderate day out-doors; the weather, mingled snow and rain, settling down into the latter. Within the car, to take off the chill, we had a stove, kept for the greater part of the time near a red heat. I soon felt more as if I was already in the tropics, than upon a journey in the direction of Canada. Before long I was obliged to commence the operation of laying aside one article after another; first the India-rubber overshoes which were parboiling my feet, then the warm vicuña gloves, then the splendid sea-otter tippet, then the ample folds of the Bay State shawl, then the lined and wadded cloak, very much as the grave-digger in Hamlet divests himself of the traditionary score of jackets. I would gladly have got rid of the pilot-cloth overalls, but as I had only half a seat in a crowded car for a dressing-room, I did not attempt that critical operation. When I had thrown off the last article of extra clothing, which could conveniently be laid aside, I was a little disconcerted at the indifferent success of my experiment in dressing for the season.

In other respects, I made the journey to Albany most comfortably, especially after the youth, who sells what he calls "meggyzines," had passed through the car with the "New York Ledger," without which the traveller might as well stay at home; and with which, he that stays at home has about as fair a chance to improve his mind, as those that travel. This comfortable condition was further owing, in no small degree, to a liberal supply of sandwiches, prepared by neat and bountiful hands before I left home, and carefully bestowed in my travelling-bag. I am surprised to see how few travellers avail themselves of this resource, on a journey, for, if there is nominally a place for dining, you are nearly sure to arrive at an unusual and inconvenient time, whereas you take your sandwiches at your accustomed hour, or just as you want them. For instance, if, in passing East or West, you leave your seat in the car to dine at Springfield, in Massachusetts, you find indeed a very good dinner prepared at the Massasoit, for which you are allowed twenty minutes. The operations of placing your shawl and bag carefully in your seat by way of retainer, of finding your way into the house, of washing and brushing, occupy the first five minutes of your time. The fear of being left behind makes you hurry from the table five minutes before the time is up. In the remaining ten minutes you bolt your dinner, pay your seventy-five cents, and returning to the car, find that your shawl and travelling-bag have been piled into another seat by a lady and gentleman (?) who have in your absence helped themselves to yours. The sandwiches on the contrary, as I have said, can be taken when you please, and eaten leisurely, which your doctor will tell you is the best sauce to your dinner. Besides this, they will not cost you, at the outside, over fifteen cents, so that you have made a comfortable meal and saved sixty cents.

Having helped you to save this handsome sum, I ought to

tell you how to invest it to advantage. Ten cents of it you will want to pay the boy who takes your valise to the hotel in Albany. With the remaining half dollar, I should advise you to pay the first three months of your subscription to some valuable weekly paper. There are several such published in different cities of the Union, and delicacy forbids a more particular indication of that, to which I think your preference will no doubt be given. If you tell me, as you probably will, that you are already a subscriber to the "New York Ledger," the next most desirable investment for your half a dollar, which occurs to me, is, to contribute it to the fund for the purchase of Mount Vernon. Or better than either, give it to that half-clad, wretched-looking creature in the corner of the car, holding, wrapped up in her threadbare shawl, a famished, blue-lipped child, that does not look as if it had had a comfortable meal for a week; and it would not be amiss if you handed them, at the same time, the remainder of the sandwiches. They have already been devouring them with their hollow, vacant, hungry eyes.—There, my friend, does not that unearthly smile repay you; have you not laid out your fifty-cent piece a hundredfold better than if you had paid it for a half-masticated meal, and a dyspeptic afternoon?

But we shall never get to our journey's end if we loiter so by the way. Let us then strain up the Becket Hills as fast as we can, dash down to Pittsfield, and so on to States Line and the Hudson, till we get to Albany, somewhat weary and a little bit dreary, just before dark. This travelling alone in the winter, of a rainy day, is not the most genial thing in the world. At the Delavan, however, we shall get a nice comfortable tea, a room, a fire, a chance to write a letter home, to let them know we are safe thus far, possibly a nap, and all for a dollar and three quarters; at half past eleven o'clock at night, not a little refreshed, in pursuance of our friend's advice above mentioned, we take the sleeping-car for Syracuse.

This *sleeping-car* is a great step forward in the march of civilization. It enables you to travel and go to bed at the same time. You lie down quietly to repose in your berth, and all the time you dash along at the rate of twenty-five miles an hour. Going from Albany to Syracuse I paid for this novel luxury one dollar, in addition to the fare; returning from Syracuse to Albany four days later I paid fifty cents. I suppose the first time, that I forgot to tell the conductor that I was going only half the way to Buffalo, and that he forgot to ask me how far I was going. Any how, I paid my dollar and no questions asked. The next time, however, I shall tell him how far I am going.

The berths, at least the lower berths, one of which I took, are made up with no little skill. The stuffed seats on which you stretch yourself at full-length, are not too hard, and you have two good rubber pillows, and two very substantial shawls by way of bed-clothing; altogether as comfortable a night's arrangement as can be expected by a man who is shooting all the while through the Valley of the Mohawk, at the rate of twenty or thirty miles an hour. I really fancied I had reached the perfection of midnight travelling; if perfection can be predicated of that, which at best is but a mitigated discomfort:

> " ——— not so sound, nor half so deeply sweet,
> As he whose brow, with homely biggin bound,
> Snores out the watch of night."

But the philosophical Latin poet tells us that something bitter bubbles up from the very fountain of pleasure. I had scarcely composed myself—not to sleep—but to the delightful dreamy doze which precedes it, in which, escaped from thought, you have just consciousness enough left to know that you are conscious of nothing—was just sinking into a state in which I am sure I could not have said the first line of the multiplication table, nor returned thanks for a complimentary toast at a public dinner,—when the door of the car opened, and two gentlemen bounded cheerily in, took their seats at the stove (my berth was next to the stove), and engaged in loud, animated, earnest conversation! The first hearty burst of question and reply went off like a pistol, and summoned me back from the misty precincts of dream-land; thought resumed her importunate sway; and a perplexed impression succeeded, that either on their part or on mine, the right man was not in the right place. For a moment I was lost in doubt whether somebody or other was not unseasonably loquacious, or I myself unseasonably drowsy. In fact I was not quite sure of my personal identity. I felt somewhat as Hodge did, when he awoke and found himself in his wagon, from which some rogue had stolen his cattle while he slept. "If I am not Hodge," quoth he, "I have found a capital wagon; if I am Hodge, I have lost a first-rate yoke of oxen."

Pretty soon, however, I found out that I was Hodge; that the sleep on which I had calculated so confidently was in a fair way to be stolen; moreover, that I had a long journey before me; that I was to speak at Canandaigua in the evening, and was likely to be a good deal the worse for wear. Accordingly, after waiting awhile for the river to run dry, I raised myself, with the most wo-begone look I could assume (and it required no effort to assume it), looked over the end of my berth, and told my conversible neighbors that I was very weary, and wanted sadly to go to sleep, but that I could not possibly do so if they continued to talk with each other. The gentleman nearest me answered with the utmost politeness, that they were not aware there was a person in the next berth who wished to sleep, and that they would cease to disturb me. For what other object than going to sleep the worthy gentleman supposed I should be packed away at midnight, in the lower berth of a sleeping-car, between Albany and Syracuse, in the middle of the nineteenth century, he did not intimate, nor have I been able to conceive. Satisfied, however, with his courteous and encouraging assurance, I sank back; the gentleman drew up the screen that separated us six inches higher, and, apparently under the impression that sound like water would not rise above its source, resumed with his companion their conversation as before!

This was a state of things to put one's philosophy, even if he had been wide awake, to the proof. The conductor presently passed along, and I made my appeal to him. I expostulated, I argued, I sought to move. I really think on this occasion I was eloquent. I pleaded for the imprescriptible right of every human being to a night's sleep, once in the twenty-four hours. I put it on the ground of contract; I had paid my dollar for a berth in a sleeping-car. Had I known that I had paid double price I could have put that point more forcibly. I threw myself on his sense of duty as a conductor; on his feelings as a man. I had travelled since 8 o'clock, A. M., and expected to travel till half-past ten the next day, before I reached my destination. I was tired; in a word, I was sleepy; and I stood, or rather, at the moment I lay, upon my right to go to sleep. I had half a mind to tell him that, as he had caused the words "sleeping-car" to be printed on the outside, and had taken my money for a berth, I could bring *assumpsit* against him, if he did not adopt all reasonable measures to let me go to sleep.

The conductor was evidently not only convinced but moved. He admitted the soundness of my argument; it was plain that he felt the force of my appeal; but, when I begged him to interpose, and oblige the talkative gentlemen to cease their conversation, his countenance fell, and leaning towards me he said, in a low voice, by way of excuse for not interfering, that "he knew they ought not to talk, but one was a high officer of the New York Central Railroad (and he named the office, but I shall not), and the other was a great president of a railroad out West." He uttered the words with solemnity, adding, for my consolation, that "the officer of the New York

Central would get out at Schenectady." This was all the satisfaction I got by my first appeal; of a second and a third he took no notice as he passed by. He probably supposed I was beside myself, to think of stopping the conversation of a high functionary of the Central with the "great president" of some other road. But the longest hour has an end; we reached Schenectady; the officer of the New York Central got out; and the "great president," like other great presidents, leaving his seat, retreated to obscurity in the rear of the car. As he passed me toward his berth, I murmured to myself, *requiescat in pace*, meaning only (I am of a very forgiving make) "may he get a good nap." With this benediction I dismissed the great president (who, like the great Macbeth, had "murdered sleep ") to that rest of which he had deprived me. For the rest of the way silence resumed her solitary reign, and I slept till we reached Syracuse.

Here an awkward space of two hours, and a very coriaceous beef-steak (partaken with the brakemen who were to go out at seven) intervened before we started for Canandaigua. On the way to Auburn, the car in which I was broke down; but without causing any disaster, or more than a few moments' delay. I arrived in safety at my destination in Canandaigua, and found myself at home under the hospitable roof of my friend Mr. Granger.

With this region, especially with Canandaigua, I have some domestic associations, by means of a connection with the family of Hon. Nathaniel Gorham of Charlestown, Massachusetts, who was associated with Oliver Phelps in the vast land purchase, which bears their joint names. Judge Gorham was a man of eminence; he presided one year in the Congress of the old confederation; and in the convention for forming the Constitution of the United States, he was called to the Chair by Gen. Washington every day for three months. In connection with Mr. Phelps, shortly after the revolutionary war, he purchased of the State of Massachusetts (which claimed, in virtue of a compromise with New York, a pre-emptive right in the property of the soil) a tract of six millions of acres in the Genesee Country, as it was called, for a few cents the acre; a magnificent speculation on paper; but, like many other magnificent paper speculations, ending in vexation and disappointment; and yielding, I believe, nothing but very moderate results to the bold and sagacious adventurers. But the country at that time was unsettled—the Indian title not extinguished—the property in the soil in one State, the jurisdiction over the territory in another—the Federal Constitution not framed, and no efficient common tribunal existing to settle controversies. Under these circumstances Messrs. Gorham and Phelps were obliged, eventually, to abandon the greater part of their princely purchase.

But, though I have hardly got to the beginning of my "Incursion," I have reached the end of my paper, and I must tell the rest of the story another time.

NUMBER SEVEN.

AN INCURSION INTO THE EMPIRE STATE.

PART II.

Unpromising weather at Canandaigua—History of the settlement—Oliver Phelps—Anecdote of Judge Gorham—Visit to Rochester—Reserved seats—Astonishing progress of the settlement—Return to Auburn—Change in the weather—From Auburn to Syracuse and detention there—Sleeping cars from Syracuse to Albany—Wakeful fellow-passengers—Collision at Albany—Kind-hearted Conductors—Return home.

It was snowing and raining when I arrived at Canandaigua; and when one has travelled, by day and by night, four hundred and twenty-one miles, to speak in the evening, a heavy rain, especially in the country, where dry side-walks and vehicles do not much abound, is rather discouraging. And so we watched the signs of the times with some anxiety, and lamented over the weather; reconciling ourselves, however, to it at last, on two grounds principally, which I mention because they contain a practical philosophy, which may be turned to account in graver cases;—one was, that our lamentations and anxieties would do no good;—the other that, though the rain was not particularly desirable for us, it was greatly wanted by the "rest of mankind," as the springs were low. And so we submitted to the rain. It did not appear greatly to tell upon the audience, and the next morning Mr. Granger handed me, as the proceeds of the evening, a generous contribution to the Mount Vernon fund. I suspect the sum was somewhat increased by individual liberality.

There is no more beautiful village, as far as my observation has extended, than Canandaigua; few places of greater interest in the history of the settlement of the country. It was here, that the settlement of the western part of New York commenced, (after the purchase of Messrs. Gorham and Phelps,) in the year 1788. In the summer of that year, Mr. Oliver Phelps, a person of truly heroic character, who is entitled to a place among Lord Bacon's *Conditores Imperiorum*, (founders of empires,) left Massachusetts, for the purpose of exploring and surveying the vast region which he and Judge Gorham had purchased,—now embracing, I believe, twelve counties,—in the western part of New York. They penetrated, what was then a savage wilderness, as far west as Canandaigua, one hundred and thirty miles west of the German Flats, then considered the utmost limits of civilization. Rev. Mr. Kirkland, (father of President Kirkland, of Harvard College,) who had long lived among the Indians as a Missionary, accompanied Mr. Phelps and his party, as a Commissioner on the part of Massachusetts. An Indian Council was held on a beautiful eminence overlooking Canandaigua Lake; Red Jacket denounced the proposed treaty; but Farmer's Brother pacified the excited chiefs, and an agreement was finally made for the extinction of the Indian title to more than two millions of acres of land. After the treaty, the land was surveyed under the direction of Mr. Phelps, on the system of townships and ranges, which has since been extended to the public domain of the United States, and forms one of the most important and admirable arrangements in the practical administration of the Government of the United States.

"In 1789 (I quote the Rochester Directory of 1827, as cited in Barber's valuable Historical Collections of New York) Oliver Phelps opened a land office in Canandaigua. This was the first land office in America for the sale of her forest-lands to settlers; and the system which he adopted for the survey of his lands by townships and ranges became the model for the manner of surveying all the new lands in the United

States. Oliver Phelps may be considered the Cecrops of the Genesee Country. Its inhabitants owe a mausoleum to his memory, in gratitude for his having pioneered for them the wilderness of this Canaan of the West."

Some idea of the hardships attending the first settlement of new countries in general, and this in particular, may be formed from the description given of this now beautiful and highly cultivated village, abounding with all the improvements of a prosperous rural district, in Mr. Spafford's Gazetteer, also cited in Barber's Collections.

"The settlement of this town (Canandaigua) commenced in 1790, and in 1797 I found it but feeble, contending with numerous embarrassments and difficulties. The Spring of that year was uncommonly wet and cold. Besides a good deal of sickness,—mud knee deep, mosquitos and gnats so thick that you could hardly breathe without swallowing them; rattlesnakes, and the ten thousand discouragements everywhere incident to new settlements—surrounded by these,—in June of that year, I saw with wonder that these people, all Yankees from Massachusetts, Connecticut and Vermont, were perfectly undismayed, 'looking forward in hope, sure and steadfast.' They talked to me of what the country would be, by and by, as if it were history, and I received it as all fable."

Oliver Phelps died on the 21st February, 1809, in the sixtieth year of his age; and future generations will do justice to his memory. So rapid has been the growth of this, in common with many other parts of the country, that the present generation loses, in its familiarity with it, an adequate appreciation of the stupendous process, by which barbarous territories, almost boundless, have within sixty years been brought into the domain of civilization. To illustrate the rapidity of this progress, I often repeat an anecdote, which has descended by tradition in the Gorham family.

On one occasion, when Judge Gorham was musing, in a state of mental depression, on the almost total failure of this magnificent speculation, he was visited by a friend and townsman, who had returned from a journey to Canandaigua, then just laid out. This friend tried to cheer the Judge with a bright vision of the future growth of Western New York. Kindling with his theme, he pointed to a son of Judge Gorham, who was in the room, and added, "You and I shall not live to see the day, but that lad, if he reaches threescore years and ten, will see a daily stage-coach running as far west as Canandaigua." That lad was the late Mr. Benjamin Gorham, who died a few years ago,—who represented Boston for several years in Congress with great ability, and who lived to witness, not merely a daily stage-coach, entering Canandaigua, but two great lines of rail-road, and a gigantic canal, traversing the State from east to west, with subsidiary communications in every direction, and without end.

The next day, (15th December,) at half-past ten, I left Canandaigua, regretting only the necessary shortness of my visit, as I have to do constantly. At Rochester we had the same menace of bad weather, which, however, gave way before evening. I met at the station President Anderson, General Smith, and Mr. Moore, and was conducted by them to the hospitable dwelling of Silas O. Smith, Esq., and to the enjoyment of all the comforts of a cordial reception and a friendly home.

At Rochester we had inadvertently incurred the risk of a pretty serious miscarriage. In order to increase the receipts of the evening, and also to accommodate some elderly persons, invalids, and ladies, who might desire a comfortable seat in the hall, without going at an hour beforehand, or who were unable to struggle for it at a crowded door, the idea of reserving a portion of the seats at a higher price, occurred to those having charge of the arrangements. It was not an entirely novel plan ; but, though a well-meant, it proved to be an unfortunate suggestion. Seats are daily reserved in many, nay, in most places of public resort, in this country and in Europe, without giving alarm to the most sensitive votary of republican equality. But it gave offence to some of our Roffensian friends,—and it became necessary, in deference to the excited public feeling, to abandon the discrimination, and to place all the tickets at the lower price. This restored harmony, at the expense, I suppose, of a hundred or two of dollars to the Mount Vernon fund; and a noble audience filled the hall, which is one of the best in the country. For myself, I am no aristocrat. I do not own a quadruped larger than a cat, and she an indifferent mouser; nor any kind of a vehicle, with the exception, possibly, of a wheelbarrow. But I am willing my neighbor should dash by me on his spirited horse, while I am trudging a-foot; or roll in his luxurious carriage, while I take a seat in the omnibus. On the same principle, if my neighbor prefers to pay a dollar for a reserved seat at a place of public resort, (especially for the benefit of the Mount Vernon fund,) it does not disquiet me in the purchase of a fifty-cent ticket. If my neighbor is an aged person, an invalid, or a lady, and is disposed to pay a double price for a little comfort of this kind, I have personally no objection,—although I had nothing to do with the proposed arrangement at Rochester, as I never have with any business arrangements connected with the repetition of my address.

The next day—though the air was somewhat shrewd—I greatly enjoyed a drive to the beautiful Cemetery and the falls of the Genesee. The river was in grand order, the falls magnificent, spanned with a rainbow, which, in cosequence of a high wind, that blew the water into spray, was of more than ordinary brilliancy. I had seen Rochester but once before, and that in 1821; and when, I believe, Carthage contended with her for the mastery. Carthage is now pretty much in the condition of its African namesake, and Rochester is a city probably of some fifty thousand inhabitants. It is one of the most astonishing examples of the growth of the new settlements in this country. The part which, in 1812, was surveyed for the purpose of settlement by Nathaniel Rochester, Charles

H. Carroll, and William Fitzhugh, emigrants from Maryland, I believe, and called " Rochester " after the senior proprietor, had, under the name of the " Mill lot," been bestowed by Gorham and Phelps on a semi-savage, called *Indian Allen*, as an inducement for building mills, to grind corn and saw boards for the few settlers at that time in this region.* Messrs. Rochester, Carroll, and Fitzhugh paid $1,750 for this hundred acre lot, on which a considerable part of the city of Rochester is built. Some of the land on the other side of the river was sold by Gorham and Phelps in 1790 for eighteen pence the acre. It is statements like these, which beguile men into land speculations, in which I shall give you the benefit of my own experience, on a small scale, another time.

Having passed a most agreeable day in the amiable family circle of my hospitable hosts, and with the advantage of making the acquaintance of many of the citizens, I left Rochester at 6 P.M., in company with my friend, the Rev. Dr. Cressy of Auburn, who had taken charge of the arrangements for the repetition of my address at that delightful village, which we reached at about half-past ten P.M.

I never would willingly travel in the dark, which deprives you of all the gratification and benefit of seeing a country with your own eyes, and thus getting an idea of it which no guide books can furnish. But in this intense condensation of existence to which we submit, crowding into one week the work of three—the leisurely survey of the country through which you pass in travelling, is one of the first things to be sacrificed. One would have thought that the vastly increased facilities of travelling, which enable one, on all the great routes, to do in eight or nine hours the work of three days in old times, would have led us to take things a little more leisurely and comfortably. Instead of this we

* Barber's Historical Collections, p. 266.

clamor for more unseasonable trains, and wish to pass these eight or nine hours under the dark, damp wings of night.

A great change in the weather took place during the night of the 16th; and in the morning Dr. Cressy's churchyard which lay beneath my windows, and the fine street which runs through Auburn, were covered with snow. The weather was not tempting abroad, though I was very desirous of seeing the penitentiary, which occupies so prominent a place in the history of prison discipline,—the "Auburn system" being originally the technical designation of the plan of social labor in the workshop, and solitary confinement at meals and at night. Prevented from going abroad, I passed the hours at home, till it was time to receive the visits of friends—in what occupation think you, gentle reader? Can there be two conjectures as to what a well-meaning man, under engagement to furnish a weekly article to the "New York Ledger," would do with a couple of leisure hours, which he was compelled, by stress of weather, to pass within doors?

The appointed hour arrives, and a full and favoring audience welcomes us to Auburn; a village, I doubt not, though seen by me only under its wintry shroud, far more "sweet" than that from which it derives its lovely name. Compelled to return to Boston by Saturday night, in order to keep my appointments for the following week, I was obliged to deny myself the gratification of a visit to its important public Institutions. And so after one more genial and refreshing hour with my hospitable host, I went, with him, and my obliging friends Mr. Morgan and Mr. Ludlow, (the latter so well known to many of the readers of the Ledger as the "Hasheesh Eater,") to the Railway station, and the train soon arriving from Rochester took us to Syracuse. The night was cold, and one feels a little catch-coldish after speaking two hours; and so the extra clothing of which we spoke rather disparagingly last week, grew mightily into favor again.

We reached Syracuse about twenty minutes after eleven,

and were to leave it for Albany by the Western train for Buffalo, due at five minutes before four; an arrangement of hours, too long to sit up and too short to go to bed, and admirably adapted to cultivate the equanimity of itinerant orators, tired of speaking and anxious to get home. Time does not "gallop withal" under such circumstances; in fact, I am strongly inclined to think that *fretting* is the very best instrument for clipping his wings. At length the Western train arrived with the most gratifying punctuality, and I again took refuge in the sleeping car. No "great president" or high official of the New York Central disturbed my slumbers, which lasted till the break of day. I could have wished, in fact I may say that I fondly expected, that they might last a little longer. I know few places or times when one is less tempted to wake up, than a cold December morning in a sleeping car, after two hours oratory at Auburn and four hours impatient waiting at Syracuse. It so happened, however, that the berths next to me, and on opposite sides of the car, were occupied by travellers from Chicago, who had probably had two nights comfortable sleep since they left home, at any rate had slept all the way from Buffalo. They were consequently prepared to wake with the dawn. They not only woke themselves, but fell into an argument, that produced precisely the same effect upon everybody else in the car. They happened to take opposite views of several important political questions. One appeared to be a naturalized foreigner, and the other was very strongly Native American. They had both gone through the late electioneering campaign in Chicago, which, as far as I could infer from their statements, was "animated" to say the least. Their accounts of it certainly were. They argued, vociferated, and shouted. It was an interchange of sentiment that might be called boisterous; taunt and retort; fling and sarcasm. Virgil tells us that the muses like alternations. I think that if the muses had been broken of their rest as much as I had, they would change their minds a little in a case of this kind. But though the alter*n*ation was decidedly an alter*c*ation, it was upon the whole good-natured. Had they got to blows, one might almost have thought that we had, during our slumbers, been transported to Washington and woke up on the floor of Congress. Happily it was in a sleeping car; the dispute was interspersed with peals of laughter while it lasted, and ended in great good humor and a general waking up.

Nothing adverse happened till we entered the station yard at Albany. Here within a few rods of our goal, our car, which was in the rear, came into collision with an Engine left standing in the wrong place. The iron coupling which attached us to the preceding car snapped like pack-thread, and we were thrown from the track. But we had reached our destination; the damage to the car was trifling, to passengers null. An engineer, as we passed out, judiciously remarked, that "we should not have got off so well had the collision taken place, while we were moving at the rate of thirty miles an hour." Probably not; but whether the carelessness which caused it might not have existed, deserves consideration.

We were comfortably housed at the Delavan at a quarter past ten. The trains from the West are so arranged, that they reach Albany about an hour after the train for Boston has started. If you happen to have business in Albany which occupies four or five hours, this is a convenient arrangement. If you are very anxious to get back to Boston by daylight, it would be a convenient thing to have the two trains connect with each other. But it is impossible that every train should connect with every other; although impatient travellers are apt to think it might.

The afternoon and evening were intensely cold. The pilot clothes and dreadnoughts came admirably in play. The kind-hearted conductor said it was the coldest night of the season. I call him "kind-hearted," because he allowed a poor young mother with a shivering infant in her arms, and not a farthing in her pocket, to keep her seat. "How could I put her out in a night like this?" You couldn't, good conductor, because you have a kind heart;—but I have fallen in with conductors, who I fear would have been less merciful.—Though not in a sleeping car, I enjoyed a glorious sleep almost all the way home. In fact so overwhelmed was I with drowsiness, that I think I could have slept through the argument of my Chicago friends, or the dialogue of the high officer and the great President. The new conductor,—also kind-hearted,—happened to recognize me though asleep, and did not wake me up for my check from West Brookfield to Boston,—for which good office he will long live in the grateful remembrance of a sleepy traveller.

NUMBER EIGHT.

THE PARABLE AGAINST PERSECUTION.

First published by Lord Kames in 1774 as having been communicated to him by Dr. Franklin—Soon discovered in Jeremy Taylor's Liberty of Prophesying—Next found in the dedication to the Senate of Hamburg of the Latin translation by George Genz of a Rabbinical work—Afterwards traced to the "Flower-Garden" of the celebrated Persian poet Saadi—Some account of Saadi—Possibly still to be found in some Jewish writer—Defence of Dr. Franklin against the charge of plagiarism—Quoted by Sydney Smith before the Mayor and Corporation of Bristol in 1829—The parable given entire from Dr. Franklin's works.

No composition of the kind is so famous, perhaps, as the "Parable on Persecution." This is owing, partly, to its intrinsic beauty both of substance and form. The moral lesson which it inculcates is of the purest and loftiest kind; and the form in which this moral is clothed is singularly attractive. Its celebrity, however, is mainly to be ascribed to the circum stances attending its publication,—or rather re-publication in a revised form,—under the name of Dr. Franklin.

In 1774 Lord Kames, in the second volume of his "Sketches of the History of Man," introduced the substance of this parable, with these words: "The following parable against persecution was communicated to me by Dr. Franklin of Philadelphia, a man who makes a great figure in the learned world, *and who would still make a greater figure for benevolence and candor, were virtue as much regarded in this declining age as knowledge.*" Such is Lord Kames' remark, in the first edition of his book, as I find it quoted by Mr. Sparks in the second volume of the works of Franklin. In the third edition of Lord Kames' "Sketches," which lies before me, and purports to be "considerably improved," the words in italics are omitted, probably for political reasons.

The parable was given as follows in his Lordship's Sketches, though not, as will presently appear, with entire accuracy, as communicated to him by Dr. Franklin:

"And it came to pass after these things, that Abraham sat in the door of his tent, about the going down of the sun. And behold a man bent with age coming from the way of the wilderness leaning on a staff. And Abraham arose, and met him, and said unto him, 'Turn in, I pray thee, and wash thy feet, and tarry all night; and thou shalt arise early in the morning, and go on thy way.' And the man said, 'Nay; for I will abide under this tree.' But Abraham pressed him greatly; so he turned, and they went into the tent: and Abraham baked unleavened bread, and they did eat. And when Abraham saw that the man blessed not God, he said unto him, 'Wherefore dost thou not worship the most high God, creator of heaven and earth?' And the man answered and said, 'I do not worship thy God, neither do I call upon his name; for I have made myself a God, which abideth always in my house, and provideth me with all things.' And Abraham's zeal was kindled against the man, and he arose and fell upon him, and drove him forth with blows into the wilderness. And God called unto Abraham, saying, 'Abraham, where is the stranger?' And Abraham answered and said, 'Lord, he would not worship thee, neither would he call upon thy name; therefore have I driven him out from before my face into the wilderness.' And God said, 'Have I borne with him these hundred ninety and eight years, and nourished him, and clothed him, notwithstanding his rebellion against me; and couldst not thou, who art thyself a sinner, bear with him one night?'"

From Lord Kames' work this parable was taken by the late Hon. Benjamin Vaughan of Hallowell, but then of London, in his edition of Dr. Franklin's writings. Mr. Vaughan, as is well known, was the intimate friend of Dr. Franklin, and published in London, in 1779, the first English edition of Franklin's miscellaneous essays. From the time of its appearance in this volume, the Parable began to attract notice, was often repeated, and greatly admired as a most happy illustration of an all-important moral truth.

Though not communicated to Lord Kames by Dr. Franklin as his own composition, it was naturally enough inferred from the manner in which it was brought forward, that such was the case. A good deal of surprise was accordingly manifested, when it was discovered, not long after, that a parable of substantially the same import was found in Jeremy Taylor's "Liberty of Prophesying;" (published in 1657,) in the following words:

"I end with a story which I find in the Jews' Books. When Abraham sat at his tent-door, according to his custom, waiting to entertain strangers, he espied an old man stooping and leaning on his staffe, weary with age and travelle, coming toward him, who was an hundred years of age; he received him kindly, washed his feet, provided supper, caused him to sit down; but observing that the old man eat and prayed not, nor begged for a blessing on his meat, asked him why he did not worship the God of heaven? The old man told him that he worshipped the fire only, and acknowledged no other God; at which answer Abraham grew so zealously angry, that he thrust the old man out of his tent, and exposed him to all the evils of the night and an unguarded condition. When the old man was gone, God called to him, and asked him where the stranger was; he replied, 'I thrust him away because he did not worship thee;' God answered him, 'I have suffered him these hundred years, although he dishonored me, and couldst not thou endure him one night, when he gave thee no trouble?' Upon this, saith the story, Abraham fetcht him back again, and gave him hospitable entertainment and wise instruction. Go thou and do likewise, and thy charity will be rewarded by the God of Abraham."

Bishop Taylor, having quoted "the Jews' Books" as the source of the Parable, search began to be made for it in every direction among Jewish writers, but without success. At length it was discovered.—In the Latin dedication to the Senate of Hamburg, of a Rabbinical work, entitled the "Rod of Judah;" the translator, George Genz, gives the story substantially as found in Jeremy Taylor's "Liberty of Prophesying." The work of Genz was published at Amsterdam, in 1651. The Latin passage is quoted at length by Mr. Sparks and by Bishop Heber, in a note to his life of Jeremy Taylor, but it approaches so near the version contained in "the Liberty of Prophesying," that it is hardly worth while to extract it in this place. There are, however, some differences. For instance, in the Latin preface of Genz the answer is, "'I am a fire-worshipper, and ignorant of manners of this kind; for our ancestors have taught me no such pious observance;' perceiving with horror from his speech, that he had to do with a profane fire-worshipper, and a person alien to the worship of his God, Abraham drove him from his table and his abode, as one whose intercourse was contagious, and as a foe to his religion."

But though there were considerable differences of this kind in the versions, it was thought highly probable, not to say certain, from the substantial similarity of the parable in the preface of Genz to "the Rod of Judah," that Jeremy Taylor derived it from that source; and as it was the preface by a Jew to a Rabbinical work, it was not inaccurately, though rather vaguely, credited by him to "*the Jews' Books.*" The inquiry of course immediately arose as to the authority on which it was given by Genz. He himself cites simply "nobilissimus autor Sadus," "a most noble author *Sadus.*" Who was Sadus?

Conjecture was not long at fault on this point. It was soon discovered in India, that this remarkable composition, which seemed like a shadow to fly as it was approached, was substantially contained, not in any "Jews' Books," (as Jeremy Taylor supposed, for the reasons just stated,) but in the *Bostan* or "Flower Garden" of the celebrated Persian poet Saadi, unquestionably the individual referred to by Genz under the Latinized name of *Sadus.* An English translation of the Parable from this ancient Persian poem was published in the Asiatic Miscellany at Calcutta in 1789, and is quoted from that work in the note of Bishop Heber to the life of Jeremy Taylor, above alluded to. It is somewhat more diffuse, and more strongly tinged with Oriental coloring than in the translation of Genz, but not materially different.

Thus the authorship of this celebrated Parable, originally brought into notice by the great American patriot and philosopher, is traced, through an English prelate, and a German Jew, to the famous Persian poet of the twelfth century. Saadi is supposed to have been born at Shiraz about the year of our Lord 1194, in the reign of Richard Cœur de Lion. He studied at Bagdad, under the most celebrated teachers of the time; but soon embraced a religious life, and made, it is said, fourteen pilgrimages to Mecca, and always on foot. He is reported to have attained the age of a hundred and two years. Some accounts say a hundred and twenty; and that, after reaching the age of twelve, he devoted thirty years to study, thirty to travel, and thirty to retirement and religious contemplations. His literary tastes and religious occupations did not, in middle life, prevent him from discharging the duty of all good Mussulmans, to fight against the infidels. He served both in India and in Asia Minor; and in the latter country was made prisoner by the Crusaders. He was employed by them with other prisoners in throwing up the trenches before Tripoli in Syria. Here he was ransomed for ten pieces of gold by a rich inhabitant of Aleppo; who also gave him his daughter in marriage, which, however, is not represented by him as the most auspicious event of his life. Having acquired a great name as a poet, traveller, and devotee, he built a house in the neighborhood of Shiraz, towards the close of his career; where, retaining of his wealth only what was necessary for his support, he gave up the rest to the poor. He was buried in the garden of his dwelling, and his tomb is still visited as that of one of the brightest geniuses that adorn the literature of his country.

The Parable on Persecution, then, is found in the *Bostan* or "Flower Garden," one of the most celebrated poems of Saadi; and in his *Gulistan*, or "Rose Garden," there is an allusion to an incident in his life, which may by possibility throw a ray of light on the remoter history of the Parable. Saadi states in the *Gulistan*, that while he was a prisoner to the Crusaders, he was set to work, "with some Jews," on the trenches before Tripoli. This was a period of high culture among the Jews of Western Asia; and there is no reason to doubt, that, among the prisoners of that race that fell into the hands of the Christians, some of them may have been, like Saadi himself, men of refinement and learning. Saadi gives the Parable as something that "he had heard once;" and nothing seems to me more probable than that a learned Jew, being a fellow-prisoner with a learned Persian, should have related to him this striking parable, of which the personages were the great Jewish patriarch, and a devotee of the old Persian fire-worship.

On this supposition, it would still remain probable, that the Parable yet lies concealed in some of the ancient "Jews' Books," and may have even been found there by Jeremy Taylor. There is no apparent reason why, if he took it from Genz, he did not name him. A learned Jewish scholar, mentioned by Bishop Heber, was strongly persuaded, that he had somewhere seen it, in a commentary on Genesis xviii. 1,— which has, however, never been found. Whatever be its source, there are few uninspired teachings, Jewish or Christian, equally impressive. It is an undoubted chapter of that great primitive gospel, which the Creator has written on the hearts and minds of men, but which, like the page of revelation, is too apt to be forgotten under the influence of partisan and sectarian passion.

But to return to Franklin's connection with the Parable. As soon as it was discovered that it was found substantially in Jeremy Taylor, Dr. Franklin, then living in England, was accused of plagiarism in the *Repository*, a journal in which the discovery was announced. From this charge a friendly writer, probably Mr. Vaughan, evidently well acquainted with

Dr. Franklin's tastes and habits, defended him, on the ground that he had never claimed it as his own; that it was published without his knowledge by Lord Kames; that Dr. Franklin had been struck and pleased with it, as he heard it or found it, and, having expanded and improved it, had it printed for private distribution.

"This great man," says this writer, "who at the same time that he was desirous of disseminating an amiable sentiment, was an extreme lover of pleasantry, often endeavored to put off the Parable in question upon his acquaintance, as a portion of Scripture, and probably thought this one of the most successful modes of circulating its moral. This object would certainly have been defeated, had he prefixed to the printed copies of the Parable, which he was fond of dispersing, an intimation of its author. He therefore gave no name whatever to it, much less his own. And often as I have heard of his amusing himself on this occasion, I never could learn that he ascribed to himself the merit of the invention."

In a letter to Mr. Vaughan, Dr. Franklin tells him that he had a copy of it bound up in a Bible, and often read it from the volume to his visitors, sometimes to the perplexity of those who heard it, and had no remembrance of having noticed it in their own reading of the Scriptures. This treatment of the sacred volume cannot be entirely approved, though nothing irreverent was intended in it, by Dr. Franklin. The last time, as far as we are aware, that the Parable has attracted public notice in England, was when it was quoted by Sydney Smith, in a sermon preached before the Mayor and Corporation of Bristol, on the 5th of November, 1828. "I told the Corporation," says he, in a letter to a friend, "at the end of my sermon, that beautiful Rabbinical story quoted by Jeremy Taylor, 'as Abraham was sitting at the door of his tent,' &c., which, by-the-by, would make a charming and useful placard against the bigoted."

I cannot better close this curious history than by subjoining the Parable entire, as communicated by Dr. Franklin to Mr. Vaughan; and the reader will no doubt concur with Mr.

Sparks in the remark, that "whoever will compare it as here given, with the sources whence it was derived, will see that its chief point and beauty consists in the dress and additions which it received from Dr. Franklin's hand."

Parable against Persecution.

1. And it came to pass after these things, that Abraham sat in the door of his tent, about the going down of the sun.

2. And behold, a man bowed with age, came from the way of the wilderness, leaning on a staff.

3. And Abraham arose and met him, and said unto him, "Turn in, I pray thee, and wash thy feet, and tarry all night, and thou shalt arise early on the morrow, and go on thy way."

4. But the man said, "Nay, for I will abide under this tree."

5. And Abraham pressed him greatly; so he turned and they went into the tent, and Abraham baked unleavened bread, and they did eat.

6. And when Abraham saw that the man blessed not God, he said unto him, "Wherefore dost thou not worship the most high God, Creator of heaven and earth?"

7. And the man answered and said, "I do not worship the God thou speakest of, neither do I call upon his name; for I have made to myself a God, which abideth always in mine house, and provideth me with all things."

8. And Abraham's zeal was kindled against the man, and he arose and fell upon him, and drove him forth with blows into the wilderness.

9. And at midnight God called unto Abraham, saying, "Abraham, where is the stranger?"

10. And Abraham answered and said, "Lord, he would not worship thee, neither would he call upon thy name; therefore have I driven him out from before my face into the wilderness."

11. And God said, "Have I borne with him these hundred ninety and eight years, and nourished him, and clothed him, notwithstanding his rebellion against me; and couldst not thou, that art thyself a sinner, bear with him one night?"

12. And Abraham said, "Let not the anger of the Lord wax hot against his servant; lo, I have sinned; lo, I have sinned; forgive me, I pray thee."

13. And Abraham arose, and went forth into the wilderness, and sought diligently for the man, and found him and returned with him to the tent; and when he had entreated him kindly, he sent him away on the morrow with gifts.

14. And God spake again unto Abraham, saying, "For this, thy sin, shall thy seed be afflicted four hundred years in a strange land;

15. "But for thy repentance will I deliver them; and they shall come forth with power, and with gladness of heart, and with much substance."

NUMBER NINE.

WASHINGTON'S DIARY.—ROBERTSON'S MINIATURES OF GENERAL AND MRS. WASHINGTON.

A portion of General Washington's Diary the property of Mr. J. Carson Brevoort—Recently printed for private circulation—Illness of Washington in the summer of 1789—Tour in the East partly to recruit his health—A considerable portion of the Diary relates to this tour—Washington consults his friends as to the expediency of the tour—Their opinion—Anecdote of Henry IV. of France, and his ministers Villeroi, Sully, and Jeannin—Robertson's miniature of Gen. Washington forms the vignette to this edition of the Diary—Account of Robertson—And his likenesses of General and Mrs. Washington—Colonel Trumbull's opinion—Photographic copies—Pine's portrait of Washington in Mr. Brevoort's possession—Gen. Washington's letter about it—An original letter of the Duke of Wellington in reply to a request to sit for his portrait to Mr. Inman.

It was known to the friends of the late Henry Brevoort, Esq., of New York, during his lifetime, that, among many other treasures of history, literature, and art, he was in possession of a portion of the original Diary of Washington. It was shown by him to persons not likely to make an improper use of it, but obvious considerations dictated the delay of its publication while many of those named in it were still living. The reasons for withholding it from the public eye have of course been steadily losing their force with the lapse of time. Mr. J. Carson Brevoort, the present possessor of the precious relic, has been able to allow its perusal with less reserve, and has occasionally permitted it to be transcribed for persons engaged in historical researches. Four years ago, while the guest of Mr. Bancroft at Newport, I enjoyed the privilege of reading a copy of it, which he had had the opportunity of adding to his invaluable collection of original documents pertaining to American history, and he was kind enough to allow it to be copied for me, with a minute accuracy, extending to the nicest details of orthography and punctuation. Within a few months, Mr. Carson Brevoort has permitted an edition of one hundred copies of it to be printed for private circulation. As soon as this fact was announced, I felt at liberty to furnish to the editor of the "Portsmouth (N. H.) Journal" at his request, the portion of the Diary narrating General Washington's visit to Portsmouth, which I had read by way of introduction to my Address on its repetition at that place. This I presume was the first occasion on which any considerable portion of this Diary was committed to the Press. No reason for limiting the number of copies of this most interesting document seems now to exist, and I venture to recommend to the accomplished owner of the manuscript, to allow an edition of it to be published for general circulation. The present publication, as may be inferred by the initials appended to the introductory remarks, B. J. L., has been made under the supervision of a gentleman, to whose labors and researches, in illustrating the localities and personalities of the Revolution, the student of our history is deeply indebted. He has in this edition of the Diary given a few valuable explanatory and illustrative remarks.

This part of Washington's Diary is one of a considerable series, of which some portions are in the Department of State at the seat of government, and other portions are believed to be in private hands. "It is in a small oblong volume," not bound in stiff covers, but sewed in old-fashioned marble paper, "about four inches in width and six in length, containing sixty-six leaves," written throughout in the well known firm and legible hand of Washington, with very few erasures, and an occasional blank left to be filled up on subsequent inquiry. It was evidently of a size intended to be carried in the coat pocket, both for convenience at the time, and in order to avoid exposing larger portions of the Diary to risk of loss at once.

The new government, as is well known, went into operation nominally on the 4th of March, 1789, just seventy years ago the present year,—but not in reality for some weeks later. Such distrust pervaded the country of the *reality* of the new order of things, that the members of the first Congress assembled too slowly to form a quorum of the two houses before the sixth of April. The oaths of office were administered to President Washington by Chancellor Livingston, in the open balcony of what was called Federal Hall, in Wall street New York, on the 30th of that month. In the course of the summer, the President was taken down by the most severe illness he had ever known, and his life for some days was thought to be in danger. He was confined to his bed for six weeks, attended by Dr. Bard, a physician of the highest reputation both professional and personal, who was thought, under Providence, by his judicious and devoted attentions, to have saved the precious life confided to his care. General Washington never entirely recovered from the effects of this attack.

To recruit his health after this severe illness, as well as for general purposes of observation, the President determined on a tour of observation in the Autumn of the year, and a considerable part of this portion of the Diary is devoted to the events of this journey, which commenced on Thursday the 15th of October, and terminated on Saturday the 13th of November. Before finally making up his mind to the proposed tour, General Washington, according to his custom, took the advice of some of those in whose judgment he confided on the expediency of the step. The following interesting extracts from the Diary will show the pains which he took in obtaining and recording the views of those whom he consulted:

"Monday 5th. [of October 1789.] Had conversation with Col. Hamilton on the propriety of making a tour through the Eastern States during the recess of Congress, to acquire a knowledge of the face of the Country; the growth and agriculture thereof—and the temper and disposition of the inhabitants towards the new government, who thought it a very desirable plan and advised it accordingly."

"Tuesday 6th. Conversed with Gen. Knox, Secretary at war, on the above tour, who also recommended it accordingly."

"Wednesday 7th. Upon consulting Mr. Jay on the propriety of my intended tour in the Eastern States, he highly approved of it, but observed a similar visit w'd be expected by those of the Southern."

"Thursday 8th. Mr. Madison took his leave to-day. He saw no impropriety in my trip to the Eastward."

The different replies of the distinguished persons consulted by Washington, on this occasion, are somewhat characteristic, and remind one of the manner in which Henry IV. of France illustrated, in the presence of a foreign Minister, the different dispositions of his three ministers Sully, Villeroi, and Jeannin. Col. Hamilton, ever prompt and decided, "thought it a very desirable plan and advised it accordingly." With Gen. Knox "he converses on the above tour," and the veteran artillerist, satisfied that his chief inclines to the measure, simply "recommends it accordingly." Jay, the most cautious and prudent of men, "highly approved of the intended tour;" but saw that in justice and policy, a similar visit would be expected in the other portion of the Union. Mr. Madison, slightly non-committal, neither advised nor dissuaded; but, "he saw no impropriety in the trip to the Eastward." Henry IV. pointed to the ceiling of the reception-room and cried with affected alarm, "See that timber, it is about to fall." Villeroi, with instant compliance, replied, "Sire, it must be replaced immediately." Sully, secure in his royal master's well-earned confidence, exclaims with the bluntness authorized by it, "Who could have given you this groundless alarm, Sire; it will last longer than you or I?" President Jeannin, with judicial caution, says, "I do not perceive, Sire, that there is anything the matter with it, but it ought to be examined by a builder."

The very first page of the Diary shows the heavy drafts made upon the time of General Washington for the purpose of sitting for his portrait.

"Saturday, the 3rd [of October, 1789,] sat for Mr. Rammage near two hours to-day, who was drawing a miniature picture of me for Mrs. Washington."

"Walked in the afternoon and sat about two o'clock for Madame de Brehan, to complete a miniature profile of me which she had begun from memory, and which she had made exceedingly like the original."

This lady was the sister of the Count de Moustier, the French Minister to the United States, and with her son, accompanied her brother to this country. They all visited Mount Vernon in 1788. After their return to France, her miniature profile was engraved, and proof impressions of it sent by the Count to General Washington. The original of it appears also to have been intended by Madame de Brehan (or Brienne) for Mrs. Washington.

An original likeness of Washington, from a miniature by Archibald Robertson painted in 1792, forms the *vignette* to the present edition of the Diary. Robertson came to this country in the Spring of 1791, at the instance of the Earl of Buchan, bringing with him, as a present to Washington from the Earl, a box made of the wood of the oak tree which sheltered Wallace after the battle of Falkirk. No impression of this miniature by Robertson had ever been made, before it was engraved in wood for the present work.

In a manuscript left by Mr. Robertson (from which an extract has been kindly furnished to me by Mr. T. W. C. Moore) he says—

"The first sittings for the original miniature of General and Mrs. Washington were in Philadelphia toward the end of December 1791 and finished in January 1792. In the succeeding month of April, the portrait (in oil) of Washington for Lord Buchan was dispatched by Col. Lear, then on a mission to Europe. His Lordship afterwards expressed his high satisfaction in a letter of thanks to the artist. The original miniatures he (the artist) retains in his own possession, and intends them to remain in his family an heir-loom and memorial of his veneration for the great and successful champion of American Liberty."

It is evident on an inspection of this likeness of Washington, that it was painted before he had begun to wear artificial teeth. The eye, also, I am told, is of a lighter blue than the eye in Stuart's portrait. Mr. William Dunlap in an article in the Atlantic Magazine of 1824, says—

"If we wish to behold Washington, when he began to wane in his latter years, when he had lost his teeth, but with full vivacity and vigor of eye, looking at the spectator, we must behold Robertson's portrait of him."

These interesting miniatures of General and Mrs. Washington are now in the possession of the granddaughter of the artist, Miss A. Robertson of New York, who two or three years ago kindly permitted a few photographic copies of them to be taken, for a pair of which I am indebted to the courtesy of Mr. Moore. Being mounted as a brooch, the miniature of the General are somewhat faded by exposure to solar light, and it is not impossible that the lighter blue of the eye may be accounted for in that way. It is scarcely possible that a colorist like Stuart, at the meridian of his power should have failed in that respect.

In the manuscript above referred to, Mr. Robertson gives an interesting account of the nervous agitation he experienced, on approaching General Washington. It is one among the numberless facts showing the awe which was felt in his presence. After speaking of his agitation and the kind attempts of Washington to overcome it, he proceeds:

"The General, not finding his efforts altogether successful, introduced me to Mrs. Washington, whose easy, polished, and familiar gaiety and ceaseless cheerfulness almost accomplished a cure. Another effort of the President to compose his guest was at a family dinner-party, at which the General, contrary to his usual habits, engrossed most of the conversation, and so delighted the company with humorous anecdotes, that he completely set the table in a roar."

It was my intention, in the commencement of this article, to extract some of the more interesting portions of the Diary, but there remains too little space for that purpose, and its fulfilment must be deferred. It may not be inappropriate to this description of Robertson's miniature, which serves as a *vignette* to the remarks introductory to the Diary, to observe that Mr. Carson Brevoort is also the possessor of the original portrait of Washington by Pine. This painting which, if I am not mistaken, has never been copied nor engraved, is one of extreme value. I hope at some future time, with the permission of the liberal proprietor to have it in my power to offer the readers of the Ledger an accurate description of it. It is the portrait with reference to which Washington gives the famous good natured but somewhat plaintive account of the heavy drafts upon his time, required to satisfy the demands for his likeness. It is in the following words :—

President Washington to Francis Hopkinson, Esq.

MOUNT VERNON, 16 *May*, 1785.

DEAR SIR—*In for a penny in for a pound*, is an old adage. I am so hackneyed to the touches of the painter's pencil, that I am altogether at their beck; and sit, "like Patience on a Monument," whilst they are delineating the lines of my face. It is a proof among many others, of what habit and custom can accomplish. At first I was as impatient at the request, and as restive under the operation, as a colt is under the saddle. The next time I submitted very reluctantly, but with less flouncing. Now, no dray-horse moves more readily to his thill, than I to the painter's chair. It may easily be conceived, therefore, that I yielded a ready obedience to your request and to the views of Mr. Pine.

Letters from England recommendatory of this gentleman came to my hands previous to his arrival; not only as an artist of genius and taste, but as one who had shown a very friendly disposition towards this country, for which it seems he had been marked.

It gave me pleasure to hear from you. I shall always feel an interest in your happiness, and with Mrs. Washington's compliments and best wishes joined to my own for Mrs. Hopkinson and yourself, I am, &c.

I venture to subjoin, by way of comparison, an original letter of the Duke of Wellington on a similar subject, in reply to an application which I made to him in behalf of our countryman, Mr. Inman. I am glad to be able to add, that a short time after the following letter was written, the Duke extended a courteous invitation to Mr. Inman to visit him at Srathfieldsaye, of which, however, he was unable to avail himself.

The Duke of Wellington to Mr. Everett.

LONDON, 22 *Feb.*, 1845.

MY DEAR SIR—I have to apologize for having omitted to return an answer immediately to your note of the 18th, received two days ago.

I am much flattered by the desire of Mr. Inman, that I should sit to him for a picture. But I am much concerned to add that, during the Session of Parliament and while the Court is in town, it is impossible for me to find time which I can devote to him.

I am bankrupt in respect to portraits and busts. I am certain that there are not less than a dozen artists in London, with commissions to paint portraits, or model busts of me. But I cannot find time to give to any one a sitting. I have not been able to give a sitting for many years. I receive the artists at my houses in the country; either Strathfieldsaye or Walmer Castle; and give them sittings at their leisure. Wilkie, Chantrey, Campbell, Mr. Lucas, Mr. Lister and others, the principal artists, have come down and passed their three or four days at my house, and I really can find no other time to give them.

In the last autumn, H. M. the Queen desired me to sit for my portrait for the King of the French, and I sat at Windsor Castle, instead of going out hunting one day and shooting another with his Royal Highness Prince Albert.

I do everything in my power to have time at my disposition! I never dine in company on the days on which the house of Parliament, of which I am a member, sits for the decision of business! Nor go out in the evening. I rise early and go to bed late.

But still my whole time is occupied, and it is absolutely impossible for me to name an hour at which I could receive Mr. Inman, and sit to him for a picture.

Ever, my Dear Sir, yours most faithfully,

WELLINGTON.

EDWARD EVERETT, ESQ., No. 46 Grosvenor Place.

NUMBER TEN.

WASHINGTON'S DIARY.

PART II.

Commencement of his tour to the Eastern States in 1789—First day's journey to Rye—Description of the road—The three different visits of Washington to this part of the country—Second day's journey to Fairfield and description of the road—Third day's journey to New Haven through Stratford and Milford—Description of New Haven—Sunday passed at New Haven—Fourth day's journey to Hartford through Wallingford and Middletown and incidents by the way—Fifth day's journey to Springfield and description of that place—Sixth day's journey to Spencer—Express received at Brookfield from Governor Hancock—Seventh day's journey to Worcester and arrangements for entering Boston—Eighth day's journey to Weston—Arrival at Boston on the ninth travelling day from New York.

General Washington commenced his tour in the Eastern States on the 15th of October, 1789, starting from New York where he then resided as President of the United States. He travelled in a chariot with four horses, and was accompanied by Major Jackson as his official Secretary, by Mr. Tobias Lear, his private Secretary, and by six servants, among whom was his man Billy, his faithful attendant during the revolutionary war. The newly appointed Chief Justice, Mr. Jay, the Secretary of the Treasury, Colonel Hamilton, and the Sercretary *at* war, (for such was at that time the official designation,) General Knox, accompanied the President for some distance from the city. "About 10 o'clock, it began to rain and continued to do so till eleven, when" they "arrived at the house of one Hoyatt, who" kept "a tavern at Kings-bridge, where" they "dined. After dinner through frequent light showers," they "proceeded to the tavern of a Mrs. Haviland at Rye, who" kept "a very neat and decent inn."

Such was the commencement of the journey, substantially in the words of General Washington. The following is his description *verbatim* of the first day's progress, which is copied as a specimen, with the punctuation and capital letters, as they appear in the printed diary.

"The Road for the greater part, indeed the whole way, was very rough and stoney, but the Land strong, well covered with grass and a luxuriant crop of Indian Corn intermixed with Pompions (which were yet ungathered) in the field. We met four droves of Beef Cattle for the New York Market, (about 30 in a drove) some of which were very fine—also a flock of sheep for the same place. We scarcely passed a farm house that did not abd. in Geese."

"Their cattle seemed to be of a good quality, and their hogs large, but rather long legged. No dwelling house is seen without a Stone or a Brick chimney, and rarely any without a shingled roof—*generally* the sides are of shingles also."

"The distance of this day's travel was 31 miles, in which we passed through (after leaving the Bridge) East Chester, New Rochelle and Mamaroneck; but as these places (though they have houses of worship in them) are not regularly laid out, they are scarcely to be distinguished from the intermediate farms, which are very close together—and separated, as one Inclosure from another is, by fences of stone, which are indeed easily made, as the country is immensely stoney. Upon inquiry we find their crops of Wheat and Rye have been abundant—though of the first they had sown rather sparingly on acct. of the destruction which had of late years been made of that grain by what is called the Hessian fly."

The interesting journey thus commenced was not the first which Washington had made in this direction. The life of man and the history of nations present few contrasts so striking, in the fortune of individuals or of communities, as that which marks the successive visits of Washington to the Eastern States. On the 20th of February, 1756, he started from New York, with one or two brother officers, travelling on horseback, and on their way to Boston. He was at that time a provincial Colonel and had been despatched by his superior officer from his station on the frontiers of Maryland and Virginia, to go to Boston to take the decision of Governor Shirley who had just been appointed Commander in chief, on a question of precedence between the Crown troops and those called out by the provinces. The fame of his gallant conduct on the disastrous field of Braddock's defeat went before him, and the public mind seemed already, by strange presentiment, to be drawn toward the future hero of the Revolution. He probably kept his twenty fifth birthday that year at New Haven. At the end of June 1775, Washington passed through New York in the same direction, not now a provincial Colonel in the British Service, and at the commencement of a war between France and England and their respective colonies, but as the Commander in chief of the armies of the Anglo-American Colonies, rushing to the field in the war of Independence. And now having, under a gracious Providence, and through trials of undescribed severity, brought that war to an auspicious close, he was commencing the same journey for the third time, and after an interval of thirty three years since the first visit, as the unanimously elected Chief Magistrate of the United States of America.

The party started the second day from the widow Haviland's at Rye at seven o'clock in the morning, and breakfasted at Stamford (which is six miles distant over a road "hilly and immensely stoney and trying to Wheels and Carriages) at one Webb's a tolerable good house, but not equal in appearance or reality to Mrs. Haviland's." They stopped at Norwalk, which is ten miles further to feed their horses, from whence to Fairfield where they dined and lodged was twelve miles.

"The superb Landscape" says the diary, "which is to be seen from the meeting house of the latter [Fairfield], is a rich regalia. We found all the farmers busily employed in gathering, grinding, and expressing the juice of their apples; the crop of which they say is rather above mediocrity. The average crop of wheat they add, is about 15 bushels to the acre, from their fallow land—often 20 and from that to 25. The Destructive evidences of British cruelty are yet visible both in Norwalk and Fairfield; as there are the chimneys of many burnt houses standing in them yet. The principal export from Norwalk and Fairfield is Horses and Cattle—salted Beef and Pork—Lumber and Indian Corn, and in a small degree Wheat and Flour."

On the third day, October 17th, the party started a little after sunrise from Fairfield, and breakfasted at Stratford, "which is a pretty village on or near Stratford River," after a drive of ten miles. At Stratford the President was received with what he good-naturedly calls "an effort of Military parade; and was attended to the Ferry, which is near a mile from the centre of the Town, by sevl. Gentlemen on horseback." From the ferry they proceeded about three miles to Milford, where "a handsome Cascade over the Tumbling dam" attracts the attention of the illustrious traveller, "but (he adds) one of the prettiest thing of this kind is at Stamford, occasioned also by damming the water for their mills; it is near 100 yards in width, and the water now being of a proper height, and the rays of the sun striking upon it as we passed, had a pretty effect upon the foaming water as it fell." The reader will not fail to observe, that is the third occasion on which Washington has already shown a taste for the beauties of natural scenery, in which it has been sometimes said he was deficient.

From Milford the party took the lower road through West Haven and arrived at New Haven before two o'clock, thus having time to walk through several parts of the city before Dinner. By taking the lower road they missed a Committee of the Assembly, who had been appointed to wait upon the President, and escort him into town, to prepare an Address, and to conduct him when he should leave the city.

"The address," says the diary, "was presented at 7 o'clock—and at nine I received another address from the Congregational Clergy of the place. Between the rect. of the two addresses I received the compliment of a visit from the Govr. Mr. Huntington—the Lieut. Govr. Mr. Wolcott—and the Mayor, Mr. Roger Sherman."

"The City of New Haven occupies a good deal of ground, but is thinly, though regularly laid out and built. The number of souls in it are said to be about 4000. There is an Episcopal Church and 3 Congregational meeting-Houses and a College, in which there are at this time about 120 students under auspices of Doctr. Styles. The Harbour of this place is not good for large vessels—abt. 16 belong to it. The Linnen manufacture does not appear to be of so much importance as I had been led to believe. In a word, I could hear but little of it. The Exports from this city are much the same as from Fairfield, &c., and flax-seed (chiefly to New York.) The road from Kingsbridge to this place runs as near the Sound as the Bays and Inlets will allow, but from hence to Hartford it leaves the Sound and runs near to the Northward."

Sunday the 18th of October was passed by the President at New Haven, and according to his general practice he attended Church both parts of the day. In the morning "at the Episcopal Church," where he was "attended by the Speaker of the Assembly, Mr. Edwards, and a Mr. Ingersoll," and in the afternoon at one of the Congregational Meeting-Houses, (so the President discriminates the places of Worship,) where he was attended "by the Governor, the Lieut. Governor, the Mayor and the Speaker."

"These Gentlemen (continues the diary) all dined with me, (by invitation,) as did Genl. Huntington, at the house of Mr. Brown, where I lodged, and who keeps a good Tavern. Drank Tea at the Mayor's (Mr. Sherman). Upon further inquiry, I find that there has been abt. ——— yards of coarse Linnen manufactured at this place since it was established—and that a Glass work is on foot here, for the manufacture of Bottles. At 7 o'clock in the evening many Officers of this State, belonging to the late Continental army, called to pay their respects to me. By some of them it was said that the people of this State could, with more ease pay an additional 100,000£ tax this Year than what was laid last Year."

The travellers left New Haven about six o'clock in the morning of the 19th, (pretty early rising, for the third week of October,) and reached Wallingford to breakfast, a distance of about thirteen miles, at half past eight. It was the anniversary of the surrender of Cornwallis, eight years before, but the Diary is silent on that as on most other historical reminiscences. At this place the White Mulberry, "raised from the seed to feed the silk worm," attracts the President's notice.

"We also," continues the diary, "saw samples of lustring (exceeding good) which had been manufactured from the Cocoon raised in this town, and silk thread very fine. This, except the weaving, is the work of private families, without interference with other business, and is likely to turn out a beneficial amusement. In the Township of Mansfield, they are further advanced in this business. Wallingford has a Church and two meeting-houses in it, which stand upon high and pleasant grd. About 10 o'clock we left this place, and at the distance of 8 miles passed through Durham. At one we arrived at Middletown on Connecticut River, being met two or three miles from it by the respectable citizens of the place and escorted in by them. While dinner was getting ready I took a walk round the Town, from the heights of which the prospect is beautiful. Belonging to this place, I was informed (by a Genl. Sage) that there were about 20 sea vessels, and to Weathersfield higher up, 22—and to Hartford the like number—other places on the River have their proportion—the whole amounting to about 10,000 tons."

"The Country hereabouts is beautiful and the Lands good. * * * Having dined we set out with the same escort (who conducted us into town) about 3 o'clock for Hartford, and passing through a Parish of Middletown and Weathersfield, we arrived at Hartford, about sundown. At Weathersfield we were met by a party of the Hartford light horse, and a number of Gentlemen from the same place with Col. Wadsworth at their head, and escorted to Bull's Tavern, where we lodged."

On Tuesday the 20th after breakfast, accompanied by Col. Wadsworth, Mr. Ellsworth and Col. Jesse Root, the President visited the woollen factory at Hartford, "which seemed to be going on with spirit." "Their Broadcloths," he remarks, "are not of the first quality as yet, but they are good; as are their Coatings, Cassimeres, Serges, and Everlastings; of the first, that is, broadcloth, I ordered a suit to be sent to me at New York—and of the latter a whole piece to make breeches for my servants. All the parts of this business are performed at the Manufactory except the spinning—this is done by the Country People, who are paid by the cut."

The diary gives the usual account of the general appearance, population, and business of Hartford, and the number of the churches there and at Middletown, bestowing that name, on this occasion, upon the places of congregational worship. He dined and drank tea at Col. Wadsworth's, and about 7 o'clock "received from, and answered the address of, the Town of Hartford."

On Wednesday the 21st the President started for Springfield. He was to have breakfasted with "Mr. Ellsworth" (afterwards Chief Justice Oliver Ellsworth) at Winsdor, but a heavy rain prevented his departure till half-past ten. He "called however on Mr. Ellsworth and stay'd there near an hour." He reached Springfield by four o'clock; "and while dinner was getting examined the continental stores," which he "found in very good order at the buildings (on the hill above the town) which belonged to the United States." "The Elaboratory," continues the dairy, "which seems to be a good building, is in tolerable good repair, and the Powder Magazine, which is of brick, seems to be in excellent order and the powder in it very dry. A Col.° Worthington, Col.° Williams, Adjutant General of the State of Massachusetts, Gen. Shepherd, Mr. Lyman, and many other Gentlemen sat an hour or two with me in the evening at Parson's Tavern where I lodged, and which is a good House."

After an interesting sketch of the road from Hartford and Springfield, (the distance is stated to be twenty-eight miles) the navigation of the river, and the character and produce of the land, the record of the 21st of October closes with the following summary description of Connecticut:

"There is a great equality in the people of this State. Few or no opulent men—and no poor—great similitude in their buildings—the general fashion of which is a chimney (always of Stone or Brick) and door in the middle, with a stair case fronting the latter, running up by the side of the former—two flush stories with a very good show of sash and glass windows—the size generally is from 30 to 50 feet in length and from 20 to 30 in width, exclusive of a back shed, which seems to be added as the family increases. The farms, by the contiguity of the Houses, are small, not averaging more than 100 acres. These are worked chiefly by Oxen (which have no other feed than hay), with a horse and sometimes two before them, both in Plow and Cart. In their light lands and in their sleighs they work Horses, but find them much more expensive than Oxen."

On Thursday, the 22d, the President left Springfield at seven o'clock, and travelled fifteen miles till he "came to Palmer, at the House of one Scott," where he breakfasted. From Palmer to Brookfield "to one Hitchcock's" was fifteen miles. "A beautiful fresh water pond and large" is "in the Plain of Brookfield;" "the fashion of the Houses" was "more diversified than in Connecticut, though many are built in their style."

"At Brookfield" (says the diary) "we fed the Horses and dispatched an Express which was sent to me by Govr. Hancock—giving notice of the measures he was about to pursue for my reception on the Road and in Boston—with a request to lodge at his House.

"Continued on to Spencer, 10 miles further, through pretty good roads, and lodged at the house of one Jenks, who keeps a pretty good Tavern."

On Friday the 23d says the President, we "commenced our course with the sun and passing through Leicester met some Gentlemen of the Town of Worcester, on the line between it and the former to escort us. Arrived about 10 o'clock at the House of ——— where we breakfasted—distance from Spencer 12 miles. Here we were received by a handsome company of Militia Artillery in Uniform, who saluted with 13 Guns on our Entry and departure." At Worcester, a Committee of the citizens of Boston and an Aid of Major Genl. Brooks (afterwards Governor) of the Middlesex Militia waited on the President to make "arrangements of military and other parade " on his way to and in the town of Boston. " Finding this Ceremony was not to be avoided though " he " had made every effort to do it," the President named the hour of ten to review the Middlesex Militia at Cambridge and twelve for entering Boston. He sent word at the same time to General Brooks, that conceiving there was an impropriety in his *reviewing* the Militia or seeing them perform manœuvers, otherwise than as a private man, he could do no more than pass along the line, which might be under arms to receive him.

After breakfast the President left Worcester under escort and at the line between the Counties was met by a troop of Middlesex Light Horse who escorted him to Marlborough where he dined and to Weston where he lodged. Here he was met by Jonathan Jackson, Esqr., the United States Marshall for Massachusetts, who proposed to attend the President while he should be in the State. On Saturday the 24th October, the President started from Weston at 8 o'clock and reached Cambridge at the appointed hour of ten. " Most of the Militia having a distance to come were not in line till after eleven; they made however an excellent appearance with Genl. Brooks at their head."

Here the Lieutenant Governor, Samuel Adams, with the Executive of the State, met the President and, says the diary, " preceded my entrance into town—which was in every degree flattering and honorable."

But we must leave the Diary for the present, proposing in another paper to give an account of this celebrated entrance of Washington into Boston, which at the time was a matter of no little public interest and comment, and on which the Diary throws new light.

5

NUMBER ELEVEN.

LOUIS NAPOLEON.—THREE PHASES IN HIS LIFE.

The Downfall of Napoleon the First—His escape from Elba in 1815—His second fall and retirement of his family at Rome—Louis Napoleon a boy at his father's table —After a lapse of twenty-one years on trial for his life at Paris—His appearance and demeanor—His imprisonment at Ham—The revolution of February 1848 and downfall of Louis Philippe—Re-appearance of Louis Napoleon as deputy, Prince, President, and Emperor—General character of his administration—Unscrupulous violence of the party press under Louis Philippe—His government overturned by leaders who aspired only to supplant his ministers—the Press of the United States.

I REMARKED in the last number, that "the life of man and the history of nations present few contrasts so striking, in the fortune of individuals or of communities, as that which marks the successive visits of Washington to the Eastern States." As far as the fortune of individuals is concerned, the name, which stands at the head of this article, exhibits a contrast of conditions, at different periods of life, quite equal to that which is presented in the career of Washington. The year 1814 was a most momentous year in the history of modern Europe. The great drama of the French Revolution seemed to have found its catastrophe. Dethroned kings recovered their sceptres; needy emigrants returned to the possession of their titles and the hope of one day regaining their estates; and what seemed to stamp with permanence the great political and social restoration, the mighty hero of this world-drama, crushed by the armies of combined Europe, had been banished to a petty islet on the coast of Tuscany. Peace was concluded between the United States and Great Britain at the close of the year, and the temple of Janus was shut.

Such was the state of things when, on the 12th of April 1815, I sailed for Europe in a ship of three hundred and fifty tons, which at that time was thought a large vessel. It was the second which sailed from Boston for England after the peace, a fact sufficiently indicative of the profound torpor into which the foreign commerce of the country had sunk during the war. Intelligence did not reach us from Europe every three days, as it does now. It was six or seven weeks, if I recollect right, after the signature of the treaty of Ghent on Christmas Eve, 1814, before the welcome news reached this country. Between that event and our arrival in Europe a new and most astonishing revolution had taken place. It was announced to us by the pilot, who climbed over the bulwarks of our little vessel off Holyhead, in the rather homely statement that "Boney had broke loose again." The suspicion, with which we were inclined to receive this news, was soon removed by the sight of the Liverpool papers, which contained the certain intelligence that the continent of Europe was again a-blaze with war.

No one of course could foretell the result for Napoleon or for Europe. Lord Byron, in a conversation which I had with him a few days before the battle of Waterloo, alluding to the conflict which was evidently impending, expressed the opinion that Napoleon would drive the Duke of Wellington. This he said he should be sorry for, as he did not wish his countrymen to be beaten, adding, however, with bitter emphasis, that he would tell me what he did wish to see,—"Lord Castlereagh's head carried on a pike beneath his windows." But in a few days the great Message of Waterloo (first brought by a clerk of Rothschild, in advance of the Duke of Wellington's courier) arrived from Belgium, and in a few weeks the curtain again fell on the mighty drama, (and this time never more to rise for the principal actor,) at St Helena.

New restorations of fugitive kings, new return of emigrant nobles, new adjustments of the political relations of Europe, and in the final result, the kindred of the fallen hero, consigned to private life at Rome.—Here it was my good fortune, in the winter of 1817–1818, to become acquainted with the venerable mother of an emperor, three kings, and one queen; and with those of her children who were living at Rome, viz.: the Ex-King Louis, (the father of the present Emperor of the French;) Lucian, who at an early period of his career lost the favor of his imperial brother; and the princess Borghese, still one of the most beautiful women of her day, and as amiable as she was beautiful.

In the course of the winter I saw for the first time, at dinner at his father's table, the present emperor of the French, than a boy of eleven years of age. The party was small, and being very near the ex-King, when we were invited to seat ourselves unceremoniously, I was about to place myself in the chair next him, and as it happened on his right hand. With a good-humored smile, as if not wholly in earnest, he requested me to let his son sit there and to accept a seat myself on his left hand.—It probably did not enter even into his fond imagination, that the lad, for whom he claimed this little remnant of royal deference, would one day sit upon the throne of his Uncle. I have no distinct recollections of him in this first phase of his life, but as a handsome, well-behaved youth, with an expression somewhat beyond his years, of mature manners, and as taking little part in the conversation of the dinner table.

Twenty one years pass, and being on a second visit to Europe in the Summer of 1840, I was present in the gallery of the house of Peers in Paris, when the handsome, well-behaved, quiet boy, with whom I had dined at his father's table in 1819, now grown up to a resolute, aspiring, fearless young man, thirty two years of age, was on trial for his life, after the miscarriage of the affair at Boulogne. Four years (I think) before, a similar attempt at Strasburg had sent him into exile in the United States and England, where he lived without attracting public notice, though doubtless cherishing the visions, which were one day to burst into startling realities for himself and Europe. Nothing had occurred in the twenty one years to call my attention to him; but when I saw him on trial for his life before the peers of France, I could not, in the extreme peril in which he stood, but recollect with emotion under what different circumstances I had first seen him. His demeanor before his judges was firm, composed, and respectful. The French criminal jurisprudence subjects the prisoner to a severe interrogatory, for a purpose wholly forbidden by our law, that of making him, if guilty, criminate himself. As far as I could judge, the young man answered with frankness the questions propounded to him, and the impression made by him on his judges,—certainly the impression on the crowded galleries—was decidedly favorable.

This attempt at the time seemed rash almost to the point of insanity. In conversing with the ex-King of Holland a few months afterwards, then living in the House of Alfieri, at Florence, he expressed the opinion to me that it was a *guet-apens*,—a snare set for his son, by the French police, in order to get the young man into their power. I have, however, since seen it stated, that the attempt was by no means so rash as it seemed; that an understanding had taken place between Louis Napoleon and the regiment stationed at Boulogne; and that, a day or two before his landing, in consequence of some vague rumor having reached Paris, that the troops could not be relied upon, and that mischief was brewing, another regiment was sent to that city.

The young man's head was spared and he was sent to the fortress of Ham, a prisoner for life. In that confinement unquestionably his character ripened for the empire. His occupations, never frivolous, assumed a severer cast. He studied and wrote on civil engineering, artillery, and the political system of his Uncle, and escaped from the fortress, a more dangerous enemy to the reigning dynasty than he went in. In eight years from his sentence in 1840, the government of Louis Philippe was overturned, as good a one, probably, as France could bear, though far too bureaucratic for a liberal government; too mild for a despotism. It promoted the material prosperity of France, but it was neither feared nor loved. After the sad death of the Duke of Orleans, it had no hold upon the army—the sole efficient prop of a French throne. The old nobility affected to despise it though they accepted its favors,—the legitimists hated it,—the republican factions swore its downfall;—and the mass of the people, who were never more prosperous than under Louis Philippe, with the fatal apathy of conservative parties, allowed it to sink. —It is not certain that anything could have upheld it much longer, for as was wittily said by one of Louis Philippe's cabinet, who escaped with him to London, "there are two kinds of government which the French cannot bear—one is Republicanism,—the other Monarchy." The catastrophe, however, was dimly foreseen, for it was said by the same ex-minister, "We knew we were living on the crust of a volcano, but we did not think it was so thin."

But the volcano burst forth in February, 1848; Louis Philippe is driven into exile as Charles X. had been before him, the streets of Paris are piled with barricades and drenched with blood, the Tuileries are sacked, Neuilly is ravaged, and "the impossible republic" is inaugurated. Louis Napoleon, enrolled as a special constable with two hundred thousand other citizens of London, at the time of the great chartist demonstration in April, is elected a member of the ephemeral chamber; his choice as Prince President soon follows; on the 2d of December, 1852, the quiet lad of 1819, by a *coup d' etat*, whose unexampled boldness is excelled only by its success, takes possession of the throne of France; and it devolved upon me, in an official capacity, to send to Mr.

Rives, the American Minister in Paris, a letter of credence to the government of his Imperial Majesty Napoleon the Third.

In that capacity he has given to France the strongest government,—equivalent, I fear, in that country to the best government,—which she has had since the downfall of his uncle.—He has completed public works, beneath which the magnificent profusion of Louis the fourteenth staggered. He has decorated and improved Paris beyond all his predecessors on the throne, and projected and accomplished the most gigantic undertakings throughout the interior and along the coasts of France. Abroad he has consolidated the conquest of Algeria,—maintained an undoubted superiority for France over the armies of England associated with hers in the Crimea;—formed a firm alliance with Great Britain, against whom his uncle waged an internecine war for twenty years; and has restored his country to her former rank in the politics of Europe.* In accomplishing these objects, the press has been fettered and the tribune silenced, and those liberties, which the Anglo-Saxon mind regards as the final cause of the political societies of men, have been grievously abridged. But France has yet to show that she is capable of enjoying them in peace.

Happening to be in Paris during the Summer of 1840, and in the habit of reading the principal journals, as well those adverse as friendly to the government, I was amazed at the virulence and ferocity with which the political war was carried on. Had the king been a military usurper instead of a prince succeeding by a species of popular choice to the throne, in the place of one who had forfeited it by violating the Constitution, he could not have been more fiercely assailed, and that by some of the most vigorous pens in France. Had the ministry, instead of holding power on the tenure of parliamentary support, been solely dependent on the will of

* This was written before the war of 1859, which has shown that the Emperor of the French, to all his other extraordinary endowment unites a military capacity of the highest order.

a despot, they could not have encountered a deadlier opposition. The government was eminently pacific, and as such, it gave France a breathing space after the conflicts and exhaustions of her mighty wars; but it was daily denounced as pusillanimous. The king and his family lavished their vast private possessions on works of public utility and private charity, and were continually libelled as selfish and sordid wretches. When the law was appealed to, for that protection of their personal characters from those outrages, to which the humblest are entitled, triumphant verdicts of acquittal were obtained by the calumniators. The unreflecting mass of the community, in the enjoyment of peace abroad and prosperity at home, were made to believe that they were the most oppressed and insulted of nations. Well aware from the history of the last eighteen centuries of the fiery susceptibility of Gallic blood, instead of marvelling at the Revolution of February, 1848, when it burst out, I had for eight years been anticipating it, and predicting it to my friends.

That revolution which extinguished the parliamentary liberties of France,—which turned into dreamy nonsense the doctrinarian wisdom of thirty years,—and joked together in one common humiliation, the leaders of the rival factions, was the work of party.—I do not mean that there was nothing to blame on the part of the king's government, but on the 23d of February, 1848, the popular leaders thought only of displacing their opponents in the ministry; on the 24th they had overturned the monarchy. On the 24th of February, 1848, they drove out a constitutional king; on the 2d of December, 1852, they were marched to prison under the bayonets of an imperial guard. The statesman who falls at the post of duty commands respect; the politician who imperils the great interests of his country to subvert a rival is a public enemy, and merits no sympathy if crushed himself by an impartial despotism.

All assumption of unconstitutional power is usurpation, but the government of Louis Napoleon has received the sanction of an overwhelming majority of his subjects. M. Berryer, in his late defence of the Count de Montalembert, says that he has seen seventeen governments in France. Of these seventeen governments, those of Louis the sixteenth and Charles the tenth,—the two out of the seventeen least respected by the people and both violently superseded,—are the only ones which ruled by a regular constitutional title. It is a fact not generally known, but of which I am well informed, that in overturning the government in 1852, Louis Napoleon, did but anticipate a movement of the Chambers against himself. The resolution was formed to arrest and impeach him and no alternative remained to him but to succumb to the venal demagogues who, under the abused name of constitutional freedom, had brought France to the brink of ruin, or to extinguish them and with them, for the time at least, the parliamentary liberties of the country.

It is painful to reflect how many eloquent pens and persuasive voices of France are silenced by the censor; but if they did not join in the clamor, (some of them did,) they held their peace, when the madness of party rage, by unremitting assaults on a mild and constitutional government, crushed it beneath a load of undeserved opprobrium. They have their reward. Would that our beloved country might profit by the example! The Press of the United States is vigorous and enterprising, and reaches the heart of the community, far beyond that of any other country. It is for good or for evil, the most powerful influence that acts on the public mind,—the most powerful in itself, and as the channel through which most other influences act. If it could learn that an opponent is not necessarily an unprincipled and selfish adventurer, a traitor, a coward, and a knave; and that our neighbors on an average are as honest and right minded as ourselves, it would increase its own power and the great interests of the country (which languish under the poison of our party bitterness) would be incalculably promoted.

NUMBER TWELVE.

WASHINGTON'S DIARY.

Washington's entrance into Boston involved, to some extent, a question of State rights —Major Russell's account inexact—General Washington's own account—Gov. Hancock abandons his ground and calls first on the President—Termination of the affair—Oratorio—Dinner at Fanueil Hall—The President requested to sit for his portrait—Postponement of the music at the Oratorio—Duck Manufactory described—Card Manufactory—Visit to the French vessels of War—Departure from Boston and continuation of the journey—Letter to Mr. Taft at Uxbridge.

The entrance of the President into Boston is the most important event mentioned in the Diary, inasmuch as it assumed, to some extent, the form of an issue between State Rights and Federal precedency. We have already seen that Governor Hancock invited the President to be his guest, during his visit to Boston. The President, in reply to this invitation, said "from a wish to avoid giving trouble to private families, I determined on leaving New York, to decline the honor of any invitations to quarters, which I might receive while on my journey; and, with a view to observe this rule, I had requested a gentleman to engage lodgings for me during my stay in Boston." On the receipt of this letter, Governor Hancock despatched a second express to the President, inviting him and his suite to an informal dinner on his arrival in Boston. This invitation met the President at Weston and was accepted.

Thus far all seems to have proceeded harmoniously, at least to outward appearance. Major Russell, however, the veteran Editor of the Columbian Centinel, and one of the committee of arrangements for the reception of the President states in an interesting letter to Mr. Sparks (Washington's writings vol. x. p. 491) that a collision of opinion and design existed from the first between Governor Hancock and the Committee of the Citizens. These two parties, according to the Major, made arrangements independently of each other, and without mutual consultation; the Governor as we have seen, inviting the President to be his guest;—the Citizens informing him that they had made provision for his accommodation. Major Russell represents that the express sent by the Citizens reached the President first, and that their invitation was accepted. This is inexact. The Governor's invitation was received at Brookfield and declined; that of the Citizens reached the President the day after at Worcester, but he had previously informed the Governor that he should go to Lodgings. The dissatisfaction of Governor Hancock did not therefore, as Major Russell supposed, arise from his having been anticipated by the Citizens, such not having been the fact.

Major Russell states another fact at variance with the uniform tradition. He says that the Governor "claimed the right of receiving and welcoming *in person* the expected guest, on his arrival at the boundary of the Capital. The Committee on their part, contended, that, as the President was then about to enter the town, it was the delegated right of the Municipal authorities to receive and bid him welcome; that it was in their opinion, the right and duty of the Governor to have met the guests at the boundary of the State over which he presided, and there to have received and bid him welcome to the hospitalities of the Commonwealth."

This was, in Major Russell's recollection the matter in controversy; and he further represents that, as the President was approaching the town, "both authorities remained in their carriages, while the aids and Marshals were rapidly posting between them. Both contended that the point of etiquette was on their side. The day was unusually cold and murky. The President with the Secretary had been mounted for a considerable time on the *Neck*, waiting to enter the town. He made enquiry of the cause of the delay, and on receiving information of the *important* difficulty, is said to have expressed impatience. Turning to Major Jackson, his Secretary, he asked, 'Is there no other avenue to the town?' And he was in the act of turning his charger, when he was informed that the controversy was over, and that he would be received by the Municipal authorities."

There must, however, be much inaccuracy in this account, written after an interval of forty four years. That a tedious delay took place is no doubt true; it is rarely wanting on occasion of extensive civic and military processions. But that Governor Hancock claimed the right of receiving the President *in person* at the entrance of the town, and was even struggling with the city authorities for an hour or two to effect that object, while the President was kept waiting, is in the highest degree improbable in itself, as it is contrary to the uniform tradition, and wholly inconsistent with the fact that, in two or three hours afterward, the Governor sent a message to the President, that he was too ill to call upon him at his lodgings. General Sullivan in his Familiar Letters, states that during the detention, which, from whatever cause, undoubtedly took place at the entrance of Boston, the President was exposed to a raw northeast wind, by which exposure he was visited by a severe cold. Many other persons were exposed and affected in like manner, and the affection became so general, as to be called the "Washington Influenza." General Washington rode on a white charger, with his hat off, not bowing to the spectators as he passed, but sitting his horse with a calm dignified air. The following is the President's own account of his *entrèe* in which the reader will perceive that there is no mention of any such collision of authorities as Major Russell records,—a circumstance too remarkable, one would think, to have been omitted had it taken place.

"To pass over the Minutiæ of the arrangements for this purpose, it may suffice to say that at the entrance I was welcomed by the Selectmen in a body. Then following the Lieut. Govr. and Council in the order we came from Cambridge, (preceded by the Town Corps, very handsomely dressed,) we passed through the Citizens classed in their different professions, and under their own banners, till we came to the State House, [the old State House at the head of State Street]; from which across the Street an Arch was thrown; in the front of which was this Inscription. 'To the Man who unites all hearts'—and on the other—'To Columbia's favorite Son'—and on one side thereof next the State House, in a pannel decorated with a trophy, composed of the Arms of the United States—of the Commonwealth of Massachusetts—and our French Allies, crowned with a wreath of Laurel, was this Inscription—'Boston relieved March 17th, 1776.' This Arch was handsomely ornamented, and over the centre of it a Canopy was erected 20 feet high, with the American Eagle perched on the top. After passing through the Arch, and entering the State House, at the So. End and ascending to the upper floor and returning to a Balcony at the No. End; three cheers were given by a vast concourse of people who by this time had assembled at the Arch—then followed an ode composed in honor of the President; and well sung by a band of select singers—after this three Cheers—followed by the different Professions and Mechanics in the order they were drawn up with their colors through a lane of People, which had thronged about the Arch under which they had passed. The Streets, the Doors, windows and tops of the Houses were crowded with well dressed Ladies and Gentlemen. The procession being over, I was conducted to my lodgings at a Widow Ingersoll's, (which is a very decent and good house) by the Lieut. Govr. & Council—accompanied by the Vice-President, where they took leave of me. Having engaged yesterday to take an informal dinner with the Govr. to-day, but under a full persuasion that he would have waited upon me so soon as I should have arrived—I excused myself, upon his not doing it, and informing me thro' his Secretary that he was too much indisposed to do it, *being resolved to receive the visit.* Dined at my Lodgings, where the Vice-President favored me with his Company."

It is plain from the clause italicized, that it was the understanding of the President that the Governor deemed himself entitled to receive the first visit, as Chief Magistrate of Massachusetts, which the President, on the contrary thought due to himself as the Chief Magistrate of the whole United States,

Massachusetts included. There is no doubt, that Governor Hancock entertained this opinion conscientiously. Had he firmly adhered to it, testifying in every other respect, all possible consideration for the President of the United States, his opinion, "though most persons at the present day, as then, would propably deem it erroneous," would have been entitled to respect, certainly as held by so distinguished a revolutionary patriot. His friends however, Mr. Sparks informs us, held a consultation with the Governor in the evening, and in compliance with their advice, he wrote the following not very well expressed note to General Washington the next day.

"Sunday, 26 October, half-past Twelve o'clock.

"The Governor's best respects to the President. If at home and at leisure, the Governor will do himself the honor to pay his respects in half an hour. This would have been done much sooner, had his health in any degree permitted. He now hazards everything as respects his health, for the desirable purpose."

To this note the President returned the following reply:

"The President of the United States presents his best respects to the Governor, and has the honor to inform him, that he shall be at home till two o'clock.

"The President need not express the pleasure which it will give him to see the Governor; but at the same time he most earnestly begs that the Governor will not hazard his health on the occasion."

The Diary of Sunday acquaints us with the result of these communications.

"Sunday, 25th. Attended Divine Service at the Episcopal Church whereof Doctor Parker is the Incumbent," [Trinity Church, in Summer Street] "in the forenoon, and the Congregational Church of Mr. Thacher" [in Brattle Street] "in the Afternoon. Dined at my lodgings with the Vice President. Mr. Bowdoin accompanied me to both Churches. Between the two I received a visit from the Govr., who assured me that indisposition alone prevented his doing it yesterday, that he was still indisposed; but as it had been suggested that he expected to *receive* the visit of the President, which he knew was improper, he was resolved at all haz'ds to pay his compliments to-day. The Lieut. Gov'r and two of the Council, to wit, Heath and Russell, were sent here last night to express the Gov'rs concern that he had not been in a condition to call upon me so soon as I came to town. I informed them in explicit terms that I should not see the Gov'r unless it was at my own lodgings."

These lodgings were in the house still standing, at the corner of Court street and Tremont street, now occupied as a grocery on the ground floor, with lawyers' offices above. As a dwelling house it was one of highly respectable appearance and character for that day.

The Diary for the following day records the sad consequence of the detention and exposure of the President on entering the town. It will be observed that he calls the war of the revolution "the dispute with Great Britain." This was frequently done by the worthies of that day, reserving the name of "War" for the struggle between England and France of 1756.

"Monday 26. The day being rainy and stormy, myself much disordered by a cold and inflammation in the left eye, I was prevented from visiting Lexington (where the first blood in the dispute with G. Britain was drawn). Rec'd the compliments of many visitors to-day. Mr. Dalton and Gen'l Cobb dined with me, and in the evening [I] drank Tea with Gov'r Hancock and called upon Mr. Bowdoin on my return to my lodgings."

Thus terminated an affair without serious consequences and without scandal, which at the moment assumed an alarming character, and might with less judicious counsel have resulted in permanent mischief.

The events of Tuesday and Wednesday, the remaining days of Washington's visit to Boston, are given in the words of the Diary:

"Tuesday 27th. At 10 o'clock in the morning, received the visits of the Clergy of the town. At 11 went to an Oratorio—and between that and 3 o'clock rec'd the Addresses of the Governor and Council—of the town of Boston—of the President &c. of Harvard College, and the Cincinnati of the State; after wch at 3 o'clock at a large and elegant Dinner at Fanueil Hall, given by the Gov'r and Council and spent the evening at my Lodgings. When the Committee from the Town presented their Address it was accompanied with a request (in behalf they said of the Ladies) that I would sit to have my Picture taken for the Hall, that others might be copied from it for the use of their respective families. As all the next day was assigned to various purposes, and I was engaged to leave town on Thursday early, I informed them of the impracticability of my doing this, but that I would have it drawn when I returned to New York, if there was a good painter there—or by Mr. Trumbull when he should arrive, and would send it to them."

A slight mishap occurred at the Oratorio. On account of the indisposition of several of the first performers, (as stated in the Centinel of the following day,) the music was postponed for a week. "Several pieces, however, were given which merited and received applause"! Of this rather serious drawback to the success of an Oratorio, viz.: the postponement of the music in consequence of the indisposition of several of the principal performers, all mention is kindly omitted in the Diary.

"Wednesday 28th. Went, after an early breakfast, to visit the duck manufactory, which appeared to be carrying on with spirit, and in a prosperous way. They have manufactured 32 pieces of Duck of 30 or 40 yds. each in a week, and expect in a short time to increase it to
They have 28 looms at work, and 14 Girls spinning with Both hands, (the flax being fastened to their Waist.) Children (girls) turn the wheels for them, and with this assistance each spinner can turn out 14 lbs. of Thread pr. day when they stick to it, but as they are paid by the piece, or work they do, there is no other restraint upon them but to come at 8 o'clock in the morning, and return at 6 in the evening. They are daughters of decayed families, and are girls of character—none others are admitted. The number of hands now employed in the different parts of the work is but the Managers expect to increase them to . This is a work of public utility and private advantage. From hence I went to the Card Manufactory, where I was informed about 900 hands of one kind and for one purpose or another—all kinds of Cards are made; and

there are Machines for executing every part of the work in a new and expeditious man'r, especially in cutting and bending the teeth, wch. is done at one stroke. They have made 63,000 pr. of Cards in a year, and can undersell the imported Cards—nay Cards of this Manufactory have been smuggled into England. At 11 o'clock I embarked on board the barge Illustrious, Captn. Penthere Gion, and visited his ship and the Superb, another 74 Gun Ship in the Harbour of Boston, about 4 miles below the Town. Going and coming I was saluted by the two frigates which lye near the wharves, and by the 74s after I had been on board of them. I was also saluted going and coming by the fort on Castle Isld. After my return I dined in a large Company at Mr. Bowdoin's, and went to the Assembly in the evening, where (it is said) there were upwards of 100 Ladies. Their appearance was elegant, and many of them very handsome; the room is small but neat and well ornamented."

The President left Boston the following morning. His departure was fixed at eight o'clock. As that hour was striking, he was seen in the door-way of his lodgings, and at the last stroke of the clock he started with his suite. The troop of Cavalry appointed to escort him did not overtake him till nearly arrived at Charlestown Bridge. On his way to Salem he visited Harvard College, where he expressed the opinion from the inspection of the drawing, that the inscription on Dighton rock, is the work of our aborigines. From Cambridge he passed through Malden, Lynn and Marblehead to Salem, where he remained over night. On the 30th he proceeded to Newburyport and lodged there. From Newburyport the following day he went to Portsmouth and remained there till Wednesday the 4th of November, when he started on the return through Exeter, Haverhill, Bradford, Andover, Wilmington, Watertown, Needham, Sherborne, Holliston and Uxbridge. Here he lodged at "one Taft's," where, "though the people were obliging the entertainment was not very inviting." The following letter written to Mr. Taft from Hartford, the second day after lodging at his house, places the gentler qualities of Washington's character in a very pleasing light. The person referred to by the name of Polly is still living.

"HARTFORD, 8 Nov: 1789.

SIR—Being informed that you have given my name to one of your sons, and called another after Mrs. Washington's family, and being moreover very much pleased with the modest and innocent looks of your two daughters, Patty and Polly, I do for these reasons send each of these girls a piece of chintz; and to Patty, who bears the name of Mrs. Washington, and who waited more upon us than Polly did, I send five guineas, with which she may buy herself any little ornaments she may want, or she may dispose of them in any other manner more agreeable to herself. As I do not give these things with a view to have it talked of, or even to its being known, the less there is said about it the better you will please me; but, that I may be sure the chintz and money have got safe to hand, let Patty, who I dare say is equal to it, write me a line informing me thereof, directed to "The President of the United States at New York." I wish you and your family well, and am your humble servant,

"GEO. WASHINGTON."

I should have been pleased to be able to extend this review and abstract of President Washington's Diary, but I have already appropriated to it as much space as can be given up to one subject. The extracts submitted to the reader will, if I mistake not, throw some new light on his character, shewing that he was as exact and methodical, as considerate and gentle, in the private relations and minor duties of life, as he was grand and heroic in its great emergencies. An edition of the diary for general circulation, accompanied with copious notes, and illustrated with accounts of his progress, the addresses made to him and his replies, and the other incidents of his reception, would be a highly valuable contribution to History.

NUMBER THIRTEEN.

ABBOTSFORD VISITED AND REVISITED.

PART I.

Invitation to Abbotsford—Arrival at Melrose—Ruins of Melrose hastily visited—Walk to Abbotsford—And reception there—Church at Selkirk—Walk to the Mushroom Park—Dogs in company, who accidentally start a hare—The house and grounds—Ornaments of the rooms—Reading of the Heart of Mid Lothian—Visit to Melrose—Manner of passing the time at Abbotsford—Charles Scott—Departure for Selkirk, but the London Mail Coach being full, return to Abbotsford—Sir Walter's fondness for animals, dogs and cats—Piper at dinner.

HAVING had the happiness, in the month of July, 1818, to make the acquaintance of Sir Walter Scott and his amiable family at Edinburgh, I was honored with an invitation to visit them at Abbotsford, after I should have returned from a short tour in Perthshire. I feel that there is a sanctity in private life, which ought to be respected, even after all concerned have passed away. But entertaining no feelings but those of veneration and gratitude toward the illustrious name, which stands at the head of this paper, and having nothing to record of him and his, inconsistent with those feelings, I trust that I shall not offend the strictest delicacy, in describing the occurrences of a few days passed within his family circle in the country,—and very much in the language, in which I noted them down at the time.

On the first of August, 1818, I took passage at Edinburgh in the Blücher Stage Coach for Melrose. Passing a bookseller's as we drove through the City, I saw the " Heart of Mid-

Lothian" advertised, and the good natured driver, by whose side I sat, was kind enough to stop while I ran in and bought it. This proved to be the first copy of that novel which reached Abbotsford, excepting the copy which had come in the shape of proof sheets to the (as yet unavowed) author.

It is another of the thousand illustrations of the marvellous power of Scott's genius, that the most remarkable ruins of the most remarkable mediæval church in Scotland, were first raised into general notoriety and classic renown, fifty years ago, by "the Lay of the Last Minstrel." I shall not attempt to describe what has been so often described before,—the ruins of the Abbey, the Tweed, and the Eildon hills which rise in front of you, cleft of old by the never-to-be repeated words of the mighty wizard. Although I expected to pass two or three days in the neighborhood, I could not resist the temptation to take in advance a hasty view of the Abbey. Those who have never seen the ruins of a grand old building,—what we call a gothic ruin especially,—can form no conception of its effect on the feelings of a young traveller. It is one of the most striking examples of the mingled interests of loveliness and desolation; art and the triumph of time and violence over art; beauty and ashes, that can be seen on earth. I did not, indeed, on this occasion, visit "fair Melrose" by moonlight, as Scott says all must do, "who would view it aright," though his daughter Sophia told me he never so visited it himself. I think, however, that I must have misunderstood her, or that she must have meant that he was not then in the habit of doing it. That he had *never* surveyed it by moonlight is hard to believe, after reading the inimitable description in "the Lay."

But whether seen by sunlight or moonlight, it is most beautiful in its decay. The lightness of the arches; the grace of the curves; the slender airy mullions still standing, though sashes and painted glass have long been gone; mysterious staircases in ruinous turrets; the fragments of pillars scattered on the pavements; broken, uncouth images piously laid up against the walls in order to preserve them from further injury; the tomb of Michael Scott and of Alexander one of the kings of Scotland,—how much is there not here,—especially when passed through the prism of some of the most admirable strains of modern poetry,—to fire a youthful imagination! But I shortened my visit, hoping before I left the neighborhood to visit Melrose in company with a greater magician than he that sleeps within its crumbling vaults.

While I was making my solitary pilgrimage to the ruins, my stage-coach companions were ordering dinner at the inn; a less ethereal gratification, but in its place not to be disdained, particularly at the end of a day's journey, and in the shape of trout from the Tweed and green peas from the gardens on its banks. After dinner I started on foot for Abbotsford, distant about three miles. In former times, and when one travelled by stage coaches and post chaises, I always, in journeying walked as much as possible; and surely there could be no occasion when one would more wish to do it, than in the approach of Abbotsford and along the banks of the Tweed, the road running for the most part by the river's side. A short hour brought me to my destination though I did not see the house till I was close upon it, so thick a shrubbery already clothed a spot, which only six years before was entirely bare.

The family were at table when I arrived, the dinner hour being earlier than I thought; but my coming in caused no stir. I was received as an old acquaintance,—I might always say friend. Mr. Scott (for such he then was) alluding to some remarks that had passed betwen us in Edinburgh about the prodigious effect of his poems in turning such a vast amount of travel into the lake region of Scotland, scarcely visited before except by an occasional antiquarian tourist,—good humoredly asked, "whether I did not forgive him the time and money he had cost me among the lochs and hills?" Starting with this genial salutation, the afternoon and evening passed with inconceivable rapidity. Sir Walter was in the best possible spirits, and Sophia, as yet "fancy free," sang us several ballads with the most touching expression and pathos.

The next day was Sunday. Sir Walter gave me my choice of going with his wife and daughters to church, or walking with him over the fields. I decided for the former, and drove with them to church at Selkirk. The intellectual portion of the service was not of a high order, but the devotional parts were performed with becoming solemnity. The singing was about such as you would hear from a well trained choir in one of our rural churches;—and it was a matter of no little gratification to me, to hear some of the fine old familiar tunes sung in the heart of the strange land amidst so many impressive associations, and by the voices of my interesting companions.

After our return home, we walked out, in the hope of meeting Sir Walter, to what was called in the family the "Mushroom park;" Mrs. Scott, the young ladies and Charles,—Walter, the oldest son being in the highlands. We took with us a pretty formidable attendance of dogs, viz., the favorite deer-hound, Maida, then quite advanced in years, a grey-hound, (who was however black and called Hamlet,) a spaniel named Finette, and Urisk, a sprite of a terrier from the isle of Skye, all well known favorites and privileged companions at home and abroad. We soon fell in with Sir Walter, who, though he had been on his feet all the morning, said he made it a rule never to turn his back on good company and joined us. We had a scramble in the park, who should pick up the best mushrooms and the most of them. The visitor was allowed, as a privileged person unacquainted with the localities, to enter into a partnership with Miss Scott, and of course their joint stock was the largest.

While we were busy searching for mushrooms, the dogs, following their instinct, were busy searching for a hare. It was really curious to see the approach to reason on the part of these poor animals. The grey-hound is swift of foot but has no scent; the spaniel has no fleetness but has an acute smell. The spaniel's nose was down among the bushes and her whole little body in a flutter of search, whisking from cover to cover like a little four-legged spirit. The lean and long-legged grey-hound, his ribs staring through his skin, without attempting to join in the search, kept close to Finette. At last the hare was started; the grey-hound bounded off like lightning in pursuit, and poor little Finette, having done her duty, came fawning round her master. All the time, the stately old deer-hound was stalking about with sovereign unconcern; and Urisk, the little cur from the isle of Skye, a frisking, bristling, weird looking lump of live hair, was playing with Charles. The poor hare took the road and was soon run down; and then the old deer-hound stalked majestically toward the game; growled sharply at Hamlet to drive him off, and seizing the hare in his teeth, brought it with great solemnity, and laid it at Mr. Scott's feet. The affair was every way out of season. It was Sunday, and the sporting season had not begun; but it had taken place accidentally, and I was not sorry to witness the sight for the first time in my life; though not without compunction for poor puss. The scene interested me the more, as tallying so precisely with Xenophon's description of the instincts of the different species of dogs, in the first book of the Cyropædia.

The rest of the day was passed in conversation, in part of a graver cast. We had sacred music after dinner, and in the evening Sophia sung national ballads and some of her father's songs. She made no pretension to execution, or the *bravura* style;—or at least she had no occasion to exhibit it in these fine old Scottish melodies;—but, to my uneducated ear, nothing could be more pleasing.

On Monday, Sir Walter told Sophia to show me the house and grounds, adding playfully that she knew a great deal more about both than he did. It was plain to see, from the manner in which he always spoke to her, that she was the object of his entire confidence and boundless love. The house was not wholly finished. For the ornaments of the hall and passages, Sir Walter had introduced casts of the carved work of the Abbey, and while I was there, the workmen were putting up masks taken from the "Corbells grotesque and grim," mentioned in "the Lay." As we walked through the grounds, I had a long conversation with Sophia about the authorship of the novels. I omit the details of what was said by her on this subject, having furnished them to my friend Mr. Allibone, for insertion in his second volume, which has not yet appeared. I will only say here, that, though she firmly believed, as I did, that her father was the author of the novels, she did not at that time know it. We passed an hour or two this day in reading the "Heart of Mid Lothian" aloud, Sir Walter taking his turn with the rest, and remarking with unconcern on the passages that struck him. He was much amused at my attempt to imitate the Scottish cadence, and said "if I would bide awhile in Tweedale, they would give me a very pretty accent."

I asked Sophia to manage to have dinner a little earlier, that we might go to Melrose, and to get her father to go with us. She said he had so often been there with visitors, when he first came to Abbotsford, that he had got tired of it, and had seldom been of late; but she thought he would go with us, which he was kind enough to do. I am not ashamed to confess that a visit to Melrose Abbey, with Sir Walter Scott and his family, kindled my imagination, at the age of twenty-four, as it has perhaps never been excited on any other occasion. I have attempted to describe the feelings awakened by the scene, in a speech at the anniversary of the Scots' Charitable Society in Boston, on the 30th of November, 1839. Nor was it, I own, without emotion "too deep for tears," that, in the solitude of my room at night, after contemplating these interesting ruins in the company of him who has made the spot which they cover holy ground, I reflected that, in all human probability, after one or two more days, I should never see him or them again. This is a reflection which not seldom mingles a shade of sadness with the pleasure one derives from meeting agreeable and congenial acquaintances and friends, in our travels through foreign countries and distant parts of our own. I must own that in two or three days I had become strongly attached to every member of the amiable family at Abbotsford. Our whole time was passed together in conversation, reading, or singing on the part of the ladies; at dusk a dance on the lawn; in walks and drives. Sir Walter poured out all the treasures of his memory, in traditions of the border times, anecdotes of celebrated characters, interspersed with constant sallies of quiet pleasantry;—and Charles contracted so great a fondness for the American guest, that he asked his father's permission to accompany me on my approaching journey to Greece and Constantinople, which, in consideration of his being under thirteen years of age, was withheld. Later in life this interesting young man was attached to the British embassy in Persia. In 1839 he wrote to me from the Foreign Office in London, reminding me of my visit twenty one years before to his father's; but many years since, he, with all the rest of the family, one after another, passed away.

It was with no common regret that I took my leave of the family. I was to go to Selkirk and there be taken up by the Mail coach for London. If the coach was full I was to return to Abbotsford. Mrs. Scott and her daughter took me to Selkirk, and left me there. Although much pressed for time, in reference to the commencement of my tour on the Continent, I could not find it in my heart to grieve, when the Mail coach drove up and was reported "full." It shows the limited amount of travel at that time, that one Mail coach daily was all that passed on that route, between Scotland and England. It was now evening. I made myself as comfortable as I could that night at Selkirk, and early the next morning walked over to Abbotsford to spend the day. I was received there as an old friend. The young ladies said that they were thankful I had come, for now they should have a good excuse for not attending their master upstairs. I inquired of them what they were studying, and they said "Tasso." I told them I could not encourage truancy and idleness, and, taking the book out of Anne's hand, began to examine them. The parents entered heartily into the humor of this scene, and begged me to be strict with my new scholars. But it ended in a hearty laugh, and that day we made but little progress in Tasso.

At dinner the veteran deer-hound made his appearance, and laid his great nose upon his master's arm. He had already been fed elsewhere, but he received a *bonne bouche* from Sir Walter's hand. After dinner a favorite cat placed herself upon the table near him. As I sat next he begged me not to be disturbed. He caressed the animal, who was evidently a pet, and said that "if cats were as well treated as dogs they would be as gentle and faithful." This I think somewhat doubtful, since, if the experience of mankind had not shown the contrary to be the case, there is no reason why they should not have secured to themselves that kind treatment which is bestowed on dogs. The habits and instincts of animals were a favorite topic of conversation with Sir Walter. He traced the practice of dogs, in turning themselves once or twice round, before they lie down, to their habit of scooping out, as it were, a bed in the leaves, while in a state of nature.

We were regaled at dinner by the gardener, in the character of piper, dressed in his tartans, and playing national airs on the bagpipe on the little lawn before the house. For this contribution to our entertainment, he was called in by Sir Walter, and rewarded with a glass of whiskey. The bagpipe at the banquet, played by the Chieftain's piper, is a part of the ancient Celtic state, still kept up in the great Scottish houses. Sir Walter clung with patriotic fondness to these national traditions.

But I must reserve for another paper the rest of these recollections, as well as a brief account,—alas, under a mournful change of circumstances,—of "Abbotsford revisited" after a lapse of twenty six years.

NUMBER FOURTEEN.

THE FOURTH OF MARCH, 1789.

Commencement of the present United States Government in New York, seventy years ago this day—Sketch of the History of the promulgation and ratification of the Constitution—Delay in organizing the new Congress—Arrival of Washington at New York and his inauguration—Question as to the titles to be given to the President and Vice President—Amusing anecdote—Causes of the prevailing apathy—The general languor of the country a circumstance favorable to a peaceful revolution—No such revolution possible in highly prosperous times—Much owing to the disinterested patriotism of the revolutionary and constitutional leaders and especially Washington—Closing reflection.

On this day seventy years ago an event took place, inferior in importance to no other, in the history of the country, if to any other in the political history of the world. On this day seventy years ago, the present Constitution of the United States became "the supreme law of the land," and New York became for a time the seat of the new government. If, as General Hamilton asserts in the last number of "the Federalist," the "establishment of a Constitution, in time of profound peace, by the voluntary consent of a whole people, is a *Prodigy*," that prodigy became an historical fact on the fourth of March, 1789. Let us dwell upon it for a moment in reverent contemplation. It is not one of the Prodigies of ancient fable, which told how

> A lioness hath whelped in the streets,
> And graves have yawned, and yielded up their dead:
> Fierce fiery warriors fight upon the clouds,
> In ranks and squadrons, and right form of war,
> With drizzled blood upon the Capitol:
> The noise of battle hurtled in the air,
> Horses do neigh, and dying men did groan,
> And ghosts did shriek and squeal about the streets.

These were the prodigies which foretold the assassination of Cæsar, and the inauguration of a despotism, doomed for fourteen centuries to master and oppress the world. Ours was the auspicious Prodigy of a well-compacted republic, formed by the counsels of unselfish patriots, pure from the stain of blood, destined, let us trust, to be the safe-guard and the blessing of far-distant ages.

The Constitution of the United States was finally proclaimed by the Federal Convention on the 17th of September, 1787, and was on that day, in pursuance of an unanimous vote of its framers, transmitted to the Congress of the Confederation, then sitting at New York, with a letter signed by George Washington, President of the Convention. The Constitution itself fixed no day when it should begin to be of force, as the supreme law of the land. It provided only that when ratified by the Conventions of nine States it should go into operation " between the States ratifying the same."

With this provision it went forth to the States and to the people, to be ratified by their Conventions. It was a season of expectation, of anxiety, and, on the part of many true patriots, of alarm. The people were divided into parties; and a document so extensive and comprehending so many details of course presented many points open to criticism. By many persons, and among them there were tried patriots and good citizens, the proposed new government seemed to be fraught with menace to the hardly-earned, dear-bought rights of the States, and liberties of the people; by others, it was looked upon as the only hope for the salvation of the country. Washington was one of those who regarded it in this light. " There is a tradition," says Mr. Curtis in his valuable History of the Constitution, (vol. II., p. 487,) " that when Washington was about to sign the instrument, he rose from his seat, and, holding the pen in his hand, after a short pause, pronounced these words :—' Should the States reject this excellent Constitution, the probability is that an opportunity will never again offer to cancel another in peace,—the next will be drawn in blood.' "

The public press was enlisted on both sides of the momentous question. Writers of great ability attacked and defended the new project of government, but the letters of Publius, under the title of "the Federalist," the joint work of Alexander Hamilton, John Jay, and James Madison have alone survived the occasion that drew them forth, and descended with a classical reputation. The first number of this remarkable series of papers was written by General Hamilton, toward the end of the month of October, 1787, on board a packet bound up the North River. They produced a great effect on the public mind, and formed an armory of weapons for the defence of the Constitution, throughout the country.

Little Delaware led off with her ratification on the 7th of December, 1787; and the remaining States followed, Pennsylvania on the 12th of December; New Jersey on the 18th of December, 1787; Georgia on the 2d of January, 1788; Connecticut on the 9th of January; Massachusetts on the 6th of February; Maryland on the 28th of April; and South Carolina on the 23d of May. Eight months had now elapsed since the formation of the Constitution, and eight States only had ratified it. In two of the five remaining States, viz.: North Carolina in the South and Rhode Island in the North, no ratification was at present expected; and the other three States, New Hampshire, New York, and Virginia were yet to act; thus conferring on any one of the three great sections of the country (for the West at that time had not been called into existence) the power of consummating the organization of the Union. In New York and Virginia a very formidable opposition was expected, and the result was doubtful; every thing for the moment seemed to depend on New Hampshire. On the 21st of June, 1788, her ratification took place, and with it the Constitution, as between the nine ratifying States, became the supreme law of the land. The ratification of Virginia followed on the 26th of June, and that of New York on the 26th of July. North Carolina delayed her ratification till the 21st of November, 1789; and Rhode Island hers till the 29th of May, 1790.

As soon as the ratification of nine States was certified to the old Congress, (and that of New Hampshire, all-important as it was in calling the new government into being, does not appear to have been officially reported till the 2d of July,) the nine ratifications were referred to a Committee to examine the same, and report an act of Congress for putting the Constitution into operation, "in pursuance of the resolution of the Federal Convention." A struggle immediately arose as to the place where the new government should be established. Most of the members from New England and the Middle States wished either that the seat of the government should continue at New York or be removed to Philadelphia; the Southern members desired a situation nearer the geographical centre of the Union. These conflicting opinions were at length reconciled, by the adoption, on the 13th of September, 1788, of a resolution which provided that, in order to carry the new Constitution into operation, Presidential electors should be appointed in the several States on the first Wednesday of January, 1789; that the said electors should meet in their several States and vote for President and vice-President on the first Wednesday of February; "and that the first Wednesday in March next" (the fourth of March, 1789,) be the time, and the present seat of Congress (New York) the place, for commencing proceedings under the said Constitution."

As originally framed, the Constitution provided that two persons should be voted for by the Electors as President and vice-President; the candidate having the highest number of votes to be President, and, in case of equality, the House of Representatives, voting by States, and each State giving one vote, was to decide.—The whole number of electoral votes for

President and vice-President, cast on the first Wednesday of February, was sixty nine. They were given unanimously for Washington, who was predestined in the public mind for the office of President. A much smaller number of votes was given for Mr. John Adams, who, however, united a large plurality over any other person, as a candidate for the second office. The State of New York took no part in the first Presidential election! She is now much more attentive to her political duties.

At length the fourth of March, 1789,—the appointed day, which was to give an organized Constitutional existence to a new Confederate Republic, about to enter on an equal footing into the family of nations,—arrived; but on that day there assembled at the seat of the new government at New York, of the Senate, only the two Senators from New Hampshire, Connecticut, and Pennsylvania, and one each from Massachusetts and Georgia. These eight punctual men met and adjourned from day to day for a week, without any addition to their number. On the 11th of March they "agreed that a circular should be written to the absent members requesting their immediate attendance." Another week passed with the same result, and on the 18th of March it was again agreed, that "another circular should be written to eight of the nearest absent members, particularly desiring their attendance, in order to form a quorum." On the 19th of March a Senator from New Jersey dropped in; on the 21st a Senator from Delaware made his appearance, and then for another mortal week no increase of the number of Senators in attendance took place. The other Senator from New Jersey came in on the 28th. No one else came till the 6th of April, when "Richard Henry Lee of Virginia appearing, took his seat, and formed a quorum of the whole Senators of the United States," viz.: twelve in number, the States which had as yet ratified the Constitution being but eleven. Such was the tardy organization of the Senate, which at first sat with closed doors, as well for legislative as executive business.

Of the Representatives, of whom the whole number from the eleven ratifying States was but fifty-nine, thirteen only assembled at New York on the 4th of March, viz.: four from Massachusetts, three from Connecticut, four from Pennsylvania, one from Virginia, and one from South Carolina. On the following day one more arrived from New Hampshire, one from Massachusetts, two from Connecticut, and one from Pennsylvania. No one else came in till the 14th of March, the house adjourning from day to day for want of a quorum. On that day JAMES MADISON, JNR. and two other members from Virginia came in, but there was still no quorum. On the 17th and 18th of March two more members from Virginia appeared, and no further arrivals took place till the 23d. On that day two members came in from New Jersey, and on the 25th another from Virginia. No additional members arrived till the 30th of March, when another member from Maryland and Virginia appeared. On the first of April, another member each from New Jersey and Pennsylvania came in, and a quorm was formed. It was five days more before a quorum of the Senate was present, and the first Congress of the United States was organized. On the 21st of April, the Vice-President, John Adams, appeared, and took his seat as President of the Senate. In his address on taking the Chair, he paid an emphatic and eloquent tribute to the newly-elected Chief Magistrate.

Expectation now dwelt on the arrival of Washington. He received the official notice of his election on the 14th of April, at Mount Vernon, and immediately started for the seat of Government. Attended from city to city by the joyous and grateful salutations of the people, he reached New York on the 23d of April. The necessary arrangements for his inauguration occupied a week, and, at length, on the 30th of April, in the gallery in front of the Federal Hall, just erected in Wall street, in the presence of the newly-organized Congress, of the municipal authorities of New York, and her sympathizing population, he took the oath to "preserve, protect, and defend the Constitution of the United States." The oath was administered by Chancellor Livingston; the Secretary of the Senate began to raise the Bible to the President's lips, but he bowed his head and kissed the sacred volume. At the close of the solemn ceremony Chancellor Livingston proclaimed "Long live George Washington, President of the United States!" He was then fifty-seven years, two months, and six days old, and he lived ten years, seven months, and fourteen days, from the time of his inauguration.

Before the arrival of the President, a Committee had been appointed by the Senate to consider "what style or title it will be proper to annex to the offices of the President and Vice-President of the United States, if any others than those given in the Constitution." This Committee consisted of Mr. Richard Henry Lee of Virginia, Mr. Izard of South Carolina, and Mr. Dalton of Massachusetts, and they reported in favor of addressing the Chief Magistrate as "His Highness the President of the United States of America, and Protector of their Liberties." The Senate was inclined to favor that style of address, which was, no doubt, suggested by the title adopted by the Protector Cromwell, and that of the States General of Holland, who, as was remarked by Mr. Madison, assumed the style of "their High Mightinesses." The House of Representatives deemed it expedient not to bestow any title on the President and Vice-President, and in the answers of the two houses to the President's inaugural speech, he was, without any titular addition, addressed as "President of the United States.'" The Senate persevered for a few days in the attempt to establish a title by legislation; the house continued to dissent; a committee of conference was appointed who could agree on no report; and the Senate, "desirous of preserving harmony with the House of Representatives," postponed the report of their Committee, and resolved that the present address be "To the President of the United States, without the addition of title."

Notwithstanding this wise decision of the two houses of Congress, grandiloquent titles were occasionally bestowed on the President in the newspapers and other publications of the day. During his tour in 1789, he was sometimes spoken of as his "Highness, the President." This is the case in the account of his reception at Worcester; and the following amusing anecdote is found in the "Massachusetts Spy" of 12th of November. It appears from Washington's Diary, under date of 6th of November, that "the house in Uxbridge had a good appearance, (for a tavern,) but the owner of it being from home, and his wife sick, we could not gain admittance, which was the reason of my coming on to Taft's." The anecdote is as follows:—

"The following is handed us for fact, and is one of the many instances, which show that it is necessary the President of the United States should have some title, or address at least, to distinguish him from other great personages, who may have occasion to travel either in their own or other States.—Towards the close of one day last week, a messenger was sent forward to inform the keeper of the Inn where his Highness intended to lodge that night, that "the President was near by, and wished to be accommodated with lodging, and a little necessary refreshment," &c. The innkeeper was absent; the landlady, supposing the messenger meant, by "*the President*," the President of Rhode Island College, for it was in the neighborhood of that State, and that of course he had his lady with him, and being herself unwell, she told the messenger she could not entertain "*the President*"—and that he must go on to the next tavern—in consequence of which the messenger, although it was late, had to send word back to his Highness that he had proceeded on to the next inn, to provide that entertainment which he could not get at the first. The landlady soon after found out her mistake, and most piteously lamented that she could not have known that it was the illustrious Washington, who intended honoring her house.—'*Bless me*,' exclaimed she, '*the sight of him would have cured me of my illness, and the best in my house and in town would have been at his service*.' This inn was in the middle of the town, and when the inhabitants who lived in the neighborhood, heard of the affair, they could not refrain expressing the greatest mortification at the unlucky adventure, which deprived many of them of the opportunity of seeing HIM whom they would have delighted to honor."

But to return to our narrative.

Thus quietly, and, if I may use the expression, unconsciously to itself, the government of the United States began its constitutional existence, seventy years ago this day in the city of New York. If we are inclined to wonder at the indifference with which, not merely the public at large, but sagacious politicians and partiotic statesmen, looked on, while the infant Republic struggled into being, we must bear in mind the lassitude produced by six years of weary expectation. Who could give assurance that the acts of the new government would command a greater measure of respect than the Recommendations of the late Congress? that the new piece of parchment would be more potent than the old?

There is one point of view, in which we must deem it fortunate that the new government came over the land and the people, as the kingdom of Heaven "cometh, not with observation." In no other way could it probably have come at all. There is no other instance in the history of the world of a political change,—proved on trial to be of the utmost importance,—which has been made at the time without bloodshed. No more important revolution than that which substituted the present Constitution for the old Confederation ever took place, in ancient or modern times. A change of government as radical as those which have caused the direst and the deadliest conflicts between the different orders of the State, the existing and the substituted powers, in Greece and in Rome; mediæval Italy; in England in the middle of the seventeenth century; and in France at the close of the eighteenth, was made on this day, in this city, seventy years ago, nearly unperceived, and still more, nearly disregarded by an often disappointed and languid people. New York would not even take a part in the organization of the new government, though established in her own metropolis. It was an experiment, and the people were tired of experiments. It promised little to gratify ambition, and its promises carried little hope of fulfilment. It offered nothing to feed the appetite for gold; unable to pay its debts, it was too poor to think of bribes. The vast extent of the Union compared with its scanty population,—the wide spaces which separated its great political centres,—the tardiness of communication between its remote districts,—the comparative feebleness of the press,—the poverty of the country, whose resources were nowhere developed, —the want of armies, navies, and public works, and the frugality of all the public establishments, were circumstances which favored a pacific revolution. It was not only *experimentum*, but *experimentum* (comparatively speaking) *in corpore vili*,—an experiment on a cheap substance; it was well if it succeeded, and no great matter if it failed. There were the State governments to fall back upon, and many good patriots were opposed to any encroachment on their equal sovereignty.

To bring about a change in the organic law, at the present day, as radical as that which was effected by the new Constitution, would be simply impossible. The magnitude of the existing interests is too great; the strength of the powers in possession too vast; and the spirit of contending opinions and ambitions too resolute, to admit of any great peaceable revolution. As it is only in a reduced state of the natural body, caused by regimen or disease, that certain heroic operations in surgery can be ventured on, so it is only in a body politic, exhausted like that of the United States from 1783 to 1789, that a radical change of organization could be made without a convulsion.

But let us not ascribe too much to circumstances, and too little to the pure and disinterested patriotism of the great and good men of the constitutional period. It is painful to reflect, that, in the great system of compensation which regulates the fortunes of governments as well as those of individuals, the days of palmy prosperity are not those most favorable to the display of public virtue or the influence of wise and good men. In hard, doubtful, unprosperous, and dangerous times, the disinterested and patriotic find their way, by a species of public instinct, unopposed, joyfully welcomed, to the control of affairs. The sufferings of the revolutionary war and the discouragements of the succeeding period had thrown what government there was,—and there was scarce any thing that deserved the name,—into the hands of unambitious men, who served the country from a sense of duty. The Presidency of the United States under the new government, that prize in pursuit of which the best interests of the country are daily jeoparded, while all its political energies are driven into the channels of party, with an expansive force which seems perpetually to threaten an explosion,—that dazzling prize was, in the year 1788 and from the moment the Constitution was promulgated, spontaneously allotted, in the public mind, to an Individual, who not only did not covet or seek it, but who recoiled from it, with unaffected reluctance to submit to its burdens and cares,—and who could only be induced, by the urgent and concurring importunities of all in whom he confided, to accept a unanimous election. Who can doubt that if, instead of such a state of things in 1788, half a dozen of the ablest men in the country and their friends, in and out of Congress, had exerted all their influence over organized parties, and called into action all the resources of political agitation, in different parts of the Union, in order to connect the question of the adoption of the Constitution with their own aspirations, the new government would have failed of adoption? It deserves the thoughtful consideration of all good citizens, whether a state of things which would assuredly have prevented the Constitution from coming into existence, will not, if persevered in, and that with ever-increasing intensity, prove fatal to its duration, in its original integrity.

NUMBER FIFTEEN.

ABBOTSFORD VISITED AND REVISITED.

PART II.

The family of Sir Walter Scott in 1818—His mode of life and study—Playful names given his daughters—A visitor recognized by the print of his horse's shoe before he was seen—Gratitude more affecting than ingratitude—German studies—Jesting anecdotes at table—A walk of a mile on your own land—Natural features of Abbotsford—Departure—Personal appearance of Sir Walter—Conversation—Opinions as to the authorship of the Waverley novels—Pecuniary embarrassments—Sad changes in the family—Visit to Abbotsford in 1844—Border Scenery—Otterburn, Jedborough—Remains of Dryburgh Abbey—Tomb of Sir Walter Scott—Melrose Abbey—Changes at Abbotsford—The Poems and Novels of Sir Walter Scott.

The family of Sir Walter Scott, at the time of my visit to Abbotsford in 1818, consisted of himself and Mrs. Scott, and his four children,—all he ever had,—Sophia, Walter, Anne, and Charles; Sophia the oldest, at this time, not being quite nineteen years of age. Walter entered the army, afterwards married, but died childless. Charles, as was mentioned in the former paper, attached himself to the diplomatic career, and died young and unmarried; as did also Anne the youngest daughter, who at the time of my visit was in her fifteenth year. Sophia, as is well known, married Mr. Lockhart, who was introduced into the family in the summer of 1818. Their only child, a young lady of the most engaging appearance and estimable character, was just entering society at the period of my second residence in England,—the image of the lovely maiden whom I had known at Edinburgh and Abbotsford, the pride and charm of her father's house. Walter, at the time of my visit to Abbotsford, was in the Highlands, for the opening of the moors.

Mr. Lockhart's life of Scott discloses the pleasing manner in which he lived with his family. Notwithstanding his Herculean literary labors, with the addition of his official duties, (which while he united the offices of clerk of the Court of Sessions and Sheriff of Selkirkshire, necessarily occupied much of his time,) he never seemed, as I was told in the family, to be in want of leisure for the engagements and amusements of the social circle. Certainly, while I was at Abbotsford, he seemed entirely master of his time; and Sophia told me that what I saw of him was a fair specimen of his country life. He no doubt worked harder in the winter, when less exposed to interruption by visitors; and he habitually employed the early hours of the morning at his desk. We learn from Mr. Lockhart's Biography, the prodigious facility and courage with which he composed his novels, well knowing, as he did, that he was writing them for the whole civilized world. It was not an uncommon thing with him, as he tells us himself, to write a chapter in the evening on a tour, and despatch it unread by mail, in the morning, to his publishers.

He lived in the most delightful confidence and familiarity with his children. They were, each according to age and sex, his companions and playmates. Sophia was the first person whom he admitted to his confidence, in reference to the authorship of the Waverley novels, except those who aided him in transcribing them for the press. This, however, he had not done at the time of my visit. He was accustomed playfully to call his oldest daughter "Miss Feuclothes," from her habit, when some little article of dress was wanted in a hurry, of *borrowing* from the wardrobe of her sister or mother, *feu* being a Scottish legal term for a rent tenure, in distinction from ownership. Anne was fonder of gay dress, and would sometimes return from her rambles in the fields, with her garments torn by jumping over the hedges. This gained her the title of "Lady Bonnierag."

On one of our walks in the fields, we noticed the print of a horse's hoof in the beaten path. Sir Walter told me that on one occasion, in walking, I think he said, with Mr. Southey, over the same path, having seen a similar print, he told Mr. Southey—(if he was the person)—that when they got back to the house, they should find a certain individual whom he named. Mr. Southey asked "if he was expected?" "No." "Have you any business with him which might require him to come and see you?" "No." "Have you had a *second sight* of him?" "Neither of these, and yet we shall find him;" and so the event proved, on their return home. After amusing himself with his guest's wonder, how Sir Walter, under these circumstances, at such a distance from his house, which was entirely out of sight, could know who had come there, the mystery was cleared up. Sir Walter was acquainted with the size and shape of the hoof of his visitor's horse. It made a print different from that made by any other horse in the neighborhood.

Some poor person, as we passed along, expressed himself in terms of warm gratitude to Sir Walter, for his kind inquiries after a member of his family who was ill. When we had passed on, I made some remark on the strong and apparently sincere language of gratitude, which fell from the poor man, prompted as I supposed by some former and more important acts of kindness on his part. Without particularly replying to that suggestion, he said, "for my part, I am more touched with the gratitude than the ingratitude of the dependent poor. We occasionally hear complaints how thankless men are for favors bestowed upon them; but when I consider that we are all of the same flesh and blood, it grieves me more to see slight acts of kindness acknowledged with such humility and deep sense of obligation."

Being fresh from a long residence in Germany, I had much

conversation with Sir Walter about the language and literature of that country, and the men of eminence whom I had seen there; especially Gœthe. I inferred from the general character of his remarks, that he had not, of late years, pursued his German studies with as much diligence as in early life, though he had never wholly neglected them. He mentioned the circumstances of his translation of Bürger's Lenore, very much as they are given in Lockhart's life.

Nothing was too playful for him at table. He related with great glee an anecdote of a lady in Edinburgh, who had a house servant from the highlands, altogether ignorant of the little refinements of civilized life, and not entirely master of the English language. A visitor was staying at the house. At the dinner hour the servant was sent up to call the gentleman, and found him brushing his teeth, a process of the nature and objects of which the Gael had no knowledge, and of which he could only form a conception from what he witnessed. He accordingly returned to the dining-room and reported that "the gentleman would immediately come to dinner;—she was sharpening her teeth."

Another of his jesting anecdotes at table was of a gentleman, who had been passing some time with friends at a country house. At length the time for departure arrived, and Andrew, his travelling servant, was directed to pack up the portmanteaus. At the last moment, Andrew was asked by his master, whether "he was sure that he had put up all their things." The answer, brought out by Sir Walter with a mischievous twinkle of the eye, at the emphasized word, was "*At least*, your Honor."

As we were walking toward Melrose, and talking on the subject of exercise, as necessary to health, he said "he thought a walk of a mile before breakfast, *and if possible on one's own land*, was highly conducive to health." Such a walk he was even at that time fully able to take. His property, I think I understood, amounted then to twelve hundred acres in rather a narrow strip on the Tweed. It was, I believe, considerably increased by additional purchases. In its natural features, when Sir Walter first became possessed of it, there was not much that was attractive, except the river. It was nearly if not entirely destitute of trees, and the space between the road and the Tweed was rather too narrow and the bank too steep, either for entire convenience or beauty. The house was very near the road, and wanted that seclusion which forms so much of the charm of rural life. As far as I could judge from the appearance of Ashestiel, where Sir Walter lived before removing to Abbotsford, the former had the advantage in natural beauty. Abbotsford was, however, greatly improved by Sir Walter's plantations, and the historical and traditionary interest of the spot was to him irresistible.

But all things on earth must have an end; and those which are most agreeable seem to come to their end the soonest. The hours of my last day at Abbotsford passed but too rapidly, and I took my leave of the family late in the afternoon, with a presentiment, too fully verified, that I should never see them more. I rode one of Sir Walter's ponies to Selkirk, where I had left my baggage in the morning, and there took the mail coach to London.

Sir Walter Scott was at this time forty-seven years of age. He looked older, for his hair, though not thin, was gray approaching to white. He was tall, full six feet in height, I think rather more. He was not very stout for a person of his stature, though the framework was that of a large, fully-developed man. There was a certain air of heaviness in the brow, which in moments of entire mental quiescence seemed hardly in character for one of the most brilliant geniuses, learned antiquaries, and genial temperaments of the age. This expression, however, was wholly superficial and transient. It was a drop-curtain between the scenes. The moment the action of the mind commenced, either in conversation—whether charming the circle with the outpourings of his own exhaustless memory or gorgeous fancy, or listening to others, which he did with a courtesy and earnestness that marked a mind ever on the watch for some accession of ideas, or in reading a favorite author to a sympathizing audience—the veil was lifted, the expression of heaviness vanished, and energetic thought rayed out from every feature. His frame was cast by nature in an athletic mould; but in consequence of early disease the right leg was a little shorter than the left. It served him, however, with the aid of a cane to walk upon, and he could hardly be said to limp.

Though a Scotsman born and bred, to say that the author of the "Lady of the Lake" and "Ivanhoe" was a perfect master of the English language, in its utmost refinement and delicacy, would be a work of ridiculous supererogation. But for conversation, like many, perhaps most, of his countrymen, he had two dialects. In his family, and still more with those in a subordinate station, and persons at work about the house and the grounds, he spoke with a Scottish accent, and made use of words peculiar to the lowland Scottish dialect. In general conversation, these characteristics were scarcely perceptible. One Scottish word, however, he frequently used, in all the varieties of company in which I saw him, either at Edinburgh or in the country; namely, "I mind" for "I remember."

In 1818, the secret of the authorship of the novels, if secret it could be called, had not been disclosed. Most persons believed him to be the author; I had never doubted it, from the appearance of the Antiquary. Some persons, however, doubted it; some ascribed them, on the most shadowy of foundations, to a brother of Sir Walter, Mr. Thomas Scott, a paymaster in the British army, stationed in Quebec; and others spoke of a certain mythical Dr. Greenfield, if I recollect the name,—whose pretensions to the authorship of these magnificent productions were maintained in some of the third rate literary journals of the day. The late Mr. Randolph, of Virginia, though a critical English scholar, was, at one time, inclined to adopt this wild notion. Long before the secret was formally disclosed, few persons of discernment or taste, in England or America, entertained a doubt on the subject.

With the announcement of the secret, and I believe some time before, commenced the pecuniary embarrassments of Sir Walter, and the convulsive struggles to emerge from them, which embittered the last years of this noble life, and finally brought down his gray hairs in sorrow to a premature grave. The life of Napoleon—a work to make the reputation of an ordinary pen—was the first symptom of the stern necessity of writing for money. There is no period of his life at which he inspires a more affectionate, a more reverent interest, than during the last sad laborious years, when he wrote under the incubus of pecuniary distress. It is an interest that quenches criticism, and extinguishes pity and sorrow, in admiration and gratitude.

Such as I have described them were Sir Walter Scott and his family in 1818. At the time of my second residence in England, (1841–'45,) parents and children,—the light of the age, the joy and beauty of the domestic circle,—all had passed away. Sophia alone survived in her child, the only grandchild of Sir Walter Scott, then just entering upon society, which she was destined to adorn but for a brief season. Unusually shrinking and timid for a well-bred English maiden, she was an object of peculiar interest with all who knew her, as the sole descendant and representative of Sir Walter Scott.

Toward the close of August, 1844, I took advantage of the general pause in political and social life, which takes place in London at that season, to make a short tour to the North. Leaving New-Castle on the morning of the 29th of August, we soon entered the region of the moors; a high, undulating country, destitute of trees, but covered with bracken and heather still in bloom, and tinting the sloping surfaces, under a favorable light, with that exquisite purple, which almost makes up for the want of woodlands in a Scottish landscape.

About Otterburn, which tells you in its name that you have entered the jurisdiction of Scott's muse, plantations and farms begin. We passed through Jedborough in the afternoon. On the left, as you enter the town, are the ruins of the Abbey, in the aisle of which Thomson went to school. Passing Ancrum moor, a bridge crosses the Teviot, where "English blood swelled Ancrum ford." The remains of Dryburgh Abbey form a fitting preparation for a visit to Abbotsford. The bridge built by the Earl of Buchan, over the Tweed, was carried away a few years before, and we crossed the river, as clear as glass, in a boat. The evening was calm, and the sun was just sinking behind the middle peak of the Eildon hills, whose sharp outline formed an indescribably graceful background. An air of desolate seclusion hangs over the remains of the Abbey. Of great beauty in themselves, they were sadly disfigured by some attempts at restoration. Scott's place of rest (St. Mary's aisle) had at that time a forlorn look. There was nothing in the way of a monument to designate or adorn it; not even a slab to protect it.

We had fortunately engaged rooms in advance at the only decent inn at Melrose, and after supping, went out at nine o'clock to see the Abbey. The moon was at the full—a harvest moon; it was impossible to see the venerable ruins to greater advantage. How many years, what varied scenes had filled the interval since my former visit! A venerable female cicerone performed her duty with no little propriety, reciting the appropriate passages from "The Lay of the Last Minstrel," with a good English cadence. The churchyard was cold and damp, and we soon took refuge in the interior. The broken fragments which I had noticed at my former visit seemed to have been somewhat cleared away. Time had evidently been gently carrying on the work begun by violence in the border wars, and accelerated, I believe, by the stern iconoclasm of the Reformation. The ancient Abbey has, however, at some subsequent period, been partially covered in, and used for Protestant worship.

The next day we visited Abbotsford; where changes of every kind had taken place in twenty-six years, since my former visit. The plantations had been greatly extended even during Sir Walter's lifetime; the hall, the armory, and library were unfinished, and but partly furnished, when I saw them before. But the saddest change was the absence of those—the venerated, the joyous, the lovely—who filled the dwelling with light and happiness. The desolate apartments were kept in perfect order; the innumerable objects of taste, and of antiquarian and historical interest contained in them, admirably preserved and arranged, but I could contemplate them only with feelings of overwhelming sadness.

The rising generation of readers do not know what we enjoyed, what they can never enjoy with the zest of a fresh appearance and contemporary perusal, in the poems and novels of Sir Walter Scott. The "Lay of the Last Minstrel" was the first of his works which attracted general notice on this side of the Atlantic, about the year 1806. It rose at once to an unexampled popularity. It was probably the first English poetry which was as extensively read and relished, at the time of its appearance, on this side of the Atlantic as at home. "Marmion" and the "Lady of the Lake" followed with sustained, perhaps augmented, reputation. "Rokeby" and the "Lord of the Isles" with some abatement of popularity,—all within about six years. The reader who takes up the series of Scott's poems, now-a-days, and goes through them as one of the volumes of the British classics, can form but a faint conception of the eagerness with which they were welcomed as they came successively fresh from the press. Overshadowed by the immense favor with which Childe Harold and the other works of Byron were received, Scott retired almost wholly from the field of poetry, and soon commenced the still more wonderfully successful series of his novels. A strict incognito was at first observed, and a degree of mystery was for several years kept up; but the authorship of the novels gradually, and with many readers speedily, ceased to be a matter of serious question. There were many strong grounds for ascribing them to Sir Walter,—the choice of localities and topics, when the scene was laid in Scotland; —the peculiar tone of the nationality; many striking coincidences with his avowed works,—and, on any other supposition, the strange and persistent inactivity of his pen, in the face of daily increasing external evidence of profitable authorship. There was just doubt enough to add the element of curiosity to the eager interest with which each delightful work in the series was successively received. That charm is broken, and new and not undeserving favorites in the department of fiction solicit the public attention. The taste of the reading world is cloyed with the excess of this fascinating diet, and the delight with which a new "Waverley Novel" was welcomed, is buried in the grave of their illustrious author.

NUMBER SIXTEEN.

THE COURT OF FRANCE IN 1818.

Impressions of the French revolution derived from Burke—Presentation at court in France in 1818—Court dress and diplomatic uniform—Mr. Gallatin and the ambassadors' reception—Appearance of Louis XVIII.—Duchess d'Angoulême—Duke d'Angoulême—The Count d'Artois afterwards Charles X.—The Duke de Berri and the Duchess—Fortitude of the Duchess when her husband was assassinated, and her heroic conduct in 1832—Concealed at Nantes behind the back of a fire-place for fifteen hours—The King and Count d'Artois as described by Burke—The fortunes of the Duchess de Berri.

It was mentioned in a former number, that I arrived in Europe in the spring of 1815, just at the time of the escape of Napoleon from Elba, and was a near witness of the final catastrophe of that world-drama, of which he was the hero. Being in Paris three years afterwards, I was curious to observe, a little more closely than it can be done through the columns of the newspapers, the state of things which had succeeded the imperial *régime*. The downfall of Napoleon, and the restoration of the ancient family to the throne of France wore, to a youthful judgment at least, the appearance of a great act of retributive justice in the government of the world. The opinions of the French revolution, which prevailed among the young men of my age as well in America as England, were mainly derived from the study of the writings of Burke. We transferred to the entire Revolution, and to its effects on the condition of France, the frightful picture drawn by his master pen of the reign of terror; and we expected to find, at the Court of the Restoration, a revival of the gorgeous illusions which he has thrown round that beautiful and unfortunate Queen, whose memory he has crowned with a brighter diadem than ever sparkled on the brow of living monarch. One glance behind the scenes was sufficient to dispel the error. About the middle of March, 1818, Mr. Gallatin, at that time the Minister of the United States at the Court of France, kindly proposed to present my travelling companion (the late General Lyman) and myself to the King and the other members of the Royal Family, at one of the regular receptions of the diplomatic body. This ceremonial required a court dress; and for this, not choosing to be at the expense of one myself, I was indebted to the liberality of several friends, whose joint contributions furnished a very tolerable, though not entirely homogeneous, costume for the occasion. We are inclined, on this side of the Atlantic, to look with some disdain on diplomatic uniforms, and court dresses. They have, at times, been put under the ban of authority, and the supposed simplicity of Franklin's dress, as the American Minister at the Court of Versailles, has been held up for imitation. But though Franklin's dress was undoubtedly simple in comparison with the uniforms, which stood alone with gold lace, worn by his European colleagues, it was far enough from the austere plainness which is commonly thought. It consisted of purple velvet garments, white silk hose, and a dress sword. Official costumes, like the other incidents and appendages of place, are often no doubt greatly caricatured in Europe; but uniformity in dress has its use in checking the absurd extravagances of individual taste and want of taste, nowhere more signally and ridiculously displayed than in the adornments of the outer man. The uniform of the American Minister on this occasion, (as I believe on all occasions and at all courts,) was remarkable for nothing but its modest simplicity; just serving the designed purpose of avoiding the singularity of citizens' common clothing when every one else is in official dress.

At twelve o'clock Mr. Gallatin took us in his carriage to the Tuileries, having three days before announced our names for presentation. We were ushered on arriving into the Ambassadors' hall, where the representatives of the various governments of Europe were assembling. Mr. Gallatin was treated by them all in a manner which indicated full appreciation of his great ability and sterling worth. His mastery of the French language, of course, placed him on a footing of familiarity with his colleagues; and his great sagacity and experience and the known moderation of his views, gave unusual importance and currency to his opinions in the diplomatic circles. There was a small side table in the corner of the apartment, from which coffee was served to those who wished it. Shortly after our arrival we were introduced to the Chamberlain in attendance.

A reception of this kind was held by the King and the other members of the Royal Family every other Thursday, mainly for the diplomatic corps, and it was considered a matter of course, that the foreign ministers and ambassadors should give their attendance. This they never failed to do, unless specially prevented. The occasion served them as an agreeable *rendezvous*, at which they not only exchanged the current news of their different countries, but were able to give an impulse to matters of business, which might be pending between the different legations. Of this there is always a great amount between the European Ministers,—and commercial relations, and the convenience and wants of travelling countrymen, furnish the American Minister with many occasions to serve his countrymen with his colleagues. The half hour of attendance in the hall of the ambassadors before proceeding to the throne-room was profitably employed in this way. At length an usher, with his rod of office, announced that the King was ready, and led the way to the presence chamber. As he passed the guards at the doorways he said, "Messieurs les Ambassadeurs;" and, under his guidance, we went up the principal staircase, which was lined with guards, to the throne-room. Having entered the room, the ambassadors and ministers arranged themselves in a semicircle, according to seniority in commission, the ambassadors, however, taking precedence of all the ministers, and they of all the *chargés d'affaires*. This principle of arrangement was established at the Congress of Vienna, and put an end to those struggles for precedence, which form so prominent a part of the diplomatic history of former times, and often led to unseemly collisions, and sometimes to bloodshed. Behind each minister stood those he was to present. Mr. Gallatin's place was about half way in the circle.

The appearance of the King was in sad contrast with what Burke had said the restored King of France must be; an energetic prince, always on horseback. Louis the Eighteenth, in consequence of physical infirmity, could with difficulty be placed in a carriage. He was rather under six feet in height and corpulent, and walked with difficulty; his round and somewhat unmeaning face indicating an amiable disposition, but no strength of character. Had he ascended the throne in quiet times, and in the natural order of succession, he possessed a temper and character to insure a prosperous reign. But the most attractive and imposing personal qualities would hardly have gained popularity for a king, restored at the point of foreign bayonets, reeking from battles fatal to the pride and power of France. But in all such qualities Louis the Eighteenth, broken by misfortune and disease, was wholly deficient.

He was dressed in a blue coat and small-clothes; a white Marseilles vest, which would have fitted a very much larger man, and stout hussar boots. He wore the English order of the garter; and supported himself with a cane, being stiff in one knee, and a great sufferer by gout. He began with the Sardinian Ambassador, at the right, and passed round the circle, saying a few words to each of the ministers, and bowing to those presented by him. Having gone the rounds, he bowed to the circle and retired.

We were then conducted through a long suite of apartments to the reception room of the Duchess d'Angoulême, the daughter of Louis the Sixteenth and Marie Antoinette, and wife of the Duke d'Angoulême, the king's nephew. In England she would have been Queen instead of Louis the Eighteenth; but the Salic law excluded her from the throne of France. At this time she was forty years old. Her face was neither beautiful nor pleasant; the lines were hard; the eye indescribably sad; the expression austere. Like several of her family, she was said to be very devout. She entered France, conducted herself with heroism beyond the men of her kindred, and rallied the friends of the family, when the tide turned against Napoleon. She had not, unfortunately, any more than its other members, succeeded in gaining any degree of popular favor. I could not, however, but look upon her with respect. She had shared that terrible imprisonment in the Temple, suffering for the want of the decent comforts of life, and had seen her father and mother led out to the guillotine. She had seen the poor little dauphin, her brother, daily subjected to the vilest indignities, and most cruel hardships; and had lived herself in hourly expectation of sharing the atrocious fate of her parents. These surely were titles to sympathy if not to favor. She conversed a little more at length with the ministers, and addressed a few words to those introduced by them. "Are you an American? Are you just arrived in Paris?" were the questions which she addressed in French to me. After having gone the rounds of the circle, she returned to her position at the head of the room, from which the company retired backward. Her husband was the Duke d'Angoulême, the oldest son of the Count d'Artois, the king's brother.

We were next conducted to the presence of the Duke d'Angoulême; a short thin man of extremely ordinary appearance; dressed in the uniform of a colonel of cavalry, with hussar boots and spurs. He appeared to affect a sort of military freedom and pleasantry in his remarks to the ministers, occasionally breaking into something of a laugh, in striking contrast with the severity that marked the manners of his wife, whom we had just quitted. He conversed with Mr. Gallatin, as the duchess had also done, on a violent gale which had lately visited the northern departments of France. His questions to me were, "Have you been long at Paris?" and "Are you attached to the Legation of the United States?"

The apartments of the Duke and Duchess d'Angoulême were in the pavilion of Flora, as it is called, the wing of the palace nearest the Seine. We were next conducted across the entire extent of the castle, to the pavilion of Marsan, occupied by the king's brother the Count D'Artois, afterwards the successor of Louis XVIII. as Charles the Tenth. He was by far the best looking of the Royal Family; in person slight but well made; active and graceful in movement; and (Burke's desideratum for a restored Bourbon) a good horseman. Aware no doubt of the importance of making the most of this hold upon the imaginations of the French populace, he almost lived in the saddle. He would have been thought a man of fair appearance in any society; though his countenance was ordinary and meaningless. He was said to be moderately popular;—more liberal in his political opinions, and more conciliatory in his temper, than his children.

We were next conducted to the apartments of the Duke de Berri, the second son of the Count d'Artois;—short and stout in person; hearty in manner, and a good deal better looking than his older brother, the Duke d'Angoulême. He was the only one of the family who spoke to me in English, which he did with ease and a good accent. The late storm still furnished the staple of the conversation; and he repeated the account which his father had given of a violent gale at

Versailles, a year or two before, which had blown down a part of the palace. He was assassinated two years afterwards, in the streets of Paris, at the door of the opera-house, and in the presence of his wife, by a madman named Louvel. Being considered as the hope of the reigning family, his death was a very serious blow to its stability, and was consequently ascribed to the procurement of its political enemies, but it seems to have been the work of a feeble intellect, thrown from its balance by the violence of party passion.

After having passed round the circle, the Duke de Berri retired for a moment, and re-entered with his wife, the daughter of the Prince Royal of Naples, and sister of the present king of that country. She had been married about two years, and was then twenty years old. She looked embarrassed and terrified; and rather crept than walked round the circle, not addressing more than half the Ministers, nor looking them in the face. She wore a dark purple dress, with heavy steel ornaments, which gave her a bluish ghostly look. She was attended by three maids of honor, one of whom, by her dazzling beauty and exquisite grace, formed a strange contrast with her mistress.

The Duchess de Berri, notwithstanding her unpromising appearance at this time, is not to be mentioned without respect. When her husband was struck by the assassin, instead of yielding to the terror which, especially in her situation at that time, might well have been pardoned, she sprang from her carriage, and, tearing the sash from her waist, strove to bind up the Prince's wounds, from which streams of blood flowed upon her as she held him in her arms. Six months after his death, she gave birth to the Duke de Bordeaux, the present representative of the elder branch of the house of Bourbon, under the name of Henry the Fifth. When that branch fell by the Revolution, which placed the head of the younger branch, the late Louis Philippe, on the throne, she alone displayed the manly qualities which showed her worthy to have filled it. Long after the male members of the family had gone into exile, she returned to France, traversed the departments, openly or in disguise, (in direct opposition to the judgment and wishes of M. de Chateaubriand and M. Berryer and the other responsible leaders of her party,) seeking to rally the supporters of the fallen dynasty, and prepare the way for its return. She was closely tracked by the police, but so complete and varied were her disguises, and so vigilant and faithful her adherents, that for five months she escaped her pursuers. Sometimes she assumed the dress of a shepherdess, at others that of a miller; at one time she was to all appearance a chamber-maid, and then a peasant's wife. Several times she was conveyed to a place of safety wrapped up in a bundle of clothes, on the back of a sturdy porter. At length, thinking herself safer in a large city, she took up her abode at Nantes, where she was betrayed by a converted Jew, who for some time had served her faithfully, and won her confidence. He pointed out the place of her residence to the police; they entered it, but could find no one within. They were accompanied by masons and other artificers to sound the walls for places of concealment, but none were found. The corner of one of the rooms contained a chimney, in which the *gens-d'armes* had lighted a fire during the night. It had been allowed to go out, but was rekindled in the morning. It appeared to the police that some change had been made in the fire-place and chimney during the night, by which the position of the burning fuel was elevated. Voices also were heard behind the chimney. The fire was now increased, and the heat rendered so great, that the Duchess de Berri, with three of her ladies, who were concealed in a hole to which the iron back of the chimney was a sliding door, was obliged to come out and surrender herself. They had remained fifteen hours in this dismal place of concealment!

The above described presentations lasted about two hours.

The narrative, after so many years, may seem somewhat arid and uninteresting, but at that time the restoration of the Bourbons, and indeed the stupendous tragedies of the reign of terror, were events so recent, as to impart some degree of painful interest, even to a merely ceremonial occasion of this kind. One could not help scrutinizing the features of the Duchess d'Angoulême, to see if they reflected, in any degree, the radiance of that "delightful vision," which kindled the imagination of Burke. Is this stricken woman, whose hard features and tearful eyes awaken mingled aversion and pity, the child of that youthful mother, whom the greatest of modern orators saw and wondered at "just above the horizon, decorating and cheering the elevated sphere she had just begun to move in,—glittering like the morning star, full of life, splendor, and joy"? Is the person, who, twenty-five years ago, was pronounced by Burke to be, nowithstanding some human frailties, a "character full of probity, honor, generosity, and real goodness," excelling Louis XVI. "in general knowledge, and in a sharp and keen observation, with something of a better address, and a happier mode of speaking and writing; his conversation open, agreeable, and well informed; his manner gracious and princely," is he the shattered form that stands before us, advanced in years, laden with infirmities, with little personal dignity, and no influence in his government, once driven from the throne to which foreign armies had conducted him, and still holding it by a most precarious tenure? Is all that remains of that Count d'Artois, "eloquent, lively, engaging in the highest degree, of a decided character, full of energy and activity; the brave, honorable, and accomplished cavalier," to be found in that unimposing and insignificant presence, destined in a few years to mount the throne, only to be driven from it by his own kinsman, into an unpitied exile? Is this timid little foreigner, that scarce sustains herself as she makes the circuit of her drawing-room, destined to be the mainstay and hope of the oldest of the Royal houses of Europe; and we may now, after the event, well exclaim with astonishment, is she, daughter of one crown prince, wife of another, to strive in vain, in two years, to stanch her husband's life-blood, as it flows beneath the assassin's dagger; and is she literally doomed in twelve years more to pass through a fiery furnace in order to escape the pursuers who are dogging her by order of her Royal relative, who has seated himself on the throne to which her son is the "legitimate" heir? What a shocking sight for men and angels, a widowed mother of the presumptive heir to the throne of France half baked alive, not under Marat, Danton, or Robespierre, but under the reign of a wise and clement prince, her kinsman!

NUMBER SEVENTEEN.

LORD ERSKINE'S TESTIMONY TO WASHINGTON.

Lord Erskine said by Lord Campbell to have saved the liberties of his country—His testimony to Washington—Sketch of his life—The Earl of Buchan—Narrow circumstances of the family—Enters the navy—Original anecdote of his surveying the coast of Florida—Passes from the navy to the army—Commences the study of the law—Brilliant début in the Greenwich Hospital case—His own account of the manner in which he came to be retained in that case—Extract from the pamphlet sent by him to General Washington—His tribute to Washington on the blank leaf.

One of the noblest testimonies to the character of Washington is that of Lord Erskine. It is written on a blank leaf in a presentation copy of a pamphlet by him, published in 1797, and entitled "a view of the causes and consequences of the present war with France." The little volume purports to be of the twenty-second edition, and it is said to have reached the thirty-seventh edition. The copy in question was sent by Lord Erskine to General Washington, and is still preserved at Mount Vernon. Before quoting this remarkable testimony, let us contemplate, for a few moments, its illustrious author, whom the present Lord Chief Justice of England pronounces the "brightest ornament of which the English bar can boast;"—who "saved the liberties of his country."

He was born (says Lord Campbell) on the 10th day of January, 1750. He states himself, in a memorandum dictated to Mr. Samuel Rogers, of which a copy lies before me, and to which I shall presently return, to have been born on the 21st of January, 1749. He was the youngest of the sons of the tenth earl of Buchan, his oldest brother being the Earl of Buchan, who sought to gain notoriety as the correspondent of Washington; and whose egregious vanity led him to aver that the most eminent men were usually childless, as evinced by the three greatest men of the age, Frederic the Second, General Washington, and himself.

The family of Thomas, afterwards Lord Erskine, was of noble, nay royal, descent, but, at the time of his birth, had sunk into very straitened circumstances. Although he early showed himself a bright lad, it was not in the power of his parents to educate him for a profession, their frugal means having been exhausted in bestowing that advantage on his older brother, Henry, who rose to eminence as a lawyer. Thomas was forced to choose between the army and the navy. He strongly preferred the former, as likely to afford, in the leisure of country quarters, greater opportunity for the improvement of his mind. Circumstances, however, made it necessary for him to adopt the other branch of the service, and at the age of fourteen he entered the navy as a midshipman on board "The Tartar" man-of-war, commanded by Sir David Lindsay. Lord Campbell, in his biography of Lord Erskine, says, "it is wonderful to think, that the period of his life, during which almost all those whose progress to greatness I have described, were stimulated to lay in stores of knowledge at public schools and universities, was passed by Erskine in the hold of a man-of-war or the barracks of a marching regiment. But his original passion for intellectual distinction was only rendered more ardent by the difficulties that threatened to extinguish it."

He remained four years on board the "Tartar," cruising in the West India seas and on the coast of America. Having had the good fortune to make Lord Erskine's acquaintance in London in the spring of 1818, I heard him say, on one occasion, that he had a very accurate knowledge of some portions of America, having, while he was in the navy, been employed in a survey of the coast of Florida; and that, while engaged in that duty, "he had turned over every muscle that lay gaping on the shore!" During his cruise he became an acting lieutenant; but on his return to England his ship was paid off, and, owing to the great number that stood above him on the list, he failed to obtain a lieutenant's commission. Determined not to sink back to the rank of midshipman, he abandoned the navy, and obtained the commission of Ensign in the "Royals" or first Regiment of foot. His father was just dead, and the purchase of this commission absorbed the whole of Thomas' patrimony.

For two years his regiment was quartered in various country towns of England, in one of which, at the age of twenty, and with no establishment but Ensign's pay, he fell in love with a young lady of respectable connections and estimable character, and married her.

This imprudent marriage turned out auspiciously. The young couple lived in uninterrupted harmony. His regiment being ordered to Minorca, Mrs. Erskine accompanied her husband to that island. In this secluded spot he passed two years, insulated from the world; but they were no doubt, as is remarked by Lord Campbell, "the most improving years he ever spent." Laboriously and systematically he went through a course of English literature. Shakespeare and Milton, Dryden and Pope, were his favorite authors. He occasionally showed the versatility of his powers by acting as chaplain to his regiment. At first he confined himself to reading the Liturgy of the church of England, but as his men were mostly Presbyterians and discontented with the use of a printed form of worship, he "favored them," says Lord Campbell, "with an extempore prayer, and composed sermons, which he delivered to them with great unction from the drum-head."

The regiment returned to England in 1772, and Ensign Erskine obtained a leave of absence for six months. He availed himself of this opportunity to mingle in general society, and produced quite a sensation in London "by his agreeable manners and graceful volubility." Boswell mentions seeing him at dinner in company with Dr. Johnson, with whom the bold young officer ventured to engage in argument, first on the comparative merits of Fielding and Richardson, and then on the miraculous destruction of the army of Sennacherib, in the Old Testament. He combated with success Johnson's absurd paradox, that Fielding was "a blockhead" and "a barren rascal;" but wandered out of his depth on the subject of the Assyrian catastrophe.

In 1772 he wrote a pamphlet, which attracted attention, on abuses in the army, and in 1774 he rose to the rank of Lieutenant. In August of that year, having attended a trial under Lord Mansfield (with whom he was acquainted) as presiding judge, and feeling that he could have argued the cause himself,—stranger as he was to the forum,—better than the counsel on either side, he conceived the thought of another change of profession, and determined to study the law. Lord Mansfield, the same day, invited him to dinner, and, being greatly struck with his conversation, and pleased with his manners, detained him till late in the evening. The ambitious lieutenant ventured to confide his newly formed purpose to the veteran magistrate, with his reasons in favor of its adoption. He was not discouraged by Lord Mansfield, who only counselled him to take the advice of his mother and other near relations. The project was warmly approved by his mother.

He was unable to execute his purpose till the following spring, when he was admitted as a student at Lincoln's Inn. The following January he was matriculated at Trinity College, Cambridge, thus, in name at least, at the age of twenty-five, beginning academical and professional education at the same time. The former, however, though he kept his rooms at Cambridge, was but a nominal affair; he was, as being of noble family, entitled to his degree without examination; and in this way was able to cut off two of the five years of law study, which would otherwise have been required of him before he could be called to the bar.

By this narrow chance was Lord Erskine enabled to enter the profession in which he earned so brilliant a reputation, and which carried him to the wool-sack. He was admitted a student of Lincoln's Inn just one week after the commencement of hostilities at Lexington. Had he retained his commission in the army but a few days longer, the news that the war had broken out would have reached Great Britain, and it would have been impossible for him to resign it with credit. He must have taken the chance of active service in America, and all thoughts of the future Chancellorship would have vanished like a sick man's dreams. For three years that he was studying the law he lived in great poverty, on borrowed money, in small lodgings, near Hampstead, practising painful economies in food and clothing, and expressing the greatest gratitude to the manager of the Covent Garden for occasional free admissions to the theatre.

He was called to the bar in July, 1778, and sprang at one bound to practice, fortune, and fame. His first retainer, procured by a fortunate accident, before he was actually admitted to the bar, was as junior Counsel, with four Counsel learned in the law, to precede him. It was the famous cause of the Greenwich Hospital. Captain Baillie, deputy governor of that institution, had written a pamphlet exposing the gross abuses which had crept into its administration, and reflecting with great, but just, severity upon Lord Sandwich, the first Lord of the Admiralty, and several subordinate officials. For this publication, Captain Baillie was suspended, and some of the underlings (at the instigation of Lord Sandwich) obtained a rule, to show cause, at next Michaelmas term, why a criminal information should not be filed against Captain Baillie for a libel.

Lord Campbell relates in some detail the manner of

Erskine's being retained in this memorable cause, but I am able to state it in some points more circumstantially from a memorandum dictated by Lord Erskine himself to Mr. Samuel Rogers, in 1816, and copied by me with Mr. Rogers' permission. As this memorandum has never, to my knowledge, been published, it will, I think, interest the reader.

"On a Sunday in June, 1778, I was engaged to dine with Agar, in New Norfolk street, who had become acquainted with me at Tunbridge Wells, but I was persuaded by a young man, William Lyon, an Attorney, to walk as far as Enfield Chase, and dine with Mr. Barnes, a wine merchant in St. Mary Axe, remarkable for the excellence of his claret. When half way, he [Lyon] challenged me to leap over a ditch by the road side. I leapt over it, but in returning, the bank gave way, and I fell and sprained my ancle. The expedition was over. I could proceed no further, and returned in a stage coach. * * * My wife was confined at this time, and at her suggestion I resolved to keep my engagement at Agar's. She said I was justly punished, and I felt that I was.

"When I arrived, the dinner was begun. A tall man drew his chair aside and I went into the gap. He talked much about the pictures, and so did I, though I knew little of the subject, turning that little to as good an account as I could. When dinner was over, he drew Agar aside, and asked who I was. Agar said I was a lawyer, and said much in my favor. 'Could he be prevailed upon to take a brief from my brother?' 'Perhaps he could,' said Agar in his pompous manner.

"I knew nothing of this conversation; but the next day, my servant John Nichols, who had served under me in 'the Royals,' and who, when he set my books in order, used always to place the Bible a-top, as that, he said, was the best book, told me, when he opened the door, that I must be in another scrape, for a cross, ill-looking man, in a large, gold laced, cocked hat, had been twice inquiring for me. 'He insists, sir, upon seeing you, and is at this moment waiting for you in Bloomsbury Square Coffee-house.' I went there, and there I found an old seaman, with a furrowed face. He was sitting gloomily in one of the boxes, with a small red trunk on the table before him, and his sword lying on the trunk. I mentioned my name. He said, 'There are my papers; will you read them over?' It ended in my taking them home. I was to be called to the bar in a few days, (6th of July,) and at a consultation held on the first of November, Bearcroft, Peckham, and Murphy were for consenting to a compromise, our client to pay all costs. 'My advice, gentlemen,' I said, 'may savor more of my late profession than of my present, but I am against consenting.' 'I'll be d— if I do,' said Baillie, and he hugged me in his arms, saying, 'You are the man for me.' 'Then the consultation is over,' said Bearcroft. 'It is,' I replied, 'let us walk in the gardens.'

"When the cause came on, the Senior Counsel exhausted the day and the patience of the Court. It grew dusk and my time arrived, when Lord Mansfield adjourned. I began next morning fresh and before a fresh audience. All crowded around me, and when it was over, Sir Archibald McDonald had known me at school, Lee had known my father at Harrowgate, and that night I went home and saluted my wife, with sixty-five retaining fees in my pocket. Had I not taken a nobleman's degree of M. A., I could not have been called to the bar for two years later. I was then in my 30th year, having been born on the 21st of January, 1749." * * *

At the foot of this memorandum, Mr. Rogers had written "Dictated by him" (Lord Erskine) "to me, as I sat with my pen in my hand, after dinner in St. James place, in 1816." S. R.

This account, it will be perceived, differs in some details from that of Lord Campbell, who relates with greater fulness the manner in which the cause was argued by the Senior Counsel. It seems altogether to have been an extraordinary affair, and not the least remarkable part of it, according to our practice, is, that a young man, just admitted to the bar, should have made the closing speech.

Of this speech, so well known in the records of legal oratory, Lord Campbell remarks that "the impression made upon the audience is said to have been unprecedented; and I must own that, all the circumstances considered, it is the most wonderful forensic effort, of which we have any account in our annals." It was a fitting commencement of that noble career, which boasts for its crowning glories the vindication of the trial by Jury in all its efficiency, the establishment of the Liberty of Speech and the Press in all its perfection, and the annihilation of the abuse of constructive treasons. This wonderful speech gained for Erskine, at one blow, the reputation of a consummate advocate.

In the pamphlet named at the commencement of the article, its author makes the following allusion to Washington:

"The pretence of a war waged against opinions, to check, as is alleged, the contagion of their propagation, is equally senseless and extravagant. The same reason might equally have united all nations in all times, against the progressive changes which have conducted nations from barbarism to light, and from despotism to freedom. It ought indissolubly to have combined the Catholic kingdoms to wage eternal war, till the principles of the reformation, leading to a new civil establishment, had been abandoned. It should have kept the sword unsheathed, till the United Provinces returned to the subjection of Spain; until King William's title and the establishment of the British Revolution had given way to the persons and prerogatives of the Stuarts; and until Washington, instead of yielding up the cause of a Republican empire to a virtuous and a free People, in the face of an admiring and astonished world, should have been dragged as a traitor to the bar of the Old Bailey and his body quartered on Tower Hill."

A copy of this pamphlet, handsomely bound in green morocco, was sent by Lord Erskine to General Washington, by the hand of Mr. Bond, of Philadelphia, with the following letter written on the blank page. General Washington's letter of acknowledgment will be found in his works, Vol. XI., p. 209.

To General Washington.

Sir—I have taken the liberty to introduce your august and immortal name, in a short sentence, which is to be found in the book I send to you. I have a large acquaintance among the most valuable and exalted classes of men; but you are the only human being for whom I ever felt an awful reverence. I sincerely pray God to grant a long and serene evening to a life so gloriously devoted to the universal happiness of the world. T. Erskine.

London, 15 *March*, 1797.

NUMBER EIGHTEEN.

THE FINANCIAL DISTRESS OF THE YEAR 1857.

PART I.

An inquiry into the causes of the distress of the year 1857 proposed—Difficulty of the investigation—The facts of the case stated—And the extent of the distress briefly described—The general paralysis of business and credit—What could have produced it, in the absence of all the usual causes of public distress?—Its probable cause to be found in DEBT—An estimate of the personal debt of the people of the United States—Its annual interest ninety millions of dollars—The business debt is vastly greater—The Corporate debt—The Bank debt and the elements of which it is composed—Banks create no additional capital—By sudden contraction of credit in times of pressure produce or increase the panic.

SHORTLY after my engagement to write these papers was announced, I began to receive letters, from different parts of the country, calling my attention to various subjects of inquiry and discussion. Among other letters I received one from a friendly correspondent in the West, personally a stranger to me, requesting me to state, if possible, the precise cause of the financial distress of the year 1857; to explain how it happened that, in a condition of great and general prosperity, the country should have been struck as with a palsy in all its business concerns, from which it has hardly yet, after a lapse of eighteen months, fully recovered; and, as this is not the first instance of events of this kind, to point out how their periodical recurrence, in something like a regular cycle, can be prevented.

My well-meaning correspondent has given me a problem, which requires for its satisfactory solution, a much wiser man than I am;—a problem which, in its entire comprehension, will not soon receive a full practical answer. Some of the topics involved in the inquiry into the causes of the distress of the year before the last, are of an abstruse and subtle character, particularly those which relate to the subject of credit, and how far it ought to be resorted to in carrying on the business operations of the community,—and the effect of a currency, composed of coin and paper, on the money value of commodities at home and abroad. These are topics, with respect to which different opinions are entertained by judicious and well-informed men. The other part of the inquiry, how the periodical recurrence of these seasons of general financial and commercial embarrassment can be prevented, embraces moral considerations, the justice of which will not be questioned in theory, but which it is extremely difficult to reduce to practice, to an extent sufficient to affect the condition of a community.

The fact itself was pronounced by my unknown but intelligent correspondent one that would be utterly incredible, had it not been matter of daily observation throughout the Union; it was nothing less than the almost instantaneous suspension of active business operations of every kind and in every branch, without any manifest assignable cause. A more than usually abundant harvest had filled the granaries of the great West to repletion, but at the season of the year when the produce of the interior is finding its way to its markets, domestic and foreign, the steamers on the great rivers and lakes stood still; the canal boats ceased to ply; and the railroad trains moved backward and forward with less than half the usual amount of travel and transportation. I had occasion just as the crisis was coming on, to travel from Boston to Buffalo, to deliver an address before the New York State Agricultural Society. Notwithstanding the great resort to the State Fair, the travel, for more than half the way, was reduced far below the average of ordinary seasons. I took passage at Buffalo, on the 9th of October, 1857, in one of the magnificent steamers which plied between that city and Detroit, and which was capable of lodging two thousand persons. It was one of three of equal or greater capacity. The number of persons actually on board at that time did not exceed fifty! The boats on the line had been for some time running to great loss, and this trip of the 9th of October was the last of the season. After that day they were laid up;—two or three weeks earlier than usual.

A similar state of things prevailed in the manufacturing regions. The factories either wholly stopped or worked on short time; and then rather as a choice of evils, to prevent the dispersion of skilled labor, and injury to the machinery by disuse. The navigating interest shared the distress. Our vessels brought home cargoes that passed into the public stores, or were re-exported at great loss. The freighting business was nearly annihilated. The all-infecting malady of the country showed itself, in its most malignant form, in the banks, and a general suspension of specie payments completed at once and indicated the universal distress. On the 6th of October, as I was leaving Boston, I was told by the President of one of the strongest and best conducted of our institutions, that, let what would happen, the banks would stand firm; and in less than a fortnight a universal suspension of specie payments had begun in New York, and extended itself throughout the country. So complete and universal was the stagnation, that it was impossible to procure a draft on New York, by which the modest proceeds of my oration on the character of Washington could be remitted, from a prosperous town in the interior of Michigan.

A short time only elapsed before the necessary consequences of such a general suspension of business were seen, in a prostration as general of credit, and in rapidly multiplying bankruptcies of individuals and corporations. Powerful manufacturing companies, or what were deemed such, failed;

substantial private houses, or houses accounted substantial, sunk; and the great industrial classes of the community, who live by the earnings of their daily labor, were thrown out of employment, and driven to straits for the support of themselves and their families. The General Government at length shared in the embarrassment of the people;—the revenue fell off, and temporary expedients became necessary to carry on the ordinary operations of the Treasury.

What produced this most extraordinary condition of things? The country was in profound peace. No hostile armies traversed and wasted it,—a frequent occurrence in Europe and the East. Our neutral commerce was not, as at some former periods of our history, swept from the ocean by the edicts of unscrupulous rival belligerents, intent upon injuring each other, and to effect that object, trampling the Law of Nations under foot. No embargo, or non-intercourse sealed our ports. No untimely frosts,—no mysterious blight menaced famine or even scarcity. No pestilence walked in darkness, nor destruction wasted at noonday. A week before the panic commenced there was the appearance of universal prosperity, and after it commenced and while it lasted, the country possessed, and that in abundance, all the solid elements of substantial well-being. Under these circumstances, how was it possible,—under similar circumstances how is it ever possible,—that an intelligent, energetic, industrious, and in the aggregate virtuous people, living under a free government, and, as far as political relations are concerned, enjoying privileges elsewhere and before unknown in the world, should, even for a short time, fall into a state of general embarrassment and profound distress such as I have described?

I hardly know whether it would be possible, even in a voluminous treatise on the subject, to return a full and satisfactory answer to this inquiry; whether, with business relations extending throughout a country so vast and with a population so enterprising and active as ours, living and acting in a highly artificial state of society, and especially under a financial system singularly complicated and confined,—it is possible to trace and analyze the remote and occult causes of such a phenomenon. They may, like the ultimate secrets of the material universe, defy the grasp of our minds.

But I am inclined to think, that there is one great efficient cause, which will fully account for a large part, perhaps the whole, of this mighty and terrible effect ; a cause so simple, so homely, so near at hand, that men overlook it, while they are exploring the metaphysics of currency, credit, and the balance of trade.

If I mistake not, the distress of the year 1857 was produced by an enemy more formidable than hostile armies; by a pestilence more deadly than fever or plague; by a visitation more destructive than the frosts of Spring or the blights of Summer. I believe that it was caused by a mountain load of DEBT. The whole country, individuals and communities, trading-houses, corporations, towns, cities, States, were laboring under a weight of debt, beneath which the ordinary business relations of the country were, at length, arrested, and the great instrument usually employed for carrying them on, CREDIT, broken down. Let us, by looking into a few particulars, see whether this is a true statement. I apprehend that the inquiry will disclose some startling facts.

I will first speak of what may be called the personal debt of the country, which runs up, in the aggregate, to an almost fabulous amount. The free population of the United States amounts, at the present time, to about 26,000,000 of individuals, which will give, in the ordinary calculation, 5,200,000 heads of families. I assume that each one of these persons is three hundred dollars in debt. This is, of course, a purely conjectural sum. Many persons may think it too large; others may think it too small; such is my own impression. I believe it will be perfectly safe to assume that, in consequence of the natural proclivity to anticipate income, to buy on credit, to live a little beyond our means, the community carries with it through life a debt of at least three hundred dollars for each family. I am aware that there are many persons who "owe no man any thing but to love one another;"—some, I fear, there are, who obey the apostolic injunction, without the benign qualification. But, on the contrary, how many there are of the 5,200,000 heads of families, who owe a great deal more than three hundred dollars; how many individuals, not included in the 5,200,000, who have larger or smaller debts! How large a proportion of the real property of the country,—the houses, the farms, the plantations,—is under mortgage; and of those who have no real property to give in security, how many pledge their credit and honor to an extent at least equal to that assured! When all these things are considered, I think it will be felt, that three hundred dollars is a moderate sum to assume, as an *average* amount of debt for every head of a family. This basis of calculation gives us fifteen hundred and sixty millions, say fifteen hundred millions of dollars as the private personal debt of the American people, or about one-half of that national debt of England, which sits like an incubus on the taxable resources of that country. The interest of this sum is ninety millions of dollars, which the people of this country have to pay annually on their personal debts. Stated in this naked form it is a frightful sum; and no small part of the straits, discomforts, and troubles of domestic life arise from this perpetual strain upon the family resources. Still, in a time of prosperity, the burden is divided among so many, that it is carried with greater or less ease, according to the amount which weighs on each individual; for though we assume for calculation an equal average amount, in point of fact the burden is very unequally divided. Some are prudent enough to be almost or quite free; others, as the popular expression is, are "over head and ears."

The business debt, whether in trade, manufactures, or

agriculture, is vastly greater; probably greater in this country, in proportion to its population, than in any other in the world. Almost all persons in business extend their transactions very far beyond their capital. A merchant or manufacturer with a capital of one hundred thousand dollars will often trade upon a million. This I have been told, by two or three persons themselves extensively engaged in trade, is not an extravagant statement of the ratio between the capital and the business of our American traders and manufacturers. If this ratio is thought too great, let us reduce it one-half, and suppose that our men of business, on an average, extend their transactions to five times the amount of their capital; that is, a person with a solid capital of a hundred thousand dollars, will buy and sell to the amount of half a million. He will, in that case, have to carry a debt which exceeds his capital five-fold. On this basis, to get at what may be called the business debt of the country, we must multiply the business capital by five. I presume not to go into the enormous amount,—the hundreds and thousands of millions, which would result from this multiplication, and which represent the business debt of the country.

This debt, it is true, unlike the personal debt, is supposed to be balanced by a still larger amount of credits. The trader who has bought four hundred thousand dollars worth of goods on credit, has sold them or expects to sell them for five hundred thousand; but he is paid in the first instance in credit, that is in debt. While things are prosperous this untold mass of debt can be carried. If all the speculative purchases and sales succeed, the debts on one side will be balanced by the credits on the other, but if any great derangement takes place, distress, perhaps ruin, ensues;—to a few individuals, if the disturbing cause is confined to a locality or a single article of commerce; to large bodies,—to the whole community, if it is of a comprehensive nature. As soon as the business debt becomes oppressive, the personal debt above alluded to begins to pinch; and it may be observed, (what I omitted to state, in reference to the ratio of capital and business,) that the capital of the country is at all times charged with the maintenance of those to whom it belongs,—a circumstance which materially impairs its efficiency as the means of doing business. Most men possessed of a clear property of one hundred thousand dollars, probably live at an expense of at least six thousand a year, which reduces to that extent the efficiency of the capital as a basis to trade upon.

Then there is the corporate debt of the country, and this of two kinds, public and private. By the former, I mean the debt of the General Government, of the States, cities, towns, and other political and public bodies; by the latter, the debt of the various private corporations, the churches, the associations of all kinds, Railroad companies, and all the other incorporated bodies which have business transactions. The amount of this kind of debt is of course enormous, many hundreds of millions, and much of it has been improvidently contracted; so that in many cases no permanent value has been created in return.

I reserve for the last place the bank-debt, which is of a somewhat peculiar nature, and which exercises by its fluctuations a controlling, sometimes disastrous, influence on all the other debt—that is, all the other business—of the country. The remark already made with reference to the ratio of the capital and business of individuals, applies with nearly equal force to the capital and business of the banks. They are, at all times, largely in debt. Their circulation is all debt; it is avowedly a promise to pay on demand. The deposits are so much debt, which the banks are equally obliged to pay on demand; and these two kinds of debt are the basis of a large part of their business operations. Besides this, bank capital, however solid, does not even profess to be any positive addition to the wealth of the community. The sums of which it is made up, of course, existed elsewhere before, and, except when hoarded, were, in some way or other, employed. The banks can do nothing but collect them into masses, available for business. This is an important public benefit, but it is not a creation of capital. The circulating paper which the banks issue, can add nothing to the capital of the country, for it is nothing but the evidence of debt. The bank borrows it from the public without interest, and lends it back to the public at six or seven per cent. That such an operation should be thought to add to the wealth of a community is not one of the least remarkable delusions of the day.

The banks then are among the largest debtors of the country. It is true they are also among the largest creditors; but their credits are on time; their debts are due on demand; and their immediately available means are notoriously inadequate to meet that demand. By rapid contractions of their credits when their debts are pressed upon them for payment, they create or increase a panic, and when it is created, they suspend payment, and drag the whole community with them into bankruptcy.

If such as we have described it is the real state of things, —if the country is burdened with this enormous amount of debt, public and private, individual and corporate, it is quite evident, that on the occurrence of any cause, real or imaginary, which powerfully affects the public mind, which produces alarm, and so checks the renewal or the extension of credit, and compels the whole business community to *demand* payment in order that it may *make* payment, a general stoppage must ensue. There is no solid basis on which to stand and resist the rushing tide. Almost everybody is under obligations beyond his immediately available means; and the few that have property are afraid to trust it in any investment. Above a million of dollars, belonging to a person who never willingly left a dollar unemployed, lay idle in the banks of Boston, during the panic of the year 1857.

The real cause of the distress, then, of the year before the last, was the overwhelming DEBT of the country, and the shock given to credit, by which alone that debt is sustained. I reserve to another occasion the application of these views, as suggesting the only practical remedy.

NUMBER NINETEEN.

THE FINANCIAL DISTRESS OF THE YEAR 1857.

PART II.

The view taken in the preceding paper best explains the periodical recurrence of a financial crisis—Origin of the term Panic—Its connection with seasons of pressure and distress—The only remedy is to keep out of debt—The abuses of credit the chief cause of great commercial revulsions—Long credits deprecated by distinguished financial authorities—The agency of banks in the dangerous extension of credit—Doubtful utility of a paper currency—Individual prudence must furnish the main protection—The soundness of these views confirmed by the manner in which the country is returning to a state of prosperity.

THE view taken in the preceding number of the real cause of the financial distress of the year 1857, viz., the mountain mass of debt under which the community was laboring, will best explain the periodical recurrence of a similar state of things. The process of running in debt is, in its very nature, a growing one. It rarely stops while it can by possibility be carried on. With respect to what I have called the *personal* debt of the country, if the means of the individual do not enable him, in the first instance, to get through the year without anticipating the next year's income, he will, the second year, besides his current expenses, have a debt,—and soon an interest-bearing debt,—to take care of. Accustomed gradually in this way to live in part on credit, he soon begins to resort to it from convenience, as he did at first from necessity. Family expenses usually go on increasing,—the happy accident which is greatly to augment one's means never turns up; and the debt, which I have supposed averages at least three hundred dollars for every head of a family, swells till it is arrested by a forced liquidation, which comes sooner or later in the case of each individual, according to the extent of his ability to carry a debt.

The *business* debt of the country goes on increasing till it can increase no longer, by a still more certain law. If the business is what is called prosperous, the trader is tempted on " to enlarge the sphere of his operations," which means, to strain his resources still further; to buy and sell more largely, and of course on credit; his personal expenditure increasing all the while, and he himself often tempted into new fields of enterprise, with which he is unacquainted. The panic of 1837 and that of 1857 were both preceded by seasons of unprecedented activity in the business world. In the former year, besides a strange expansion in every other direction, the public lands were purchased in such fabulous quantities, that it became necessary to relieve the plethora of the treasury by a distribution of the surplus revenue! The crisis came, however, before the last instalment was paid.

In the year 1857, business of all kinds had been quickened by the influx of California gold, which gave a fallacious strength to the banks, and tempted them not merely to aid, but to stimulate, speculation. On this occasion, the West became again the great field, where golden visions of sudden wealth were to be realized. The stock of railroads through tracts of country to which the Indian title was but recently extinguished, and town lots in pathless wildernesses, were sought with avidity throughout the older States. A few highest prizes in this lottery, drawn by " fortunate individuals," turned the heads of thousands, who dreamed of the same good luck, and awoke ruined.

But the business debt like the personal debt has its limits; —it cannot go on forever. The time comes at length when borrowing must cease and paying must begin. An uneasy feeling begins to pervade the community. The banks and the men of solid wealth, who watch the signs of the times with care, understand the portents. A crisis is perceived to be coming on,—and with the unerring, but not always wise, instinct of self-interest, the individuals and the institutions of the creditor class, seek, not to avert the storm, but to secure themselves from its fury. Further accommodations are now refused, credits contracted, loans called in. The ship is put under snug canvas, and men wait in feverish anxiety for the white squall to burst. It may come from a quarter and in a shape absurdly disproportioned in appearance to the effect produced;—as in the failure of the Ohio Trust Company the year before the last. The whole debt of that institution was a small percentage on the aggregate of the money transactions of the New York banks for one day; and yet, as far as any individual cause can be pointed out, its failure gave the alarm, which ended in the temporary prostration of the credit, and suspension of the business of the whole country.

But even the dictionaries teach us that it is idle to inquire into the cause of a Panic; that is the immediate cause;—the word is used to signify a great and general alarm, without any apparent adequate cause. In the oldest heathen mythology, Pan blew his conch shell, when the Titans were fighting with the gods. The audacious rebels had stood undaunted against the thunders of Jupiter, but they fled at the blast of this harsh clarion. Having succeeded so well on this occasion, Pan accompanied Bacchus on his expedition to India, where on a certain occasion he gave a wild scream, which filled the echoes of the mountains and put the enemy to flight. These old fables—(what foundation of fact they may have had in the experience of infant humanity, who can tell?)—struck to the heart of the race, and have given a name to saddest realities in every period of history. Old dynasties have sunk,—mighty battles have been lost,—revolutions have been commenced by Pan-ic fears. One of the most authentic signs of the last dread consummation is "men's hearts failing them for fear;" and when this takes place, no form of disorganization and ruin is just matter of surprise. The cracking of a seat, or a mischievous cry of fire, will, in an instant, set assembled thousands of intelligent persons frantic with terror, and cause them to trample each other to death, in their insane haste to escape from the building. A great, strong ship strikes an iceberg, and discipline is sometimes instantly subverted, all hope of escape in the life-boats blasted, by the fierce haste with which they are lowered into the sea and overcrowded in the dismay of the moment, and hundreds of lives lost when all might have been rescued. Almost all the great battles of ancient and modern times, from Pharsalia to Waterloo, have probably been decided at last by Panic. Miracles of valor are performed by brave men, blood flows like water;—at length a wild cry is heard, on one side or the other, that all is lost,—and with that cry all *is* lost.

It is so in a financial Crisis; a cry of alarm is raised perhaps by a feeble voice, perhaps from an insignificant quarter; but its foundation, in the general state of things, is felt by too many persons to be just. All, alike the creditor and the debtor class, know that the country is staggering under a load of debt. Most persons in active business unite the two characters of creditor and debtor; and, either coerced by the necessity of meeting his own engagements or from the desire of securing what is due to him, every man demands payment at the same time, and general bankruptcy ensues. From a condition of careless and joyous prosperity, the community passes in a week into one of embarrassment, terror, and for too many persons, hopeless ruin. Individuals indebted to the extent of from five to ten times their capital; banks that have one specie dollar in their vaults, for from five to six of their deposits and circulation, are struck with the panic. All grasp at once at the means of paying their debts, and find the debts many times larger than the available means of payment.

What, then, is the remedy! Unhappily it is so simple, so destitute of all financial refinement, so much at war with the speculating character of the age, that the very mention of it will, with many persons, excite no feelings but those of pity and derision. It is just to *keep out of debt.* As far as personal expenses are concerned, live within your means. Leaving out of view a small class of exceptional cases, in which large future accessions of fortune can be depended on, your means will never be much ampler than they now are. If your trade, your business, your profession does not support you now, it never will; because you will generally find that your expenses will steadily increase with your earnings or your income. Your family will grow, your wants will multiply, the standard of comfortable living will be constantly rising; or, on the other hand, you will have sickness in your family, or some unexpected burden will come upon you;—in short, if you get into the habit of borrowing and living on credit, nine times out of ten you will never get out of it. You will live under the harrow all your life, and sooner or later be compelled to seek relief by painful and mortifying sacrifices.

So too of the business debt. I am well aware that the astonishing growth of this country in material wealth is ascribed by many persons to the great facilities which have existed for doing business on credit. Without intending at all to question the utility of credit rightfully understood and kept within proper limits, I would rather say, that the country has prospered, not in consequence of the facility with which credit has been obtained, but in spite of its abuses. The vast body of land within the territorial limits of the country;—its almost boundless means of internal and external communication by ocean, river, and lake,—the average fertility of much of its soil, and the abundance and variety of its staple products; its free political institutions; the energy and enterprise of the Anglo-Saxon race, and the yearly accession from abroad of an immense amount of adult labor,—these are the main causes of the rapid growth of the country. Facilities of credit have in some cases and under some conditions safely supplied the place of solid capital and anticipated its creation. But this advantage is to be offset by the ruinous public enterprises, and the untold amount of private bankruptcy, which have been the disastrous result of easy borrowing at home and abroad.

I heard a gentleman of acute observation and large experience say, many years ago, that he had made out two lists, one of a considerable number of farmers, and the other of merchants, starting with fair prospects in life;—the one class to live upon the produce of their farms, tilled for the most part by their own hands, and this under the comparatively imperfect system of agriculture which prevailed in the last generation; the other to take their chances in the lottery of commerce. At the end of the term for which the comparison was made, the farmers were the more prosperous body. None of them had become very rich;—a few only had wholly failed in life, and those few from causes not essentially connected with agricultural pursuits. The greater part had lived and brought up their families in comfort. Of the merchants, by far the greater part had wholly failed; and one or two only had greatly prospered.

I know of no circumstance so likely to produce this effect, as doing business mainly on borrowed means; keeping your all at the mercy of events, over which you have no control; the probity or the solvency of others; political influences at home; the chances of peace and war abroad; your own continued health; in a word, the innumerable contingencies of life.

Nor let it be thought that this idea of greatly limiting the use of credit is the mere theoretical fancy of a person, who knows nothing practically of the subject. The President of the Bank of Commerce in New York writing to Mr. Nathan

Appleton in Boston, a few days before the suspension of specie payments in 1857, says "when will your banks confine themselves to short dates, and cease to encourage the pernicious system of long credits—credits ramified to the last degree, *from which spring most of your difficulties?*" Mr. Appleton in reply says, "I have always been opposed to the system of long credits, but I recollect very well that it was in consequence of eight months being the established credit given by the New York importers, that we were obliged to submit to the same in our manufactures." These two gentlemen differed only as to what may be called long credits, and where the responsibility of favoring them rests.

The banks, of course, are mainly responsible for the undue expansion of credit, which has proved so pernicious. These institutions are created in many cases for the benefit of a few individuals, principally active in getting them up. Their capital is often to a considerable degree fictitious, paid in one day and borrowed out the next, not in the discount of business paper, but to be employed in speculations, wholly unjustifiable on any sound banking principles. Where a solid capital is actually paid in, a desire to increase the profits of the bank often leads it to push its accommodations beyond the limits of prudence and safety. In the month of January 1857, the banks of New York owed one hundred and four millions of dollars to their depositors and bill holders, and they had eleven millions of specie in their vaults. In other words, they were carrying a fearful debt themselves, to enable their customers to carry one equally fearful. In a little more than nine months, under the influence of no assignable cause but panic, banks and customers in New York and throughout the greater part of the Union, were involved in one common bankruptcy.

Banks of deposit and discount, confining their operations strictly to business paper of short date, would no doubt be of great convenience in carrying on an active commerce.

They would insure the safe keeping of large sums of money; bring idle funds into active use; facilitate payments, and hasten the consummation of business transactions. But it may well be doubted whether banks of circulation, that is, banks authorized by the States to create a paper currency, which, having no real value, is accepted by the public as if it were solid money, are not in the long run, an injury rather than a benefit to the community. They have directly and indirectly had the chief agency in causing those periodical seasons of pressure and distress, which have so often occurred in this country, and with such disastrous consequences to individuals and the public.

It must be admitted, however, that there is very little hope of a remedy. Although the public mind is probably almost unanimous in the conviction, that a National Bank, once deemed by many persons absolutely essential for the collection of the revenue and the regulation of the currency, is by no means necessary either for the government or the people;—there is not the least probability that the States will forego the power of establishing local banks, and clothing them with the right to create a fictitious currency. Such being the case, the country is too likely, in time to come as in time past, to suffer every twenty or twenty-five years the enormous evils resulting from the inflation of credit, and the arbitrary expansion and contraction of a circulating medium, resting on misplaced confidence and not on a basis of solid value.

There remains then no remedy, but that not entirely efficient, yet still very important one, which each individual is able to apply to his own affars. The man who lives within his means, will in prosperous times pass through life with as great a freedom from pecuniary distress, as our imperfect nature admits. Even he may suffer from ill health on his own part or that of others, paralyzing his activity or burdening his means, and a general stagnation of business may, by no fault or imprudence of his own, fatally cripple his resources. These are misfortunes, for which there is no help. They belong to the imperfections of our social nature; but even these will be resisted and sustained far more successfully by the unembarrassed man, than by one already staggering under a load of debt.

So with reference to business, no individual, however prudent, can place himself wholly beyond the reach of those frightful storms, that from time to time burst upon the trading community, with the fury of a typhoon, sweeping all before them to destruction. But even in times like these, the man who has contented himself with moderate gains, has kept his liabilities within his means, conducted his business on a substantial basis, and eschewed gigantic speculations, will be most likely to go through the crisis unscathed; and in all ordinary cases be successful and prosperous, in life; while those who pursue the opposite course, strain their credit to the utmost, and trade on a capital far beyond their solid property, besides leading a life of splendid anxiety and ostentatious care, are the most likely to be prostrated by the first blast which sweeps over the country.

It may be remarked, in conclusion, that the justice of the foregoing views, both as to the cause of the distress of 1857 and the only security against the recurrence of a similar calamity, is confirmed by the manner in which a partial recovery has been brought about. No new branches of business have been established, no new markets have been opened. There has been no fortunate change in affairs domestic or foreign, for the pressure was not caused by any thing adverse in our political condition at home or abroad. It is not years of plenty succeeding years of famine; nor health returning after the visitations of pestilence. The change has been brought about simply by arresting the augmentation of debt, relieving the money market of gigantic borrowers, looking desperate concerns in the face and treating them accordingly;—in short, by settling up old accounts. Great sacrifices have attended the process; but they would have been greater had they been longer delayed. If the country would learn wisdom by experience, all would be well. But in matters of this kind, men seldom learn by any experience but their own; and that is apt to come too late. They gain wisdom and nothing else.

NUMBER TWENTY.

TRAVELLING IN FORMER TIMES.

First visit to New York by packet from Newport in 1810—Exodus from Dorchester to Connecticut River in 1635, in fourteen days—Madam Knight's journey to New York in 1704—Extracts—Franklin's voyage to New York in 1723—Abandons vegetable diet by the way—Franklin's reasons in 1754 for recommending Philadelphia as the seat of a provincial Union—Anecdote of General Adair and General Root—Rapid journey of Cardinal Wolsey from Richmond to Bruges and back—Washington's first journey to the Eastern States in 1756—Travelling by stage coach fifty years ago—"Waking up the wrong passenger"—Indifferent accommodations both for passengers and baggage—Anecdote of a German traveller—This mode of travelling sometimes very pleasant.

The generation now coming forward in life can have but a faint idea of the change, which has taken place within thirty years, in the facilities of travelling, as we in our turn probably form an inadequate conception of the state of things which existed before the establishment of stage-coaches. My first visit from Boston to New York was made in August, 1810, in a coasting packet from Newport, and if I mistake not we were out two nights and a part of three days. A second visit was made in December, 1814, in a stage-coach, and occupied three days of very diligent and severe travel, and this state of things lasted several years longer.

Changes are made with such rapidity in this country, that a couple of centuries have witnessed results, which in Europe have filled up the whole period from the dawn of civilization. When the first settlers of the Connecticut River emigrated from Dorchester, in Massachusetts, about one hundred men, women, and children, they were fourteen days in making the distance, which is now daily crossed over by the express train in three hours. This was the first movement in that great march of emigration from the coast to the interior, which fills so important a space in the annals and in the "destiny" of America. The history of the country contains few pages of greater interest, than those which record this first *Exodus* to the American promised land. The touching narrative is admirably given by Dr. Ellis, in the thirteenth volume of Sparks' American Biography.

Such as there described were the men and women, such the toils and hardships, by which this beautiful and prosperous America, now filled with its rapidly multiplying millions, approached and traversed in every direction by steam boat and steam car, on ocean and land, on river and lake, was settled but little more than two centuries and a quarter since.

Madam Sarah Knight was a heroine of a different character, and made her journey from Boston to New York on horseback in October, 1704. She was a person of thrift and went to settle important affairs; and as her business, going and coming, required her to stop in several places, her diary does not enable us to calculate the time which was then absolutely necessary for a journey from New York to Boston, the distance being then estimated at two hundred and seventy miles. About a fortnight is supposed to be the time usually employed on the journey. Madam Knight's journal, a most curious record, was first published in New York in 1825, and was reprinted in Littell's Living Age for 26 June, 1858. The following extracts will show the style of travelling between Boston and New York in 1704:

"In about an how'r, or something more, after we left the Swamp, we come to Billingses, where I was to Lodg. My Guide dismounted and very Complacently help't me down and shewd the door, signing to me wth his hand to Go in; wch I Gladly did—But had not gone many steps into the Room, ere I was Interrogated by a young Lady I understood afterwards was the Eldest daughter of the family, with these, or words to this purpose (viz) Law for mee—what in the world brings You here at this time a night?—I never see a woman on the Rode so Dreadfull late in all the days of my versall life. Who are You? Where are You going? I'me scared out of my witts—with much more of the same Kind. I stood aghast, Prepareing to reply, when in comes my Guide—to him Madam turned, Roreing out: Lawfull heart, John, is it You?—how de do! Where in the world are you going with this woman? Who is she? John made no Ansr. but sat down in the corner, fumbled out his black Junk, and saluted that instead of Debb; she then turned agen to mee and fell anew into her silly questions, without asking me to sitt down.—I told her shee treated me very Rudely, and I did not think it my duty to answer her unmannerly Questions. But to get ridd of them, I told her I come there to have the post's company with me to-morrow on my Journey, &c.

I paid honest John wth money and dram according to contract, and Dismist him, and pray'd Miss to shew me where I must Lodg. Shee conducted me to a parlour in a little back Lento, wch was almost fill'd wth the bedstead, wch was so high that I was forced to climb on a chair to gitt up to the wretched bed that lay on it; on wch having Stretcht my tired Limbs, and lay'd my head on a Sad-coloured pillow, I, began to think on the transactions of ye past day."

The following was Madam Knight's experience at Rye:

"—Early next morning set forward to Norrowalk, from its halfe Indian name *North-walk*, where about 12 at noon we arrived, and Had a Dinner of Fryed vension, very savoury. Landlady wanting some pepper in the seasoning, bid the Girl hand her the spice in the little *Gay* cupp on ye shelfe. From Hence we Hasted towards Rye, walking and leading our Horses neer a mile together, up a prodigios high Hill; and so Riding till about nine at night, and there arrived and took up our Lodgings at an ordinary, wch a French family kept. Here being very hungry, I desired a fricasee, wch the Frenchman undertakeing, mannaged so contrary to my notion of Cookery, that I hastened to Bed superless; And being shewd the way up a pair of stairs wch had such a narrow passage that I had almost stopt by the Bulk of my Body; But arriving at my apartment found it to be a little Lento Chamber furnisht amongst other Rubbish with a High Bedd and a Low one, a Long Table, a Bench and a Bottomless Chair,—Little Miss went to scratch up my Kennell wch Russelled as if shee'd bin in the Barn amongst the Husks, and suppose such was the contents of the tickin—nevertheless being exceeding weary, down

I laid my poor Carkes (never more tired) and found my Covering as scanty as my Bed was hard. Annon I heard another Russelling noise in ye Room—called to know the matter—Little miss said shee was making a bed for the men; who, when they were in Bed, complained their leggs lay out of it by reason of its shortness—my poor bones complained bitterly not being used to such Lodgings, and so did the man who was with us; and poor I made but one Grone, which was from the time I went to bed to the time I Riss, which was about three in the morning, Setting up by the Fire till Light, and having discharged our ordinary wch was as dear as if we had had far Better fare—wee took our leave of Monsier and about seven in the morn come to New Rochell a french town, where we had a good Breakfast."

New York at that time contained about four thousand inhabitants. Madam Knight's description of her residence there, of the style of building, and the manners and customs of the People is extremely curious; but we have no room for further extracts.

Benjamin Franklin made his runaway journey to New York by water in 1723. He had a favorable wind most of the time, and was three days on the water. An incident occurred on the way, which induced him,—a youth of seventeen, to abandon an exclusively vegetable diet, which he had some time before adopted, on the recommendation of an author named Tryon. They were beclamed off Block Island and the crew employed themselves in catching Cod of which they "hauled up a great number." Till then he "had stuck to the resolution of eating nothing that had had life." Following the doctrine of Tryon, he considered "the taking of every fish a kind of unprovoked murder," since none of them had been or could be guilty of any injury, "that might justify the massacre." He had, however, unfortunately for the Tryonic theory and Benjamin's practice under it, been formerly a great lover of fish. It is the weak side of people, especially of hungry apprentices, in a certain part of the country that shall be nameless. "When it came from the frying-pan," says young Benjamin, "it smelt remarkably well." What was the dead letter of Tryon's treatise, compared with a treat like that? "I balanced for some time between principle and inclination, till, recollecting that when the fish were opened I saw smaller fish taken out of their stomachs, then thought I, 'if you eat one another, I don't see why we may not eat you,' so I dined upon Cod very heartily."

In 1754 a convention was held at Albany to concert a plan of Union between the Colonies. In the articles adopted by this convention, it was recommended that Philadelphia should be the place where the first meeting for the proposed Assembly should be held. The reasons for the various provisions embraced in his plan were stated in a memoir drawn up by Dr. Franklin. The statement of the grounds for selecting Philadelphia throws considerable light on the facilities for travel at that time. It is as follows:

"Philadelphia was named as being nearer the centre of the colonies, where the commissioners would be well & cheaply accommodated. The high roads through the whole extent are for the most part very good, on which forty or fifty miles a day may very well be, and frequently are, travelled. Great part of the way may likewise be gone by water. In summer time the passages are frequently performed in a week from Charleston to Philadelphia and New York; and from Rhode Island to New York through the Sound, in two or three days; and from New York to Philadelphia, by water and land, in two days, by stage-boats and wheel carriages, that set out every other day. The journey from Charleston to Philadelphia may likewise be facilitated by boats running up Chesapeake Bay, three hundred miles. But if the whole journey be performed on horseback, the most distant members, vizt. the two from New Hampshire and from South Carolina, may probably render themselves at Philadelphia in fifteen or twenty days;—the majority may be there in much less time."

This primitive mode of travelling by horseback has, within my recollection, had its advocates, and that on the score of rapidity. Much amusement was caused at Washington by a friendly argument between Gen. Adair of Kentucky and Gen. Root of New York, on the comparative advantages of travelling on horseback and in stage-coaches, on the score of safety and speed, Gen. Adair declaring for the saddle. They started each for his home and by the conveyance which he preferred. Gen. Adair made the journey in safety on horseback and returned to Washington the same way the next December; while Gen. Root, travelling in a stage-coach, was overturned and suffered a severe injury which detained him on the road for the greater part, if not the whole, of the interval between the long and short sessions.

Notwithstanding the great superiority of the means of conveyance at the present day, a journey was sometimes made in old times with prodigious speed. Cardinal Wolsey owed his first advancement, in no small degree, to the rapidity with which he made the journey from London to Bruges in Flanders and back again, on an important mission to the Emperor of Germany, confided to him by Henry the Seventh. Having received his despatches from the King at Richmond, he arrived in London at four o'clock on Sunday afternoon, in season for the Gravesend barge, by which he reached that place in about three hours. The distance is about thirty miles by land as the river winds; he must have been strongly favored by wind and tide. There he took post-horses, and, travelling all night, reached Dover, about forty-five miles, on Monday morning, just as the packet was ready to sail. In less than three hours he was at Calais, and immediately starting with post-horses for Bruges, distant sixty or seventy miles, the residence at that time of the Emperor Maximilian, he arrived there the same night. Wolsey was immediately admitted to audience by the Emperor, and having despatched his business successfully was sent back to Calais by the Emperor the next day, under an escort of horse. He arrived at Calais as the gates of the city were opening Wednesday morning; stepped on board the packet just ready to sail and reached Dover at ten. Post-horses were in readiness, which conveyed him to Richmond, a distance of seventy miles, that night, after an absence of a little more than three days. Having taken some repose, he appeared before the king, as he was going from his bed-room to mass on Thursday morning. The king at first, supposing that he had not yet started on his mission, chided him for his delay. He was astonished at finding that he had been to Bruges and returned. The king next inquired if he had fallen in with a courier despatched the day before with additional instructions, relative to a matter which had been overlooked. Wolsey had met him on his own return, but having himself perceived the omission in his instructions, had "been so bold" (said he) "in mine own discretion, perceiving that matter to be very necessary, to despatch the same!" Hume erroneously gives Bruxelles instead of Bruges as the residence of the Emperor.

General Washington on his first visit to the Eastern States in 1756, travelled on horseback, starting from New York on February the 20th. It is not precisely known, I believe, how long he was on the way, probably a week. It appears from Hempstead's journal cited in Miss Caulkin's excellent history of New London, that he passed through that place, both going and coming.

"March 8th. Colonel Washington is returned from Boston and gone to Long Island in Powers' Sloop; he had also two boats to carry six horses and his retinue, all bound to Virginia."

The journey to New York from Boston by stage-coach, and this too after that mode of conveyance was brought to a very considerable state of perfection, was in my youth, in the winter season at least, an affair of three days. It was two days from New York to Philadelphia, and two from Philadelphia to Baltimore, by the way of Columbia. From Baltimore to Washington in 1814 was a pretty hard day's travel, and the weariness and discomfort of the journey were quite as formidable as the length of time required for its performance.

If my recollection serves me, a single daily stage-coach

carrying the mail, plied regularly at this time, 1814, between Boston and New York. It purported to start at about three o'clock in the morning; to sleep at Ashford the first night, and at New Haven the second, and arrive at New York on the evening of the third day. As there was generally rather more travel than one coach could accommodate, though not often enough for an extra carriage, it was necessary to engage your place two or three days beforehand. An hour or more before the time nominally appointed for starting, a messenger came around from the stage-office to "wake up the passengers." The old-fashioned brass knockers had not wholly disappeared at that time, so that the benefit of the operation, when the person to be aroused did not "wake easy," was sometimes extended to the neighbors. Occasionally a mistake would be made in the street number of the house, and expostulations of an animated kind would ensue between the messenger and the wrongly waked person, drowsily inquiring from his open chamber window, of a freezing wintry night, as to the precise object of the visitation. Hence the expressive proverb of "waking up the wrong passenger." As the messenger had often an extensive circuit to make round the town, those who stood first on his list, were sometimes called an hour and a half or two hours before the time; which gave them the advantage of getting thoroughly waked up.

At length came the vehicle rattling along, a four-horse coach, containing three seats inside and places for two beside the driver, which fell to the lot in cold weather of the last applicants; in summer they were the places of preference. Seats on the top of the carriage, like those in use at the present time, were not then known. Each of the three seats inside was supposed to accommodate three persons of whatever size or weight, small children being thrown into the bargain and bestowed on the knees of the adult passengers;—an arrangement which became a superior test of patience and good nature, before the long and weary day was over, especially if the child, besides not being your own, was troubled with a catarrhal affection or the whooping cough. The middle seat when I first began to travel had no strap or other support to the back. When that improvement was first introduced it was regarded as one of the great discoveries of the age. The baggage was not suspended with the body of the vehicle on springs, but it was placed on a frame-work extending backward from the hindmost axle, where it partook, without any mitigation, the concussion of the carriage. The consequence was that, unless your trunks were packed with great skill and their contents tightly strapped inside, your garments of every kind were nearly ruined by a journey of two or three days.

I remember to have witnessed a sad but not unamusing spectacle caused by the neglect of proper precautions in this respect, on the part of an inexperienced German traveller in Pennsylvania. He was returning from Philadelphia, with a moderate-sized portmanteau of which the contents had been very loosely bestowed. With a few articles of clothing, which seemed to be principally shirts and stockings, he had placed in his trunk a quire of printed music paper, a quantity of hard biscuit, a dozen of oranges, and a bag of silver dollars. The specie had broken from its place of deposit and had circulated freely, in every direction, through the trunk and the music paper, the oranges, and the biscuits, (like some chemical substances very different in nature while separate, but brought into intimate union by the intervention of a new element,) had, by the action of the dollars, been compounded into a mass,—not to say mess,—in which it was difficult to trace the slightest resemblance to either ingredient. The appearance of things when the trunk was opened, and the wobegone looks of its proprietor, might have furnished a plausible argument for preferring a convertible paper currency to hard coin,—at least for travellers in a stage-coach.

It was a matter of some moment to see your baggage securely strapped on at the outset, and as the coach was usually changed two or three times in the course of the day, it was necessary, whenever this was done, to exercise a little supervision over the process, and to see that light articles, such as valises and umbrellas and bandboxes, (these last regarded with unqualified horror by the male travellers,) carried in the interior of the coach, were removed at each exchange of vehicles. It was generally understood that the first applicant had the choice of seats, qualified however, in all cases, by the claim of the gentler sex to the best accommodations. There was room also for the display of courtesy and the want of it, in occasionally relieving, by an exchange of positions, your unfortunate fellow passenger, who was swaying all day long on the middle seat, without support to his back.

When the coach was crowded with unsociable and taciturn passengers, its floor encumbered with bags and other small articles greatly encroaching upon the space for extending the legs, the weather a drizzling mixture of rain and snow, the roads rough, the drivers surly and the beasts jaded, one arrived at the journey's end late at night, in a condition which a victim of the rack would scarcely have envied. But with a moderately filled vehicle,—a good natured, and, still more, a congenial circle of fellow passengers, a light elastic air, a December sun gleaming over sparkling fields, a road like marble, a succession of spanking teams with drivers as fearless as skilful, who generally went down hill at full gallop,—the breakfast and dinner table plainly but bountifully and wholesomely served by active and tidy hands, at those nice old country taverns, which have almost wholly ceased to exist; —under these circumstances, a journey in the stage-coach was a positive enjoyment. After a lapse of forty years I recall a journey like this, in company with Daniel Webster and Judge Story, as having afforded some of the happiest, the most instructive, and most joyous hours of my life.

NUMBER TWENTY-ONE.

TRAVEL IN EUROPE.

No Railroads or Steamers in Europe in 1818—Fulton's first passage to Albany—Stage-coaches, posting, and vetturino in Europe—Travelling on foot and on horseback—The ancient Roman roads almost wholly lost—Visit to the Continent in 1818—Guide books—Hon. T. H. Perkins and tribute to him by John Quincy Adams—Stone Henge—Wilton House—Old Sarum—Salisbury Cathedral—Passage from Southampton to Havre—Freedom from care at sea—Transition from England to France and points of contrast—French custom-house—Anecdote of a dyspeptic Bostonian.

In the last number I alluded to the great facilities for travelling at the present day in America, compared with the state of things in former times. The difference is as great in Europe as in the United States, although, in reference to the practical arts, an old country might be expected to be far in advance of one so recently settled as the United States. In 1818 there was not a Railroad in Europe, with the exception of the tram roads used in connection with the coal mines, nor was there, if my memory serves me, on any of its waters, salt or fresh, such a thing as a steam vessel of any dimensions, with the exception of a small steamer on the river Clyde. Eight years before that time, the passage from New York to Amboy was regularly made in a steamer, and more than ten years before, Fulton had made his memorable voyage from New York to Albany in the same way;—a slow and tedious passage, but an era in human affairs;—the most important ever made since the voyage of Columbus.

In England forty years ago, persons, who did not use their

own carriages and horses, travelled in the stage-coach, (a remarkably compact and expeditious vehicle, usually making ten miles an hour, carrying from four to six inside, and from eight to twelve on the top;) or posted, that is, made use of their own carriages and took post-horses, one of which is ridden by a postilion, at convenient stations, where also post-carriages might be found, for those who did not make use of their own; a much more expensive, but otherwise far preferable mode of travelling, as it took you over roads not traversed by stage-coaches, and enabled you to choose your own hours. When three travelled in company and divided the expense, it did not exceed that of the stage-coach. In France you had the stage-coach under the name of the *Diligence,* (a name rather ominous of the rate of speed,) and a system of posting analogous, as far as the supply of horses was concerned, to the English. Both these modes of travelling were also found substantially in most other countries of Continental Europe.

A third mode of travelling a good deal resorted to by persons not pressed for time and studying economy, was by what is called *vetturino.* It is not yet wholly obsolete, though like stage-coaches and post-horses nearly susperseded by railroads. The *vetturino* conveyed you by contract with the same carriage, horses, and driver, for the whole of the proposed journey and for a stipulated price. For persons who travel, not to kill time but to employ it usefully; to see a country, not merely to be able to say they have seen it; to visit a city and examine its objects of interest, not "to do" a city, this mode of travelling has its advantages.

Two other modes of travelling were resorted to in Europe forty years ago, not yet nor likely to be ever wholly disused, with the results of which, on one or two occasions, I shall endeavor to make the reader who knows locomotion only as it exists in the railroad train, better acquainted. There are parts of the old world of the highest interest to the intelligent tourist, which he can explore only on foot. If he would enjoy any thing but the mere music of the verses in the poetry of Scott, (and that I must admit is an exquisite enjoyment,) he must visit the scenery of the Lay of the Last Minstrel and the Lady of the Lake on foot. Sophia Scott told me that she once did this with her father in a drenching rain, which he persisted in calling "a Scotch mist." Much of Wales and the Lake region of Westmoreland and Cumberland can be seen to advantage,—or rather seen at all,—in no other way. When Wordsworth protested against allowing the district of country, which he so much venerated, from being invaded by railroads, he did not reflect that no railroad would ever penetrate their lovely and sacred retreats. The only effect of their construction would be to take the place of the stage-coach and the post-carriage, along one or two principal lines of travel, and thus multiply a hundred fold the numbers who would come to worship with him at the shrine of that Nature, which he feared to desecrate. So, too, the weird recesses of the Harz Mountains, the secluded valleys, the bewitched heights, the solemn caves, the dreary dripping mines, the ruined castles, moss-grown with the legends of eight centuries, can be approached only on foot. Last of all the imperial Alps admit of none but the pedestrian to their crystal halls. As you approach their glittering battlements,—the inmost citadel of nature's glory and power,—lazy affluence must fain alight from her chariot, the arm of the engineer is palsied, and the grim necromancer of steam admits the presence of a Force mightier than his own.

As soon as you leave Europe for the East, (in fact, in many parts of Europe,) vehicles of every kind are unknown, and you travel on horseback, on camels, and in the further East on elephants. In my time, there were no vehicles for travellers in the lower part of the kingdom of Naples. We had to travel for four days on horseback in districts which, in the time of the Romans, were traversed by the Appian way, the *Regina viarum*, (the queen of High ways,) and which now in this respect are as completely in a state of nature, as the central plateau of our continent. In the year 1819 the facilities for reaching Tarento were no greater than they were in the time of Pythagoras. The same was the case throughout Epirus, Thessaly, Macedonia, Thrace, and the whole of Greece proper, where the great paved roads of antiquity had entirely disappeared, vehicles of every kind were unknown, and there was no communication but by bridle paths in any part of the countries named. Few things testify more loudly and sadly to the desolation of those once prosperous regions, and the barbarism of the Turkish rule. The Romans pushed their military roads to the very limits of their empire. The Appian way, paved with blocks of granite, gneiss, or lava fourteen inches thick, was carried through Epirus and Thessaly ; but its very route, except by conjecture, is lost. No trace of it, if I remember aright, east of the Adriatic, is to be seen on the surface of the ground. Ages of civilization may exist without producing roads like the Appian way, but once produced one hardly knows how they can be made, or allowed, wholly to disappear. In Italy itself this great road, in common with all the other great military roads of the Romans, has almost wholly vanished. It forms if I mistake not, the foundation of the modern road, only across the Pontine marshes.

In August 1818, after five delightful months in England and Scotland, divided principally between London, Cambridge, Oxford, Wales, the Lake region, Edinburgh, and the highlands of Perthshire, I left London for the continent, with scarce any object in view but to reach Italy and more especially Rome, as expeditiously as possible. Goethe I think quotes a remark of Lessing, that when you are going to Rome, you should be tied up in a sack on crossing the frontier of Italy, and not be taken out of it till you reach the eternal city. I began to practice on the spirit of this rule from the time I left

London, hurrying rapidly through regions of which almost every league has its memorable historical event, its ancient tradition or monument, its venerable ruin, its beautiful landscape, its remarkable collection of works of art, its important industrial, benevolent, or literary establishment. These are objects of curiosity and interest, which, under all circumstances, one must take more or less from the guide books; and if in a few important localities we linger on the spot,—observe more carefully and describe more fully and accurately in our letters or journals,—we generally find in the works of professed tourists, who travel for the avowed purpose of making a book, a minute and elaborate description which puts our hasty *memoranda* to shame; although the germ of these elaborate descriptions is not seldom itself to be found in the friendly Reichard, or, in these modern days, the not less friendly Murray.

I took the stage-coach to Southampton, avoiding the beaten road by Dover and Calais, in order to see a part both of England and France, which I had not before seen. At Southampton, I found my honored friend Col. Thomas H. Perkins, of Boston,—the friend of more than forty years, to whom I delight to pay this passing tribute. President John Quincy Adams said of him, in my hearing, in the House of Representatives of the United States, that "he had the fortune of a prince, and a heart as much above his fortune, as that was above a beggar's." On meeting me at Southampton, he said, "Come let us pass a little time together. I visited a part of this very neighborhood with your brother, (the late Alexander H. Everett,) seven or eight years ago, and nearly thirty years ago I travelled with your father from Boston to Philadelphia,—a great journey in those days."

Accordingly we went together to the objects of interest in the neighborhood, and scarce anywhere are they more numerous or important. Within a moderate distance from each other, you may contemplate the monumental records of almost every stage of ancient and modern civilization;—Stone Henge, Old Sarum, Salisbury Cathedral, Wilton House,—memorials of almost every period and form of human culture. Stone Henge is the most imposing relic of that ancient Druidical period of which we know next to nothing historically, beyond a few sentences in Strabo, Cæsar, and Tacitus. Cæsar thinks the Druids were acquainted with letters, but it is probable that the knowledge of writing among them was confined to Greeks, who had fled from home and taken refuge in these remote and (as the Greeks deemed them) barbarous races. But if the Druids, the dominant caste of the primitive Celtic races, were unacquainted with the great instrument of civilization, it is the more extraordinary that they possessed the knowledge of mechanics, required for such a structure as Stone Henge. Inigo Jones says that, "by the grace of God," he could raise stones as great or greater to their places, which is no doubt true. With the resources of modern art much greater feats of engineering are daily performed. But the Druidical architects not only wanted our modern mechanical powers, but could have hardly had the aid of that other potent assistance, (alluded to by Inigo Jones,) in rearing the temple for their sanguinary rites. The galleries of Wilton,—kindly opened to our inspection,—contain valuable specimens of Grecian art, and some paintings of the great modern masters. Old Sarum is now a wheat field; before Lord Grey's reform bill, it sent two members to parliament, who were nominated by the proprietor of the said wheat field, whoever he might be; Manchester in the mean time, with a hundred and fifty thousand inhabitants, sending no member. This certainly was a stupendous departure from the principle of geographical representation, on which our legislatures are constituted. But it would be a mistake to say that in a system like the English, constructed not on theory but on tradition, the members from Old Sarum represented nothing but the wheat field. They represented the bull-dog tenacity with which the Anglo-Saxon clings to his legal traditions, after they have become legal fictions, and thus converts them back into realities, making temper do the work of logic. They represented the whole of that old parliament which once sat (I forget when) at Old Sarum. They represented by-gone centuries, gradually struggling toward our modern constitutional ideas. They represented York and Lancaster, Plantagenet and Tudor,—in a word, the great, solemn, monumental past. Then there is, in this region, Salisbury Cathedral, one of the most beautiful of those magnificent mediæval piles, in which so much of the devotion, the art, and the social vitality of four centuries of modern history are embodied. We call the ages, which produced the earlier forms of this mysterious architecture, "the dark ages;" and dark in some things they were. But with respect to art, this arrogance would be more excusable, if, instead of the portentous abortions of modern public architecture, we produced any thing which can for a moment compare with the cathedrals of "the dark ages" for purity of conception, sublimity of thought, unity of design, richness and tastefulness of decoration, or even mechanical execution.

We had a fine sail from Southampton to Havre. The distance is one hundred and ten miles, but we made it in less time than it took in the Spring, to cross from Calais to Dover. A lovely August night, fresh smells from either coast healthfully borne on the salt sea-breeze, the heavens blazing with their eternal watch-fires to their uttermost depths; a smooth summer sea, slightly ruffled by a favorable wind;—an encircling universe of glory, loveliness, and mute praise! A short sea-voyage, when you are free from sickness, and at a pleasant season of the year, is beyond all question the occasion, on which the pulses of animal life beat with the greatest firmness and elasticity. The exquisite purity of the air carries healthful excitement to the inmost fibre of the lungs; the ordinary cares of *terra firma* (Horace to the contrary notwithstanding) do not follow you on shipboard. There is no door bell at sea; there is no mail at sea. The pathways of the sea are not paved with deafening blocks of granite. There are no news at sea; no public meetings, nor committee meetings, nor orations; the *Columbian Semi-weekly Musquito & Hemisphere* is not published at sea; there is nothing but the sky above, the ocean around and beneath, now and then a dancing vessel in sight, and the winds of heaven,—the pure bracing winds,—speeding you on your way. The Halcyons brood on the sea.

Favorable winds sped us on our little voyage. We sailed after sunset and arrived at Havre at sunrise. One night had carried us from England to France; from the Teuton to the Celt; from a language of Saxon origin to one of Latin origin; from the common law to the civil law; from Protestanism to the Gallo-Roman church; from acts of parliament to royal ordinances; from the neat and tasteful stage-coach, with its nicely caparisoned horses, and driven four in hand by the bluff coachman, to the lumbering diligence, half baggage wagon and half stage coach, drawn by five fiery Norman steeds, loosely tied together by rope harness, and straggling over the road, guided by postilions sunk to the thighs in gigantic trunk boots; and, though last not least, from the spit to the *casserole*, and the honest joint that tells its own story, to the sometimes questionable dainties of the French *cuisine.*

The English or American traveller landing on the continent in those days, (and I believe the case is not very different now,) first feels that he has reached a foreign country when he passes through the French custom-house. The poor maniac who shot the Secretary of Sir Robert Peel, mistaking him for Sir Robert himself, labored under the delusion that he was pursued by fiends. With this impression on his mind he fled from place to place, seeking rest and finding none. At length he crossed from Dover to Calais, and saw, to his amazement, the footstep of Louis XVIIII. deeply cut into the granite pavement of the quay! His diseased fancy converted this piece of loyal adulation into a work of diabolical agency. He was soon beset by the clamorous porters at the landing, and the tide-waiters of the *douane*, and felt that in them his worst visions were confirmed. For myself I had never had occasion to echo the complaints of travellers on this subject. Taking care always to have my passport duly countersigned and to carry nothing contraband in my portmanteau, I have never encountered a custom-house officer on any frontier or at any port, who was proof against patience, good humor, and a five-franc piece.

One of our countrymen, however, who made the passage with us from Southampton to Havre on this occasion, a respectable retired merchant from Boston, seeking relief in travel from chronic dyspepsia, had an amusing scene with the custom officers at Havre. The unfortunate gentleman was troubled with an eager appetite, which of course it was not proper he should indulge. To prevent his doing so was the arduous duty of his sisters, who were travelling with him. To elude their vigilance, he usually carried in his great coat pocket a private store of gingerbread or sponge cake, carefully wrapped up. As he was considerably reduced by ill health, but travelling in garments made while he was well, the concealed parcel of cake as he landed on the quay, caused the pocket of the coat, (which hung with a fulness ever suspicious to custom-house officers,) to project still more suspiciously. The attention of the tide-waiter was awakened, and he suspected no doubt that a case of fine English cutlery, or a package of cigars, was about to be smuggled into France. He accordingly walked round and round our dyspeptic traveller, who saw that all was not right, but who, speaking no French, could neither give nor understand an explanation. At last the officer indicated by signs that the contents of the protruding pocket must be disclosed. The watchful sisters by this time had taken the alarm, and the idlers on the quay began to congregate about the party. Our invalid felt guilty, not of breaking the laws of France, but those of the domestic empire, and his conscious blush gave new impulse to the suspicions of the officer. The questionable packet was at length, with some difficulty, produced, carefully tied up. The string, in the trepidation of hastily untying it, (a common case,) ran into a hard knot. More delay, more suspicion, deeper blushes. At length the irritated gentleman tore open the parcel, and with a look between the comical and the disconsolate, pulled out a great cake of gingerbread and thrust it into the officer's face. A general laugh ensued, and the troublesome article was allowed to pass duty free.

NUMBER TWENTY-TWO.

HAVRE AND ROUEN.

The importance of Havre owing to its position at the mouth of the Seine and the American trade—St. Pierre—Conflict of races in Normandy—Lillebonne—The council-hall of William the Conqueror swept away by a cotton spinner—Detention at Rouen—Ugo Foscolo—Thomas Moore—Béranger—Society at Paris in 1817-1818—Importance of Rouen—The Cathedral—Heart of Richard Cœur de Lion—Church of Saint Ouen—William the Conqueror could not write his name—Deserted at his death—Place de la Pucelle, where Joan of Arc was burned—Reflections on her fate—Her statue by the Princess Marie, daughter of Louis Philippé—Voltaire, Schiller—Corneille—Regrets that he had not chosen the Maid of Orleans for a heroine—Overturn of the diligence.

Parting at Havre with Col. Perkins, who was travelling in a different direction, I continued the journey to Paris with my friend, Mr. Delavan, so well known for his exertions in the temperance cause, whose acquaintance I had had the pleasure of making at Southampton. Of antiquarian interest there is but little at Havre, of which, however, the foundation dates from the early part of the sixteenth century. It owes its importance principally to its position at the mouth of the Seine, which makes it in reality the seaport of Paris, and gives it no small share of the foreign commerce of France. It was originally founded by Francis I., but the guide book tells us that its growth in modern times is owing to a cause little foreseen in his day, and connected with a discovery which had been lately made in foreign parts by a Genoese mariner. "The declaration of the Independence of the United States formed the groundwork of the present good fortune of Havre." If the benefits accruing to the commerce, manufactures, population, and general prosperity of the leading States of Europe were duly estimated by them, they would feel with how little reason they view with jealous and even hostile eye the growth of this country. To say nothing of their participation in all the general advantages of a friendly commercial intercourse with the American continent, I took the liberty in an official communication to the representatives of the two leading powers of Europe a few years since, to express the opinion, that but for the refuge afforded in the United States to the starving millions of the old world in 1847, and the employment given to their industry by the raw materials of our agriculture and the demands of our consumption, an explosion would have taken place, which would have shaken society to its foundation. I have within a few weeks read a pamphlet of a French adventurer in Central America, who speaks of the United States, in the coolness of his hatred, as a nuisance to the other powers of the earth, which ought to be abated, not remembering to how many cities of France, besides Havre, such an event would carry desolation!

St. Pierre is, I believe, the only native of Havre who has distinguished himself as a writer. His birth at Havre perhaps led him in after life to engage in the enterprise for the colonization of Madagascar. The world may be said to be indebted for "Paul and Virginia" to the fact, that Havre is a seaport carrying on a familiar commercial intercourse with the colonies of France.

In pursuance of the plan already alluded to, of loitering as little as possible by the way, I took the diligence in the evening for Rouen. I passed consequently by night through the region where many of the most important scenes were acted, of that long struggle between the Norman and Saxon, and afterwards between the Anglo-Norman and the Gallo-Norman races, which fills the most memorable ages of early English history. That long conflict has exercised as great an influence over the fortunes of the modern world, as the old struggles of Persia and Greece, and of Carthage and Rome, did upon the fortunes of the ancient world. It will be felt in our language, literature, manners, political institutions, and religious belief, for ages to come, and till new convulsions shall create a new chaos and a new re-organization among the families of men.

The road from Havre to Rouen passes through Lillebonne, a city which stands on the site and retains substantially the name of *Julia bona*, (Julia the good,) in which very remarkable remains of a spacious Roman theatre have been excavated. It is overlooked from a commanding position, by the ruins of a castle, which was one of the residences of William the Conqueror, and in which he is said to have consulted his barons on the project of invading England. The guide book says that " the great Norman hall, in which, according to the tradition, William met his barons in council, has been entirely swept away by the present proprietor, a cotton-spinner." Not the least notable of the sweepings of King Cotton's besom! The "present proprietor" would, I think, have done better to imitate the policy which William the Conqueror pursued in England, and to preserve, and, if need be, render commodious for modern use, rather than to "sweep away" the Council Hall, in which the most momentous event of modern history was decided upon!

I had expected, on leaving Havre for a night's drive, to be able to continue our journey from Rouen, where we arrived in the morning. We found, however, that all the places in the diligence for Paris, except one, had been pre-engaged at Rouen, an accident, we found on inquiry, to be of frequent occurrence, and therefore supposed by impatient travellers to happen on purpose, for the sake of detaining them for a day in that city. All these little annoyances have of course vanished with the construction of railroads. But although we were unable to get a couple of seats for ourselves, I succeeded in obtaining one for my faithful Luigi, a respectable young man from the shores of the Lago Maggiore, who had been recommended to me in England in the spring, by Ugo Foscolo, as a person who could at once perform the duty of a travelling servant and an Italian master. He had lived and travelled with me in these capacities for several months, gradually adding to them that of humble friend.

Having named Ugo Foscolo, one of the most original characters and eminent writers of modern Italy, the reader will pardon me, I am sure, for dwelling a few moments on my recollections of him, as preserved from a familiar acquaintance during the spring and summer of 1818. A native of one of the Ionian Islands, but of a Venitian family, he had received a very superior classical education. He was a critical Greek scholar, and wrote and spoke the Latin language with fluency. He had been an officer of cavalry in the army of the Cisalpine republic, and was one of the deputies from that republic to the Congress held at Lyons after the return of Napoleon from Egypt. Here he pronounced, on behalf of his constituents, a remarkable discourse, in which he censured the preceding French governments with unsparing severity, earnestly appealing to Napoleon, of whom he was at that time the eulogist and admirer, to correct their abuses. He filled, for a short time, the chair of polite literature at Pavia, and after the suppression of that and the other professorships of classical literature and belles-lettres, lived in discontented retirement, brooding over the oppression of his countrymen, to whom the only alternative offered was that of the French or Austrian yoke. When I knew him he was living in straitened circumstances in England. He had delivered lectures on Dante, Boccaccio, and Petrarch, in London, which were afterwards published, in different works, and form perhaps the acutest commentary on "the all-Etruscan three." With the exception of Alfieri, if he is an exception, Foscolo was, at that time, the most vigorous of the modern Italian writers. His Jacopo Ortis is an Italian *Werther*, but, though an imitation, had a great influence at the time of its publication on the reading classes. I greatly value a copy of it given me by himself, as also a copy of a curious satire on his literary contemporaries, written in the language and style of the Vulgate. We occupied the greater part of an afternoon passed at his retired rural lodgings, in reading this piquant composition, of which he explained to me the personal allusions; but they have long since lost all interest except for the literary antiquary. He used to complain of the late English hours, which, he said, destroyed health and eyesight. He quoted with great applause Dr. Franklin's new mode of lighting large towns, viz., by sunshine. I dined with him on one occasion at the hospitable table of the elder Murray, with a party consisting of some of the most distinguished literary celebrities of the day, among others Mr. Thomas Moore, who sang several of his own songs. It will readily be believed that the hours were winged with geniality; they were, however, prolonged till two o'clock in the morning. Foscolo and myself walked home to our lodgings together at that unseasonable hour, (he was then living in London,) and at every pause in the conversation he muttered "troppo lungo," (too long.) If the reader will look into Lord Broughton's (Mr. Hobhouse's) "Illustrations of the fourth canto of Childe Harolde," he will perceive that Ugo Foscolo is well entitled to the place which I have given him in these desultory recollections. He is mentioned by Lord Byron, in his preface to the same poem, with ten or twelve others of his countrymen, as persons who "will secure to the present generation in Italy an honorable place in most of the departments of science and belles-lettres."

Having stated that, on the occasion above alluded to, I heard Mr. Thomas Moore sing some of his own songs, I may add that I had a similar gratification, the preceding winter at Paris, in hearing several of Béranger's songs, and especially the *Dieu des bons gens*, sung by himself. It was my good fortune occasionally to meet this remarkable man at the tables of General Lafayette, Benjamin Constant, and one or two other persons belonging to the circle of liberal statesmen in France. Besides the two named, the Abbé de Pradt, then at the height of his popularity, the baron Alexandre von Humboldt, Bishop Grégoire, Mr. Gallatin, M. Manuel, General Foy, M. David d'Angers, the sculptor, and Talma, the great tragedian, were of these parties, where the conversation, it is scarcely necessary to say, was most brilliant and fascinating. Béranger was often an honored and favorite guest, though somewhat reserved in his manners. Amidst all the delicacies of the French *cuisine*, the material repast, which, by the way, was of a brevity to satisfy Ugo Foscolo himself, was, beyond comparison, the least attractive part of the banquet. The highest political and social questions of the day were discussed by men of master minds, trained in the great vicissitudes of the revolution, the empire, and the restoration. No one shone to greater advantage on these occasions than Mr. Gallatin, whose memory was a vast storehouse of discriminating observation and important fact, and whose acuteness surpassed that of most men whom I have known. These dinners rarely passed off without one of his own songs from Béranger, often the last composed by him. Like Thomas Moore, he had scarce any thing of a voice, but in the case of both, exquisite poetry, the deep pathos of an aggrieved nationality, and conscious influence over public sentiment, more than supplied the want of mere musical execution.

But I have wandered far (not I trust to the discontent of the reader, who will not be offended with these somewhat disconnected recollections of great men who have passed away) from the little Lombardian travelling servant recommended to me by Ugo Foscolo. Having no occasion for his services on the way to Paris, I took the only vacant place for him, in the diligence that started in the morning, and remained myself to pass the day at Rouen, one of the most important cities of France. As a manufacturing town it is one of the most considerable, and it has a depth of water in the Seine which admits vessels of two or three hundred tons. It possesses architectural monuments of extreme magnificence and beauty; and its historical associations, as the capital of lower Normandy, are of the most rich and varied character. It will readily be supposed that a day's observation of such a place could add nothing to the stock of information contained in the guide books; in fact, could but embrace a portion of the objects worthy the traveller's attention. But here, as in so many other places, even a day's observation gives a distinctness of impression, especially as to localities, not to be got from books alone, and leads you to read with greatly increased relish and profit.

The Cathedral of Rouen is one of the grandest of the structures of this class. It is severely criticized by Mr. Galley Knight, and other learned amateurs, for incoherent mixture of style and excess of ornament, portions of it being built in a declining age of art; but the entire effect upon an uncritical eye is extremely imposing. Its interior is not far from four hundred and fifty feet in length, and the nave is about ninety feet in height. There are three magnificent rose windows in the nave and transept; and in the last chapel, on the southern side of the nave, is the monument of Rollo, the first duke of Normandy. Several of the chapels contain painted glass windows, of great age and beauty. Within the choir a piece of colored marble, sunk into the pavement, indicates the spot where the heart of Richard *Cœur de Leon* was buried. His rude statue, which disappeared in the time of the Huguenots in the sixteenth century, was discovered under the high altar about twenty years after my visit. His "lion heart" shrunk, but in perfect preservation, was found at the same time, wrapped in thick silk and enclosed in a leaden case. It was removed to the Museum. Richard had bequeathed it to the city of Rouen, from the especial affection which he bore to the Normans.

The church of St. Ouen, nearly as long as the Cathedral, and of somewhat greater height, is justly deemed one of the noblest specimens in the world of this style of architecture. It has suffered from time, from fanaticism, and from political Vandalism. The Huguenots made bonfires in it, to burn the images of the saints, the wood work of the altars, and the vestments of the priests; and the terrorists of 1793 set up a blacksmith's forge in one of the chapels for the repair of arms; godless unbelief and the sternest orthodoxy meeting on the same platform of desecration. It is, however, in the main, well preserved, has been judiciously restored, and the essential parts of it having been built within one generation and in the best age of the art, it far exceeds the Cathedral in purity of taste, and unity and harmony of design. Some of the finest painted glass in Europe is to be seen in this noble church. It is said that the master architect murdered one of his journeymen, from jealousy of the superior taste and skill which the youth had exhibited in one of the exquisitely beautiful rose windows.

The Museum of Rouen contains objects of great curiosity. I have already mentioned one of them, the poor shrunken remains of the Lion Heart, for whose living pulses Europe and Asia were too small. What a moral antithesis; the heart of Richard Cœur de Lion wrapped, not in plaited mail, but in grave clothes, encased, not in burnished steel, but in mortuary lead, and exposed to view in a museum! The same museum contains another relic, which illustrates in a different way the vanity of human greatness,—a charter of William the Conqueror, authenticated, not by his signature, but his ⋈ mark. The stern and politic chieftain, who accomplished what Julius Cæsar imperfectly attempted, and Napoleon wholly failed to achieve; who ingrafted the fiery courage and haughty spirit of the Norman on the persistent endurance and judicial method of the Saxon; who gave nerve and blood to muscle and wind, and thus laid the foundation of a power which, after eight hundred years, girdles the globe, could not write his name! The great Conqueror of the British Islands died in the suburbs of Rouen, and his poor remains, deserted by his courtiers, neglected by his children, stripped by his servants, were left to be conveyed by charitable strangers to their last resting-place at Caen. Such are the terrible homilies, in which Providence, taking Death for a text, preaches humility to the great ones of the earth!

But there is a spot in Rouen, the *Place de la Pucelle* (Maiden place) which teaches the lesson in sadder terms than the deserted death-beds of remorseless monarchs. In this *Place*, about twenty years only before the invention of the art of printing was consummated, and a complete edition of the Bible was issued from the press; in this *Place*, in the century that witnessed the discovery of America, an innocent girl, who united every thing in her person and history, which could command admiration and merit gentle and honorable treatment, was burned alive! Her crime was, that she had kindled such enthusiasm in the hearts of her craven countrymen, as enabled them to wrest a portion of their soil from the foreign conqueror. Her betrayers and accusers were the unworthy Frenchmen whom she had rescued from vassalage; her executioners were the English prelates and nobles, who meanly revenged upon the poor fettered girl the shameful defeats they had suffered in the field from the maiden champion. A monument unworthy of her memory stands upon the spot where she perished at the stake; a nobler monument, the work of a king's daughter, is dedicated to her memory at Versailles. King Louis Philippe, in 1840, spoke to me, with moist eyes, of this admirable work of his daughter, and added, with gratified paternal feeling, that the inhabitants of Domrémy, the native place of Joan of Arc, had petitioned him for a copy of it, which he, I think, has since erected in that village. I know of no bitterer satire on the France of the eighteenth century,—no more striking proof that she stood in need of some fierce and burning process of regeneration,—than that her greatest and most popular writer in that century,—Voltaire,—should have made this almost sainted heroine the object of his abominable ribaldry, and left it to a foreigner,—Schiller,—to celebrate her poetical apotheosis, in a strain not unworthy of the theme.

About two centuries after the acting of this terrible tragedy in the *Place de la Pucelle*, the noblest tragic writer of France, the great Corneille, was born at Rouen. His statue adorns the bridge which spans the Seine. One cannot but lament, that, instead of bestowing the immortality of his genius on the legends of the mythical Spanish champion, he had not held up the inspired Maid of Orleans, (inspired, beyond the measure of ordinary humanity, with faith, patriotism, and courage,) to the reverence of his countrymen. He might have rescued her by anticipation from the infamies of Voltaire, and won for France, what now belongs to a foreign muse, the credit of having first rendered due honor to her gentle heroism and spotless name.

My poor Lombardian, who preceded me twelve hours from Rouen, reached Paris but a very little time before me. The diligence in which he was travelling broke down, and the passengers were obliged to while away their time in the high road till it could be repaired. Luigi assured me that, when they crept to light from the *Interior* in the centre of the vehicle, the *gallery* behind, the *Coupé* in front, and the *Boot* above, they amounted, all told, to twenty-three, besides the Conductor, an indefinite amount of luggage and merchandise being bestowed in the Imperial. Such was the *Diligence* in France forty years ago!

NUMBER TWENTY-THREE.

WILL THERE BE A WAR IN EUROPE?

The vast importance of this question—Comparative strength of the parties in a military point of view—The leaders described, the Austrian Emperor Francis Joseph, the King of Sardinia Victor Emmanuel II., the Emperor of the French—The German Confederation in its relations to the contest—Hungary and the possibility of a new revolution—The general spirit of disaffection in Italy and the strength which it lends to Sardinia as the champion of Italian nationality—Qualified in practice by the hostile feelings of the Italian States toward each other.

"Will there be a war in Europe?" This is a question which, more than any other relating to human affairs, now occupies the thoughts of reflecting men throughout the civilized world. Before this paper sees the light, the question may have been decided, and a page of fearful significance for good or for evil,—importing prosperity or devastation to fertile regions, permanence or downfall to established governments, life or death to tens of thousands of our fellow-creatures,—may have been turned in the volume of contemporary history. If the question is decided for peace on any basis that promises a durable settlement of the existing controversies, a period of amost unprecedented prosperity will open on the world, affording the various states of Europe ample opportunity to recover from the exhaustion of their recent struggles, with the energy of a mighty re-action. The abundance of recently discovered gold, and the unexampled perfection to which the mechanical arts, and the facilities for transport and travel have been brought, with the astonishing development of mental energy and inventive sagacity which are everywhere manifesting themselves, seem to mark out the present time as one of the most auspicious for further improvement and progress, that the world has ever seen. If the great question is decided for war, all admit,—the rival leaders in the British parliament unite in proclaiming with anxiety,—that it will be a contest of fearful range and of desolating violence.

The parties to the contest are such, in the present state of the political equilibrium of Europe, as to foreshadow the tremendous proportions of the struggle. They will be, at the first outbreak, Austria on the one side, and on the other Sardinia and her ally, France. The army of Austria, on its ordinary peace establishment, is usually reckoned at four hundred thousand men, capable of being carried, by calling out the reserve, very nearly to six hundred thousand. This army is in a state of effective organization and perfect drill. The regular army of France for the year 1857 was estimated at 450,000, with sixty-two thousand seamen in the imperial navy. The official paper denies that the regular force has been augmented the present season. But if not professedly augmented, the regiments have undoubtedly been filled up to their complement, and the actual state of the army (what rarely happens in time of peace) carried up to the returns. As for Sardinia, whose population is estimated in the French imperial Almanach for this year at 4,300,000, (only a third larger than the State of New York,) her regular army is about fifty thousand, which is now said to be rapidly swelled by volunteers from every part of Italy. These armies are not, like the undisciplined rabble of Turkey and China, armed with rusty guns, and protected by shields emblazoned with painted lions. They are provided with the last improvements in ordnance and the munitions of war, and trained to perfection in their use. The lazy tactics of the last century have long since been discarded. Celerity of movement, in overwhelming masses, artillery flying over the field on the wings of the wind, rifled musketry of fearful range, throwing to an incredible distance balls of a murderous weight and configuration, are now introduced into the armies of Europe. In a word, the arts of destruction are not a whit behind the arts of peaceful culture, in the perfection to which they have been carried. If the Austrian and Franco-Sardinian forces take the field against each other, it will be a shock of arms scarcely witnessed before in the world.

The sovereigns by whom these great powers will be put in motion,—probably commanded in person,—are all supposed to be animated by courage and military ambition. The Emperor of Austria, Francis Joseph, now twenty-nine years of age, was, at the age of eighteen, called to the throne of the Hapsburgs, at a period of perilous convulsion, by the abdication of his imbecile uncle, the Emperor Ferdinand, and the voluntary renunciation of the right of succession by his father. He was thought, even at that immature age, to evince a capacity for sovereign power in arduous times. Under the influence of his mother, the Archduchess Sophia, and the advice of wise counsellors, coming in aid of no ordinary tact, firmness, and resolution, he carried the empire through the immense perils of the crisis,—brought the revolutionary struggle to a close,—appeased Hungary, in appearance if not in reality,—harmonized the various races subject to his rule,—preserved the neutrality of his empire in the Crimean war, though sorely pressed and greatly tempted by France and England to take an active part,—and maintained, when strained almost to rupture, relations of friendship with the great rival German power, the King of Prussia. With eleven years prosperous experience of power, the youthful Sovereign is said to retain an impatient recollection of the humiliations of his family and Empire in the war of the French Revolution, and to burn to wipe out the names of Austerlitz and Wagram from the history of Europe.

The King of Sardinia is by ten years the senior of the

Emperor of Austria, and acceded to the throne on the abdication of his father in 1849. This prince is also animated by personal ambition, civil and military. He has sought to place himself at the head of the liberal party of Italy. Parliamentary institutions and popular reforms have been introduced into his dominions. The religious houses have in many cases been suppressed, and lands held for ages in mortmain appropriated to the service of the State. The government is carried on by a responsible ministry, the trial by jury is adopted, and the liberty of the press established. In short, the political organization of England has been imitated, and as much of the spirit of constitutional government borrowed with it, as is at all compatible with the fiery temperament of the Latin races. Besides concurring in these attempts to liberalize the government of his own dominions, Victor Emmanuel II. has assumed the stand of champion of Italian nationality and independence. He is supposed to aim at the fusion of all the States of Italy into one system, of which Sardinia is to be the head. The English premier, in his speech of April 18th, ascribes much of the anxiety and distrust which exist on the part of Austria, and which have compelled her to clothe herself in the panoply of War, to the disposition shown by the King of Sardinia to encourage disaffection to their governments in the other Italian States, and especially in the Austrian provinces, (the Lombardo-Venetian kingdom,) and to his somewhat rhetorical exclamation at the opening of the Piedmontese Chambers, that there was "a cry of anguish" from the other parts of Italy, to which he could not remain indifferent. Nor is the military spirit of this prince less apparent. Without the slightest possible interest in the Crimean war, he allowed a considerable part of his forces to be subsidized by England for that contest. The Sardinian government, it may be proper to state, has shown at all times a friendly disposition toward the United States, and affords us, in the commodious harbor of Spezia, an admirable rendezvous for our vessels of war in the Mediterranean.

The third and the most important party to the impending war is the Emperor of the French. His power also may be said, like that of the Emperor of Austria and the King of Sardinia, to date from the memorable years of 1848–'49; for though his accession to the empire took place in December 1852, the way was prepared for it by his election as President of the French republic; in fact, by the subversion of the throne of Louis Philippe. It is generally thought and said in Europe, that the question of peace or war rests *exclusively*,—and at present inscrutably,—within his bosom. This, however, is probably an error. It may be true that the precise time, at which the causes shall take effect that are now working together toward an outbreak in the South of Europe, may depend very much upon the will of the Emperor of the French. But that it is in his power wholly to neutralize their action, and substitute a good understanding between Austria and Sardinia for the present hostile disposition of those powers to each other,—and diffuse content and acquiescence in the present state of things, throughout the Italian peninsula, is, as it seems to me, an extravagant and wholly unfounded supposition. Without at all undervaluing the importance of the participation of Napoleon III. in the approaching contest, it would, as I think, be a great mistake of its causes and character to suppose that it is, so to say, *got up* by him, though this appears to be the opinion of very many persons at home and abroad.

Such are the Leaders on both sides of the great impending struggle, and the forces at their command. But there are many subsidiary circumstances, which will modify the complexion of the contest and seriously affect its character. Assuming for the present, that the other three great European powers, Russia, Prussia, and England, will preserve their neutrality in the struggle, (which will, however, in each case

10

most assuredly be what England through her Premier has announced for herself, viz., " an *armed* neutrality,") there are still very formidable auxiliary forces, which must inevitably be drawn into the struggle. On the side of Austria, there is the German Confederation, of which she is the head. Many of its members will from inclination march under her banners; all owe her a qualified allegiance. The war contingent of the Federal body has already been called out by the diet at Frankfort. In a cause to which Germans as a people were hostile or indifferent, this would be a matter of little account, but the public mind in Germany is vehemently excited on the side of Austria. The course pursued by Louis Napoleon has been assailed with great bitterness by the leading German Journals. The memory of the mortifications to which Germany was subjected during the reign of Napoleon I. has been studiously rekindled. And whatever may be the justice with which the benefits accruing from his subversion of the crazy machinery of the old German empire, are urged, (and they are plausibly urged in the *Idées Napoleoniennes,*) great political changes forced by a foreign potentate on a proud people, at the point of the bayonet, can never be the foundation of an efficient popularity. In a war of opinion between Austria and France, not touching the political rights or material interest of Germany, she would march as one man, under the banner of her old imperial leader.

The condition of Hungary is, however, not to be forgotten. A few years only have elapsed since Austria was obliged to rely upon Russian bayonets to quell the disaffection of that portion of her empire;—the abode of fourteen millions of inhabitants, bound together by a language of their own, by community of oppressions resented for ages, and the late convulsive struggle for independence. How far the recent hatreds of that struggle have been softened by the lapse of ten years and the conciliatory government of the present Emperor, is uncertain; but it seems hardly in human nature that any material change in the public mind should have taken place. None such is indicated in the expressions of opinion occasionally put forth by Kossuth. If Hungary should find the opportunity for a new revolt, in the withdrawal of the main body of the Austrian army, to a war in Italy, it would strike a fatal blow at the Imperial power; especially in the present friendly relations of Russia and France, which would prevent the former, as in 1848, from coming to the rescue.

On the Italian side of the great controversy, facts of nearly equal significance will materially affect the strength of the hostile parties. Sardinia herself is but a second-rate power, but she represents both a physical and a moral force of the most formidable character. She represents the traditionary hatred toward the "barbarian;" the passionate longings of Italy for political independence; the fervid dream of a patriotic nationality, which has glowed unsatisfied in the Italian imagination for three or four hundred years. Clothed in no constitutional forms,—hopeless of any such forms, in the judgment of the cool observer,—this feeling operates with so much the greater intensity. The moment an attempt is made to turn it into a reality, the gravest practical obstacles present themselves; but while it is confined to the aspirations of the ardent and generous children of the one Italian soil, and comprehends within the range of its heart-sick and long-deferred possibilities, all who—on whichever side of the Apennines, and whether they breathe the refreshing gales of the Adriatic or the Tuscan sea—cherish the gorgeous vision of a regenerated and united Italy, it mingles in the contest with the force of twelve legions.

Unhappily however for Italy, the bright vision vanishes like a perturbed spirit, at the breaking of the chilly dawn of real life. The Sardinian hates the barbarian from beyond the Alps, but he hates his Lombardo-Venetian brother on the other side of the Po, not less intensely. The Genoese has not yet forgotten that he was robbed of his sea-born independence, and made subject to the crown of Turin, by that Congress of Vienna which sat to redress the wrongs of revolutionary France. Tuscans, and Neapolitans, and Sicilians, and subjects of the Ecclesiastical state, have for ages regarded each other with aversion and scorn; and it is probable, at this moment, if the practical sense of the People of the various Italian States could be fairly polled, not one of them would exchange its present allegiance to become subject to Sardinia.*

But I must not forget that before this paper sees the light, a blow may have been struck which may render all anticipations baseless and nugatory.

* I leave this sentence as it was written ten months ago. To what extent the unbiassed feeling of the People of the Grand Duchies favors annexation to Peidmont does not yet clearly appear; but events have shown that the traditionary feuds alluded to in the text are less operative, at the present day, than they appeared to be twenty years ago. The establishment of liberal institutions in Sardinia and the Austro-Sardinian war in 1849, were events well calculated to win for Sardinia the sympathies of patriotic citizens in every part of Italy.

NUMBER TWENTY-FOUR.

ANOTHER VOLUME OF WASHINGTON'S DIARY.

Another portion of Washington's Diary in the possession of J. K. Marshall, Esq.—Description of the manuscript and its contents—Circumspection of Washington in receiving foreigners—General appropriation bill for 1790—Tour on Long Island—Presents to foreign ministers on taking leave—Chasms in the Diary—The President starts on a Southern tour—In great danger in crossing from the Eastern shore of Maryland to Annapolis—Reception there—Continues his journey to Georgetown—Conference with the proprietors of the lands on which the city of Washington was to be erected—They agree to a cession of lands for public purposes—District of Columbia; Alexandria retroceded to Virginia—Description of the city of Washington.

It may be recollected that, in the first number of these papers, I mentioned, as one of their objects, to give publicity to such remaining memorials of Washington as might be brought to my knowledge in visiting different parts of the country, for the purpose of repeating my discourse on his character. With this object in view, three papers of the series have been devoted to an account of his journey in the Eastern States in 1789, as related in his own Diary, lately printed for private circulation. On occasion of a late visit to Richmond, Virginia, I learned from my friend Mr. Jno. R. Thompson, the Editor of the Southern Literary Messenger, that another portion of the Diary was in the possession of Mr. J. K. Marshall, of Fauquier County in Virginia, a son of the late Chief Justice. At my request Mr. Thompson made application to Mr. Marshall for the loan of this interesting relic, and for permission to make use of it. This permission was kindly and promptly granted, and the precious manuscript safely forwarded to me by Adams' Express, to which I am almost daily under obligations for the most important services. As this portion of the Diary has never been printed, and as it contains matter of the highest interest, I am persuaded that my readers will thank me for offering them an account of this important memorial of Washington from his own pen.

This portion of the Diary, like that described in the ninth number of these papers, is contained in a small manuscript volume, originally bound in marble paper covers. It is seven inches long, by four and a half wide, and contains, like its predecessor, sixty-six leaves. It commences where that terminates, viz., with the 12th of March, 1790, while the seat of the government of the United States was still in New York. About half of the manuscript is occupied by the daily occurrences of the Spring and Summer of 1790,—brief memoranda of the despatches received and forwarded, of conferences of the members of the Cabinet and the Vice-President, who appears to have been consulted by the President in common with the Secretaries, the titles of Acts of Congress submitted for his signature, the names of persons entertained by him at dinner, and the manner in which he took his daily exercise. There is scarce a line which does not throw light on his marvellous prudence and practical wisdom, and much curious information is contained on matters of detail in the administration of the government and the State of public affairs, for which, however, we have no room on the present occasion.

The following extract will show the circumspection of President Washington in receiving strangers :—

"Information being given by Mr. Van Berkel [the Dutch Minister] that Mr. Cazenove just arrived from Holland and of a principal mercantile House there had letters for me which he wished to deliver with his own hands and requesting to know when he might be presented for that purpose, it was thought before this should be done, it might be proper to know whether they were of a public nature, and whether he was acting in a public character. If so, then to let them come to me through the Secretary of State—if not then for him to send them, that the purport might be known before he was introduced, which might be at the next Levee where he might be received and treated agreeably to the consequence he might appear to derive from the testimonial of the letters. It being conceived that etiquette of this sort is essential with all foreigners to give respect to the chief magistrate and the dignity of the government, which would be lessened if every person who could procure a letter of introduction should be presented otherwise than at Levee hours in a formal manner."

In mentioning the signature of the bill for the support of the government for 1790, the President gives the items of appropriation contained in it. Let them be quoted for the amazement of this generation!

"By this last [bill] was Grant[d]

dollr cents	
141.492—73	for the civil list.
155.537—72	War department
96.979—72	Invalid Pensions
10.000—	President—for contingent services of government.
147.169—54	for demands enumerated by the Secretary of ye Treasy in wch the light H° on Cape Henry is includ[d]
120—	To Jehoiakim McToksin
96—	" James Mathers
96—	" Giffard Dally.
551.491—71	Total amount."

Such was an appropriation bill for the support of government two generations ago! By way of comparison, I subjoin the official statement of the aggregate of the appropriations made at the last session of Congress, reminding the reader at the same time, that the bill appropriating several millions for the Postal service failed to pass.

Legislative, executive, judicial, civil, and miscellaneous	10.939.365 50
Diplomatic and consular - - - - - - - - - - -	1.047.745 00
Indian Department, revolutionary, invalid, and other pensions - - - - - - - - - - - - - - - - -	3.270.535 14
Army fortifications and Military Academy - - - -	15.248.657 28
Naval service - - - - - - - - - - - - - - -	10.527.163 55
Ocean Steam mail service - - - - - - - - - -	341.229 16
	$41,374.695 63

On Tuesday the 20th of April the President started on a little tour through the Western end of Long Island, going down the South side of the Island and crossing over to the Sound, proceeding as far East as Huntington. This little circuit occupied five days. The observations of the President are characteristically minute and accurate, but we have no space to quote them.

The following extract relates to a practice, long since disused, of making a farewell present to foreign Ministers on their leaving the country. Such presents are still interchanged in the diplomatic service of Europe; but as the Constitution of the United States forbids the American Ministers to receive similar presents, they have long since ceased to be offered to foreign Ministers leaving this country.

"Fixed with the Secretary of State [Mr. Jefferson] on the present which (according to the custom of other nations) should be made to Diplomatic characters when they return from that employment in this Country—and this was a gold medal, suspended to a gold Chain—in ordinary to be of the value of about 120 or 130 Guineas—Upon enquiry into the practice of other countries, it was found that France generally gave a gold snuff-box set with diamonds; and of diff^{t}. costs; to the amount *generally* to a Minister Plenipotentiary of 500 Louisdores—That England usually gave to the same grade 300 guineas in *specie*—and Holl^{d}. a Medal and Chain of the value of, in common, 150 or 180 Guineas the value of which to be encreas'd by an additional weight in the Chain when they wished to mark a distinguished character.—The reason why a Medal and a Chain was fixed upon for the American present, is that the die being once made the medals could at any time be struck at very little cost & the chain made by our artizans, which (while the first should be retained as a memento) might be converted into Cash."

Very important memoranda are made, in this portion of the Diary, on the subject of consulting the Senate on questions of foreign policy, on the famous Yazoo land sales, on the dispositions of the British government relative to the surrender of the Western posts, and other topics of importance in the politics of that day. They are necessarily, though with reluctance, omitted.

From Sunday, 9th of May, to June the 24th, there is a chasm in the Journal, which is accounted for as follows:

"A severe illness with which I was seized the 10th of this month and which left me in a convalescent state for several weeks after the violence of it had passed, and little inclination to do more than what duty to the public required at my hands occasioned a suspension of this Diary."

The Diary is resumed on the 24th of June, and under the 29th we find the following entry, which I quote in illustration of the statement already cited, in reference to the presents to foreign Ministers.

"On a consultation with the Secretary of State to-day, it was thought advisable to direct him to provide two medals, one for the Marq. de la Luzerne, formerly Minister Plenipo from France to the United States of America, and the other for Mr. Van Berkel, late Minister from Holland; and to have the Dies with which they were to be struck in France, sent over here.—The cost of these Medals would be about 30 guineas;—but the chain for that designed for the Marq. de la Luzerne (on acct. of his attachment and services to this country) was directed to cost about 200 guineas—the other about 100 Guins."

No entry is made in the Diary between the 14th of July, 1790, and the 21st of March, 1791. The session of Congress was prolonged to the 12th of August, 1790, and it is probable that even the systematic diligence and resolute punctuality of the President broke down under the incessant labors of the office, and compelled him wholly to omit these daily *memoranda.* The new Congress met at Philadelphia, and the next entry in the Diary is under date of 21st March, 1791, and to the following effect:—

"Left Philadelphia about 11 o'clock to make a tour through the Southern States. * * *
In this tour I was accompanied by Maj[r]. Jackson—My equipage & attendance consisted of a chariot & four horses drove in hand—a light baggage-wagon and two horses—four saddle horses besides a led one for myself and five servants to wit my valet de chambre, two footmen, Coachman & Postilion."

Proceeding through Delaware and down the Eastern shore of Maryland, the President crossed the bay from Rock-Hall to Annapolis, and on this passage appears to have been in great danger. His own narrative cannot fail to command the reader's attention.

Thursday 24th. [of March] Left Chestertown about 6 o'clock—before nine I arrived at Rock Hall where we breakfasted and immediately after which we began to embark—the doing of which employed us (for want of contrivance) until near 3 o'clock—and then one of my servants (Paris) & two horses were left, notwithstanding two boats in aid of the two ferry Boats were procured. Unluckily embarking on board a borrowed boat because she was the largest, I was in imminent danger from the unskilfulness of the hands and the dullness of her sailing, added to the darkness and storminess of the night—for two hours after we hoisted sail, the wind was light and ahead—the next hour was a stark calm—after which the wind sprung up at S[o]. E[t]. and increased until it blew a gale—about which time and after 8 o'clock P. M. we made the mouth of the Severn River (leading up to Annapolis), but the ignorance of the people on board with respect to the navigation run us aground first on Greenbury (?) point from whence with much exertion & difficulty we got off; & then having no knowledge of the channel, and the night being immensely dark with heavy and variable squals of wind—constant lightning and tremendous thunder—we soon grounded again on what is called Hornes (?) point where finding all efforts in vain, & not knowing where we were, we remained, not knowing what might happen, till morning.

Friday 25. Having lain all night in my Great Coat & Boots, in a berth not long enough for me by the head, & much cramped; we found ourselves in the morning within about one mile of Annapolis & still fast aground—Whilst we were preparing our small Boat in order to land in it, a sailing Boat came off to our assistance in wch with the Baggage I had on Board I landed, and requested Mr. Man at whose Inn I intended lodging to send off a Boat to take off two of my horses & chariot which I had left on board and with it my Coachman to see that it was properly done—but by some mistake the latter not having notice of this order and attempting to get on board afterwards in a smaller sailing Boat was overset and narrowly escaped drowning.

Was informed upon my arrival (when 15 guns were fired) that all my other horses arrived safe that embarked at the same time I did, about 8 o'clock last night.

Was waited upon by the Governor (who came off in a boat as soon as he heard I was on my passage from Rock-Hall to meet us, but turned back when it grew dark & squally) as soon as I arrived at Man's tavern, and was engaged by him to dine with the Citizens of Annapolis this day at Man's tavern, and at his house tomorrow—the first I accordingly did.

Before dinner I walked with him, and several other gentlemen to the State house (which seemed to be much out of repair)—the College of St. John at which there are about 80 students of every description—and then by the way of the Governor's (to see Mrs. Howell) home.

It thus appears that the President of the United States, travelling with every facility which the state of the communications at that time afforded, was five days in accomplishing the journey from Philadelphia to Annapolis, now easily made in six hours.

The city of Washington was not yet laid out, and the President pursued his journey from Annapolis to Georgetown, in order to bring the proprietors of land at this last-named city and Carrollsburg (which I suppose to be the region extending east and west from Capitol Hill) to terms of agreement as to the cession of land for the public buildings. Contrary to his usual practice, he went from Annapolis to Bladensburg on Sunday, and dined and lodged there. The following day he was met by a large party of citizens from Georgetown, headed by Mr. Thomas Corcoran, (Father of Mr. William W.

Corcoran of Washington city,) by whom he was addressed, and was by them escorted to Georgetown, where he arrived at an early hour.

His first care on arrival was to examine the surveys of Mr. Ellicott, who had been appointed "to survey the district of ten miles square for the federal seat, and also the works of Majr. L'Enfant, who had been engaged to examine and make a draught of the grounds in the vicinity of Georgetown and Carrollsburg on the Eastern Branch." The President made arrangements to examine them himself the following day, and attended a public dinner given by the Corporation at Suter's tavern, where he lodged. At seven o'clock in the morning of the 29th, "in a thick mist and under a strong appearance of a settled rain (which however did not happen)" he set out to institute this examination, but from the unfavorableness of the day he "derived no great satisfaction from the Review."

Finding the landholders of Georgetown and Carrollsburg "at variance with each other, and that their fears and jealousies were counteracting the public purposes and might prove injurious to its best interests," the President invited a conference of those concerned, and succeeded in bringing them to unite in a satisfactory arrangement. The proprietors alluded to agreed "to surrender for public purposes one-half of the land they severally possessed within bounds which were designed as necessary for the City."

Thus were the District of Columbia, ten miles square, and the City of Washington, laid out. The District originally contained the Cities of Washington and Georgetown on the Maryland side of the Potomac, and the City of Alexandria on the Virginia side. Such an arrangement was not indicated by the geography of the region, though wearing in theory and on paper an agreeable appearance. The citizens of Alexandria, after fifty years' experience of Congressional government, prayed to be restored to the genial tutelage of their parent

State: and all that part of the District lying on the right bank of the Potomac was a few years since retroceded to Virginia.

The situation of Washington is of unsurpassed beauty for an inland town. The sweep of the river, as you look from the balcony of the library on the Western front of the Capitol, the line of the Virginia hills beyond, especially when seen in the early part of the day, the encircling heights which stretch from Georgetown round to the North, destined at no distant period to be crowned with all the beauties of villa architecture, forest, and garden, (this anticipation has begun to be realized,) the noble streets and avenues before and beneath the eye, lined already in many places with stately private dwellings and magnificent public edifices, form altogether a panorama of extreme richness. Some errors no doubt may be pointed out by a fastidious taste in the plan of the city. Desolate spaces, neglected amorphous spots, abortive attempts at premature display,—the necessary incidents of a town called into being, in the first instance, by the exigencies of the public service, and sustained by a government patronage alternately profuse and parsimonious,—offend the eye on a close survey of the national Capital. But for natural advantages, beauty of position, the rapid progress already made in the comforts and refinements of social life, and in its capacity for almost indefinite improvement, under the fostering care of a paternal government, Washington fully justifies the interest taken by its illustrious Founder in its selection as the seat of republican empire.

NUMBER TWENTY-FIVE.

WASHINGTON'S SOUTHERN TOUR.

Washington's Southern tour in 1791 less known than his Eastern tour in 1789—Departure from Mount Vernon 7th of April—Accident in crossing the ferry at Colchester—Fredericksburgh—Richmond—Locks in the James River Canal—State of public opinion in Virginia on the assumption of the State debts and the Excise law—Petersburgh and the President's account of it—Innocent artifice to escape an escort—Halifax, N. Carolina—No stabling at Allen's—Arrival at Newbern and description of that place—Its present condition and appearance—Arrival at Wilmington and account of that place—The mode of taking the first census described by Washington—Present condition of Wilmington—Recent visit of the writer to North Carolina—Its general prosperity—Raleigh—Chapel Hill.

Of Washington's Southern Tour little in detail has been published. Of his tour in the Eastern States, two years before, some of the incidents, and particularly his relations with John Hancock at Boston, attracted general notice at the time, and have been narrated at some length in different publications. They furnish the matter of several pages in General Sullivan's "Familiar Letters" in Mr. Sparks' edition of "the Writings of Washington," and in the volume of Mr. Irving's Life of Washington just issued from the press. In addition to this, that portion of the Diary of Washington which contains the account of his Western tour, had within the past twelvemonth, as the readers of these papers have seen, been printed for private circulation.

Of the Southern tour, equally interesting in itself, much less has been said. It has been dismissed with a single paragraph in the Standard lives, and the portion of the Diary which contains the record of it, and which, as stated in my last number, is now in the possession of Mr. James K. Marshall of Fauquier County, Virginia, (a son of the venerable Chief Justice,) has never been committed to the press. I have for these reasons felt confident, that I should gratify the reader by copious extracts from this portion of the Diary, containing as they do the impressions of its illustrious author recorded at the time, as to the principal cities in the Southern States of the Union, and the various occurrences of his tour.

Having completed the business which engaged his attention at Georgetown, as related in my last number, the President, on the 30th of March, 1791, left that city, dined at Alexandria, and reached Mount Vernon in the evening. Here he remained one week, "visiting his Plantations every day," and on the 7th of April recommenced his "journey, with horses apparently well refreshed, and in good spirits." On crossing the ferry at Colchester, with the four horses hitched to the chariot, by the neglect of the person who stood before them, one of the leaders got overboard, when the boat was in swimming water and fifty yards from the shore. With much difficulty he escaped from drowning before he could be disengaged. His struggles frightened the other horses in such a manner, that one after another in quick succession they all got overboard, harnessed and fastened as they were. With the utmost difficulty they were saved, and the carriage escaped being dragged after them. "The whole of it," says the Diary, "happened in swimming water and at a distance from the shore. Providentially,—indeed miraculously, by the exertions of People who went off in boats and jumped in the river as soon as the Batteau was forced into wading water—no damage was sustained by the horses, carriage, or harness." The President this day dined at Dumfries —"after which," says the Diary, "I visited & drank tea with my niece Mrs. Tho's Lee."

Starting at 6 o'clock the following day, the President breakfasted at Stafford Court House, "and dined and lodged," says the entry, "at my sister Lewis's in Fredericksburg." Saturday the 9th was appropriated to "a public entertainment given by the Citizens of the town." On the following day, Sunday the 10th, he breakfasted with General Spotswood, dined at the Bowling Green, and lodged at Kenner's tavern; in all a journey of thirty-five miles. He reached Richmond to dinner on the 11th at 3 o'clock, having "breakfasted at one Rawlings's" by the way. On his arrival he "was saluted by the Cannon of the place—waited on by the governor & other gentlemen—& saw the city illuminated by night."

The President remained in Richmond from Sunday, the day of his arrival, till Thursday. His first care was to inspect the locks on the James River Canal, a work in which he ever took the deepest interest. He records with evident satisfaction the impressions made upon his mind, chiefly by Col. Carrington, the marshal of the district, with reference to the popularity of the general government. He "could not discover that any discontents prevail among the people at the proceedings of Congress. The conduct of the assembly respecting the assumption" [of the state debts] "he (Col. Carrington) thinks, is condemned by the people as intemperate & unwise, and he seems to have no doubt but the Excise law —as it is called—may be executed without difficulty, nay more that it will become popular in a little time." Col. Carrington evidently painted things *couleur rose.* On Wednesday the President attended a public entertainment given by the Corporation of Richmond. "The buildings in this place," he remarks, "have encreased a good deal since I was here last but they are not of the best kind. The number of Souls in the City are ——." A blank is here left as in other similar cases for more accurate information. The industry of Richmond in all its branches was then in its infancy, and those topics which usually occupy so much of the President's attention are not mentioned.

The next day, Thursday the 14th, he went to Petersburg. Passing through Manchester he "received a salute from Cannon & an escort of horse, under the command of Capt. David Meade Randolph, as far as Osborne's, where" he "was met by the Petersburgh Horse & escorted to that place & partook of a public dinner given by the Mayor and Corporation & went to an assembly in the evening * * at which there were between sixty & seventy ladies." The President's account of Petersburg is in the following terms:

"Petersburgh which is said to contain near 3000 souls is well situated for trade at present, but when the James River navigation is compleated & the cut from Elizabeth river to Pasquotanck is effected, it must decline & that very considerably. At present it receives at the Inspections nearly a third of the Tobacco exported from the whole State besides a considerable quantity of Wheat & Flour—much of the former being manufactured at the mills near The town—Chief of the buildings in this town are under the hill & unpleasantly situated but the heights around it are agreeable.

"The Road from Richmond to this place passes through a poor Country principally covered with Pine, except the interval lands on the River which we left on our Left."

The President's anticipations of the falling off of Petersburg from a population of 3,000 have not been fulfilled. By the census of 1850, it was 14,010, a trifle smaller than that of Norfolk. It cannot at this time be much if any below twenty thousand.

On Friday the 15th the President started from Petersburg, practicing a little artifice as to the time of his departure, of which I recollect no other instance in his whole career, and which, involving no departure from the strictest truth, and resorted to for the best of reasons, will not be blamed. It is described in the following words:—

"Friday 15th. Having suffered very much by the dust yesterday—and finding that parties of Horse and a number of other gentlemen were intending to attend me part of the way to-day, I caused their enquiries respecting the time of my setting out, to be answered that I should endeavor to do it before 8 o'clock, but did it a little after five, by which means I avoided the inconvenience above mentioned."

This day the President breakfasted after travelling twelve miles at "one Jesse Lee's, a tavern newly set up on a small scale," and proceeding fifteen miles further dined and lodged "at the House of one Oliver, which is a good one for horses & where there are tolerable clean beds. For want of proper stages" he "could go no further."

The President started the next day at about 5 o'clock, and travelling most of the time under a heavy rain, was compelled, for want of stopping places, to proceed as far as Halifax in North Carolina, a distance of forty-eight miles, arriving at six o'clock in the evening. He passed the following day, Sunday the 17th, at Halifax, which he describes as "a place said to contain a thousand souls & apparently in a decline." At the invitation of Colonel Ashe, (the representative of the district in which Halifax was situated,) and several other gentlemen, General Washington attended a public dinner at that place.

On Monday the 19th the President started at six o'clock, "dined at a small house kept by one Slaughter twenty two miles from Halifax, & lodged at Tarborough fourteen miles further. We were received at this place" the President benignantly remarks, "by as good a salute as could be given with one piece of artillery." On the following day (19th April) they "dined at a trifling place called Greenville 25 miles distant & lodged at one Allans 14 miles further, a very indifferent house, without stabling [for the horses], which for the first time since I commenced my Journey were obliged to stand without a cover."

The President left Allan's on the 20th before breakfast, and "under a misapprehension went to a Col? Allan's, supposing it to be a public house, where we were very kindly & well entertained without knowing it was at his expense until it was too late to rectify the mistake." They crossed the Neuse at a ferry ten miles from Newbern, were they arrived to dinner and were exceedingly well lodged.

"This town," says the President, "is situated at the confluence of the Nuse and Trent, and though low is pleasant. Vessels drawing more than nine feet of water cannot get up loaded. It stands on a good deal of ground, but the buildings are sparse & altogether of wood; some of which are large & look well. The number of souls are about 2000. Its exports consist of Corn, Tobacco & Pork,—but principally of naval stores & lumber.

Thursday 21st. Dined with the citizens at a public dinner given by them & went to a dancing assembly in the Evening,—both of which was at what they call the pallace—formerly the government house & a good brick building but now hastening to ruins. The company at both was numerous—at the latter there were about 70 ladies."

Newbern still, as in General Washington's time, "though low is pleasant." Its population by the Census of 1850 was 4,681, and is now considerably increased. It has a railroad connection with Beaufort and Goldsboro', and with the main lines which traverse the State. Its once splendid Palace, erected by the ostentatious Tryon, and ruinous in President Washington's days, has vanished from the face of the earth; —an open street passes over the site; but the substantial brick stables remain. The grass-grown streets, shaded by elms and lined with gardens, give to Newbern an air of repose, which reminds you of some of the small German residences. The situation at the confluence of the Trent and the Neuse is magnificent. The traditional culture of a provincial metropolis is visible at Newbern; and the honored memory of Judge Gaston is freshly cherished. But I have experienced its hospitable welcome too recently to speak of it with impartiality. I had the pleasure on the 12th of April of repeating my discourse on the character of the great man whose visit I am now recording, to a crowded audience, and with a net receipt, for the benefit of the Mount Vernon Fund, of $593.

The President left Newbern on the 22d April, " under an escort of horse & many of the principal gentlemen," dined at a place called Trenton, at the head of the boat navigation of the Trent, crossed that river on a bridge, and " lodged at one Shrine's 10 miles further—both indifferent houses." On the 23d, " breakfasted at one Everet's 32 miles, bated at a Mr. Foy's 12 miles further & lodged at one Sages 20 miles beyond it,—all indifferent houses."

On Sunday the 24th the President " breakfasted at an indifferent house about 13 miles from Sage's & three miles further met a party of Light Horse from Wilmington, & after them, a committee and other gentlemen of the town, at which he arrived, under a federal salute, at very good lodgings about two o'clock. Here says he, " I dined with the committee whose company I asked." The country betwen Newbern and Wilmington is described by the President as being, with the exception of a few places, the most barren he ever beheld, especially in the parts nearest Wil mington, where it is " no other than a bed of white sand." In some places however, " if ideas of poverty could be separated from the land, the appearances of it are agreeable, resembling a lawn well covered with evergreens and a good verdure below, from a broom of coarse grass, which having sprung up since the burning of the woods had a neat and handsome look, especially as there were parts entirely open & others with ponds of water, which contributed not a little to the beauty of the scene."

" Wilmington," says the President, " is situated on Cape Fear River, about 30 miles by water from its mouth, but much less by land. It has some good houses pretty compactly built.—The whole under a hill which is formed entirely of sand. The number of souls in it amount by enumeration to about 1000, but it is agreed on all hands that the Census in this State has been very inaccurately & shamefully taken by the Marshall's deputies; who instead of going to Peoples houses, and there on the spot, ascertaining the nos. have advertised a meeting of them at certain places, by which means those who did not attend (and it seems many purposely avoided doing it, some from an apprehension of its being introductory to a tax & others from religious scruples) have gone with their families unnumbered. In other instances it is said that these deputies have taken their information from the Captains of Militia companies; not only as to the men on their muster rolls, but of the souls in their respective families, which at best must, in a variety of cases be mere conjecture, whilst all those who are not on their lists, widows & their families &c pass unnoticed.

Wilmington unfortunately for it has a mud bank miles below over which not more than ten feet of Water can be brought at common tides; yet it is said vessels of 250 tons have come up. The qty of shipping which load here annually amounts to about 12,000 tons. The exports consist chiefly of Naval stores and lumber. Some Tobacco, corn, Rice & Flax Seed with Porke. It is the head of the tide navigation, but inland navigation may be extended 115 miles farther to and above Fayette's ville which is from Wilmington 90 miles by land and 115 by water as above." * * *

Monday 25th, Dined with the citizens of the place, at a public dinner given by them—went to a Ball in the evening at which there were 62 ladies,—illuminations, bonfires &c.—

The population of Wilmington by the census of 1850 was 7,264. In the period which has since elapsed, and under the stimulus of the railroads which connect it with the conterminous States North and South, it has greatly increased, and amounts no doubt at the present time to ten or twelve thousand. Its natural features have of course not changed since President Washington's time; the "mud bank" still obstructs the navigation, and has as yet been attacked with but partial success, under liberal appropriations of the federal government. Wilmington is however the seat of an active trade in the staples of the country. Its population, as far as I was able to judge from a short visit, intelligent, enterprizing, and rather more than usually harmonious among themselves. The river prospects from elevated positions are remarkably fine. An immense audience, assembled in Thalian Hall on the 11th April last, honored the repetition of my address on the character of Wilmington, and the net receipts of the evening, $1091 80-100, were, in proportion to the population, far beyond those of any other place in the Union.

I reserve for another paper the account of the President's tour in South Carolina and Georgia, of which as of his tour in Virginia and North Carolina, scarce any thing has hitherto been published. I may be permitted, by way of filling up this Number, to say that nowhere have my anticipations of an agreeable tour been more completely fulfilled than in the last named State. In the course of a week I visited Wilmington, Newbern, Raleigh, and Chapel-Hill, speaking at each of those places. Communications between the principal places in North Carolina is rendered expeditious by about eight hundred miles of railroad, traversing the Eastern and central portions of the State. It was not in my power to visit the mineral district about Charlotte or the mountain region of the West, which form a very important and attractive portion of the territory. I have already said a few words of Newbern and Wilmington. Raleigh, the political metropolis of the State, and Chapel-Hill, the seat of the University of North Carolina, honored my address with crowded and favoring audiences. The net receipts at the former were $515; at the latter $615 60-100. I found at both places a highly intelligent social circle. Raleigh was adorned at very great expense to the State, with a superb statue of Washington by Canova, at a time when, if I mistake not, with the exception of Houdon's, there was no other statue of Washington in the United States. It was unfortunately destroyed by fire when the Capitol was burned a few years since. A copy of Hubard's cast from Houdon's Washington has lately been placed in the Capitol grounds. Raleigh itself constitutes, in its name, the noblest monument to the illustrious but unfortunate pioneer of North American colonization. It will preserve his gallant deeds and generous traits of character in honored remembrance, ages after the crowned pedant who sent him to the block is recollected only to be despised. The University at Chapel-Hill is second to none of the Southern Seminaries, except the University of Virginia, in the number of its Students, and it stands in well earned high repute as a place of education.

NUMBER TWENTY-SIX.

WASHINGTON'S SOUTHERN TOUR CONCLUDED.

Departure from Wilmington—The Swash crossed—Arrival at Georgetown, S. C.—Capt. Alston's plantation—Description of Georgetown—Arrival at Charleston and reception and festivities there—Description of Charleston—No mention of cotton among the exports—Journey resumed on the 9th of May—Mrs. Gen. Green—Arrival at Savannah—Military operations in 1779—Savannah described—Road through Waynesborough to Augusta—Reception at Augusta—Description of that place—Return to the North by the way of Columbia, Camden, Charlotte, Salisbury, and Salem.

Having sent his horses across the river the day before the President started for Charleston on the 26th of April, 1791, breakfasted at Mr. Ben Smith's, and lodged at one Russ's, " an indifferent house," having made but twenty-five miles. On the following day the party breakfasted at William Gause's, dined at a private house, (' one Cochran's) and lodged at Mr. Vareen's, ' two miles short of the long bay.' " To this house," says the Diary, " we were directed as a tavern, but the proprietor of it either did not keep one, or would not acknowledge it. We therefore were entertained (& very kindly) without being able to make compensation."

The following day they were piloted by Col. Vareen across the Swash, (which at high water is impassable and at times, by the shifting of the sands, is dangerous,) to the long beach of the ocean. The tide being favorable, the party followed the beach to the place for leaving it, an estimated distance of sixteen miles. They dined at Mr. Pauley's, a private house, and " being met on the road & kindly invited by a Dr. Flagg," they lodged there, after a day's journey of thirty-three miles.

The record of the 29th is as follows :—

"We left Dr. Flagg's at about 6 o'clock and arrived at Captain Wm. Alston's on the Waggamaw to breakfast. Captain Alston is a gentleman of large fortune and esteemed one of the neatest Rice planters in the State of S°. Carolina and the proprietor of some of the most valuable grounds for the culture of this article.—His house which is large, new, and elegantly furnished stands on a sand-hill, high for the Country, with his rice fields below; the contrast of which with the lands back of it and the Sand & piney barrens through which we had passed is scarcely to be conceived."

The President was met at Capt. Alston's by General Moultrie, Col. Washington, and Mr. Rutledge, (son of the chief justice of S. Carolina,) who had come out to escort him to Georgetown. The next day they crossed the river, after a descent of three miles "under a salute of cannon & by a company of infantry handsomely uniformed." The President dined with the citizens in public, and "in the afternoon was introduced to upwards of fifty ladies, who had assembled (at a tea party) for the occasion."

"Georgetown," says the Diary, "seems to be in the shade of Charleston— It suffered through the war by the British, hav'g had many of its houses burnt. It is situated on a peninsula between the river Waccamaw and Sumpter *Creek* about 15 miles from the sea—a bar is to be passed, over which not more than 12 feet of water can be bro't except at Spring tides; which (tho' the inhabitants are willing to entertain different ideas) must ever be a considerable let to its importance; especially if the cut between the Santee & Cowper Rivers should ever be accomplished.

"The inhabitants of this place (either unwilling or unable) could give no account of the number of souls in it, but I should not compute them at more than 5 or 600. Its chief export Rice."

The population of Georgetown by the Census of 1850 was 1628.

On Sunday, 1st of May, the party left Georgetown, and crossing the Santee River at a distance of twelve miles, breakfasted and dined at Mrs. Horry's, about fifteen miles from Georgetown, " & lodged at the plantation of Mr. Manigold about twelve miles further."

On the 2d of May, the party breakfasted at the country seat of Gov. Pinckney, about eighteen miles from the place where they had lodged, and then came to the ferry at Haddrel's point, six miles further, where they were met by the Recorder of the city, Gen. Pinckney, and Edward Rutledge, Esq. in a twelve oared barge, rowed by twelve American captains of ships, most elegantly dressed. There were a great number of other boats with gentlemen and ladies in them, and two boats with music:

"All of which," says the Diary of the President, "attended me across; & on the passage were met by a number of others. As we approached the town a salute of artillery commenced, and at the wharf I was met by the Governor, the L^t. Governor, the Intend^t. of the city, the two Senators of the State, Wardens of the city, Cincinnati, &c. &c. and conducted to the Exchange where they passed by in procession—from whence I was conducted in like manner to my lodgings,—after which I dined at the Governor's (in what he called a private way) with 15 or 18 gentlemen" * * *

"The lodgings provided for me in this place were very good—being the furnished house of a Gentleman at present in the Country; but occupied by a person placed there on purpose to accommodate me, and who was paid in the same manner as any other letter of Lodgings would have been paid."

"Tuesday the 3d breakfasted with Mrs. Rutledge (the Lady of the chief justice of the State who was on the Circuits) and dined with the citizens at a public din^r. given by them at the Exchange.

"Was visited at about 2 o'clock, by a great number of the most respectable Ladies of Charleston—the first honor of the kind I ever had experienced & it was as flattering as it was singular."

"Wednesday the 4th. Dined with the members of the Cincinnati, and in the evening went to a very elegant dancing Assembly at the Exchange,—at which were 256 elegantly dressed & handsome ladies."

"In the forenoon (indeed before breakfast to day) I visited and examined the lines of attack & defence of the city & was satisfied that the defence was noble & honorable altho the measure was undertaken upon wrong principles and impolitic."

"Thursday the 5th. Visited the works of Fort Johnson on James' Island & Fort Moultree on Sullivan's Island; both of which are—in Ruins; and scarcely a trace of the latter left—the former quite fallen.

"Dined with a very large company at the Governor's and in the Evening went to a Concert at the Exchange at wch there were at least 400 ladies—the number and appearance of wch exceeded anything of the kind I had ever seen."

On Friday the 6th, the President rode through the principal streets of Charleston, dined at Major Butler's, and went to a ball in the evening, at the Governor's, "where there was a select company of ladies." On Saturday, the 7th, he visited the Orphan House before breakfast, "where there were 107 boys & girls." He also viewed the city from the balcony of ——— church, "from whence the whole is seen in one view to great advantage, the gardens & green trees which are interspersed adding much to the beauty of the scene." On Sunday the President "went to crowded churches in the morning & afternoon," but the names of the churches are left blank. General Washington staid an entire week in Charleston, being a considerably longer time than was given by him to any city North or South. His summary description of it is in the following terms:

"Charleston stands on a Peninsula between the Ashley & Cowper Rivers and contains about 1600 dwelling houses and nearly 16,000 souls [population in 1850 42,985], of which about 8,000 are white— It lies low with unpaved Streets (except the footways) of Sand. There are a number of very good houses of brick & Wood but most of the latter— The Inhabitants are wealthy—gay—hospitable; appear happy and satisfied with the general governm[t]. A cut is much talked of between the Ashley & Santee [Cowper] Rivers, but it would seem I think as if the accomplishment of the measure was not very near— It would be a great thing for Charleston if it could be effected— The principal Exports from this place is Rice, Indigo and Tobacco; of the last from 5 to 8000 Hhd have been exported and of the first from 80 to 120,000 Barrels."

No mention yet of cotton among the staple products of the South. As late as 1794, it was not known to Chief Justice Jay, when he negotiated his treaty with England, that it was likely to be an article of United States Commerce. So recently has this great element of trade and of the wealth of nations made its appearance on this side of the Ocean!

On Monday the 9th of May the President resumed his journey for Savannah, "attended by a corps of the Cincinnati, & most of the principal gentlemen of the city, as far as the bridge over the Ashley River." After breakfast they proceeded, "with a select party of very particular friends,"—to Colonel Wahington's, at Sandy Hill, a distance in the whole of twenty-eight miles. On the following day the friends and attendants, with the exception of Gen. Moultrie and Major Butler, took leave and the party proceeded to breakfast "at Judge Bee's & dined and lodged at Mr Obrian Smith's."—On the 11th the President was entertained at dinner "by the parishioners of Prince William" and lodged at Judge Hayward's.—He enters an apology in his journal, at this place, for visiting Col. Washington, on the score "of friendship & relationship," and for lodging at Mr. Smith's and Judge Hayward's, on the ground of necessity, "there being no public houses on the road."

Starting on the 12th at 5 A. M. they arrived at Purisburg, on the Savannah River, twenty-two miles distant, to breakfast. Here they were met by Messrs. Jones, Col. Habersham, Mr. Jno. Houston, Genl. McIntosh, and Mr. Clay, a committee from the city of Savannah. They descended the River in boats, the President in an eight oared barge, rowed by eight American captains. "In my way down the River," says the Diary, "I called upon Mrs. Green, the widow of the deceased Gen! Green, (at a place called Mulberry Grove,) & asked her how she did." The wind and tide being against them, it was six o'clock before they reached the city, where they "were received under every demonstration that could be given of joy and respect." The President dined in public at a late hour in the evening. On the following day he dined with the Cincinnati, "and in the evening went to a dancing assembly, where there were about 100 well dressed & handsome ladies." On the 14th, in company with the principal gentlemen of the place, he took a survey of the city. He expresses himself in the following circumspect manner of the siege of 1779:

"I visited the city & the attack & defence of it in the year 1779 under the combined forces of France and the United States commanded by the Count de Estaing & General Lincoln.—To form an opinion of the attack at this distance of time and the change which has taken place in the appearance of the ground by the cutting away of the woods &c is hardly to be done with justice to the subject, especially as there is remaining scarcely any of the defences."

There was a public dinner this day, "under an elegant bower" on the bank of the river, and in the evening "a tolerable good display of fire-works."

On Sunday the 15th, after morning service, "& receiving a number of visits from the most respectable ladies of the place, (as was the case yesterday,)" the President started for Augusta, under a general escort of the citizens, dined with Mrs. Green at Mulberry Grove, and lodged at one Spencer's.

"Savanna," says the Diary, "stands upon what may be called high ground for this country—It is extremely sandy which makes the walking very disagreeable; and the houses uncomfortable in warm & windy weather, as they are filled with dust whenever these happen. The town on three sides is surrounded with cultivated rice fields which have a rich and luxuriant appearance. On the south or back side it is a pine land.—The harbour is said to be very good and often filled with square rigged vessels but there is a bar below over which not more than 12 [feet] water can be bro$^{t.}$ except at spring tides.—The tide does not flow above 12 or 14 miles above the city though the River is swelled by it more than double that distance.—Rice & Tobacco (the last of which is greatly encreasing) are the principal exports—lumber & Indigo are also exported, but the latter is on the decline and it is supposed by Hemp & Cotton.*—Ship timber vizt. live oak and Cedar is (and may be more more so) valuable in the exp[t]."

On Monday the 16th and Tuesday the 17th the places where the party breakfasted, dined, and lodged, are recorded. Of Waynesborough the Diary states that it "is a small place, but the seat of the Court of Burke's County—6 or 8 dwelling houses is all that it contains. An attempt is making (without much apparent effect) to establish an Academy at it, as is the case also in all the counties."

On the 18th the President was met by "Governor Telfair, Judge Walton, the Attorney General, and most of the principal gentlemen" of Augusta, escorted into town, "& received under a discharge of artillery." He dined "with a large company at the Governor's and drank tea there with many well dressed Ladies." On the 19th there was an Address presented by the citizens of Augusta to which the President replied; a dinner with a large company at the Court House, and an Assembly in the evening at the Academy, "at which there were between 60 and 70 well dressed ladies."

The 20th was devoted to the survey of the remains of "the works which had been erected by the British during the war & taken by the Americans," of "the falls" in the river, and the neighboring country. Tobacco is mentioned as the principal article of growth and export from this region, and as likely so to continue.

"Augusta" says the Diary "though it covers more ground than Savanna does not contain as many inhabitants, the latter having by the late Census between 14 & 1500 whites & about 800 blacks."

The numbers of the population of Augusta are left blank in the Diary. By the Census of 1850 the numbers of the two cities stood, Savannah 15,312 and Augusta 9,569.—

* A word or two appears to be wanting here, but the sense is plain.

From Augusta the President proceeded to Columbia, where he was detained a day longer than he intended, one of his horses being badly foundered by the length of the journey from Augusta, the want of water, and the heat of the weather. He was entertained at dinner at Columbia by the gentlemen and ladies of that place and the vicinity, "to the amount of more than 150 of which 50 or 60 were of the latter."

The following is the President's description of Columbia, then in its infancy:

"Columbia is laid out upon a large scale; but in my opinion it had better been placed on the River below the falls. It is now an unreclaimed wood, with very few houses in it & those all wooden ones. The State house (which is also of wood) is a large and commodious building, but unfinished. The town is on dry, but cannot be called high ground, and though surrounded by Piney & sandy Land is itself good. The State house is near two miles from the River, at the confluence of the Broad River & Saluda.—From Granby the River is navigable for craft, which will, when the river is a little swelled carry 3000 bushels of Grain—when at its height less and always some. The River from hence to the Wateree below which it takes the name of Santee is very crooked it being according to the computed distance near 400 miles—Columbia from Charleston is 130 miles."

Want of space compels the omission of the President's description of his journey to Camden, and onward to Charlotte, and his account of those places. His remarks on the encounter of Green and Lord Rawdon and of Gates and Lord Cornwallis are extremely interesting; but no room remains for further extracts. He passed through the towns of Salisbury and Salem, where he examined the Moravian Settlements, and here this volume of the Diary concludes.

No apology seems necessary for occupying so much space with these memoranda. They relate to a portion of General Washington's personal history never before described in detail; they present in his own language the impressions made upon him, by the principal places which he visited; and they afford most interesting materials for comparing the state of the country in 1791 with its condition at the present day.

NUMBER TWENTY-SEVEN.

ADAMS' EXPRESS AND THE EXPRESS SYSTEM OF THE UNITED STATES.

Scene at Embarcation at New York for Charleston—Quantity of packages put on board by Adams' Express—The Expressage not to be confounded with commercial transportation—Miscellaneous nature of articles transported by Express—Connection of the Express with the periodical press—Want of all facilities for the conveyance of small parcels in former times—Sketch of the Origin and progress of the Express System—Wm. F. Harnden—Alvin Adams—His associates—And successors—Present state of Adams' Express and extent of its operations—Importance of the Express system compared with commercial exchanges—Comparison of the Express with the Post-office—Origin and functions of the Post-office—Growing importance of the Express.

Having occasion, a little more than a year ago, to visit South Carolina and Georgia, for the purpose of repeating my address on the character of Washington, I embarked at New York on board the fine steamer "Columbia," for which I was favored with a free passage by the liberal proprietors of the line, Messrs. Spofford, Tileston & Co. Going on board about half an hour before the sailing of the vessel, my attention was drawn to the animated scene on the quay, scarcely less varied and striking than that which is witnessed on the departure of a first-class passenger ship for Europe. Carriages filled with passengers of either sex and of every age and their friends; porters staggering under the weight of heavy trunks; a discouraged maid with a lap-dog under her arm looking as if she wished the troublesome pet would jump into the water; the usual throng of newsboys, venders of oranges, Stewart's mixed candy, and popped corn, with lookers-on of every description and in every body's way, all crowding and jostling each other in the narrow space; the fierce roar of the steam as if impatient for departure; the busy windlass hoisting in merchandise in packages of every shape, which clear their way before them, as they bound over the sides of the vessel, and then plunge into the hold; the spasmodic energy of the crew crowding a good morning's work into half an hour; the sharp voice of the first mate directing the movement; the occasional yelp of an unwary cur caught at disadvantage among the warring elements; the confused plunging of an obstinate dray-horse, who, to the dismay of his driver and the gathering multitude, persists in backing into the dock; the majestic port of the solemn policeman as he penetrates the crowd; the cordial hand-shaking of friends parting soon to meet again; the tearful farewells of anxious relatives bidding good-bye to their pale invalids, bound to the tropics, foreboding too truly that they shall see them no more on earth;—all this made up a scene, and occasionally as I have witnessed it, ever makes up a scene,—which furnishes much food for thought as a tolerable epitome of the tragi-comedy of life.

I was particularly struck, on this occasion, with the successive arrivals and unloading of the wagons of Adams' Express. I think there were at least four of them, which came down to the quay, drawn by sleek, powerful, and docile horses, and delivered their contents on board the ship, in the course of the half hour; in packages of every size and shape, from large tierces, barrels, and bales, to boxes of moderate dimensions, and of every imaginable shape and character. In addition to packages, large enough to go separately and safely, there were two or three coffers of great size and strength, braced with iron, and double locked, containing—as I was told—parcels whose contents were highly valuable; specie, packages of bank notes and bonds, jewelry, and articles of every kind, too small or too valuable to be separately transported. The addresses on the separate packages and parcels showed the vast range of territory embraced in this system of communication, and formed a little gazetteer of the South Atlantic and Gulf States.

Astonished at the amount of articles thus moving southward, I inquired if it was unusually large that day, and I was answered in the negative; about the same quantity was despatched twice every week from New York to Charleston. This, it will be remembered, is independent of what may be forwarded from New York by the steamers to Norfolk, Richmond, and City Point, to Savannah and New Orleans, and all that goes by land to the Atlantic States of the South, by the way of Philadelphia, Baltimore, Washington, Richmond, and the cities of North Carolina. I then asked whether the movement took place only from North to South, and I was answered that it was about equal in the opposite direction, and as might have been expected, that the ebb and flow of this mighty tide, in the long run, balanced each other.

It is scarcely necessary to say, that this stupendous system of communication is far from being confined to the seaboard or to the intercourse between New York and the region South of it. When the steamers start from Boston for Maine and the British provinces, Favor's Express presents the same spectacle; and from every considerable Atlantic city, on all the lines of railway that penetrate the interior, from Louisiana to Maine, from New York to Minnesota, the same permeating net-work, under the management of some one of the great Express companies, will be found in activity. Nor is it confined to the Eastern portion of the Continent; the steamers bound to the Isthmus of Panama, and connecting with those that ply to San Francisco, perform their part, in like manner, in carrying on this wonderful system.

It would be a great mistake to confound the *Expressage* of the country, with its commercial and manufacturing exchanges, properly so called,—a different affair conducted by different agencies.—These latter indeed probably form a more active home trade than exists in any other country, for there is no other country uniting, in the same degree, extent of territory, variety and importance of natural products, boldness of speculation on the part of the people, energy in the transaction of business, recklessness in the use of credit, ingenuity and vigor in creating, and profusion in consuming. But the transportation of the heavy masses of merchandize is not, in ordinary cases, the "mission" of the Expresses. Their business is to carry parcels of considerable value in proportion to their size; precious articles, one thing of the kind; miscellaneous packages, transmitted to meet the infinitely varied wants of social and domestic life; parcels in reference to which speed is of importance; things, in fine, too small in amount, too multifarious in character, too widely scattered in distribution to enter into the great regular movements of Commerce; but which fill up the little interstices of life with comforts, luxuries, and objects of taste and convenience. To enumerate them all would be impossible; but besides packages of every kind of valuable merchandise despatched in urgent or exceptional cases, the Express conveys a volume transmitted to a friend at a distance; a watch which has been sent up to town to be repaired; a daguerreotype of an absent relative; an engraving in a gilt frame; specie balances interchanged by banks in critical times; a small cask of hams of Southern curing and flavor; a piece of plate as a bridal present to a distant friend; a pair of shoes of metropolitan fabric; specimens of natural history, fossil, pickled, recent; live rattlesnakes, the boxes judiciously marked "to be handled with care;" delicate fruits from suburban forcing-houses despatched to the interior; a fresh salmon from the Penobscot, packed in ice, or a maskinonge from Sault St. Marie; a buffalo robe from the plains; a box of Cincinnati or St. Louis Champagne; patent medicines in great quantities; at some seasons, mountain piles of newspapers, the "Ledger" overtopping them all;

pickled oysters for the craving West, denied that luxury by nature; a box of Congressional documents; in a word, every conceivable article of convenience or necessity, the growth or manufacture of every part of the country, despatched by interest, duty, friendship, or affection to the other.

There is one highly important service rendered by the Express system to the cause of public improvement, which ought to be more particularly signalized,—I mean that to which I have just made a passing allusion, its connection with the periodical press. During the uncertain and stormy weather of the autumn and winter, and when the ordinary freight trains are not to be fully depended on, great quantities of the magazines, weekly newspapers, and other journals are conveyed by the various Express companies to the cities of the South and West, as far as St. Louis and New Orleans.

Accustomed as we are to this immense accommodation, we can hardly comprehend how people lived without it, and yet the Express system is of quite recent growth. When I came forward in life nothing of the kind was known. There were, as I have stated in a former Number, two great modes of conveyance from place to place, in stage coaches by land, and sailing packets along the coast. By neither conveyance was there any arrangement for transmitting parcels, small or large, beyond what the traveller took with him, as a part of his personal baggage; the amount of which was greatly restricted. The stage coaches had no boxes for the convenient deposit of packages and gave no receipt for them. The carriages and drivers were changed two or three times a day; there was no system of "booking" a parcel, and of course no security for its transfer from driver to driver. A small bundle might occasionally, with an equal chance of miscarriage, be forwarded for a stage or two, if you were personally acquainted with the driver, and he was willing to take it, "seeing it was you." The coasting vessels were a safe conveyance, subject of course to be blown off to the West Indies; but they had no arrangements for receiving or distributing small parcels. The chief reliance, accordingly, was on the kindness of travelling friends, by whom a small parcel could occasionally be sent. This was an uncertain and otherwise inconvenient resort; though for very valuable parcels necessarily depended upon. Few persons of character, who had occasion forty or fifty years ago to travel between the large cities, but would be requested by the cashiers of banks and the brokers to take charge of packages,—often extremely valuable packages,—of bank notes.

This very imperfect state of things gradually passed away, with the extension of railroads through the country. The change at first was slow, for though railroads had made considerable progress by 1830, the first regular Express in the United States was started between New York and Boston in 1839. It was projected by Wm. F. Harnden, who gave up a place as conductor upon the Boston and Providence railroad, and commenced business as a travelling messenger between the cities just named. His enterprise, like most important enterprises, began upon a small scale. Mr. Harnden was able at first to transport the articles confided to him in a valise, and distributed them on foot in the two cities that formed the field of his labors. He continued for seven or eight years in this employment, which gradually and steadily grew in his hands. At length he engaged in other undertakings, which were less successful, at home, and extended his Express operations to Europe, but without satisfactory results. His name, however, is inseparably connected with the origin and development of the Express system of the United States.

In May, 1840, a new era in the system commenced, and the *Expressage* of the country may be said to date, if not its origin, at least its establishment on a firm and systematic basis from that year, when Mr. Alvin Adams, in connection with P. C. Burke as a partner, engaged in the business.

Burke soon retired from it, and the establishment was conducted by Adams alone.

Alvin Adams came to Boston from Vermont, a poor orphan boy, to seek his fortune, at first in an humble capacity, afterwards with some success in trade. He was not long in perceiving, in the Express business, the elements of a lucrative occupation, capable of almost indefinite expansion. Connecting himself with Ephraim Farnsworth as a partner in New York, he engaged actively in the conveyance of parcels between the two cities by the Worcester and Norwich route, while Harnden's Express adhered to that of Providence and Stonington. Farnsworth was soon succeeded by Wm. B. Dinsmore, Esq., the present energetic and intelligent President of the Adams' Express Company. On entering the partnership, Mr. Dinsmore removed the office from William street, New York, where it was at first established, to No. 17 Wall street. His only assistant at the outset was a bright youth of the name of Hoey, who, with the aid of a wheelbarrow, distributed the contents of the Express between Boston and New York. This person was in 1857—and probably is now—at the head of the city transportation business of Adams' Express in New York, with a force, at that time, of fifty men, forty horses, and twenty wagons at his command.

In 1843 Adams' Express associated with Messrs. Sanford of Philadelphia, and Shoemaker of Baltimore, extended itself as far South as Alexandria, in Virginia. It has since been pushed to the farthest South. The above facts are derived from a very interesting article in the New York Daily Tribune of the 10th of October, 1857, in which will also be found other curious details relative to Adams' Express, and to the establishment of the other American Expresses, viz. those of Thompson & Co. from Boston to Albany and Springfield; of Gay & Kingsley to New York by the way of Fall River and Newport; and of Wells, Fargo & Co.'s great

Western, or, as it is more properly called, American Express.—This last named enterprising house forwarded the first Express west of Buffalo in 1845, which has been prosperously conducted ever since, and has grown up into an establishment of first-rate extent and importance. No small portion of the specie remittances from California to New York are conveyed by Messrs. Wells, Fargo & Co. The general Expressage to California is shared by them with Freeman & Co., late junior partners of Adams & Co. The houses of Adams & Co. and Wells, Fargo & Co. are the two leading establishments in the Expressage of the United States.

Adams' Express, though subsequent in time to Harnden's is, as I have hinted, entitled to the credit of having first established the business on a permanent foundation. It is now supposed to have associated with itself, in private partnership, several of the minor establishments, which still retain their original separate names. Its lines of communication, as I have been informed from a reliable source, now run not only South as far as New Orleans but West as far as St Louis. By friendly or tacit understanding with other Expresses, its territorial limits extend from Boston to New York via Springfield and New Haven; from New York to Pittsburgh via Philadelphia; from Pittsburgh to Cleveland, Ohio, and thence to Cincinnati; from Cincinnati to Indianapolis, and thence to St. Louis. The points upon these several lines are common to Adams' and the other Expresses. All South and West of them is, by mutual understanding, within the territorial limits of Adams' Express; all North of these lines is served by other Expresses. Such connections, however, exist between the various establishments that packages, if I mistake not, are received by all of them to be forwarded to every part of the Union.

At the present time, as I learn from the same authentic source, Adams' Express employs 3783 men; it has 972 agencies, and its messengers travel daily 40,152 miles on the railroads and in the steamers;—a distance equal to once round the globe and two-thirds round it a second time. I have made no attempt to estimate the pecuniary value of the articles, daily conveyed by Express throughout the country, further than to satisfy myself that it runs far into the millions. It is not easy to rate too high the importance of such establishments, in promoting the general improvement and comfort of the people. Commerce is, by all admission, one of the great civilizers of nations and of men. But the Express system, though in many respects auxiliary to Commerce, goes beyond the great wholesale exchanges of trade, and penetrates further and more directly into individual life. It reaches the fireside, without passing through the hands of the jobber and retailer. It conveys just the article that supplies your want and suits your taste, at the time. It transports it in quantities so small as to be beneath the gigantic grasp of Commerce, and it extends to articles of which trade takes no cognizance. A single copy of a book ordered to a remote village in the West, which it could never reach in the course of trade, —sent for to answer some particular purpose,—may render a service to the officer, the engineer, the missionary, which he would willingly pay with its weight in silver. The Photograph of a relative or friend, transmitted from the other side of the Union, may impart a happiness to a fond and sorrowful spirit, which silver and gold cannot buy.

In this respect the Express resembles the Post-office, which is greatly undervalued, when it is regarded only as an instrument for carrying on the commercial correspondence of the country. Of inestimable importance indeed in its connection with commerce, the Post-office did not derive its origin from the wants of trade, nor, taking the aggregate of the social interests into consideration, does its great utility consist in supplying those wants. The Posts, of antiquity, were, no doubt, like those of the Mahometan governments at the present day, established for the purpose of carrying on the military and other official communications of the State. If they afforded any facilities for private correspondence, it must have been irregular and incidental. The Postal arrangements, in the early periods of modern European history, were no doubt of the same kind; and had no direct connection with trade. The first approach to the modern system is said to have been made by the University of Paris, at the beginning of the thirteenth century, for the convenience of the vast multitudes of students, who resorted to it from every part of the world. If this supposition be well founded, it was Education not Trade, which gave the germ of the Post-office system to the civilized world; and to reward this service the compensation of the professors of the University of Paris was, till quite modern times, charged upon the revenue of the Post-office.

However this may be, it scarce admits a question, that the province of the Post-office in reference to the moral, the political, the social, and domestic interests and relations of the country, is decidedly more important than its immediate connection with commerce, important as that is. In fact, when I contemplate the extent to which the moral sentiments, the intelligence, the affections of so many millions of people, —sealed up by a sacred charm within the cover of a letter,— daily circulate through a country, I am compelled to regard the Post-office, next to Christianity, as the right arm of our modern civilization.

But the Express system is rapidly rising into scarcely inferior consequence. It steps in where correspondence stops. It transports the material objects, which correspondence can only announce. It conveys across the continent the cherished symbols of love, friendship, and duty. It extends to the frontier the luxuries and comforts of the seaboard, and brings back every article of value or interest peculiar to the frontier. In conclusion, let me not forget that the Mount Vernon cause is under the greatest obligations to the liberality of the various Express companies throughout the Union.

NUMBER TWENTY-EIGHT.

AT PARIS, IN 1818.

The fête of St. Louis—His name in the United States—The festivities of the day contrasted with those usual in this country—A Mat de Cocagne described—Preparations for departure—Gen. Lyman—Relations with Coray, the celebrated modern Greek scholar and patriot—Brief account of his life and services—Transmits to this country the Address to the People of the United States of the Messenian Senate at Calamata—Its effects here—Contributions for the relief of the Greeks distributed by Dr. Howe—Death and autobiography of Coray.

In the twenty-second Number of these papers, I conducted my reader on the journey toward Italy, by the way of Southampton, Havre, and Rouen, as far as Paris. The day after our arrival at Paris, was the *fête* of St. Louis, the patron and military Saint of France, the only one of her sovereigns, says Sismondi, who has received the honors of Canonization. Bourdaloue, one of the first preachers according to Voltaire, (an impartial judge, perhaps, on such a point,) "who made reason eloquent," remarks, in his splendid panegyric of St. Louis, that "the other saints honored in the Christian world were given by the church to France, but as for St. Louis, France gave him to the church." We Americans ought to care something about St. Louis. One of the great central cities of the West bears his name, which in its origin was identical (Ludovicus, Chlodovicus,) with that of Clovis, the founder of the French Monarchy. Indeed as the great predominance of the name of Louis, under the old *régime* in France, may be ascribed to its having attained the honor of Saintship, in the person of Louis IX. he may be considered, in effect, as having given his name to one of the United States. He thus enjoys,—he a half-mythical French monarch of the thirteenth century,—an honor not conferred upon any of the wise and the good of our own history.

St. Louis owes his title, it may be presumed, to his having led two crusades from France against the Mussulmans in Egypt and Africa; expeditions which, as he conducted them, would, at the present day, at least, secure for a Sovereign a place in the insane asylum rather than in the Calendar. Apart from his fanaticism, however, he was, in the main, a wise and virtuous prince. When, however, we find Bourdaloue comparing him not merely to Moses but to God himself, because "he conducted his victorious arms into Egypt," and call to mind the egregious imbecility which really characterized every step of his insane expedition into that country, and resulted in the shameful defeat and total annihilation of his army, and his own captivity, we cannot but feel that, of all human vanities, panegyric of this kind is among the vainest.

I passed the day in witnessing the festivities with which France, in the nineteenth century, celebrated the birthday of her patron saint of the thirteenth. In some parts of the United States that shall be nameless, the day would have been "ushered in;" that is, "sleep would have been murdered" the night before, by tin trumpets, India crackers, and sporadic fire-arms, and the tired population would have been effectually roused at sunrise by a tumultuous ringing of bells and discharge of artillery. At noon we should have had an oration, containing a tolerably comprehensive history of the crusades in general and of those of St. Louis in particular, with his biography in considerable detail. To this would have succeeded a procession through the streets of the civic fathers and their invited guests, headed by a band of music; a public dinner, with a succession of patriotic toasts and still more patriotic speeches, from those who habitually do the oratory on these occasions, with a star or two perhaps from a distance; a display of fireworks in the evening, and at half past nine—the best part of the display—forty thousand spectators of all ages and of either sex, wending their way home, weary, pleased, and sober.

The celebration at Paris was differently managed. Mass was performed in Nôtre Dame, St. Germain l'Auxerrois, and some of the other churches; but there was no oration, no procession, no public dinner; no firing of crackers in the streets over night, no ringing of bells, no salvos of artillery at dawn. Little or no notice, that I could see, was taken of the day in the streets. The shops were open as usual,—in fact, they are open on Sundays, except some of those kept by Protestants;—the *cafés* and *restaurants* perhaps a trifle more resorted to, but they are almost always full;—no perceptible augmentation of the gay and busy throng on the Boulevards. In the *Champs Elysées* alone some provision was made, partly by individuals on their own account, but rather more by the government, at least so I judged, for the public amusement. There were all kinds of rarée shows, menageries, marionettes, temporary circuses, mountebanks, and jugglers, booths for the sale of toys, flash jewelry, and fancy articles, gambling tables, popular sports of all kinds, curious gymnastic apparatus, and theatres erected of slight materials for the occasion, in which every act seemed a catastrophe and every scene the winding up of the plot; the two principal actors being a head of brigands and the commander of a force sent to arrest them, who rarely failed to kill each other, and the other personages of the drama consisting of platoons of *gens d'armerie*, detached for the ostensible purpose of carrying on the action of the piece, by an eternal uproar of musketry, but really to be on hand in case of need to suppress disorders among the spectators.

What most attracted me was the *Mâts de Cocagne*, which I had never seen before, and with which I was greatly amused. A *Mât de Cocagne* is a good-sized mast, such as might suit a topsail schooner, erected in the ground, its surface smeared all the way up with soap and grease, and on its top a box containing silver forks, watches and cheap jewelry, destined as a prize to reward the successful climber. No one person can hold out strong enough to attain the object, which can only be accomplished by several clubbing together. Those who undertake it begin by wiping off the lubricating substances with wisps of straw, as high up as they can reach, and this done they are then allowed to throw sand on the mast to render it less slippery. This preparation enables one person to climb to a certain elevation, wiping and sanding the mast, as far up as he can sustain himself, by clinging with his legs round the part already sanded. When he is tired out, he slips down to the ground, plants himself firmly on his feet, clinging tight round the mast, while a confederate mounts on his shoulders, and from the elevation thus gained, wipes and sands, and so fits for climbing another portion of the mast. He in turn slips down, at length, fatigued; but plants himself on the shoulders of the first, who is still clinging to the mast if his strength holds out. A third one then mounts upon the two, thus standing one above the other, and so on till the whole mast, delubricated and sanded, is brought into a condition in which a fresh and strong associate can climb to the top and take possession of the prize for himself and colleagues. No ladders or hooks of any kind are allowed; and the climbers are searched to prevent their having any steel points or other contrivances concealed under their garments. The only artificial aid permitted is the wisp of straw and the sand, of which they are allowed to carry up as much as broad deep pockets made for the purpose will hold. The effort of course is to attain the object by a party consisting of as few confederates as possible. It usually takes, as I was told, the greater part of the day to climb to the summit and get possession of the valuables there deposited. The toilsome efforts to ascend, —the persons at the bottom often giving way under the weight of those standing upon them, two or three deep, and all coming down with a run,—the appearance of a remarkably meagre or unusually rotund climber,—with other incidents of such an undertaking, furnish the day's amusement to the *gamins* of Paris and bystanders generally, and lead to the exchange of a deal of coarse pleasantry, interspersed with an occasional scuffle between the friends of the climbers and those who criticize their operations too pointedly. These last demonstrations are however kept within bounds by the aforesaid *gens d'armerie.* Upon the whole, if one wishes to study the humors of the *bas peuple* of Paris, there are few places where he can pass a couple of hours to greater advantage than near a *Mât de Cocagne.*

We have nothing exactly like it in this country, but it does not badly symbolize the life of those, who toil and strain to climb a slippery mast of another kind, mounting on the shoulders of confederates, flinging dust in the eyes of the public, and occasionally a little mud in the faces of rivals, and find when they reach the top, that the prizes in the basket are of little value in themselves, and not half numerous enough to satisfy their associates, who are apt to quarrel over the division of the spoils.

At Paris I rejoined my friend the late General Lyman of Boston, with whom as a travelling companion I was to visit Italy and the East,—a person of great worth, and admirably fitted as a traveller by an ever active spirit of observation, gentlemanly manners, and even temper. We remained no longer at Paris than was necessary to make the last preparations for the journey before us, and particularly to get our passports duly countersigned.

I availed myself of the opportunity thus afforded to visit a few friends, whose society I had enjoyed the winter before, and particularly the celebrated Coray, the most learned and sagacious, as it seems to me, of the scholars of Modern Greece, and second to none of her sons, in the services rendered by him in preparing the way for her liberation. Having in view a visit to Greece, I had eagerly sought his acquaintance on arriving at Paris in the Autumn of 1817, and had diligently cultivated it during the whole of the following winter. He was then seventy years of age, and of rather infirm health, but in the full possession of his faculties. My conversation with him, in our frequent interviews, naturally dwelt most on the subjects uppermost in the minds of both of us,—the ancient literature of his country, the condition and prospects of Modern Greece, and the hopes of her regeneration;—but he had seen much of the world; he possessed the principal languages of Modern Europe; had been a general reader, and had, from observation and books amassed a fund of various and useful knowledge, which I have rarely seen equalled. He was good enough to encourage the repetition of my visits,—a benignant smile ever welcomed me, even when he was suffering severe pain,—and I never left him without having heard something that was worth remembering, or learning something which I did not know before.

This remarkable man was born in Smyrna, in 1748, and was the son of parents in straitened circumstances. His opportunities of education were of course slender; but he early displayed uncommon aptitude for learning, with an insatiable thirst for knowledge. Native teachers were few and incompetent;—the instruction which they gave, as he tells us, was meagre, the flogging abundant. Happily he formed the acquaintance of the Chaplain of the Dutch Consul, who desired to learn of him the pronunciation of the Romaic, and who in return instructed young Coray in the Latin. He early imbibed, from the perusal of Demosthenes, a passionate love of liberty and a galling sense of the tyranny under which his countrymen were groaning. Brought up in trade, he was sent at the age of twenty-four to Holland to engage in business. Here he lived six years, closely confined to his duties, but passing two evenings in a week at the house of a friendly clergyman, to whom the chaplain above named had given him letters of introduction. These six years were not only agreeably but profitably passed. In 1779 he returned by the way of Vienna, Trieste, and Venice to Smyrna. His views in life had by this time undergone a change; the astonishing career of the unfortunate Rhigas had already commenced and kindled his enthusiasm; he determined to abandon the career of a merchant, which if successful marked him out as an object of oppression and plunder on the part of the Turkish government, to be avoided only by remaining in voluntary exile. He took up instead the profession of medicine, which, if he remained in Turkey, was the safest calling, while it furnished superior opportunities for cultivating those literary pursuits, to which he looked as fitting him to act extensively on his countrymen. Resisting the temptation of an eligible marriage which his parents wished him to contract, he repaired to Montpelier, in France, and there for several years devoted himself with diligence to the study of his profession, supported at first by small remittances from his father, and when this resource failed, by a little frugal aid from his old friend the chaplain, and by translating medical books from German and English into French. In 1789, and after having taken his degree of Doctor, he came to Paris. The Revolution was just breaking out, and the ten years which followed his arrival in Paris were passed by Coray in wise obscurity, and as far as concerned the bloody game of which he was a spectator, in entire inaction. He was all the time, however, by his own solitary studies and a diligent but carefully guarded correspondence with his countrymen, not only in Turkey but in the various States of Europe, educating himself and them for great events. He saw, a half century before the Emperor Nicholas announced it, that Turkey was "a sick man;" and conceived the hope that, in the general despoiling of the estate to which he looked forward, Central Greece at least would go free.

The course he pursued to accomplish the great object which he had at heart was characterized by the long-suffering of Providence. He did not seek, in the first instance, to stir up revolt, the fatal error, in some countries, of political regenerators,—but he aimed to improve the minds of his countrymen; to facilitate to them the study of the noble authors of their ancient language; to purify the modern dialect from the barbarisms that had crept into it, and thus if possible to establish an identity between ancient and modern Greece. In addition to this, his prefaces and notes to a series of the ancient writers furnished him the opportunity of inculcating many seasonable lessons of patriotism among his readers. His editions were published at the expense of his prosperous countrymen at Vienna, Trieste, and elsewhere, and widely circulated; but he did not confine himself to these indirect methods. When, after the death of Rhigas in 1798, meanly given up with his associates by Austria to the Turkish government, the Patriarch of Jerusalem was compelled to issue a general address to his countrymen, exhorting them to submit unresistingly to the Ottoman power, Coray published a fervent and high-toned reply. In 1801 he addressed another patriotic appeal to his countrymen, exhorting them to rely on the aid and protection of France. The great movement in Greece in 1821 took him at first somewhat by surprise; he had not anticipated so early an explosion; and in fact it had been prematurely brought about by the rupture of Ali Pacha of Albania with the Porte the year before. But though fearful at first that the time had not come for a successful revolt throughout the whole of the region, whose population was substantially of the Greek church,—as the event sufficiently proved to be the case,—he cordially entered into the movement, and though too old—73—to repair to Greece with a view of rendering active service, he contributed materially by his wise counsels, by his correspondence, and by his publications, to animate the zeal of his countrymen and to give it a right direction.

When I was leaving Paris for Italy and Greece, Coray furnished me with letters to his countrymen in the principal cities which I was likely to visit in European or Asiatic Turkey, a circumstance to which I was indebted for the freest access to the persons whose acquaintance a youthful traveller could most wish to form,—the patriotic merchants the learned professors, the promising young men, in short the *élite* of modern Greece. The relations thus formed naturally gave me the deepest interest in the impending future of the native land of literature, philosophy, and art.

When the revolution broke out in Greece in 1821, a deputation from the first provisional Congress was despatched to Paris to confer with Coray, and take measures with him for enlisting the sympathies of Western Europe and America. They brought with them the Address of the Messenian Senate of Calamata to the People of the United States. This manifesto was forwarded by Coray to me, and at the earliest moment at which it seemed likely to attract attention was translated and published with the accompanying letter of the Deputies, in the papers of the day. The interest with which these appeals were read was the immediately exciting cause of the enthusiasm for Greece which pervaded the United States; and which found expression in public meetings throughout the country, in the magnificent speech of Mr. Webster in Congress, and a year or two later in the liberal and substantial contributions to the relief of the sufferers by the war, which were forwarded to Greece, under the care of Dr. Howe, and there distributed by him in a manner which has earned for him and his countrymen the abiding gratitude of thousands.

Coray lived to the age of eighty-five, and died at Paris in 1833, active almost to the last in his literary pursuits, and happy in the liberation to which he had so much contributed, of a portion of his country,—though not satisfied at seeing what was called the Independent government the sport of the rival interests of the great powers of Europe. He brought down his Autobiography, published by his friends since his death, to the year 1829.—I have several letters from him, beautifully written in a character very nearly resembling that of the Didot editions of the Greek classics; and I seize with pleasure the opportunity of paying this grateful tribute to his honored memory.

NUMBER TWENTY-NINE.

THE ILLUSTRIOUS DEAD OF 1859—PRESCOTT, BOND, HALLAM, VON HUMBOLDT.

The value of their example to young men—Traits of Mr. Prescott's character, which are within the reach of imitation by others—William Cranch Bond the Astronomer—Remarkable variety and union of qualities, scientific and practical—His amiable temper and disposition—His enthusiasm for Astronomy—Liberal appreciation of others—Visit of Jenny Lind to the Cambridge Observatory—Succeeded in the Observatory at Cambridge by his son George P. Bond—Scientific reputation of Mr. Bond, Jnr.

Since I commenced these Papers at the beginning of the year, four persons of great eminence in the scientific and literary world have passed away, two in this country and two in Europe. With all of them it was my happiness to stand in friendly relations,—with three of them I was intimately acquainted. They were all four men who in their respective departments have left no superior. The lives and characters of all of them are full of instruction and encouragement, especially to young men.

There is no brighter example than Prescott's of what may be accomplished by a resolute spirit and a firm purpose. I have already had an opportunity of paying my humble tribute to his memory, before the Massachusetts Historical Society, but I would gladly dwell upon it for a few moments in the columns of The Ledger. Undoubtedly he possessed by nature an admirable talent,—intellectual powers of a very high order. But he owed his brilliant success in a very considerable degree to his moral qualities, his fortitude under severe trials; his resolute war against formidable obstacles; his unwearied perseverance; and even in some measure to the humbler agencies of system and method in his studies, in his exercise, and in his affairs. It is for this reason, that I call his example instructive to young men, because in these he may be imitated by persons who do not possess his admirable natural gifts. All men can be systematic in the arrangement of their regular occupations; punctual in their hours and especially in their appointments where others as well as themselves are concerned; and resolute in adhering to plans either of employment or relaxation; and those who are so even with natural talents far inferior to Prescott's, may in a long life bring much to pass. All men whose health requires and whose means admit it, might like him leave their beds before sunrise, in our cold New England climate, for a ride of several miles before breakfast,—and yet the number of persons who have the moral energy to pursue such a course of healthful exercise, through a northern winter, is perhaps not greater than of those gifted by nature with his brilliant mental powers.

In another respect Mr. Prescott's example is of inestimable value in pointing out to our young men of leisure and fortune the true path to usefulness and fame. The number is rapidly increasing throughout the country of those who enter life with large inherited means and still larger expectations. These young men, almost as a matter of course, enjoy the best advantages for instruction at school and at college; but it is not so much a matter of course, that they make as good use of these advantages, as those who, in straitened circumstances, are compelled to make strenuous efforts and severe sacrifices to obtain an education. We have, however, a few young men of fortune and leisure, who, without devoting themselves to professional pursuits or seeking the increase of their wealth by engaging in business,—a very hazardous step in such cases,—employ their time in reading, in cultivating a taste for science or letters, or in forming a library or a collection of works of art or specimens of natural history. There are others who resort to the country, and occupy themselves in agricultural pursuits. The possession of fortune at the outset of their career, enables persons of this class, not only to set an example of a useful and virtuous employment of time, but to enrich the community by valuable literary, scientific, artistic, and utilitarian treasures, books, pictures, statuary, collections illustrative of science;—in agricultural pursuits, implements of husbandry, animals of improved breeds, and costly experiments and improvements. Of those who have devoted leisure and fortune to the pursuits, by which, while the mind of the possessor is improved, the community is benefited and honor reflected on the country, Prescott is the brightest example in the United States;—while the almost insuperable difficulties under which he labored, will ever encourage those, who enter life under unfavorable circumstances of any kind, not to yield to despondence. What would not the country have lost, if, abandoning, on account of his infirmity, all effort at literary distinction, he had, like so many young men of wealth, plunged into dissipation, or merely wasted his time in the club room, the drawing room, or on the race course!

William Cranch Bond, another of the noble four to whom I have alluded, was an example not less bright though of a different kind. There is no man now living who watches the stars with a keener, more patient, more skilfully trained or more wary eye than he did. Though he may be excelled by individuals, in some single branches of his department, there is probably no living astronomer, who, as much as he did, unites respectable scientific knowledge, acuteness and precision of observation, conscientiousness and patient accuracy in recording its results, ingenuity as a horological machinist, and mechanical dexterity of a more ordinary kind. Witness for his scientific knowledge, and the accuracy with which his observations and researches are recorded, the published volumes of the annals of the Observatory at Cambridge, and his memoirs communicated to the American Academy of Arts and Sciences. Witness for the acuteness of his observations, his discovery jointly with his son of the new ring of Saturn, his discovery of the eighth satellite of that planet,—perhaps even of a second satellite of Neptune. For his wonderful skill as a scientific machinist, it is sufficient to allude to his apparatus for registering astronomical observations adopted in the Royal Observatory at Greenwich, which, with electric speed and automatic precision, does the work of two observers, far more minutely, as well as accurately, than it could be done by human eyes and fingers.

Nor was he less remarkable for mechanical skill of a lower kind. Witness the extraordinary feat of setting up the great Equatorial at Cambridge, taking it from the fourteen boxes, which contained its hundreds of pieces, the mass together weighing five tons, the extremely complicated apparatus such as he had never seen before, the directions in the German language, of which he had but an imperfect knowledge, and putting them all up in their places on the pier, in two days!

While his scientific talents and attainments commanded admiration, his amiable qualities of temper and heart gained him the love of all who knew him. He had struggled hard from poverty and obscurity into the light of day. No early opportunities of academical education cheered him onward. Every step of his early progress was taken under disheartening difficulties, and he had hardly reached the goal of his career—the noble observatory at Cambridge—before the declining sun of life cast long shadows over the plain, and the glow of triumph was chilled. But although frugal of speech, tranquil as the sky in demeanor, and all but impassive in outward appearance, the fire burned within him. A more generous spirit, or a warmer heart, never glowed in the human breast.

But notwithstanding the strength and kindliness of his temper, exercised in all the social relations of life, his home was in the heavens. His nightly walk was with the stars. The position and bearings of every fixed luminary, the orbit of every moving body; every law and every perturbation; the whole range and sweep of the heavens, from the outskirts of the milky way, the faintest nebula, the unfathomed regions of space, (as far as modern science has explored them,) down to the nearest planet, and our own satellite, were as familiar to him as the features of the surrounding landscape. Brought up in poverty, dependent all his life on a laborious mechanical occupation (that of a watchmaker) for a portion of the income necessary to the support of his family, I am persuaded that the discovery of the eighth satellite of Saturn gave him greater pleasure, than it would to have fallen heir to a fortune. On the 22d of September, 1847, I received a letter from him from the Observatory, (I was then connected with the University at Cambridge,) in which he said, "You will rejoice with me, that the great nebula in Orion has yielded to the powers of our incomparable telescope." I met him an hour or two after the receipt of the letter, and his sweet calm face glistened with triumphant joy, like an angel's.

He emulated the peacefulness of the stars. It was as impossible that with envious feeling, or selfish wish, or by uncharitable speech he should seek to detract from his neighbor's rights or fame, as that Jupiter and Saturn should come in conflict in their orbits. He thought the heaven and heaven of heavens a field wide enough for all who love to penetrate their depths and survey their glories. I am persuaded that a word designed or calculated to injure another man's reputation, especially that of a brother Astronomer, never dropped from his lips or his pen. So valuable was his time, so precious the use of his "incomparable telescope," so austere the simplicity of his manners, that to strangers visiting the Observatory, as a mere object of curiosity, he sometimes seemed unduly reserved and even repulsive; but with a brother observer, or a sincere lover of science, however humble his attainments, or with a friend, he was the most patient, communicative, and sympathetic of men.

Not less than "the music of the spheres" he loved the harmonies of the human voice. He was an especial admirer of Jenny Lind, and having myself the good fortune to be acquainted with her, he requested me to arrange with her a visit to the Observatory. Saturn happened at that time to be in a most favorable position for observation. While she was gazing upon it through the great telescope, a meteor of unusual brilliancy shot across the field leaving behind it for some seconds a brilliant pathway. He regretted that it was not a permanent body to which, in commemoration of her visit, he might attach her name. As he was adjusting the telescope, he entered into some general explanation of the great facts of Astronomy, and the mechanism of the heavens, rising from the sun to the surrounding luminaries, from the solar family to the sidereal system of which it is a part, and from that to the mighty whole of which our universe with all its hosts, is but a member,—orb above orb, system above system, universe above universe.—The last time I saw him, which was on the occasion described in the fifth number of these Papers, I recalled this visit to him, and spoke of the pleasure with which I had listened to what he said. He answered, "But what Jenny Lind said to me in reply was better;—'AND GOD ABOVE ALL!'" I rejoice that the respectful allusion to him in that Paper, describing a visit to the Observatory for the purpose of observing the Comet, must have fallen beneath his eyes before they were closed on this world to open on the nearer vision of those glories which he had watched on earth with such reverent gaze.

The friends of American science are well pleased that his mantle and his place, at the head of the Cambridge Observatory, have descended with his name. To equal patience, acuteness, and skill as an observer, Mr. George Phillips Bond unites the advantages, to which his venerable father, though a respectable geometer, did not lay claim, viz., those of rare mathematical talents, and thorough mathematical training and education. He was for years the trusted associate of his father's labors and studies. In Professor Loomis's valuable work on the "Recent Progress of Astronomical Science," a brief but interesting sketch is given of the researches of the Messrs. Bond, father and son, down to the year 1856.—It is there stated that Mr. George P. Bond "has been the independent discoverer of *eleven Comets*, but unfortunately it subsequently appeared, that each of these, save one, had been previously discovered in Europe. The Comet of August 29th, 1850, he discovered seven days in advance of the European Astronomers. Two other Comets he discovered on the same night that they were seen in Europe, viz., those of June 5th, 1845, and April 11th, 1849. Having found this species of observation too severe a trial for his eyes, he has for the past three or four years given up comet seeking." Mr. Geo. P. Bond's Memoir in the Mathematical, Monthly on Donati's comet, (which attracted the wondering admiration of the world last Autumn,) is a most successful attempt to popularize science. The engravings accompanying it are of surpassing beauty. The non-scientific world is under great obligations to Mr. Bond, for bringing the observations made at Cambridge and his views upon the subject of Donati's comet, down to the level of readers not versed in the mysteries of the calculus.

No men of science in this country are more honorably referred to in the "Cosmos" than the Messrs. Bond. The observations of Mr. Bond, jun. on the nebula of Andromeda, and his delineation of that most extraordinary object, have attracted the notice of European Astronomers. "For the first time, I believe," says Dr. Nichols in his Architecture of the Heavens, "first at least in so marked a manner,—the existence of *dark lines* WITHIN nebulæ, [these Italics and Capitals are Dr. Nichols',] or as part of their structure, was noticed by Mr. Bond." This important paper and another purely demonstrative, on "Some methods of computing the ratio of the distances of a Comet from the Earth," in the third volume of the new series of the Memoirs of the American Academy of Arts and Sciences, and still more his remarkable paper on the Rings of Saturn in the fourth volume of the same series, have, with his other publications, given Mr. Bond, jun. a high place, not merely among the observers but among the geometers of the Age. His conclusion from his observation of the phenomena of Saturn's rings, that they cannot be solid bodies, confirmed as it has been, by the subsequent demonstrations of Professors Pierce and Maxwell of the mechanical conditions of the Saturnian system, are certainly among the most brilliant results of Modern Astronomical Science.

I propose in another paper, to pay an humble tribute to the other illustrious dead of the year.

NUMBER THIRTY.

THE ILLUSTRIOUS DEAD OF 1859—PRESCOTT, BOND, HALLAM, VON HUMBOLDT.

Simultaneous death of Hallam and Prescott—Hallam the first standard writer of history in England after Hume, Gibbon, and Robertson—Compared with those writers—Brief account of the History of Europe in the middle ages—Of the Constitutional history of England—Of the introduction to the Literature of Europe for the fifteenth, sixteenth, and seventeenth centuries—Personal History—Loss of his two sons—Henry counsels his father not to accept the title of Baronet—Receives the honorary degree of Doctor of Laws from Harvard College—Letter of acknowledgment.

By the arrival of the next steamer from Europe, after the death of Prescott, the public mind received another shock in this country by the news that a brother Historian had passed away in England. Hallam had gone beyond the age of four score, and had for several years ceased from his literary labors. His death left nothing to regret as to the completion of his works, or the maturity of his fame. He enjoyed his well-earned reputation, in a serene old age; the lapse of time had alleviated the weight of the heavy bereavement which he had suffered in the loss of his two noble sons; and he found pleasure in the reflection that, though bereft of them, his lineage would not wholly perish. In the last letter which I received from him, not written, except the signature, with his own hand, he says:

"I return you many thanks for your kind recollection of me, though the pleasure of receiving your letter was much diminished, by the recollection that we can never meet again in this world. I continue on the whole in pretty good health, but I am become very lame and infirm and unable to walk. Still I should be thankful that I am free from organic complaints, which so often affect people at my very advanced age. I have the happiness of living in the same house with my daughter both here and in the country, for we have a house in Kent, about twelve miles from town, where we pass half the year. I have two grandchildren, one of them only a few weeks old, so that I have a hope of surviving in my posterity."

It was certainly a noticeable coincidence, that two such lights in the intellectual firmament as Hallam and Prescott, shining with such brightness in the same department of polite letters, should have been extinguished within a few days of each other. Having during my residence in England, from 1841 to 1845, been honored with the intimate acquaintance, I may venture to say, the friendship of Mr. Hallam, and with his correspondence since my return, the reader will, I am sure pardon me, even after the lapse of a few months since his decease, for placing on record, in these columns, my impressions of his literary and personal character.

After the last of the three great English historians of the Eighteenth Century had passed away, no writer appeared in the same department sufficiently distinguished, to be considered as keeping up the line of the succession in that country. In this country historical studies had hardly commenced. Many valuable works had certainly appeared, on both sides of the Atlantic, within the domain of history, or closely bordering upon it, but nothing which could be fairly placed on a level with Hume, Gibbon, and Robertson. At length, after mature preparatory studies and being then forty years of age, Mr. Hallam in 1818 published his first, and in the opinion of some persons his ablest work, "A View of the State of Europe in the Middle Ages." This work did not claim to be a History, narrating a series of events woven into unity political or territorial, but it was rather a series of historical dissertations, presenting a comprehensive view of the chief matters of interest to a philosophical inquirer, in the period called the middle ages. A work of this kind necessarily wanted something of the epic attraction of a great historical work, properly so called; but for those who read, not for amusement but instruction, it had its counterbalancing advantages. Without possessing the same charm of style as either of the three great writers of the eighteenth century, it is, in some important respects, of higher merit than either of them. In consequence of the great advance of philological studies, during the last half of the eighteenth and the first quarter of the nineteenth centuries, the learning of Hallam is more accurate and critical than that of Gibbon, though not displayed in an equal array of citations, which in "the Decline and Fall of the Roman Empire" are multiplied with superfluous profusion, and which are, in some cases, from authorities since become obsolete. It is a still greater merit of Mr. Hallam's work,—as indeed of all his works,—that they are wholly free from the taint of irreverence, which poisons Gibbons magnificent and truly monumental history. There is a gravity and dignity in the speculations of a few of the sceptical writers, which commands your respect, however you may deplore their tendency and recoil from their results. But the irony and the veiled sarcasm of Gibbon resolve themselves at last into nearly the worst fault of a writer, Insincerity; while an ill restrained pruriency occasionally manifests itself, which excites no feelings but those of pity and disgust. Mr. Hallam's history far exceeds Hume's in range of topics, in depth of investigation, and extent and accuracy of research; in a knowledge not only of the common but of the civil law, and especially in conscientious dealing with his authorities, in which respect, Hume, either from indolence, or a certain philosophical indifference, was far from exemplary. I cannot think Hume ever intended knowingly and wilfully to mistake or garble the writers whom he quotes; but those who follow in his track will occasionally find traces of a carelessness, which must have sprung, either from an unwillingness to encounter the toil of a laborious collation of authorities, or a lofty preference of his own theory of what ought to be true, over the homely reality of actual fact. In all the qualities of a first-rate historian, Hallam is far superior to Robertson, with the exception, perhaps, of a certain attractive ease and winning flow of style, (mere style in distinction from the manner of treating a subject,) by which you are borne along in the pages of the illustrious Scotsman, whose great advantage lies in the interest of his subjects. Mr. Hallam modestly replies, that he had more in view the instruction of the young than the improvement of mature readers. "I dare not," says he, "appeal with confidence to the tribunal of those superior judges who, having bestowed a more undivided attention on the particular objects that have interested them, may justly deem such general sketches imperfect and superficial; but my labors will not have proved fruitless, if they shall conduce to stimulate the reflection, to guide the researches, to correct the prejudices, and to animate the liberal and virtuous sentiments of INQUISITIVE YOUTH." Mr. Hallam's History of the Middle Ages immediately assumed and has ever maintained the character of a classical work.

After an interval of nine years, "The Constitutional History of England from the beginning of the reign of Henry the Seventh to the close of the reign of George the Second," was published. This too is a work of standard excellence. Discussing questions which, at that time more than now, divided opinion in England, Mr. Hallam's opinions did not in all points command universal assent. By the Tory journals and the Tory politicians it was characterized as the work of a "decided partisan." But this was itself mere partisan disparagement. Mr. Hallam himself says, with a noble consciousness of impartiality, that no one will suspect him of being a "blind zealot." The adverse judgment just quoted has not been confirmed by the verdict of the generation which has filled the stage since his work appeared. It has, on the contrary approved itself more and more as a fair, unprejudiced Treatise. Such in all probability will be the verdict of after time; such is the light in which it is, and no doubt always will be, regarded in this country, where the Constitutional History of England will always be studied with nearly as much interest as our own. In America Mr. Hallam's work will no doubt always be regarded as founded on those true principles of Constitutional law, which are common to all representative governments. Mr. Hallam's work afforded, what was greatly wanted, a corrective of the political theories of Hume. It is owing, I am confident, in no small degree, to the gradually increasing influence of Mr. Hallam's "Constitutional History," that the theoretical Toryism of former times, and which was still vigorous under George the Third, has almost wholly disappeared in England. His work, I am inclined to think, is generally accepted as an accurate deduction of the history and a fair statement of the principles of the British Government. It has often been said, and never to my knowledge contradicted, that it was from this work, under the guidance of the late Lord Melbourne, that the present Sovereign of England received her education in the Constitution of the Kingdom, of which she was one day, with a rare union of manly vigor and female gentleness, to wield the sceptre.

Mr. Hallam's third great work, "Introduction to the Literature of Europe for the fifteenth, sixteenth, and seventeenth Centuries" was published twelve or thirteen years later, and when he was now about sixty years of age. This, with the exception of a supplementary volume of notes to his History of the Middle Ages, was his last work. It was prepared under a cloud of sorrow, which gathered over his house, in consequence of the untimely decease of his eldest and much loved son. It is a work of vast erudition, but, from its encyclopedic character, of unequal execution. There is however no quackery in it. When he has occasion to speak of an

Author whom he has not read, he tells you so; and when he pronounces a judgment as his own, you know that it *is* his own,—the fruit of his own inquiry and reflection. It is not like so many similar works, a compilation without acknowledgment from former writers. On the contrary, it is a work of original research, and that too not seldom in unfamiliar quarters. Thus he first pointed out the similarity of thought between the celebrated passage on the Universality of Law, at the close of the first book of Hooker's Ecclesiastical polity, with a passage in the now nearly forgotten work of the Jesuit Suarez, (*de Legibus et Deo Legislatore*) 'of Laws and God the Lawgiver." Impartiality, good sense, pure taste, freedom from extravagance, and a clear and expressive though rather elaborate style, characterize this, as they do all his works.

Of personal history there is but little to record in the life of Mr. Hallam. He was educated to the law, but never engaged in its practice. He, however, attached great importance to his legal studies, as one of his qualifications for writing the Constitutional History of England. He speaks with emphasis of Hume's deficiency in this respect, though he treats his great predecessor with commendable impartiality, considering the antagonism of their political views. In his family relations, he was at once the happiest and the unhappiest of men;—the happiest in being the father of two sons of rare endowments and brightest promise; the unhappiest in being called to part with them in the morning of their days. Arthur died at the age of twenty-two; his memory has been embalmed in the crystal tears of Tennyson. Henry, on whom Mr. Hallam's affection had centred with twofold tenderness after the loss of his brother, died at the age of twenty-six, leaving his father broken-hearted, but for the hope of a reunion in a better world. I had the pleasure occasionally to see the last named of the brothers at their father's table; and in 1843 it was my good fortune to meet him at the rooms of my young friend, Mr. Charles Bristed, in Trinity College, Cambridge. An interesting memoir of this most amiable and hopeful young man, from the pen of Mr. Bristed, has been reprinted in England.—One trait of generous feeling and honest filial pride has been related to me of him by a common friend. When Sir Robert Peel tendered to Mr. Hallam the hereditary title of Baronet,—the highest title of honor ever bestowed in England on a man of letters, till Lord Macaulay was raised to the peerage,—Mr. Hallam said he would be governed by his son's wishes. Henry on being consulted, answered that as far as his feelings were concerned, he was content to be known as the son of Henry Hallam, a name to which no title should give added dignity.

Mr. Hallam, like all the distinguished authors in England, was, in proportion to our population, more extensively read in this country than at home. This arises from the greater cheapness of the American Editions, and the more extensive diffusion of education throughout all classes of the community. I reflect with pleasure, that, on my proposal, he received in 1848 the honorary degree of Doctor of Laws from Harvard College, and not till the same year, from his own Oxford. The following letter, acknowledging his degree, though it has been published before, will I think be generally interesting to my readers; but few of whom I suppose have seen it.

"CLIFTON, 26 *Oct.*, 1848.

"MY DEAR MR. EVERETT.—It has given me the greatest satisfaction to receive the Diploma of the Senate of Harvard College conferring on me the high honor of Doctor of Laws, an honor even enhanced by the eulogy which, through the medium of a very classical Latinity, that distinguished body has been pleased to bestow upon my several publications.

I have already in the present year received a similar honor from my own University, that of Oxford. It will be my pride for the remainder of my days, to reflect that not only at home, where I might better expect it, but in a land which it has not been permitted me to visit, my labors in the field of literature, deficient as I feel them to be, and perhaps unequal to what I had once hoped to have been their extent, have obtained a reward of public approbation, so ample and so honorable, as has been allotted to them. The admiration of literary merit, (and I must not now be understood as referring to myself,) has become of late years very characteristic of America. It displays itself with a noble, and we may say juvenile enthusiasm, which we are far from equalling in Europe. Nothing is more likely to maintain that natural affection between those who spring from common ancestors and speak a common language, which every wise and good man on each side of the ocean desires to see.

I request you to return my most sincere thanks to the Fellows of Harvard College. To yourself I need not say that I am peculiarly indebted, not only for the share you have had in conferring this honor upon me, but for many testimonials of your friendship, during the too short period of your residence in Great Britain.

Believe me, my dear Mr. Everett, very faithfully yours,

HENRY HALLAM."

NUMBER THIRTY-ONE.

THE ILLUSTRIOUS DEAD OF 1859—PRESCOTT, BOND, HALLAM, VON HUMBOLDT.

The year 1769 famous for the birth of great men—The memory of Humboldt associated with America—His unsuccessful plans before coming to this continent—His great reputation founded on his American works—His place at the head of the men of Science of the day—Great age to which his literary labors were protracted—Accustomed to sleep but four hours in the twenty-four—His social disposition—Acquaintance of the writer with Mr. von Humboldt in 1818—His liberal appreciation of others—Sits to Mr. Wight of Boston for his portrait—Remarks on the assertion that he was an Atheist.

Last of the Illustrious dead of the year in order, first in renown, stands the great name of Alexander von Humboldt, who, at the close of a life prolonged to fourscore years and ten, and passed in studious activity to the last, was placed by general consent at the head of the Philosophers of the Age. The year in which he was born, 1769, is distinguished for the birth of more great men than have been born, perhaps, in any other year; Napoleon, Wellington, Cuvier, von Humboldt. Schiller and Canning have been added to the list; but Schiller was born in 1759 and Canning in 1770. The current year will, in all human probability, be long remembered in history for military and political events of extreme importance; it will certainly be long remembered for the decease of the four great men whose names stand at the head of this article, (and who knows what names the remaining months may add to the solemn list?*) but it cannot fail to be spoken

* Washington Irving and Lord Macaulay died after this was written.

of, in after times, as the year in which Humboldt died. It is good to pause upon such an event, and to hold up a name like his to reverent contemplation. The ancient Egyptians sat in judgment on their dead Pharaohs. The historian does not tell us how the tribunal was composed, or the impartiality of its sentences secured. The enlightened Public opinion of the world is the great Tribunal to which the mighty of the earth are amenable; and who would not prize the bloodless wreath decreed at that bar to Cuvier, and Humboldt, before the golden crown or the blood-stained laurels of monarchs or conquerors? The career of men so illustrious as Humboldt cannot be expected, in many points, to furnish examples for the mass of mankind;—and yet with all the superiority of native talent, which makes him an exception to the ordinary conditions of humanity, there is much in his life and character with which all men sympathize,—which all may emulate as all admire.

We at least in America should neglect no act of appropriate homage to his great name. The foundations of his fame were laid on this continent. Here the most laborious years of his life were passed; for his expedition to Siberia in after life, less laborious even while it lasted, was accomplished in less than a twelvemonth. It seemed indeed as if a Providential interposition guided him to the new world; for it was only after three other projects had been baffled, that the path was unexpectedly opened to America. Having educated himself as a scientific traveller, he first conceived the plan of travelling in Egypt, but the French expedition made it necessary to abandon that design. He next thought of attaching himself to the voyage of circumnavigation, which the French government was preparing under Admiral Baudin. The war with Austria broke out, and diverted the funds assigned by the Directory to this expedition. "Cruelly deceived," says he, "in my hopes, and beholding the plans which I had been forming for several years of my life destroyed in a day, I sought, as at a venture, the most expeditious manner of quitting Europe, and plunging into some enterprise which might console me for what I suffered." With these feelings, and having made at Paris the acquaintance of Mr. Skiöldebrand, the Swedish consul at Algiers, he formed a plan for exploring the Alpine region of Central America. The Swedish frigate, which was to transport the Consul, Mr. von Humboldt, and his friend and companion M. de Bonpland, had not arrived at Marseilles. For two months they expected her in vain, and then learned that she had suffered severely in a storm, and, having put into Cadiz to refit, could not be expected at Marseilles till the Spring. They engaged their passage in a Ragusan sloop for Tunis; war broke out between the Tunisian regency and the French Republic, which made it unsafe to proceed by that conveyance, and they passed into Spain, hoping to find there the means of transit to America. The Minister of Saxony at Madrid procured for his countryman, then thirty years old, a favorable introduction to the President of the Council of the Indies, which resulted in full permission to explore the dominions of Spain in America and the East. This permission was not withdrawn on the fall of M. de Urquijo from power. "During the five years," says Mr. von Humboldt, "that we traversed the new Continent, we perceived not the least appearance of distrust; and it is grateful to me here to recollect, that, in the midst of the most afflicting privations, and struggling against the obstacles which arise from the savage state of the country, we have never had to complain of the injustice of man." Thus it was only after the thrice experienced disappointment of previous projects, that Mr. von Humboldt entered on the great work of exploring the central regions of this Continent; an enterprise most agreeable to his taste and the most likely to reward his investigations, but which, owing to the jealousy of the Spanish government, he had not in the outset ventured to contemplate.

It will not, I think, be denied that the great reputation of Mr. von Humboldt was built upon his American expedition, and the scientific, historical, statistical and miscellaneous works for which it furnished the materials. No one, of course, would claim for that remarkable series of publications, that it stands on a par, as a Philosophical treatise or a digest of natural science, with the "Cosmos." The want of systematic unity alone would oppose such a claim; but it will be agreed, I think, by the students of Mr. von Humboldt's writings, that but for the voyage to America, and the researches connected with it, the observations in every department of natural history which he had made during the progress of the voyage, and the subsequent studies required for the preparation of the numerous works in which the results are given to the world, and which occupied him for twenty years after his return, "Cosmos" would hardly have been composed. Even the remarkable work written in later life, *Examen critique de l'histoire de la Geographie du nouveau continent* (critical Examination of the History of the Geography of the new Continent) was the natural fruit of this American expedition.

It is admitted that Mr. von Humboldt stood at the head of the men of science not only of his own age, but I think we may add, with the diffidence which belongs to such a judgment, of any age. He takes this rank not only in virtue of what he was, but in spite of what he was not. Like Bacon he owes his position in the intellectual world to his grasp of the whole domain of science, and the majestic range of his generalizations. Among the contemporaries of his long life are names that take precedence of his, in almost every department, such as Cuvier, La Place, Sir Humphry Davy, Gauss; I omit the living, which will readily occur to the reader. As there was no one speciality, to which he exclusively gave himself, so there is no disparagement in saying, that in almost every branch of science, there were individuals, who had pushed their researches beyond his. But it belonged to

Humboldt to take an imperial survey of the whole field of Science, and to mould the mass of materials, derived from the individual researches of others, into one grand system;—himself an Intellectual Cosmos, combining the Geographer, the Antiquary, the Geologist, the Chemist, in short every separate title in his own person, akin to the scientific "Cosmos" of his own formation.

Nothing is more characteristic of his career as a philosopher, than the length of time during which his labors, both as an investigator and a writer, were carried on; the continuance of his physical and intellectual activity, long after attaining the age at which the majority of men, weary of toil, satisfied with success, or reconciled to the want of it, sink into repose. He was sixty years old, when, at the often repeated request of the Russian Government, he undertook with Gustavus Rose and Ehrenberg, that expedition to the Oural and Altai mountains of which the fruits are recorded in his *Asia Centrale; Recherches sur les chaines de montagnes et la climatologie comparèe.* "Researches on the mountain chains and comparative climatology of Central Asia." He tells us, in the preface to the first published portion of "Cosmos," that with the exception of the first forty pages of the work, it was wholly written and for the first time, in the years 1843 and 1844, and consequently when he was seventy-four years of age. A fifth volume has been finished within the past year.

But this length of days, however remarkable, is not the only measure of his astonishing vigor of body and mind. It may concern at least those who are not so far advanced in life as to have their habits hopelessly fixed, to know another of the facts, which account for the vast amount of intellectual labor which he was able to perform. Living within a few months to the age of ninety, he lived for all purposes of scientific research and literary labor, another life of forty or fifty years, in consequence of having accustomed himself, from the time he grew up to manhood, to little more than four hours' sleep in the twenty four. I think I can state this on his own authority, for I heard it asserted in his presence, and listened to by him with an assenting smile. If then we consider four hours of daily study, as a pretty good day's work, at least for one whose time must have been so much broken in upon, and who worked to so much purpose, we may compute that, in contenting himself with four hours' sleep, in lieu of the seven or eight required by most men, he really added forty or fifty working years to his four score years and ten. Whether this was the result of the excellence of his constitution, abstinence from the great causes of weariness and exhaustion, cheerful temper, or in some degree of all combined, I cannot say; probably the latter.

At any rate, his disposition was eminently genial. My acquaintance with him began in the winter of 1817–1818 at Paris, where I frequently met him in society. His company of course was eagerly sought, and no individual of eminence was more frequently seen, as far as my means of observation extended, at the dinner table and in the *salons* of Paris. He was then apparently engaged in those geographical researches, of which the results are given in the work above named, on the history of the Geography of this continent. I passed many happy and instructive hours with him at the Institute in looking over the early maps of this country. He was good enough to give me, on leaving Paris, letters to his brother William, at that time the Prussian Minister in London, with whom it was my happiness in that way to become intimately acquainted. In the year 1842 Baron Alexander von Humboldt came to London, (in the suite of the King of Prussia, who visited England to attend the Christening of the Prince of Wales,) and I had the pleasure of renewing my acquaintance with him during his brief stay. It is scarcely necessary to say that, at a time when London was more than usually thronged with the celebrities of Europe, he was the centre of the greatest attraction.

Enjoying his world-wide fame, his feelings were proportionably catholic. Nothing more characterizes his works than the total absence of the spirit of invidious criticism—the canker which eats so deeply into our modern literature. When other authors are named, (and how few are the contemporary writers of solid scientific merit, not named in some part of the long series of his works?) the amplest justice is always done them. He was wholly free from that carping disposition, which can see nothing in a work of science, literature, or art, but its defects; and from that hateful temper, which seeks to build its own reputation or that of a favorite on the ruins of the reputation of a competitor.

I reflect with pleasure that it was in my power, through the medium of my much valued friend Mr. D. D. Barnard, then our Minister at Berlin, to aid a meritorious young artist, Mr. M. Wight, in procuring an opportunity to paint the portrait of Baron Humboldt. This of course was a favor not likely to be asked of a person of such eminence, whose time was so precious, and whom so many artists were eager to paint and to model. Mr. Wight, however, succeeded so well in a portrait of Mr. Barnard, who enjoyed the intimacy of Baron Humboldt, that, on seeing it, he consented to give our young countryman four long sittings. In this way he was able to make an admirable likeness of the Illustrious Philosopher, which has been well engraved in this country.

I was not without hope of seeing him again in the course of the present season. Disappointed in this, it is a subject of pleasing, though sad reflection to me, that the same kind feelings, of which he gave me many valued proofs and assurances in my younger days, were manifested to my children, while on a visit to Berlin last August. "With the scarce legible hand of the old man of eighty-nine," he addresses words of friendly salutation to them and of kindly remembrance to me, from "the traveller of the Cordilleras and the

Steppes of Siberia,"—the joint character in which he wished to be known in after times.

The strange assertion has lately been made, that "Cosmos" is a system of philosophical Atheism, slightly veiled, from motives of prudence, and that even the name of God does not occur in it. This last statement is notoriously inaccurate, and for the first assertion there is not, as far as I know, the slightest foundation. Humboldt, in this as in his other works, proposes to treat only the phenomena revealed to the senses; but he recognizes the reality of spiritual and moral relations, though justly considering them above the province of demonstrative science. Between him and his brother, William, undeniably a man of the deepest religious convictions, there prevailed an entire sympathy, and he cites with approval from the works of the latter, passages which recognize the truth of the Christian religion. On the appearance of the Chevalier Bunsen's "Signs of the Times" in 1855, Humboldt rose from its perusal, and on the same day addressed a letter of two sheets to the Author, expressive of his sympathy and approval. In his "Cosmos" he refers to the Hebrew Scriptures with respect, and even bestows on the Hundred and fourth Psalm that much honored name of "Cosmos," which he had appropriated to the crowning work of his literary life. He distinctly recognizes the purifying influence of the new faith, in contrast with the decaying paganism of the Ancient world. So far is it from being true, that he "knows nothing of a God in Creation," that he asserts in terms, that it was the tendency of the Christian mind to prove, from the order of the Universe and the beauty of nature, the greatness and goodness of the Creator;" and he traces the growing taste for natural description observable in the writers of the new faith, to the tendency "to glorify the Deity in his works."

In denying the imputed Atheism of Humboldt, (on which I may speak more at length on a future occasion,) I build nothing on the occurrence of the name of the Supreme Being in his publications. No writers more freely use the great and sacred name than those of the Pantheistic or, what is the same thing, Atheistic School, meaning, however, not the All-wise All-powerful BEING, who created and who rules with sovereign intelligence the Heavens and the earth, but the aggregate of existing things; making men and beasts, and trees and stones, and dust and ashes, part and parcel of what they call God.

NUMBER THIRTY-TWO.

ITALIAN NATIONALITY.

Reasons of State and Public opinion mingled in the present struggle—Growth of liberal views in Italy—How far the feelings of the masses will affect the result of the contest—The different views of the different parties—Elements of nationality possessed by the Italians—A compact geographical position—A fusion of the original races—One language—A common faith—In all these respects their claim to an independent nationality equal to that of any of the great powers of Europe—To what is the want of it owing?—By no means to the degeneracy of the population.

The eyes of the civilized world are now turned to Italy. To whatever quarter of the globe the descendants of a European stock are scattered, or European languages spoken in the old world or the new, the arrival of every mail is watched for news from Italy. The steamers are too slow; the electric telegraph itself is too slow, to satisfy the intense and universal desire for Italian news. To speculate on the probable course of events, in a struggle like this, is as idle as it would be to speculate on the cast of the dice; particularly when your anticipations are to be recorded in papers, which, like these, are not to be read till a month after they are written. Let us resign the eventful future to the sole arbiter of its mysteries—Time—and dwell for a moment upon the renowned and beautiful field of the mighty contest. Haply we, too, separated by the world-dividing ocean from the conflict, —may derive a salutary lesson from the contemplation.

Two elements totally different mingle in this Titanic struggle, the policy of the Monarchs who conduct it and public opinion. There is so much of personal motive and feeling, so much secret and partially disclosed diplomacy, so much local history which never can be known at a distance, comprehended in all questions of State policy, that they can rarely be judged of with entire accuracy by contemporaries. On questions of this kind appearances at times mislead, deceive, betray ; the Truth is told by Events, and by them only in a continuous series, brought up to a decisive result.

The other element, and more efficient with every year of modern progress, is the spirit and feeling of the masses of the community,—of the People. This has always of course, in the long run, had a vast influence in determining the march of public affairs, especially in all cases where religious convictions are appealed too. But in casting the eye over the pages of Italian History for the last three centuries, it will not be easy to find one great political and territorial arrangement, which has been decided by any thing but State Policy ; the rival interests and power of the Emperor of Germany, and the Kings of France, Spain, Sardinia, and Naples.

This state of things has certainly been changing within the last hundred years. Nowhere was there a quicker or a keener sympathy felt within the American Revolution than in Italy. One of the very best histories of the revolutionary war is the work of an Italian. The Grand Duke Leopold of Tuscany was a liberal and enlightened, though eccentric prince, and encouraged the diffusion of liberal ideas. The Italian publicists of the last century, Beccaria, Galiani, Filangieri, were men of enlarged and generous views. All the substantial conquests gained for rational Liberty, through the influence of the French Revolution, were gained as much for Italy as for France. Her modern popular literature ;—the writers who have won the hearts of the Italian race, however politically or territorially divided, Alfieri, Foscolo, Niccolini, Manzoni and Silvio Pellico, in their best days, and their associates, are all eminently popular. In this way and through these agencies, rendered more powerful and sometimes misdirected by the various secret revolutionary societies, a very powerful public opinion has been formed in favor of political reform, free institutions of government, independence of the stranger, and Italian Nationality. The real strength of this opinion remains to be seen, and with reference to the sentiment of Italian Nationality particularly, time only can show how far it will overcome the previously existing repulsions that have existed between the minor nationalities, so to call them, into which Italy in the lapse of time has been broken up. Thus far, this recently created element of popular strength has disclosed a power and vitality for which, as we apprehend, few persons were prepared. Without firing a gun or shedding a drop of bood, it has won for the allies the greatest territorial acquisition which up to this time (22d of June) they have gained; it has given them the beautiful Grand Duchy of Tuscany and Lucca, the most important and significant occurrence which has yet taken place.

How far this Italian feeling may operate in Lombardy is, at this moment, a question not less important than the strength of Verona and the depth of the Adige. Rivers and fortresses will prove frail bulwarks to the Austrian armies in Lombardy if the masses of her population, rallied by Garibaldi, sustained as they will be by the advancing armies of Sardinia and France, shall rise against them.—And if Tuscany, Parma, Modena, and Lombardy revolt—swept away from Austrian control by popular feeling—how long will the reigning dynasty in Naples be able to resist the torrent? The Papal power alone, from its mixed secular and ecclesiastical character, the latter of which must be respected, perhaps protected by the Emperor of the French, stands upon a somewhat different footing. With respect to all the other Italian States, the embarrassing question already is, not how the Allies shall gain them, but what they shall do with them; not how they shall be rescued from the dominion or the influence of Austria, but under whose dominion and influence they shall fall.

Shall there be a great Italian Republic, coextensive with the Peninsula? Such is the programme of Mazzini and of those whom he represents. These extremists are not a small or feeble handful; on the contrary, it is by him and them, in the present generation, that much of the Italian enthusiasm has been kindled. As usually happens in such cases, they have labored, and more politic and less unselfish reformers have entered into their labors. An Italian Republic is certainly not the programme of the King of Sardinia, nor of Count Cavour, although an Italian Kingdom, coextensive with the Peninsula, may be. But this again surely is not the programme of Sardinia's all-powerful Ally. He is not leading armies into Italy, sevenfold as large as those with which his uncle conquered it, in order that the royalties and the vice-royalties, which the great chieftain won for himself and his family, may be tossed in a heap into the lap of Victor Emmanuel. What the programme of the great "neutral" powers of Europe may be, in reference to Italy, in case it should all be won from the Austrian dominion and influence, is a question wrapped in still greater mystery. The popular voice in England undoubtedly is "Italy for the Italians," and the government of England, into whatever hands it may fall, must respect this unanimous voice. The policy of England will have a great influence over that of Prussia; and if England and Prussia do not interfere, certainly Russia will not. But in all these considerations we see how fearfully the two elements of State policy and popular will are combined in the solution of the great problem.

"Italy for the Italians." What is Italy and who are the Italians, that there should be any doubt or difficulty on the subject; why are they not,—why have they not always been,—a great integral self-sustained member of the national family of Europe? No part of the European Continent seems to be so favorably situated,—at least none more favorably situated, if we except England,—for an independent power. Surrounded by the ocean for more than half the circuit of its coasts, separated by the Alps on the North and on the West, from its powerful neighbors, Nature would seem to have given to Italy in an eminent degree, the first requisite of an Independent Nationality, a compact and defensible geographical position, safe from foreign violence, and possessing within itself every facility for intercommunication between its different parts. In all other material circumstances which nourish the pride of Nationality, a delightful though various climate;—a soil productive of every thing for the food of man from wheat and rice and Indian corn to the olive, the grape, the fig, and the sweet orange;—ports once crowded with the commerce of the world, Genoa, Leghorn, Naples, Palermo, Venice;—mines of iron and copper,—quarries of marble,—broad, navigable lakes,—one noble river and many of the second class,—magnificent forests,—fertile plains, —what is there to be further desired, as far as natural advantages go, toward a liberal patriotism?

The next basis of national unity is a common origin and kindred blood; and here the Italians present as strong a claim to an independent national existence as any of their neighbors. It is true one may, following back their annals, come to the times when invading barbarians broke in upon the unity of the Latin race; nay, one may go back to the *Italia avanti i Romani*, the "Italy before the Romans," when a dozen different races, indigenous and foreign, occupied the Ausonian territory. But as these primitive races, which flourished before the period of authentic history,—(of which no memorial now exists, but ruined specimens of gigantic masonry, a few unintelligible inscriptions, and tombs filled with pictured vases, weapons, and golden ornaments, mute witnesses of a buried world of refinement and power),—were fused into the Italians of the Roman age; so the intruders of later periods, Gauls and Ostrogoths and Lombards, have, from the origin of the political organization of Modern Europe, been fused into the Italian People. This Italian People as we know it, has under various local names, in different portions of the Peninsula, and with various political fortunes, occupied the country for twelve centuries; as their predecessors did for twelve centuries before them. On the score of common origin, the inhabitants of Italy at the present day, have a much stronger claim to be considered a nation than the subjects of the Austrian Empire, in which at least four great races are comprehended,—the Italian, the German the Sclavonian and the Magyar, to say nothing of numerous sub-races, of radically different stock and speaking languages utterly unintelligible to each other.

This brings us to the next great bond of nationality, a common language. From that intellectual chaos,—that second Babel,—into which the civilized world fell, after the downfall of the Roman Empire, the extinction of its language as a spoken tongue, and the establishment of the barbarous races in its conquered provinces and in Italy itself, she was the first of all the newly organized peoples to emerge with a new national language and literature. The English language, as written in the time of Dante, is almost as unintelligible at the present day to all but the English antiquary as a foreign tongue. This Italian language thus early formed,—softened and mellowed in the lapse of five hundred years, but not become obsolete, spoken by the masses with great dialectical differences in the different parts of the Peninsula, but perhaps not greater than those of the English language as spoken in Somersetshire and the lowlands of Scotland, is still the language of Italy.—Dante and Petrarch and Bocnaccio and Ariosto and Tasso, and all the noble line of their successors are read with equal delight by all who read any thing, from Milan to Syracuse and from Genoa to Venice.

Last there is the great bond of a common form of faith, and that from peculiar local causes, operating with a force not known in any country. The Roman Catholic religion is established in every part of *Italy* as the religion of the State, and with the exception of the protestants of the mountain of Savoy, now tolerated throughout Sardinia, and of the protestant chapels attached to foreign legations in the Italian residences, no other form of Christian worship is known.—The acknowledged head of the Roman Catholic faith throughout the world is established in Central Italy, and the devout Italian Catholic regards his country as charged, in a peculiar sense, with the custody of his church. There is nothing like this in most of the States of Europe. England has six or seven millions of Catholic subjects in Ireland, besides the division of her Protestant subjects between the establishment and the various dissenting communions. A similar state of things exists in Prussia; and Catholic France and Austria have a considerable Protestant population. Under constitutional governments like that of England, this diversity of communion, taken in connection with an established church, is the source of manifold embarrassment. It is the great root of bitterness in Ireland, and has caused vast trouble in Prussia. When the contending churches, instead of being branches of the common Faith of Christendom, stand opposed to each other like Christianity and Mahometanism, in the Turkish Empire, they make a genuine and prosperous nationality impossible. They admit no relation, at least as far as modern historical experience goes, but that of dominant and subject races.

On all these grounds, then, of geographical position, race, language, and religion, the Italians might fairly claim to stand as an independent State, in the great family of Nations. There is really no other people in Europe which unites, in the same degree, the four great elements of a prosperous nationality; not either of the great contending powers whose armies now cover her soil; nor England, Prussia, or Russia, who, with hands on their swords, are anxiously watching the progress of the struggle. What, then, *is* wanting to the

Nationality of the Italians; and how does it happen that the People, whose forefathers gave law to the world, have for centuries taken the law from France, from Spain, and from Germany?

I shall attempt an answer to this important question in another paper; in the mean time, I will only observe, in a few words, that the cause of this unhappy state of things is *not* to be sought as is perhaps generally supposed in the degeneracy of the People. Trusting to the hasty generalizations of tourists, who pass a few weeks in the large towns and see the outside of Italian life and manners—the general poverty of the peasantry—the indolence of the Lazzaroni—the swarms of beggars and of monks, in some portions of the country—who see something and hear more of the dissoluteness of manners in high life—and the want of occupation which must exist where there is but little commerce, few manufactures, and no political career, and almost all the springs of industry feel the pressure of arbitrary government, we hastily agree with them, that the people themselves must be degenerate. This, however, is far from being the case. The physical development of the population in Italy, male and female, is, in the aggregate, as far as my observation has extended, quite equal to that of the population of any other part of Europe. Nowhere are finer forms or faces to be seen in places of public or private resort. The Italians are a temperate people, and the climate allows them to live much in the open air; and this in the large towns leads to social and companionable habits, and is everywhere favorable to health. In intellect they are surely not a degenerate race. Their universities still boast accomplished men of science and distinguished scholars in all the faculties; and though the provision for popular education is in none of the Italian States to be compared with that which is made in Prussia, England, and this country, it is respectable in Tuscany, Sardinia, and even Lombardy; and about equal in the other portions of the Peninsula to what it is in most parts of Europe. I attended the meetings of the Association for the Promotion of Science in Italy, which was held at Florence in 1841. About a thousand persons were present and it appeared to me that the discussions and the memoirs compared fairly with those of similar bodies, at which I have been present in England and this country. At the close of its meetings the entire Association was invited to dine by the Grand Duke, and conveyed in carriages at his expense to the halls where the entertainment was served. Each member also received a present of a bronze medal of Galileo, with a copy in quarto of a new volume of his experiments.

Every branch of Letters, except those which can exist only under free constitutions, flourishes and has always flourished in Italy. Some of the most eminent writers scientific and literary of the present day, astronomers, physiologists, antiquaries, publicists, historians, poets, and authors of popular fiction, are Italians. Their museums and libraries are unsurpassed in Europe. Italy is still the land of Art. In the highest walks of painting and sculpture she is excelled by foreigners, but here is an atmosphere of artistic culture, which still draws the foreign artist to her soil. Most of the distinguished German, English, French, and American Artists have studied their art in Italy. In music she still reigns supreme, or divides the empire with Germany alone. Surely it is the extreme of arrogance or igorance to speak of such a people as degenerate.

NUMBER THIRTY-THREE.

ITALIAN NATIONALITY.

It has failed to exist for want of a comprehensive patriotic sentiment—Difficulties in the way of the formation of such a sentiment arising from the multiplication of local governments—Benefits and evils of this multiplication—Probable consequences of the present struggle—Will not result in a republican confederacy—Nor probably in the immediate establishment of an Italian monarchy—But may prepare the way for such an event in future—Lessons to be drawn from Italian history—All other circumstances favorable to an Independent nationality unavailing without a comprehensive patriotism.

I ATTEMPTED in the last paper to show that Italy possesses the great elements of an Independent Nationality,—a compact geographical position, a population fused for twelve centuries into a homogeneous mass, a common language, and a uniform faith; and I urged that whatever else might be the cause why she never has attained an Independent Nationality, it was not the degeneracy of the People. What, then, is wanting? If I were to answer this question, in the words of Washington's Farewell Address, and say that she wanted "Unity of Government," I should be thought merely to say the same thing in other words, affirming that the Italians are not one people, because they are not one people. But the answer would be more significant than it seems. When General Washington said to his fellow citizens, "The Unity of Government which constitutes you one People, is justly *dear to you*," he gave utterance, not to a policitcal truism, but to one of the most important lessons that ever fell from the lips of

Patriot or Sage. Italy, since the Roman Empire broke up, has wanted "Unity of Government," which alone could enable her to stand in the family of Nations as "one People;" one in power, one in counsel, one in patriotism; and she has wanted this Unity of Government, because, to use the simple phrase whose venerable homeliness carries with it a sort of Scriptural solemnity,—because such a unity was not "dear to her." Her populations, in no period of their modern history, had deduced from the various elements of nationality, to which I have alluded, an Italian Patriotism and a National Love.

I admit the enormous difficulties that lay in the way of the formation of such a sentiment. The disintegration of the Roman power in Italy, which held the population together by a Unity of Government, which if not "dear" was strong, took place gradually. Had it passed away in one struggle, like the British power in the Anglo-American colonies, or the Spanish power in the Seven United Provinces, some other Unity of Government might, by the wisdom of man and the exigencies of events, have been substituted in its place. But it was broken up piece by piece. The removal of the seat of Government to Constantinople struck the whole peninsula with a heart-sickness, and changed it, from the seat of Empire into an exposed province. Barbarians and semi-barbarians of every race and from the four quarters of the globe, fell upon her; the Ostrogoths, the Lombards, the Franks, the Saracens, the Normans, each fastening upon the tempting or the assailable side, and then the great secular struggle of the Emperors and the Popes rending her vitals. In the mean time, and in the darkness of the Middle Ages, various local governments, some extensive like Venice, some confined to a few cities or a single city like Florence, and Pisa, and Genoa, sprang up, and became in some cases powerful principalities; Venice and Genoa by their commerce and maritime resources assuming the port and wielding the power of great sovereignties; carrying on war, making foreign conquests, and founding colonies.

Three flagstaffs stood and still stand, or did a few years ago, in the place of St. Mark at Venice, which once bore the banners of her three foreign tributary kingdoms. The peninsula was covered with these independent governments, some powerful, many weak, all jealous of each other, and the most of them engaged in hereditary feuds and eternal wars.

Two consequences resulted from this state of things—one a prodigious quickening of the faculties of men, under the influence of popular institutions in the free cities and little independent republics. A species of municipal liberty was enjoyed, under which the civilization of the modern world grew up in Italy long before it dawned on the West of Europe. The merchants of Florence were the bankers of Europe; the traders of Venice pushed their commercial relations to the furthest East; the mariners of Genoa discovered hidden Continents, before the intelligence of the countries, that now bear sway over fallen Italy, was thoroughly awakened. Nor were learning, and the arts, and the reviving study of antiquity behind her material development. This was the bright side of that multiplication of governments, which kindled a generous emulation and kept aloof the paralyzing effects of a despotic centrality.

But liberal emulation degenerated into bitter feuds and local wars. Duchy was arrayed against duchy; city against city; Milan and Piedmont; Florence and Pisa; Venice and the Ecclesiastical State; in short, at one time or another almost every little principality was at war with some other; or, rather, at no time was there general peace. This state of things cut off all free communication between the different parts of the country. There were probably generations of men in Florence, of whom not an individual ever saw Pistola, except in arms; generations of Neapolitans, of whom not an individual could go in safety to Rome or Venice. In addition to the controversies, that were strictly local and personal in their origin and causes, the great war of Guelf and Ghibelline, the Emperor and the Pope, filled all minds with bitterness and prevented the very thought of "Unity of Government" from being practically conceived for ages. There were several strong principalities, of limited extent indeed, but possessing a vigorous organization, such as the Republic of Venice, the Kingdom of Naples, the Duchy of Milan, the Republic of Florence, and above all the Ecclesiastical State; but they were without sympathy with each other, and upon the whole afforded no basis for a Unity of Government. There was no political arrangement, which could have been conceived and proposed, that would have been "dear" to the populations of these various States, and which would have been embraced by them with patriotic affection.

And so they remained rivals and enemies of each other, and by necessary consequence were obliged to throw themselves into the bloody game of foreign politics; invaded by overwhelming armies with every vibration of the balance of power between Germany, France, and Spain; to say nothing of remoter complications. The successive wars, expeditions, conquests, treaties, and transfers are known to the reader of modern history from the time of Charles VIII. to the Congress of Vienna; a dark and tedious tale.

Another chapter is now commenced in this eventful history. Armies such as never entered Italy before are now in Lombardy; transported by railroads, with a rapidity not dreamed of in former wars; provided with means of destruction, which in range and efficiency transcend those of the old ordnance, almost as much as fire arms exceed bows and arrows; put in motion by orders which fly with electric speed; and certainly sustained by a popular sentiment on the part of the Italians themselves, such as has never accompanied invading armies before. Will this mighty contest, urged with these overwhelming forces, result in any "Unity of Government" for Italy?

That it is not likely to result in a republican government,

either simple or confederate, or in the establishment of any form of polity like the United States, may be considered as certain. A preliminary step would be necessary to that result which cannot possibly be taken, viz., the conversion of the existing monarchies into republics; the existing *monarchies* I say, for whatever the names of the Italian States (except San Marino,) they are all monarchies, and, with the exception of Sardinia, all absolute monarchies. That there is a probability that any of these absolute governments great or small, will become a republic, no person will say who is at all acquainted with the country. There can consequently be no "United States" in one sense of the word, because there will be no States, if by that is meant republican States, to unite.

Will the contest now waged result in establishing a "Unity of Government" of another kind; a monarchical Government, embracing all Italy? As an *immediate* consequence of the movements now in progress, this event is as much out of the question as the other. The ulterior objects of the war are hidden in the deep recesses of Louis Napoleon's mind. He has revealed a portion of his thoughts, a small portion; which is to drive the Austrians from Italy, and he has disclaimed all designs of personal aggrandizement. If, therefore, he succeeds, as in all human probability he will; if no chance shot from a Tyrolese rifle, no malarious fever in the marshes of the Po arrest his career,—(for these are human possibilities)—it is as certain as any thing depending on the vicissitudes of war, that the Austrian rule over Lombardy and Venetia will terminate with this or the next campaign. To all appearance Lombardy at least, if not Venice, will be annexed to Sardinia, a very considerable augmentation of power for the aspiring, energetic, and liberal Sovereign of that kingdom. Parma and Modena, with Tuscany already revolutionized, will follow the fate of the Lombardo-Venetian territory, as far as their late rulers are concerned. Essentially Austrian in their personal and political relations, they can never come back unless some new turn of the wheel of fortune shall cause such a general reaction, as, having once happened within the present generation, may by possibility happen again. With this qualification, we may set down the three principalities just named as lost to Austrian control, and to their hereditary princes. Will they too be annexed to Sardinia? This may well be doubted. A Sardinian Commissioner appeared at Florence and took possession of the abdicated government of Tuscany; but the cousin of the Emperor has followed upon his heels with a French army, and is installed in the Crocetta.—This may be nothing but a measure of precaution to hold Tuscany for the Allies, or it may be a measure of preparation for the establishment of the cousin of Louis Napoleon, with his Sardinian bride, in a new kingdom of Etruria.

With these stirring events in Northern and Central Italy, tending however not to any "Unity of Government," but to the aggrandizement of Sardinia and the establishment of a prince of the Napoleonic dynasty in the heart of the Peninsula, will Naples and the Ecclesiastical State remain unshaken? In Naples the elements of disaffection are widely diffused. An odious Sovereign has gone to his account; that his mountain-load of unpopularity is buried in his grave is not so clear. If the new king as is reported, should wisely turn from his brother's evil ways,—throw open the prisons, lighten the burden of taxation, and reform the traditionary abuses of the State, he may maintain himself on his precarious throne.—But if it should enter into the Imperial plan to realize the *Idées Napoleoniennes*, in Southern Italy; and if the new King shall pursue the line of his government which earned for his father the hatred and contempt of his people and of Europe, the chosen instrument of redress is at hand in the person of Prince Murat.

These are the territorial changes most likely to be made, and to which, arguing from the present premonitions, the minds of men involuntarily turn. They may possibly be made by popular choice. Some great changes *must* be made, to meet the expulsion of the Austrians from Italy, and these now indicated seem to be more probable than that Sardinia will be allowed to monopolize the harvest of the war, which is the alternative possibility. But in these changes, it is scarcely necessary to say, there is no near approach to a "Unity of Government," none to an Independent Italian Nationality, comprehending the entire Peninsula.

But though these events constitute no *near* approach to such a Unity, they seem to be a first step in the right direction. It is much to throw off the foreign yoke from the fairest portions of Northern and Central Italy. Sardinia by extension in that quarter will have been built up into a very considerable Power; and in the lapse of time, by the same process by which the present Monarchy of Spain was consolidated by Ferdinand and Isabella, and the Kingdom of France grew by the successive annexation of Burgundy, Navarre, and the other feudal dependencies, and Prussia has been elevated in a century and a half from a feeble electorate into one of the leading powers of Europe, the Sardinian Monarchy may gradually draw to itself the other Italian States and form at last one powerful Italian Government. This will hardly be the work of one generation.

In the mean time, the state of Italy and the march of events are replete with instruction for us. The history of this beautiful country for ages and its present condition teach us, that the strongest inducements to "Unity of Government," —geographical position, ties of common origin, language, and religion, capacity to do each other unbounded good or evil,—strength if they hold together,—weakness and subjection to foreign powers if the body politic is broken into fragments; —are all of no avail, without some deeper principle of Union. It would be idle at this time;—for the last thousand years it would have been idle;—to say to the Italians, broken up into ten or twelve governments, "it is folly and madness for you to continue thus disunited." Men as individuals and as communities will often do foolish and mad things, and the example of Italy shows that they will persist in doing them through long ages of subjection and suffering.

Again, if before the disintegration of the Roman power in Italy commenced, men had said to themselves "this fine country will never be so unwise as to allow itself to be broken up;—this intelligent people will surely hold together forever; Nature has thrown the circling seas around their coasts, has piled up this great Alpine wall on the frontier, has poured out a noble river through her Northern valley to bind together the States which line its banks; and, in the diversity of natural products, has made each section essential to the prosperity of every other, while internal dissension will be the ruin of all;—they never can, they never will break up,"—if he had said this, he would have uttered words of wisdom, but alas, as the event has proved, not words of prophecy.

The example then of Italy teaches us, in characters written in tears and in blood, that it is not natural advantages, nor capacities for mutual good and harm;—not the material benefits of Union, not the certain woes of separation,—which create and preserve a Unity of Government, though they add strength to the tie when it exists; but it is a generous sentiment pervading the population, a comprehensive patriotism, a reciprocal respect for local interests and feelings, fusing natural elements, however dissimilar and remote, into a well-compacted whole. It is by these alone that a people can be formed, and an independent Nationality asserted.

NUMBER THIRTY-FOUR.

THE LIGHT-HOUSE.

The greatest dangers of the sea are in nearing the land—To obviate some of these light-houses have been erected—The Colossus of Rhodes—The Pharos of Alexandria—Great improvements in modern times—Fresnel—Feelings in contemplating a light-house—The Fitzmaurice light—Number of light-houses in England, France, and the United States—Dangers sometimes of their multiplication—Anecdote of a narrow escape—Minot's Ledge described—Destruction of the iron screw-pile light-house in April, 1851—The violence of the gale described—A new light-house of solid masonry in progress of erection under Capt. Alexander—Progress of the work—An eclipsing light a beautiful object—Via Crucis, via Lucis.

Most persons who navigate the ocean have found out that the greatest dangers of the sea are near the land. In mid-ocean, in a good staunch ship, the skilful sailor feels comparatively safe. There are of course perils even with full sea-room. There are dangers even there, from lightning, and hurricanes which no strength of timbers can resist, icebergs, collision with other vessels, and fire; but all these may be equally encountered on nearing land, with the additional perils of a lee shore. These last are always great, however well aware the navigator may be of his precise situation. He may be driven by a force of winds and currents, which no human skill can withstand, upon frightful rocks or treacherous sands, well knowing beforehand that he is speeding to certain destruction. But it happens not seldom on nearing land after a long voyage, especially in the night, and still more in weather so thick as to prevent taking the sun, that the wretched vessel, ignorant of her position, goes without warning to her doom.

To obviate this danger, as far as it can be done by human art, it has been the practice of the civilized nations to mark the approach to their sea-ports, and the position of dangerous points on the shore, and of sunken ledges and shoals, with light-houses. This practice began in antiquity. Some persons have supposed that the Colossus of Rhodes was a light-house; but the Pharos of Alexandria, which, in the French language, has given its name to structures of this kind, and which was built by one of the Ptolemies in the fourth century before our Saviour, is the oldest of which we have any authentic accounts.

It would be out of place, in a paper of this kind, to attempt a minute description of the great improvements which have been made in light-houses in modern times. As far as their illumination goes, the most important of these improvements may be traced to the elder Fresnel in France, whose system has been adopted in our own, and most, if not all, other countries. It has earned for him the distinction of being "classed with the greatest of those inventive minds, which extend the boundaries of human knowledge, and he will thus at the same time receive a place among those benefactors of the species, who have consecrated their genius to the common good of mankind, and wherever maritime intercourse prevails, the solid advantages which his labors have procured will be felt and acknowledged."

I confess I never behold one of these noble buildings without emotion, I had almost said without reverence, especially when guided by it in safety along an iron-bound coast or between sunken ledges, to the desired haven. Piloted by its trusty beams, streaming over the midnight waters, the skilful navigator shoots boldly along within a hundred rods of some grey promontory, on which the storms of fifty centuries have roared and burst. He has not perhaps for a week had an observation of the sun, but that friendly light in making land more than supplies its place. Unlike most other works of public utility, it is not built for the exclusive benefit of the country at whose expense it is erected. Its light is kindled for all mankind, like the sun which rises on the evil and on the good. In storm and in calm, in summer and in winter, for friend and enemy, citizen and alien, a land-mark by day, and a beacon by night, it stands and shines a beauty and a blessing.

There is nothing I read about with greater pleasure than light-houses, the difficulty of building them on sunken rocks, such as the Eddystone, Bellrock, Skerryvore, and our own Minot's Ledge; the triumphs of the engineer over the tides and the tempest; and the modes of lighting them, which have been so much improved in modern times, by means of lenses, mirrors, newly invented and powerful illuminating substances, revolving and colored lights, and other arrangements for identifying and discriminating light-houses, and preventing their being confounded with each other. It has been said that a narrow and dangerous passage, like the Bosphorus, might, at moderate expense, and by the application of the Fitzmaurice light, be made as light as day, all the way up from the Dardanelles to the Black Sea. Light, I fear, of a different kind, must stream into the Divan at Constantinople, before any thing like this can be expected.

I suppose there is no country in the world that maintains so many light-houses as the United States. In the seventh edition of the Edinburgh Encyclopædia it is stated, that the number of lights in England is 71, in Scotland 51, in Ireland 44; in all one hundred and sixty-six. The number of French lights is given in the same work at upwards of one hundred. By the statement in the report on the Finances for 1857–8, the last which I have seen, the number of light-houses, light-boats, and beacons, on the Atlantic, Gulf, Lake, and Pacific coasts, corrected to 1st of January, 1858, is four hundred and ninety, including those built and building. The average annual cost of each light-house and light-vessel is stated in the same document to be $1,286; or about $643,000 per annum; a sum larger than the entire appropriation for the support of Government, in the first year of President Washington's administration. Whoever will carefully read that list of light-houses, with the marginal notes, will get an idea, not easily to be derived from any other source, of the vast coastwise reach of this country, and the extent of its maritime resources. I think he will also get some new views of the beneficent operations of that United Government, which embraces it all in one jurisdiction, and which moves along the coasts of either ocean, of the Mexican Gulf, and the great inland seas, studding their headlands, and marking their shoals and reefs, with these beneficent structures.

As there is scarce any such thing as unmixed good, even the multiplication of light-houses has its dangers. They may sometimes be confounded with each other, and so betray a vessel into the very danger they were intended to point out. I once heard a pilot say there were too many light-houses on Long Island Sound. He probably would have found it difficult to name any one which he would wish to take away; certainly not if he had occasion to make the port or incur the risk, on account of which it was built. The resources of modern art have been very successfully applied in contriving arrangements by which light-houses may readily be discriminated, and, if the expectations which have been formed of the Fitzmaurice light should not be disappointed, an artificial day may yet be produced along the whole extent of the coast of Long Island Sound.

I was, on one occasion, the near witness and almost the victim of the dangers attending the confounding of light-houses as you near the land. On my first visit to Europe, in the spring of 1815, in a sailing vessel of three hundred and fifty tons, which was thought a sizeable ship in those days, we were in greater danger from the time we approached the Irish and Welsh coast, than in any other part of the voyage. The weather was so thick that we could not see the ship's length before us, and the wind blew us strongly on a lee shore, which we did not at first know to be such, having had no observation for a day or two. The first land we made was an island, with a light-house upon it. When the light-house was first descried through the haze, we took it for a vessel, and steered directly for it. It was apparently not above two miles off. Presently the man at the mast-head cried out, with a frightful voice, "A Light-house. Breakers!" Our captain was led by his reckoning to think it was Waterford light, and supposed that we were driving on the Irish coast. The ship was immediately forced to starboard, to weather the supposed point on the coast of Ireland. In a moment the Captain cried with a yell and an oath, which I have never forgotten, "It's Small's,"—a light-house on the Welsh coast. We were driving head-on toward the breakers. The ship, which in another moment would have struck, was put about; we passed the light-house on the right in safety, but at a very short distance, and within full sight and hearing of the awful breakers we had so narrowly escaped!

Minot's Ledge or Minot's Rocks, form one of the most dangerous points on our north-eastern coast. They lie off Cohasset, in the State of Massachusetts, seventeen miles south-east from Boston. Within thirty years and principally within fifteen years prior to 1848, ten ships, fourteen brigs, sixteen schooners, and three sloops struck on these dangerous rocks, and of these forty-three vessels, twenty-seven were total losses. The outer rock is forty-eight feet long and thirty-six feet broad, at mean low-water level. It being deemed impossible to construct at a moderate cost a light-house of solid masonry on such a rock, exposed to the full sweep of the Atlantic, it was determined to erect a screw-pile iron light-house, on a plan which had been successfully adopted on other points of our coast, and in Europe. This was done at small expense and under a skilful engineer between 1847 and 1849. Either, however, from some suspicion of want of solidity in the rock, into which the iron piles were bolted, or the impossibility of resisting a column of water, driven with such tremendous leverage under the floor of the lantern, it soon began to be doubted whether the structure would stand. A letter written at the light-house by the keeper, after the gale of December 1850, gives a fearful description of its effect upon the building.

"At intervals," says he, "an appalling stillness prevails, creating an inconceivable dread, each gazing with breathless emotion on the other; but the next moment the deep roar of another roller is heard, seeming as if it would tear up the very rocks beneath, as it burst upon us. The light-house quivering and trembling to its very centre, recovers itself just in time to breast the fnry of another and another wave, as they roll in upon us with resistless force."

The same letter says, "the Northern part of the foundation is split, and the light-house rocks at least two feet each way."

On the 16th April, 1851, a terrible storm swept the coast of New England. In the afternoon the light-house on Minot's Ledge was last seen from the shore; at eleven o'clock at night the fog-bell was heard between the fearful pauses of the tempest; no light was seen in it that night; and in the morning its broken fragments, scattered on the shore, proclaimed the fate of the ill-starred structure, and of the two unfortunate keepers, Joseph Wilson and Joseph Antonio, who were lost in it. The iron piles had remained firm in their beds, but had been bent and snapped about six feet from the rock; and the lantern, after having fallen to an inclination of about twenty degrees, thus presenting its flooring to the rushing waves, seemed to have been driven forward with a force that tore the piles asunder.

After the disastrous result of the experiment of the screw-pile light-house, nothing remained but to build a tower of solid masonry, at whatever cost. The work was projected by General Totten, the accomplished head of the Department of Engineers, and its execution confided to Captain B. S. Alexander, who had already given satisfactory proofs of his ability as a constructing engineer. The tower is now in progress of successful erection, a cone thirty feet in diameter at the base, to be seventeen feet and a half at top; ninety feet high, the lower forty feet to be solid. The greatest difficulty has been in forming the foundation-pit in the rock, which was to be cut down two or three levels, and the whole circle of thirty feet finely hammered. To give greater solidity to the work the levels are fastened to each other by galvanized iron bolts, and the solid masses of hewn granite dovetailed and cemented together. "On Tuesday morning, the first day of July, 1855," said Capt. Alexander last October, "just as the sun tipped the wings of the seagull, as it took its flight over the wave, we struck our first blow on the Minot. The first year we worked upon it 130 hours; in 1856, 157 hours; in 1857, 130 hours and 21 minutes; in 1858, to September 30th 208 hours,—in all 625 hours 21 minutes." As the work advances in height above the level of the tide, it will of course admit of a full day's work; and Captain Alexander expressed the opinion last October, that if no unforeseen cause of delay occurred, it might be finished in two years. It will when completed take rank with the Eddystone and Skerryvore as a piece of fearless engineering.

Among the ingenious devices for distinguishing lighthouses from each other, where there is any danger of confusion, are the arrangements, to which I have already alluded, for revolving, eclipsing, flashing, and intermittent lights, which, with the addition of white and red color, are capable of almost indefinite variety. A more pleasing spectacle is not to be seen on earth than a revolving or intermittent light, which disappears for a few seconds; then sparkles white or red; beams out gradually to its full illumination; wanes and disappears but to return; seen of a moonless night upon some lonely promontory which rears its grim buttresses from the moaning waters, and enabling the homeward bound vessel to thread its way to its destined port through narrow channels and roaring breakers, regardless of the tempest ready to burst from the overhanging cloud. Such an eclipsing light, seen during the contemplative watches of a sleepless night on the 8th of July, 1855, suggested the following lines:

THE ANTITHESIS OF LIFE:

Via Crucis, Via Lucis.

It goes in and comes out, now it fades, now is bright,
And it guides by its darkness, as well as its light.
So a word fitly spoken is potent to teach,
But silence sometimes talketh better than speech.
Force winneth the battle, force driveth the throng,
But patient endurance, through weakness, is strong.
A gay sparkling glance is right joyous to see,
But a deep thoughtful eye hath more witchery for me.
The king rules his realm by a word, by a whim,
But the babe that can't speak,* from his cradle, rules him.
So the pride of this life treads the path of renown,
But the way of the Cross is the way of the Crown.

* Written shortly after the birth of the Prince Imperial of France.

NUMBER THIRTY-FIVE.

PRINCE METTERNICH.

Should he be classed with the Illustrious dead of 1859?—His success civil not military—Not cruel nor bloodthirsty—His government mild for an absolute despotism—Is Lombardy an exception?—Anecdote of Silvio Pellico and the other conductors of the Conciliatore—Metternich's first service at the Congress of Rastadt—The four coalitions—His conduct as the Austrian minister in France—Anecdote from Capefigue of doubtful authenticity—Was he the projector of the marriage of Napoleon I. with Marie Louise?—Rules Austria in peace for thirty-three years—Sinks at last in 1848—His exile, return, and the close of his career as a private man.

I HAVE in some late Numbers of this series spoken of the ILLUSTRIOUS dead of 1859, Prescott, Bond, Hallam, and Humboldt; all surely entitled to that designation. Since those papers appeared, another name has been added to the list of the distinguished dead of this year, to which the epithet "illustrious" must with greater hesitation be applied. If talent in his peculiar vocation, rank, power, and—during a long course of years—success, make a man justly "illustrious," then was Prince Metternich entitled to that appellation. He belonged to the privileged class of his native country; he possessed by nature all the personal endowments which, in the old world, most promote success in life. He received a thorough German education for a public career; he married in his youth a daughter of the prime minister, and rose from step to step in positions of trust, responsibility and power, till he became, under a feeble and confiding sovereign, the real ruler of the oldest and one of the most powerful monarchies of Europe. This position he filled for forty years, in the most difficult times,—in a period of general political disorganization, and in direct collision with the great military genius of the age, of whom more and longer than any other individual he was the direct antagonist. All this, in the ordinary estimate of human endowment and performance, must be admitted to make a man illustrious; and yet I should be ashamed to class him with the great intellectual princes who have enlarged the bounds of human knowledge; who have traced the pathways of Providence in the fortunes of nations; who have discovered new worlds in the depths of the heavens; or like Humboldt have ruled with serene mastery over the whole empire of science.

Some things, however, may be said to the honor of Metternich's genius and career, although his character is one with which I have no sympathy. In an age when every thing bowed to the supremacy of the sword, and single battles decided the fate of Empires;—when men rose from the ranks and shook the world;—Metternich attained the elevation which I have described, without the *prestige* of military reputation. I am not aware that he ever held any rank in the army; he certainly never served. He rose with fair but not commanding advantages of birth, under the most intensely aristocratic government in Europe, by the force of talent, education, manners, untiring industry, and a resolute purpose. I do not deny that first and last he had many adventitious aids, as he had some drawbacks; but, in an age in which, in almost every country, England not excepted, the greatest soldier was the greatest man, Metternich's undisputed ascendancy was earned not in the field but in the cabinet.

It may also be said to the credit of Metternich, that, though his principles of government were those of unmitigated despotism,—the exercise of sheer power,—there does not seem to have been any thing tyrannical and still less any thing blood-thirsty in his nature. He started with the principle of the Right Divine. He interpreted *Dei Gratia* literally ;—he was a strict constructionist of the straitest sect in that school. But having laid down this theory of government, and practically placed his administration on this platform, he studied the good of the subject. He would not, it is true, allow him to study his own good, by any intermeddling with public affairs. He enforced a severe censorship over the press; he annihilated political journalism; he shut out all foreign literature, which he deemed dangerous to Church or State, with greater jealousy than he did the plague,—for you could enter Austria from Smyrna or Alexandria after a reasonable quarantine, but there was no quarantine for a pestilential volume. But the highways, as I know from experience, were safe in the loneliest passes of the Carpathians,—private justice, when no reasons of State interfered, and although a little apt to get buried under a cartload of written pleadings, (but that is the fault not of the government but of the code,) was faithfully, if not promptly, administered; common schools were encouraged, scientific institutions and scientific researches patronized, and, in a word, the material well-being of the people was cared for.

In his person, Prince Metternich was a man of courteous manners, and temperate and industrious habits,—a hard worker, a patron of art, a collector of books, paintings, and statuary, a lover of music, a hospitable and genial host. With every thing to turn his head and harden his heart, he was, individually, what may be called an unaffected, honorable, and amiable man. Wielding for forty years absolute power under weak princes,—reminding you of the Mayors of the palace in the early French Monarchy, under the reign of the *insensati* (silly) Kings, there are probably few rulers to whose door less wanton cruelty can be laid,—at any rate less shedding of blood.

His government of Lombardy and Venice may be thought to furnish an exception to this remark; it was no doubt an iron rule, but this only in one respect, viz.: that all political action and word were forbidden under the severest penalties, enforced by a military police and an unrelenting criminal code. Regarding the Austrian power not as established and accepted, but simply as encamped in Lombardy, every thing that looked like the manifestation of disaffection, or even open opposition to the government was regarded, not merely as dangerous, but as treasonable, and as such repressed. But there was some show of moderation even here. Men were not taken out of their beds and shot, nor blown away from the mouth of cannons; but they were sent to the Piombi of Venice and to the Spielberg in Moravia.

I made the acquaintance of Silvio Pellico at Milan in 1819, and of some of his liberal friends. They were just commencing the publication of a political journal, which they called the "Conciliatore," which means in Italian pretty much what it means in English. To an American it seemed a remarkably milk-and-water concern. It had the fault, happily almost unknown in this country, of discussing political questions with good temper, and confuting your adversary without calling him hard names. In short, it might be called tame. In the few numbers which had come out at that time, I did not see the Italian equivalents of the expressive epithets of "hypocrite," "coward," "swindler," or "liar" applied to a single official from the throne to the police station. The Emperor was not even called a "fool," nor the vice-regal Archduke a "tyrant." It is plain that poor Silvio and his associates had very little idea of the beauty of a free press; and they suffered accordingly. Like all "conciliators" between the extremes of opinion, they pleased the ultraists of neither party. Those who sought the emancipation of Italy at the point of the dagger, disdained their moderation; while the Public Prosecutor looked upon it as a mere pretext to insinuate the treason which they dared not openly teach. I deemed it an act of kindness to intimate these views to the conductors of the *Conciliatore*, and half in jest told Silvio, that I should hear of him and his associates in the Spielberg in three months. The prophecy proved true with a little difference of time; and this was under the government of Prince Metternich.

The London "Times" has given us a sketch of the career of the great statesman,—principally borrowed from Vapereau's *Dictionnaire des Contemporains,* or from some common source,—which has been generally copied, and need not be here repeated. He figured in Imperial ceremonials, while yet a youth of seventeen, at the coronation of the Emperor Leopold, but he commenced the business of life at the Congress of Rastadt. This was a diplomatic meeting, called to make the territorial arrangements, required to carry into effect the secret articles of the treaty of Campo Formio, concluded between Austria and France in 1797. Metternich attended on behalf of the Westphalian Princes; and the fruitless negotiations of this body protracted to the year 1799, ended at last in an event,—the assassination of the French ministers and the seizure of their papers,—which, the historian tells us, at the time "excited the utmost indignation and horror throughout Europe;" but which now—so full has Europe supped of horrors, in the sixty years which have elapsed—will be words without meaning to the most of my readers.

Of the great coalitions in Europe, by which the four other leading powers strove to arrest the progress and shatter the system of Napoleon, Metternich was incontestably the contriver and the head. Their vitality and strength were due to his energy and tact, and to British subsidies. No one, I suppose, of any party, will now blame an Austrian Minister for seeking to stop the march of Napoleon the First to Universal Empire. Granting his ulterior objects to be as beneficent as they are represented in the *Idées Napoleoniennes,* it could not be expected that the dynasties, whose extinction was the condition of his success, should acquiesce without a struggle in their doom. Had Metternich been as liberal in his general principles of administration, and as regardful of the "nationalities" as Kossuth himself, it could not be expected of an Austrian Minister to lie down in the dust before the chariot wheels of a foreign conqueror. That he should, as the Austrian representative to the French Imperial Court, endeavor to mislead Napoleon as to his own feelings and the policy of his government, is certainly not to be justified by the rules of a severe morality, which makes the truth on all occasions the first duty of governments and of men. But it could hardly be expected of the envoy of the weaker and the menaced government, pitted against the most consummate diplomatic finesse, backed by the most overwhelming military power in modern history, to practice upon the rules of Roman or Christian virtue. There is a proverb which need not be repeated, relative to the length of the spoon, which it is convenient to use, when you sup with a personage who shall be nameless. A similar precaution will not be severely blamed by the charitable, on the part of the foreign minister, compelled to cope with M. de Talleyrand.

An anecdote is related by Alison, on the authority of Capefigue, of which the authenticity may be doubted. It is to this effect, that when M. de Metternich was at first accredited to the French Court, Napoleon remarked to him, "you are very young to represent so powerful a monarchy." His reply is said to have been, "Your Majesty was not older at Austerlitz." As Napoleon himself was at the moment but thirty-seven, and had been for several years at the head of the French government, it does not seem probable that he should have thought thirty-three very young for an Austrian Minister. The reply ascribed to Metternich is still less likely to have been made. Such an allusion to a battle, in which the armies of his country were defeated, and the Sovereign he represented was humiliated, never passed the lips of a patriot or a gentleman, and Metternich was both. It is one of the epigrams, which sensation writers put into the mouths of the great personages they attempt to describe.

After Wagram, despairing of further resistance to Napoleon, and intent upon building up Austria, from the ruins of four vast wars, which she had fought, though unsuccessfully, in thirteen years, Prince Metternich, being placed at the head of her government, on the retirement of Count Stadion, came to the conclusion, that a durable peace and intimate relations with France were absolutely necessary to the successful promotion of this policy. With this in view, acting upon the traditions of the House of Austria,* which had passed into a proverb three centuries before, he determined to promote a marriage between Napoleon and an Austrian archduchess. Alison appears to represent Metternich himself as having stated to the late Lord Londonderry, that it was his first care, on acceding to power, "to arrange and bring about the marriage." The common account gives the credit of this "arrangement" to Fouché. A more probable opinion is, that it was the conception of Napoleon himself;—not a man to have matches made for him by his own ministers or those of any other government. By whomsoever conceived, it was an inauspicious thought; but one which might well catch the imagination of an Austrian Minister, weighing sacraments, and duties, and affections in the scale of a worldly ambition. It was one of the great mistakes of Napoleon the First. Napoleon the Third did a wiser and a worthier thing, when, disdaining to engraft his dynasty on the reluctant royalties of Europe, he raised a "parvenue" partner, to use his own ex-

* The following celebrated epigram is ascribed to Mathias Corvinus, King of Hungary:

Bella gerant alii, tu, felix Austria, nube,
Nam quæ Mars aliis dat tibi regna Venus:

which may be imperfectly rendered,

"Let others war, thou, Austria, wed the throne,
Mars gives them crowns, by Venus thine are won."

pression, selected for her amiable personal qualities, to his imperial throne.

From the downfall of Napoleon, Metternich ruled Austria under her nominal Sovereigns, for thirty-three years. He it was who, availing himself of the religious mysticism which had taken possession of the Emperor Alexander of Russia, projected, with that monarch, the Holy Alliance. At the great European Congresses which were held under its auspices at Aix la Chapelle, Laybach, and Verona, he was the great representative of the political system of the three absolute governments of the North and East of Europe. He took to himself the credit of having, mainly by his skill and firmness, staid the advances of what he called revolutionary ideas, but what the enlightened masses of the civilized world regard as progress and reform. He had some reason to look upon the fruit of his labors with complacency, for to all appearance they had been successful. Every revolutionary movement in Italy, from Lago Maggiore to Calabria, had been crushed; and though France and Spain had adopted liberal institutions, those powers were neither of them in a condition to set on foot a dangerous propagandism in foreign States. In Russia, Prussia, and his own Austria his system reigned. The territorial arrangements of the Great Captain, with whom he had waged so fearful a struggle had, for the most part, proved transitory, and while every Sovereign who had ruled when the Congress of Vienna was in session, and almost all his colleagues and associates had disappeared from the stage, he was still in the possession of his faculties, his power, and his honors.—He is said, however, to have felt that the ground beneath his feet was hollow. He had chained the tempest but he heard it roaring in its caverns. It is constantly told of him, that he was accustomed to say "things will last as long as I do,—but after me the deluge." The deluge burst before he expected it. The rains descended, and the floods came, and the winds blew. They prostrated his government, his system, and his fortunes. He reluctantly yielded up the seals of office to his imperial master, who cowered before the rising storm; and while the rabble of Vienna was sacking his princely residence, and madly scattering gilded furniture and priceless works of art in fragments over his trampled lawns, he fled for his life to England. The deluge subsided, and he returned to his estates and his honors, but never more to the possession of power. He enjoyed, however, some years of tranquil retirement, consulted by his successors and happy in his children, and died before his aged eyes were again pained by the sight, with which they had so often been sadly familiar, the inauguration of another tremendous era of Austrian Calamity.

NUMBER THIRTY-SIX.

SEVEN CRITICAL OCCASIONS AND INCIDENTS IN THE LIFE OF WASHINGTON.

Instances of an overruling Providence in the lives of distinguished men, and signally in the life of Washington—His brother Lawrence an officer in the expedition under Admiral Vernon against Carthagena—Plan for placing George in the British Navy, and a midshipman's warrant procured—His mother opposes the plan, and it is abandoned—Accompanies his brother to Barbadoes at the age of nineteen and takes the small-pox—Terrific nature of that disease before the discovery of Vaccination—Appears in the American Army in 1775 and afterwards—Great dangers to which Washington was exposed on his mission to Venango—Hazards of an excursion at that time in the districts occupied by the Indians—Their cruelties—Narrow escape of Washington on the return—Concluding reflection.

In the biographies of distinguished persons, we sometimes read the account of very narrow escapes from great dangers, or of incidents not seemingly very important at the time, but on which it appears in the sequel that the whole course of after life depended. Such escapes and such incidents irresistibly lead the mind to acknowledge a controlling Power, which watches over great and precious lives, and shapes the course of otherwise unimportant events to the accomplishment of momentous results. Modern Philosophy, I am aware, disdains these inferences, and prefers to see in these, as in all else that happens in the world, nothing but a blind fate or a mechanical necessity; as if that system did not present equal difficulties as a philosophical theory, while it extinguishes the light of an overruling Providence in the world; without which our life is a weary and cheerless pilgrimage.

I know no person in whose life these narrow escapes and

these critical occurrences are more numerous and striking than they are in that of Washington; and as his services in peace and war, and his whole public career and character stand, in many respects, without a parallel in human history, I find it impossible not to trace the hand of a protecting, guiding, and overruling Power on occasions which, in the life of an ordinary man would have passed without notice.

One of the events, in which these remarks find their application, was the project formed by the relatives and friends of Washington, when he was but fourteen years old, to place him in the Navy of Great Britain. He possessed by nature the military turn, which had been manifested by several members of his family, not only from their first arrival in this country, but before the emigration from England. His elder brother, Lawrence, belonged to one of the battalions of American troops, which sailed from America to reinforce the army under General Wentworth and Admiral Vernon, in the unsuccessful expedition against Carthagena in 1740. Several other Virginians were in the same expedition. Among them Mr. William Fairfax and Captain Dandridge, a relation, I presume, of the lady who afterwards became General Washington's wife. Captain Lawrence Washington and Captain Murray are named as the commanders of a battalion of two hundred Americans, who, on the 19th of March, 1740, aided in the assault, "with wonderful resolution and success," of a battery which commanded the entrance into the harbor of Carthagena. This is the only occasion on which I find his name in Rolt's history of the war; but his conduct is known to have been such as to win for him the respect of his superiors. He formed an intimate personal acquaintance with the Admiral, who fortunately escaped from that most disastrous expedition against Carthagena, without loss of the credit acquired by the capture of Porto Bello. On the return of Captain Lawrence Washington to America, at the close of the war, he gave to his newly erected mansion at Hunting Creek, the ever memorable name of Mount Vernon, in honor of the popular naval hero under whom he had served.

It was natural that these circumstances should make the naval service of Great Britain a familiar subject of conversation in the family circle; and that George, then a boy under fourteen, being a frequent resident at Mount Vernon, should have his juvenile imagination kindled with the tales of naval prowess and glory, which were so often repeated in his presence. It is not known whether the idea of entering upon that career originated with himself or was suggested by his brother and other friends. At all events a Midshipman's warrant was obtained for him, and it is even said, that his clothes were packed to go on board ship. His mother alone never cordially approved the plan, and her misgivings increased as the time for putting it in execution drew near. Mr. Sparks quotes a letter from Mr. Jackson, a friend of the family, apparently written from Fredericksburg to Captain Lawrence Washington at Mount Vernon, in which he says:

"I am afraid Mrs. Washington will not keep up to her first resolution. She seems to dislike George's going to sea, and says several persons have told her it was a bad scheme. She offers several trifling objections, such as fond, unthinking mothers habitually suggest; and I find that one word against his going has more weight than ten for it."

She persevered in her opposition, and the project was abandoned. Had Washington at the age of fourteen entered the navy of Great Britain, then engaged in the war of 1744 with France, as soon afterwards in that of 1756, one of two things would unquestionably have happened. He would either have fallen a victim to the hardships and exposures of the service, or he would have lived and grown up an officer —no doubt a gallant and distinguished one—in the British Navy. I cannot therefore but regard the abandonment of this plan, when it was on the point of being consummated, and in consequence of the mother's opposition, as an occurrence in

Washington's life well worthy to be ascribed to an overruling Providence.

The second event, in reference to which, though of an entirely different character, I am disposed to make a similar reflection, occurred on occasion of his voyage to Barbadoes a few years later. This was the only occasion on which Washington ever left the American continent. His brother, Captain Lawrence, whose constitution, naturally feeble, had been impaired on the fatal expedition against Carthagena, by the effect of the climate, fell into a decline, and was ordered to the West Indies; his much loved brother, George, was selected to accompany him. They sailed for Barbadoes in the month of September, 1751, and arrived there in five weeks, George being then nineteen years of age. He had scarcely been a fortnight in the island, when he was attacked with small pox in "the natural way." The attack was severe, but skilful medical attendance and the assiduities of his brother and friends were successful. He recovered in about three weeks, but he showed slight marks of the disease the rest of his life.

The reader of the life of Washington, perhaps, passes over this incident as one of comparatively little consequence. Contrasted with the stirring events of his military and political career, it hardly attracts notice. But it may be doubted whether in any of his battles he was in equal danger. The small pox, a century ago, when vaccination was unknown and inoculation not universally practised, was a name of terror. Of all the shocks that flesh is heir to, few transcended this loathsome disease, in the havoc which it caused and the dismay which it inspired. Wherever it appeared, all the moveable population fled in consternation. By the young and the fair it was dreaded worse than death: to survive it with features, once beautiful, but ploughed into ridges, was a life-long sorrow. It carried off one fourth-part of those whom it attacked, and of the survivors many who lived, disfigured for life, were left with enfeebled frames and morbid predispositions. If it entered an army, it was a foe more to be dreaded than embattled hosts; if it broke out in a populous city, those who could not fly were decimated. So frightfully contagious was it, that no attendance could be procured for the sufferer, except from those who had passed the ordeal.

But fearful as this malady was, in the extent of its ravages, it belongs to that class of diseases of which, by a mysterious law of our nature, our frames are, generally speaking, susceptible but once. Of those who survived it, it has been calculated that the proportion to whom a second attack proved fatal, was, under the most favorable circumstances, but one in seventy-five. This reduced it far below the level of many other diseases as an object of alarm; and in diminishing its terrors, diminished in the same proportion one of its most disastrous effects.

Thus it came to pass that, in the morning of his days, by a visitation which was at the time of the most alarming character, Washington became (humanly speaking) safe from all future danger from this most formidable disease. The war of the Revolution had hardly begun before the importance of this circumstance was apparent. The small pox broke out among the British soldiery in Boston, in the autumn of 1775; and reports were brought to General Washington, (which he charitably discredited,) that it was intended by the enemy to communicate it, by means of those who left the city, to the American Army. It did make its appearance outside the lines of circumvallation, and as a measure of precaution, the soldiers of the besieging army were inoculated. At this time, however, that practice was still viewed by many with dislike; and the fear of the disease, either by natural or artificial contagion, was one great cause which discouraged enlistments. It prevailed in the army in Canada, (where Major-General Thomas, of Massachusetts, died of it the next spring;) at Ticonderoga; and in 1777, at Morristown. On this last occasion of its appearance, Washington remarked in a letter to

Patrick Henry, then Governor of Virginia, where inoculation was forbidden by law:

"You will pardon my observations on Small Pox, because I know it is more destructive to the army, in the natural way, than the enimies' sword, and because I shudder whenever I reflect upon the difficulties of keeping it out!"

Such was the fearful character of the danger from which Washington was protected from the age of nineteen. The loathsome pestilence, which in 1751 menaced the life of the youthful Virginian traveller in Barbadoes, was in reality a charm which rendered the Beloved Commander of the American Armies in 1775, and in the following years of the contest, all but invulnerable, in the presence of a foe "more destructive than the enemy's sword." If to refer this to an overruling Providence be a superstition, I desire to be accounted superstitious.

On the memorable expedition of Major Washington to the post of the French military Governor at Venango in 1753 —his first entrance into active public duty of that kind—he was exposed to dangers from which his escape was all but miraculous. The journey of five or six hundred miles was made in the winter season, through a country as yet unsettled, and a considerable part of it still traversed by the natives of the continent, many of whom were under French influence. Perils of no ordinary kind attended him every step of the way. Few persons, probably, at the present day have an adequate idea of the danger, which at that time attended any excursion from the settled portions of the country into the districts still occupied by the native tribes. Frontier war even among civilized races is ever unrelenting; the collisions of the civilized and barbarous races in the mutual reactions of provocation and vengeance, have in all times been deplorably merciless. In 1753 a new element was added to the bitterness of border warfare, by the efforts of the Provincial governments both of France and England to secure the co-operation of the natives in the approaching struggle. It is scarcely necessary to say to those who are familiar with the dark accounts and traditions of Indian warfare, what this co-operation implied. The native races, not yet broken by the power nor enervated by the contact of the dominant races, still practised those revolting cruelties on their prisoners, which cannot be read without sickening horror. After Braddock's defeat—two years later than General Washington's journey to Venango, the English soldiers who surrendered themselves as prisoners, were, within sight and hearing of Fort Duquesne, made to undergo at the stake for hours, the most exquisite tortures which the human frame could support, or savage ingenuity inflict. Such were the perils to which Washington was exposed, in voluntarily undertaking this dangerous expedition. Traders from the Anglo-American settlements had already been made prisoners, in some cases sent to France, in some, it was said, put to death in the wilderness, where a life more or less, even in time of peace, was of little account.

Having fulfilled his mission, and fearing that sinister influences might be exerted over the Indians on his return, he was compelled to accelerate his departure. As he traversed the woods with his pack on his back, attended by a single companion, their treacherous savage guide at night-fall turned, and at a distance of fifteen paces, fired but without result, at Washington and his companion. Escaped from this imminent peril, but well knowing that the Indians were on their trail, they pursued their journey foot-sore for the whole of a December night, till they reached the Alleghany river then filled with drift ice. It could be crossed only on a raft which they labored all day with "one poor hatchet" to construct. In attempting to cross the river on this raft, Washington while using the setting pole, was thrown with violence into the water where it was ten feet deep, and saved his life only by clinging to a log. Unable to force the raft to either shore they passed the night, in garments which froze to their bodies, upon an island in the middle of the stream. Had the morning found them there, unable to reach the left bank, the tomahawk and the scalping knife would, in all human probability, have been their fate. But the cold which was so intense, that Washington's companion—hardy woodman as he was, froze his feet—froze the river between the Island, where they had passed the night, and the left bank of the Alleghany, and at dawn they crossed in safety.

I have no metaphysics to bandy with those who can reflect on the career which was in reserve for Washington, and who can see nothing in his escape from the rifle of his guide, from capture from the pursuing savages, from imminent danger of drowning, and from his unsheltered exposure in frozen garments for a livelong December night, but the ordinary adventures of a bold young man on the wilderness frontier. I see rather in these perils and in these escapes, the hand of Providence ;—and hear in them a voice, which in the language of the devout poet, announced the high purpose :—

> "To exercise him in the Wilderness :
> There shall he first lay down the rudiments
> Of his great warfare, ere I send him forth
> To conquer."

NUMBER THIRTY-SEVEN.

SEVEN CRITICAL OCCASIONS AND INCIDENTS IN THE LIFE OF WASHINGTON.

Braddock's expedition in 1755—Washington a volunteer aid—Falls ill on the way and sent back to the reserve—Joins the army the day before the engagement—Beautiful scene of war on the morning of the battle—Surprise and total defeat of General Braddock's army—Gallant conduct of Colonel Washington throughout the engagement—Great danger to which he was exposed—Interview with an Indian Chieftain on the Kanawha in 1770—Prediction in 1755 of his future career—Reflection by Mr. Sparks—Washington's visit to New York in 1756, where he is the guest of Beverley Robinson—Makes the acquaintance of Mary Philipse—She marries Captain Orme and adheres with her family to the royal cause.

THE next instance of a Providential interposition in the life of Washington, to which I shall allude, took place two years later. The mission to Venango, which I mentioned in my last Number, was undertaken by direction of the Governor of Virginia, for the purpose of ascertaining the strength of the French on the north-western frontier, and their probable designs in that quarter. The following year, (1754,) though the war was not declared in Europe till 1756, a small military force was sent in that direction, under Colonel Washington, which after some partial success, was forced by the greatly superior strength of the enemy to a disastrous retreat. It is mentioned by the historians as a striking coincidence, that he was compelled, under capitulation, to evacuate "Fort Necessity," (so called to indicate the straits to which he had been reduced,) on the 4th of July 1754;—the day to be afterwards rendered, and in no small degree by his inestimable services, forever memorable in the annals of America.

Such were the courage, skill, and energy displayed by the youthful commander in these trying scenes, that he came out of the campaign not only without reproach but with enhanced reputation.

The following year a great effort was made by the mother country to repair the disasters of 1754, and to secure an ascendency on the banks of the Ohio; for this was the limit of Anglo-American ambition before the seven years' war. The wildest imagination had not yet grasped the mighty domain which stretches westward to the peaceful ocean and the setting sun. Early in the spring of 1755, two regiments of regular British troops, commanded by General Braddock, a brave and experienced officer, but arrogant, passionate, and self-willed, arrived in Virginia, and were moved westward toward the passes through the Alleghanies. Colonel Washington had retired from the army, disgusted by the regulations, which gave precedence to officers holding under the royal commission over their seniors of the same rank in the provincial service, thus placing him under those whom he had commanded in the former campaign. Influenced, however, by strong attraction toward military life, and animated by fervent patriotic zeal, he accepted the invitation of General Braddock, (to whom he had been made known by reputation, as the officer of the greatest experience and ability in the provincial service,) to join his military family as a volunteer aid. On the passage through the mountains Colonel Washington was attacked by a fever, with such violence that the surgeon was alarmed for his life, and the General required him to fall back upon the reserve, which was proceeding slowly with the baggage and heavy artillery. To this Washington consented, only on condition that he should be allowed to join the main body before an engagement. Placed under the care of the surgeon in a wagon, reduced by disease, and suffering from the uneasy motion of the vehicle, he remained with the reserve two weeks, and was only able to return to Head Quarters on the 8th of July, the eve of the battle of the Monongahela, a day disastrous beyond all others in the annals of America.

Weak and exhausted, but strong in the spirit, Washington mounted his horse the following day. He was often heard to say in after life—

> "That the most beautiful spectacle he had ever beheld was the display of the British troops on this eventful morning. Every man was neatly dressed in full uniform, the soldiers were arranged in columns, and marched in exact order,—the sun gleamed from their burnished arms, the river flowed tranquilly on their right, and the deep forest overshadowed them with solemn grandeur on the left." *

The army was within less than fifteen miles of Fort Duquesne, (afterwards Pittsburg,) and confidently expected to effect its reduction in the course of the day.

Washington, though but one night in camp, had in vain besought General Braddock to accept the proffered aid of the friendly Indians, and employ them in reconnoitering the broken and wooded region through which the army was to pass, on the way to its destination. The advice was disdainfully rejected by the General, who placed full reliance on the discipline and steadiness of King's troops. Unhappily he knew the game of war only as it was practised in those days by rules of art, with the regularity of a chess board. The terrific tactics of the wilderness; the crack of the rifle from the invisible foe; the fearful war-whoop; the stealthy savage creeping on his belly through the thicket up to the saddle girths of his startled enemy; the gleaming scalping-knife; and the effect of these unexperienced terrors on the imaginations of European troops were unknown to him.—His army,

* This beautiful description is taken from Mr. Sparks' life of Washington, in the first volume of his edition of Washington's writings. Since the appearance of this invaluable work, no one has had occasion to write or to speak of Washington, without feeling himself under the highest obligations to Mr. Sparks. A very interesting monograph on Braddock's expedition by Winthrop Sargent, Esq. appears among the publications of the Pennsylvania Historical Society.

in magnificent array and in order of battle, had in the course of the morning crossed the winding stream twice without accident, and the advance under Colonel Gage, (afterwards the last Colonial Governor of Massachusetts,) was ascending the first elevation above the meadow, when a sharp volley from an unseen enemy in the woods was heard. Presently a heavy discharge followed in front and on the flanks; the advanced party in dismay fell back on the main body hastening up to their relief;— a force of two hundred French and six hundred Indians (numbers far inferior to those of the British army) rushed from the thicket; the dismayed regulars fired at random on friend and foe; and after a wild and murderous conflict of three hours, fled panic stricken from the field of slaughter.

Washington was in the thickest of this murderous action, conducting himself, according to the testimony of a brother officer, with "the greatest courage and resolution." His fellow aids, Captains Orme and Morris, were disabled by their wounds, and he only remained to convey the orders of his unfortunate chief. "I expected every moment," said Dr. Craik, his friend and physician, "to see him fall." Of eighty-six officers in the engagement twenty-six were killed, and thirty-seven wounded; and of the privates, about twelve hundred in number, the killed and wounded amounted to seven hundred and fourteen. If these numbers, augmented in proportion to the size of the armies, are applied to the losses sustained in the recent engagements in Lombardy, it will be immediately perceived that, in the number of the killed and wounded, the battles of Magenta and Solferino do not compare with the ever memorable battle of the Monongahela.

Washington was not merely exposed to what may be called the ordinary and unavoidable dangers of such a day, but to a risk, (as afterwards appeared in a very extraordinary manner,) most imminent and peculiar. In the year 1770, in company with his friend, Dr. Craik, he descended the Ohio on a tour of observation as far as the great Kanhawa, and there the incident occurred, avouched by Dr. Craik, which I give in the language of Mr. Irving :—

"Here Washington was visited by an old Sachem, who approached him with great reverence, at the head of several of his tribe, and addressed him through Nicholson, the interpreter. He had heard, he said, of his being in that part of the country, and had come from a great distance to see him. On further discourse, the Sachem made known, that he was one of the warriors in the service of the French, who lay in ambush on the banks of the Monongahela, and wrought such havoc in Braddock's army. He declared that he and his young men had singled out Washington, as he made himself conspicuous, riding about the field of battle with the general's orders, and fired at him repeatedly, but without success; whence they concluded that he was under the protection of the Great Spirit, that he had a charmed life, and could not be slain in battle."

Washington himself, at the time, was not unaware of the danger to which he was exposed, nor of the Power by which it was averted. In a letter to his brother, he says, "By the all-powerful dispensations of Providence, I have been protected beyond all human probability and expectation; for I had four bullets through my coat, and two horses shot under me, yet I escaped unhurt, although death was levelling my companions on every side." His remarkable preservation, through the dangers of this dreadful day, attracted general notice, and Dr. Daveis, of Virginia, afterwards President of Princeton College, in a discourse a few weeks afterwards, before a volunteer company of Hanover county, alluded to "that heroic youth Col. Washington, whom I cannot but hope Providence has hitherto preserved in so signal a manner for some important service to his country." It is doubtful if a mere human prediction, inspired by early promise, was ever so remarkably fulfilled in after life. It is one of those striking cases where the foresight of a wise man becomes prophecy. The expedition under Braddock was the most formidable which had ever been, at that time, undertaken in British America, and its result spread dismay throughout the continent. It furnishes a most signal illustration of the paralyzing power of Panic, to which I have alluded in a former number of these papers; and it brought down upon the ill-fated Commander's grave the bitterest reproaches of his Government and the country. Washington alone, of all in conspicuous stations, came out of the havoc of the day, not only with untarnished, but with enhanced honor; and a reverent anticipation, as we have seen, of some momentous connection between his career, and the fortunes of the country, took possession of the public mind. It is impossible to withhold assent from the reflections of Mr. Sparks:

> "Contrary to his will," says this judicious writer, "and in spite of his efforts, he had gathered laurels from the defeat and ruin of others. Had the expedition been successful, these laurels would have adorned the brow of his superiors. It might have been said of him, that he had done his duty, and acquitted himself honorably, but he could not have been the prominent and single object of public regard; nor could he by a long series of common events, have risen to so high an eminence, or acquired in so wide a sphere, the admiration and confidence of the people. For himself, for his country and mankind, therefore, this catastrophe, in appearance so calamitous and so deeply deplored at the time, should unquestionably be considered as a WISE AND BENEFICENT DISPENSATION OF PROVIDENCE."

In a career like Washington's, there is scarce any thing, that can be called private life; his domestic relations even connect themselves with the public interests. The year after Braddock's defeat, Colonel Washington went to Boston with two brother officers, from his post on the Virginia and Maryland frontier, to take the decision of Governor Shirley, the recently appointed Commander-in-Chief of all the royal forces on the Continent, on the questions of precedence between the Crown and Provincial officers, which continually embarrassed the service. Going and returning, he was the guest at New

York of an early friend and school-mate, Beverley Robinson, son of Colonel John Robinson, the Speaker of the House of Burgesses of Virginia, whose happy compliment to Washington's modesty is so well known. Mr. Beverley Robinson had lately married one of the nieces and heiresses of Mr. Adolphus Philipse, a great landholder, whose manor-house is still to be seen on the banks of the Hudson. In the family circle of Mr. and Mrs. Robinson, Washington formed the acquaintance of her sister, Mary Philipse, a young lady "whose personal attractions," according to Mr. Irving, "are said to have equalled her reputed wealth. * * * That he was an open admirer of this lady, is an historical fact; that he sought her hand and was refused, is traditional and not very probable." His public duties hastened his return southward, and Captain Morris, his brother aid-de-camp in the battle of the Monongahela, became his successful rival. These facts are usually mentioned only as a personal anecdote of no great importance in the life of Washington; but it would not be extravagant to ascribe to them an important, not to say decisive connection, with his subsequent career. At that time no thought of the future wrongs of America and of her conflicts with the Mother Country had entered the minds of men. Washington had been the associate and was the friend of many officers in the royal service; he desired and sought employment in it himself. In no part of the British dominions was the sentiment of loyalty more warmly cherished than in these transatlantic colonies. If then at the age of twenty-five, with these predispositions, if he had formed a matrimonial connection, such as that in question, with a lady of great personal attractions and wealth, already connected by marriage with a friend of his youth, is it a reproach to his memory to say, that he too like his successful rival, might have adhered to the royal cause and have been lost to America? That like him when the appeal was made to arms he might have gone "home" to

England? There the lady, I believe, died as late as 1825, having lived to see the young officer, her admirer in youth, become the great leader of the American Revolution, the first President of the United States, and to survive him twenty-five years.

NUMBER THIRTY-EIGHT.

SEVERAL CRITICAL OCCASIONS AND INCIDENTS IN THE LIFE OF WASHINGTON

Washington desires in early life a commission in the Royal Army—Exclusion of Colonists from promotion in the Royal establishments—His taste for military life—His distinguished services in the seven years' war attract no notice "at home"—At its close, having no hope of advancement, he retires from military life—After an interval of seventeen years, re-appears commander-in-chief of the armies of United America—At the battle of Princeton, Washington, in his own opinion, ran the greatest risk of his life, being between the fire of both parties—Colonel Trumbull's picture—Reputation acquired by Washington abroad by the surprise of the Hessians and the battle at Princeton—Testimony of the historian Botta.

The circumstances which decide the course of events in after life generally date from early years, and not obtaining notoriety at the time, are afterwards, even in the case of very eminent men, liable to be forgotten. It has already been seen by how narrow a chance Washington was in his boyhood prevented from becoming a British naval officer, and thus entering a career which would have withdrawn him infallibly from the scene of his subsequent service and glory. Probably without reference to any thing but the removal of a lad of fourteen years from home, and to the necessary discomforts and dangers of the service, his mother opposed this arrangement, and in so doing gave to the country the great leader of the Revolution, and the first President of the United States. In like manner, a strong desire and a fixed purpose of his own, formed at a period of life when men become (as far as that is ever the case) the masters of their own destiny, led Washington to seek a commission in the Royal army. This object, so long as he remained in active service under the provincial government, during the old French war, he sought to effect in every way in which a young man of merit and honor can seek his own advancement. If he had succeeded, he would have followed the fortunes, as he must have shared the dangers, of military service; have fallen in action on some hard fought field in America, Europe, or the East, or have risen to distinction in the Britsh army; and thus, when the war of American Independence broke out, have been found, not at the head of its newly mustered armies, but in the ranks of its veteran enemies.

Less attention, perhaps, than they merit has been given to these early views of Washington, and the steps taken by him to carry them into effect. Accustomed as we are to an Independent government, and to all the consequences which flow from it, we do not form a lively conception of the state of things which existed when the seat of power and the fountain of honor were on the other side of the Atlantic; and when the only ordinary channel through which advancement could be sought or obtained in the Colonies, was that of the Royal favorites who were sent out to govern them. This, in fact, is one of the great vices of Colonial rule, which unfits it for a mature stage of national growth. It was unquestionably an active though not an avowed, perhaps not a consciously admitted, cause of the disaffection to the mother country, which prevailed on this side of the Atlantic, and which terminated in the separation. The cause of the colonies was, from the supposed necessity of the case, argued on narrow grounds. The right of the Imperial Parliament to tax America was denied, while an unlimited right of commercial regulation was admitted, under which the trade and navigation of the Colonies were subjected to the most oppressive restrictions, and manufacturing industry placed under the ban. The same great and liberal minister, (Lord Chatham,) who rejoiced that America resisted the acts of Parliament, which laid a trifling duty on tea, would not allow the Colonies to manufacture "a hobnail," and was willing that a water-wheel should be abated as a nuisance. The loyal metaphysics of the "Sons of Liberty" found a constitutional argument against the tax on Colonial imports, but admitted the right, and hardly murmured against the policy of prohibiting Colonial manufactures, and restricting the navigation of the Colonies to the mother country. But it no doubt was a grievance equally felt, if not openly resented, that the paths of promotion, generally speaking, were shut upon the children of the country. It was only in exceptional, almost accidental cases, that a native could rise in the Royal army or navy, or in the Civil administration of the Colonies. Advancement in the Imperial government was out of the question, on any other condition than that of expatriation. All lucrative and honorable places in these Colonies, as in all Colonies, then as now, except so far as wisdom has been learned from experience, constituted the *appanage* of younger sons and the prey of needy courtiers. Posts of trust and emolument were appropriated, not for the purpose of rewarding merit or employing talent in the field of service, but to gratify the caprice or to consummate the bargains of the minister and his friends. It is unhappily but too easy for bad men to get into office, even when they are chosen by those who suffer, if they choose amiss; but this penalty furnishes some protection against an injudicious or corrupt choice. To impose by a sheer act of power an incompetent or a worthless magistrate, on a remote community, is at once a wrong and an insult. But this is, and almost by necessary operation, the genius of metropolitan rule over distant colonies. The insolence to the natives, of the young men sent out to govern Hindostan, is said to have been an active cause of the revolt, which has but just been suppressed at such hideous sacrifice of treasure and life.

Washington's taste, as I have said, was for the army; he inherited and early manifested a fondness for military life. He had, in an eminent degree, the spirit of subordination and command, the physical and moral courage, the energy, the system, the resource, the fortitude that never fainted, the wariness never surprised, and, above all, the ascendency over his associates, which make the consummate chief. That he gained few brilliant victories proves nothing to the contrary till it can be shown that, with the materials at his command, and with the odds to which he was opposed, it was possible to gain them. The common sense of mankind is a far sounder judge in this respect than the astute strategist. The chieftain, whose reputation rises in the midst of disasters, like Washington's in his youth, after the calamitous campaigns of 1754 and 1755, and who retains the confidence of a bleeding country, through years of exhaustion and despondency, may well afford to dispense with the glory which accrues from fortunate encounters. The entire series of Napoleon's victories does not reflect greater credit upon his skill as a commander, than the retreat from Moscow, which completed the loss of the largest and finest army which had ever been mustered in Europe.

With this hereditary aptitude for military service, Washington embraced with eagerness every opening for its pursuit, which Colonial life afforded; but this could only raise him to the humbler posts. He accepted, and that before he was of age, every opportunity of service within the gift of the Colonial government of Virginia; and at the age of twenty-one undertook a most dangerous mission in the winter, which, as he truly says himself, no other person could be found to accept, and which at the most imminent peril of his life, could, if it succeeded, gain him little but the credit of a faithful messenger. It so happened, that in performing the humble errand, he had the opportunity of displaying high military qualities. His modest diary showed a young man of the brightest promise. It was published in London; the growing interest attached to the movements of the French on the banks of the Ohio gave an unexpected importance to the mission and to its narrative; and it would undoubtedly have made the professional fortune of any youthful officer in the royal army. It did not earn a compliment for the Virginia Major. His prudence and fortitude, early ripe, won for him the following year, notwithstanding its disasters, the unbounded confidence of the Colonial government, but they attracted no notice "at home." Braddock came, the most self-sufficient of men, and gave his undivided confidence to Washington; a confidence well repaid on the terrible ninth of July. It is evident that the unfortunate general had perceived the claims of such a man to promotion, on the score of policy, if not of justice. Governor Dinwiddie, in a letter to the minister, spoke of him as "a man of great merit and resolution," and added, "I am confident that if General Braddock had survived, he would have recommended him to the royal favor, which I beg your interest in recommending." But the only notice earned by his bravery and conduct on that fatal day, was a good-natured rebuke from George II. and an ill-natured sneer from Horace Walpole.—For three succeeding years of fruitless application to Lord Loudon and his successor, he endeavored to obtain a royal commission. They asked his advice, followed his counsels, or lived or died to lament their rejection of it;—applied to him,—a provincial colonel,—for plans of march and of battle; yielded to him the post of danger when responsibility was to be assumed or peril braved; and left him, where they found him, in the Colonial service. Perceiving that all hopes of promotion in the British army were vain, and satisfied with the attainment of the great object of the war in the middle colonies, by the capture of Fort Duquesne and the expulsion of the French from the Ohio, he retired from the field, after five years of arduous and faithful service; the youthful idol of his countrymen, but without so much as a civil word from the fountain of honor. And so, when, after seventeen years of private life, he next appeared in arms, it was as the "Commander in chief of the army of the United Colonies, and of all the forces now raised, or to be raised, by them." Such was the policy by which the Horse Guards occasionally saved a major's commission for a fourth son of a Duke; by which the Crown lost a Continent; and the people of the United States gained a place in the family of nations! The voice of history cries aloud to powerful governments, in the administration of their colonies, "Discite justitiam moniti."*

I have thus mentioned six occasions in the early life of Washington, of great personal danger, or on which his entire future career seemed to be suspended on a very narrow chance of events, which would have given it a totally different complexion. A few years elapse, and he is brought to the all-important position for which, through all these perils and by all these preparations, he had been trained by Providence. It would be a highly instructive and not a difficult task to point out the parallelism of the two wars, and to show in specific instances, how the one served as a school of preparation for the other. This would be aside from my present purpose, and I close the list of the imminent dangers to which the life of Washington was at different times exposed, by one which, in his own estimate, was greater than any other.

The year 1775 was taken up by the organization of the army in Massachusetts; a work, like much which Washington had to perform, of boundless importance and difficulty, but of no *éclat.* The year 1776 opened with the grand operation of expelling the royal forces from Boston, without a conflict, which Washington however intended, if necessary, to hazard. This great success was followed by the unfortunate battle of Long Island, the loss of New York, the retreat

* Take warning, and learn to be just.

through New Jersey. At these great reverses, the confident began to doubt, the disaffected to exult, and the timid to despair. It was then that Washington planned the surprize of the three regiments of Hessians at Trenton; a veteran force, commanded by a skilful officer, and trained in the best military school of Europe.—This was not certainly an expedition which any punctilio of military honor required the Commander-in-Chief to lead in person; it was an affair of detachments, which might with propriety have been left to subordinates. But the crisis was too momentous for any other guidance than his own. On the night of the 25th of December, he threw his little army of twenty-four hundred men and twenty small field-pieces across the Delaware, then running with drift ice, (thrice as wide as the Mincio in any part of its course, where it flows between banks, from the Lago di Garda to the Po,) under a storm all the way of snow, rain, and hail, and with the weather so cold that two of his men froze to death on the march, and taking the enemy completely by surprise, captured a thousand men. The inability of the two other detachments to cross the Delaware prevented a similar surprise of those portions of the enemy's force which escaped from Trenton, or were stationed lower down.

Having recrossed the river with his prisoners, he speedily returned to New Jersey to follow up his success, and dexterously eluding the greatly superior army of Lord Cornwallis, who had been sent from New York to check his progress, and who boasted on the evening of the 2d "that he would bag the fox in the morning," Washington made a night march on Princeton, and there on the 3d of January, engaged and destroyed one regiment, and captured and put to flight two others. It was in this engagement, which forms the subject of Trumbull's noble picture, that for a while he was exposed, as he himself told Colonel Trumbull while painting it, to greater danger of his life than even at Braddock's defeat. In the heat of the action, the hostile forces were for a short time in close conflict, and he between them, within the rear range of the fire of both.

"His Aid-de-Camp, Colonel Fitzgerald," says Mr. Irving, "a young and ardent Irishman, losing sight of him in the heat of the fight, when enveloped in dust and smoke, dropped the bridle on the neck of his horse and drew his hat over his eyes, giving him up for lost. When he saw him, however, emerging from the cloud, waving his hat, and beheld the enemy giving way, he spurred up to his side. 'Thank God,' cried he, 'your Excellency is safe.' 'Away, my dear Colonel, and bring up the troops,' was Washington's reply, 'the day is our own!'"

The action was unusually bloody; of the enemy a hundred were killed, three hundred wounded, and large numbers taken prisoners. The gallant Mercer and other brave officers fell on the American side, but Washington escaped unhurt!

Colonel Trumbull represents him as standing by his favorite white charger on that momentous day. As the march from the bank of the Assanpink, the action, and the pursuit, lasted thirty-six hours, during which he scarcely left the saddle, there is no doubt that Washington must have ridden two or three horses in the course of the day. I have been informed, however, at second hand, from one who was in his body guard, that when the seventeenth British regiment broke, General Washington, then mounted on a favorite roan hunter, leaped the stone wall that crossed the eminence, and perceiving the enemy in full retreat, gave the *view halloo*, and, in unconscious response to the boast of Lord Cornwallis the night before, exclaimed to the officers about him, "It is a regular fox chase!"

Well might he exult in the event of the day, for it was the last of a series of bold and skilful manœuvres and successful actions, by which, in three weeks, he had rescued Philadelphia, driven the enemy from the banks of the Delaware, recovered the State of New Jersey, and, at the close of a disastrous campaign, restored hope and confidence to the country "achievements so astonishing," says the Italian historian Botta,* "gained for the American Commander a very great reputation, and were regarded with wonder by all nations, as well as by the Americans. Every one applauded the prudence, the firmness, and the daring of General Washington. All declared him the Saviour of his country; all proclaimed him equal to the most renowned commanders of antiquity, and especially distinguished him by the name of the AMERICAN FABIUS."

* Cited by Mr. Sparks, Vol. I., p. 234.

NUMBER THIRTY-NINE.

FONTAINEBLEAU, BURGUNDY, AUTUN, TALLEYRAND.

Leave Paris en route for Italy—Passports—Couriers—Fontainebleau and its historical recollections—Appearance of a wine-growing region—The Côte d'or—Autun, its antiquity and architectural remains—Epigram about the two Bishops of Autun—Character of Talleyrand—His emigration to America, and intention to become a citizen of the United States—Anecdote of Benedict Arnold—Talleyrand's course in this country—His friendship for General Hamilton—Curious anecdote of Aaron Burr, related by Talleyrand—Miniature of General Hamilton—Talleyrand's character as a statesman—The Duke of Magenta born at Autun—Another anecdote of Benedict Arnold.

On the 3d of September, 1818, after the then usual amount of delay and extortion, in procuring the requisite countersign to our passports at the foreign office and four or five legations, and the usual annoyance of finding, at the last, that several things had been neglected that ought to have been attended to, I started with my companion for Italy, intending, however, to make a hasty circuit in Switzerland by the way. There are few things, not less serious in themselves which more annoy American travellers in Europe, than the regulations about passports, which are in truth at times a source of unreasonable delay and vexation. The passport system, however, serves one valuable purpose, of which Americans, when occasion requires, derive the full benefit; but of the importance of which we are not duly sensible; and that is the aid which it affords to the pursuit and arrest of criminals fleeing from justice. It happened to me several times, in the course of official duty abroad, to have occasion to render aid to the parties interested who had come from the United States, in pursuit of embezzlers and other offenders fleeing from America. In all these cases, the necessity of having the passport countersigned in every new jurisdiction furnished important assistance in tracing and detaining the fugitive. In a region like the European Continent, divided among numerous Governments, wholly independent of each other, it will be readily seen, that the means of escape to a foreign territory must be much greater than in the United States, where so vast a territory is comprehended in one federal jurisdiction. Of course, however, the passport system is subject to great abuses for political purposes. Some of those have been brought upon *bonâ fide* American travellers, by the officials of the United States, who have in some cases undertaken to give American passports, (which are in terms certificates of citizenship,) to persons not entitled to them, either by birth or naturalization. This abuse has diminished the unhesitating respect which in former times was paid to the starry *vignette.*

Our travelling party consisted only of our two selves and a courier, one of those extraordinary persons, whose services every American travelling in Europe has found so important; —an attendant who knows a little,—sometimes a good deal, —of four or five languages; is conversant with the manners and customs of all countries; familiar with all routes in all directions;—acquainted, probably to some extent in league, —with landlords in all the towns where you are to stop. Our courier was a Neapolitan, who had conducted many Americans through Europe, and who was attached to an officer of the French army, in the terrible retreat from Moscow. On that dreadful flight, he resolutely maintained, though a man of veracity for his calling, that he rarely drew off his master's boots at night without bringing away one of the extremities of the feet which they covered. I retain a most kindly recollection of Francisco, whose fidelity was beyond suspicion, and who was one of the most indulgent persons to his employer that I ever knew. He would frequently let us have our own way. He amassed a handsome fortune in his vocation, and I renewed my acquaintance with him, after an interval of twenty-three years, at Naples, where he was living in 1841 as a respectable property holder.

There is something at almost every step of the way from Paris to Switzerland (as indeed there is in every part of Europe) to engage and reward the attention of the traveller; —the memory of some great battle, from the time of Julius Cæsar to that of Napoleon; some noble mediæval pile, or still more impressive architectural ruin; some venerable monastic establishment; the birth-place of some great man; some delightful landscape; some important institution; but all these objects have become too familiar from the guide-books and the professed tourists, to bear a description from the wayfarer who travels post through the country. We lingered awhile at Fontainebleau, which had not then recovered somewhat of its original magnificence under the restoring hand of Louis Philippe. Its immense extent, disproportioned to its height, its weather-stained brick corridors and faded splendors, at the time we saw it, produced rather a disappointing effect; but a little effort of the imagination sufficed to people it with the most stirring recollections. Louis the Seventh, in the twelfth century, laid its foundations, after his return from the second crusade, while Thomas à Becket was bidding defiance to Henry in England, and the Northmen were creeping down from Greenland to the coasts of Labrador and Newfoundland in America; and from "the Court of the White Horse," to which Catherine de Medici gave its name, Napoleon took his affecting leave of the remnants of the Old Guard on his departure for Elba. What a range for the imagination between those extremes! The *Fac Simile* of Napoleon's abdication, the little round table upon which it was written, and what purported to be the pen with which the sad words were traced, were exhibited in the room where the paper was signed; but have since, I believe, disappeared. Every intervening century and sovereign, from the founder of the old castle in the twelfth century to the present day, has left some recollection at Fontainebleau;—and its green moss-grown courts and silent halls remind you of marriages, murders, and abdications;—recall the names, besides native sovereigns, of the Emperor Charles V., Queen Christina, Pope Pius VII.; of Diana of Poitiers, Madame de Maintenon, and Henrietta Maria, the wife of Charles I.; and present you with specimens of the architecture and the arts, from their infancy in the fourteenth century to their second bloom in our own day.—The noble forest of Fontainebleau, equal in extent to two townhips of public land in the United States, exhibits no doubt a portion of the original growth of the country, preserved from the time when, within its dark recesses, the Druids burned their sacrificial victims in wicker cages. Our guide, as he approached "*La Croix du grand veneur*," * where a spectral huntsman in black appeared to Henri IV. not long before his murder, repeated the legend with a solemn air of belief. I had seen but a few days before, in the museum at Paris, the dagger which the maniac Ravaillac, climbing up the carriage wheels of the gracious monarch, as he drove slowly through the streets of Paris, plunged to his heart.

The first entrance into a wine-growing region, at least in France and Germany, disappoints the traveller, who has formed his ideas of a vineyard from the descriptions of the poets. There is nothing luxuriant in its appearance, as it is seen at a moderate distance from the road-side. The vines are pruned down to the height of a few feet, and planted in straight rows, which do not compare in richness and beauty to a field of Indian Corn in the tassel, undoubtedly the most

* "The Cross of the great Huntsman," an obelisk at the intersection of two main roads through the forest.

graceful and pompous robe in which bountiful nature arrays herself this side of the tropics. Seen, however, sufficiently near to disclose its opening clusters, purple or yellow, bursting or ready to burst with their nectarous juice, the aspect of a vineyard realizes the warmest images of Anacreon or Hafiz. We were about five weeks before the vintage was to commence, but the golden slopes of the *Côte d'or*, as we passed them, were clothed with its promise.—The Saône wound through the meadows on the left, and on the right vineyard above vineyard, and terrace above terrace, covered with plants bending beneath their melting clusters, rose to the very summit of the hills. It is on these hillsides alone, that the richest grapes can be matured, for it is necessary to combine protection from the winds of the north (that dreadful *bise* at which the readers of Madame de Sevigné have shivered for two centuries, whether they have felt it or not, which, though fully developed only in the south of France, begins in Burgundy to assume its character, and, under a cloudless sky and brilliant sun, sweeps over the earth day after day, with a dry, steady, withering chill,) with a degree of heat which can only be had in an exposure to the sun, under an angle of from thirty to sixty degrees. The promise of the vintage this year (1818) exceeded that of any season since the famous Comet year of 1811, and wherever we entered into conversation on the road we heard the language of joy and confidence.

On our way to Lyons, we passed through Autun, but saw it to some disadvantage, at least as far as comfort and accommodation are concerned, in consequence of the crowd and confusion incident to the great September fair. Few places exceed it in historical interest. It was an important city of the ancient Gauls, before the invasion of Julius Cæsar, at least if, as antiquaries suppose, it was the Bibracte of the Ædui. The name of Autun is abbreviated from that (Augustodunum) by which the Romans indicated its importance. For nearly two centuries after it was honored with this appellation, it was a seat of refinement and art, to which the young men of Gaul were sent for their education. Considerable masses of the Roman walls still exist, showing the extent of the ancient city; and architectural remains of a highly interesting character, though not of the purest age of art,—especially two Roman gates,—attract the notice of the traveller. Some portions of the Cathedral, particularly the spire, are also greatly admired by the student of mediæval architecture.

The Cathedral of Autun reminds one by natural association of its prelates. Two of them have obtained, in very different ways, what may be called a classical celebrity, recorded in the following epigram:

> Roquette, dans son tems,
> Talleyrand, dans le notre,
> Furent evêques d'Autun;—
> Tartuffe fut le surnom d'un,
> Ah! si Moliere eût connu l'autre!

which may be poorly translated as follows:—

> Two bishops have adorned Autun,
> Roquette and this his modern brother;—
> Tartuffe preserves the name of one,
> Oh! had Moliere but known the other!

It may seem the height of romance for an American even to say a civil word in favor of the last named of these celebrated bishops of Autun, but the French Revolution brought a good many men into power much worse than M. de Talleyrand. He belonged to the most ancient *noblesse* of France; but having, in consequence of his lameness, been placed in the Church, he early, like Lafayette, Mirabeau, and many others of the French aristocracy felt, as Louis XV. had felt and said before them, that the old French Monarchy could last no longer; that it was rotten at heart. He therefore adopted the revolution, but fled disgusted and horror-struck from its bloody excesses. He came to this country, and took the preliminary steps to become a citizen of the United States. I saw in Peale's museum, many years ago, the official notice of this intention, signed by himself, and it afterwards passed into the possession of the late Mr. Edward D. Ingraham, of Philadelphia.

M. de Talleyrand, having been ordered by the British government, (under the influence of the panic with reference to everything French which had seized them,) to leave England, took passage for the United States at Plymouth, where he happened to find himself in the same inn with Benedict Arnold. Not being particularly acquainted with the relations in which this wretched man might still stand with America, Talleyrand offered to take letters for him to the United States. This civility Arnold declined, saying, "I am the only man in the world that does not dare write to his native country." The little volume of "Recollections" of Mr. Rogers, lately published, contains a most remarkable counterpart to this anecdote, given on the authority of the Duke of Wellington. "When Lord Londonderry attacked Talleyrand in Parliament and I defended him, saying, in everything as far as I had observed, he had always been fair and honest, Talleyrand burst into tears, saying, 'He is the only man that ever said anything good of me!'"

Arrived in the United States, M. de Talleyrand was far from imitating the unwise conduct of his countrymen in America, who threw themselves into the political controversies of this country, and allowed themselves to be made use of, to embarrass the administration of General Washington. He of course entered into no personal relations with the President, but he formed an intimate acquaintance and contracted a warm friendship with General Hamilton, whom he considered, and in after life often spoke of, as the most sagacious and best informed of American Statesmen, especially in reference to European politics. He carried with him, on his return to France, a miniature of General Hamilton, painted at his request. When Aaron Burr was in Paris, and requested an interview with M. de Talleyrand, then Minister of Foreign Affairs, the latter added this clause to the cold official note appointing a time for the reception: "The Minister for Foreign Affairs thinks proper to inform Mr. Burr, that a portrait of General Hamilton is hanging in his office;" an intimation which of course prevented the visit. This miniature, or a copy of it, with a little receptacle on the back containing obituary notices of General Hamilton, cut from the American newspapers, was after his decease sent by M. de Talleyrand to the family in the United States. The curious anecdote just given was related by M. de Talleyrand himself to the son and grandson of General Hamilton, on a visit made by invitation to Vallençay, a few years before his death, on which occasion his distinguished attentions showed the honor in which he held the memory of their illustrious and lamented relative.

In reference to the political course of M. de Talleyrand as a French Statesman, it cannot be denied that he was a politician of the same school with the celebrated Austrian Minister, whose character formed the subject of the thirty-fifth paper of this series. But still more than Metternich, he is entitled to the credit of having studied, sometimes no doubt from a false point of view, the interests of the country of which he was a citizen, and of the government which he served. To this he sacrificed the favor of his all-powerful master, whose Spanish policy,—the great and fatal error of his reign,—was adopted and pursued in direct opposition to the counsels of M. de Talleyrand.

Before leaving Autun, it may be remarked that it is the birth-place of General M'Mahon, who was created a marshal of France by Louis Napoleon, on the battle-field of Magenta, for having "saved the army." As the name indicates, his family is of Irish extraction, and is one of those which, with self-sacrificing chivalry, followed the fortunes of James II. The new-made duke of Magenta was born at Autun, in 1807.

Having mentioned Benedict Arnold in the foregoing paper, I cannot refrain from repeating another anecdote of him, related by Mr. Sabine, which throws a dismal light on the repute in which he was held in a community where it might have been expected, if anywhere, that he would have been kindly viewed. After the revolutionary war, he established himself in some sort of business at St. John's, New Brunswick, which was principally settled by American loyalists. His warehouse and the merchandize in it, being fully insured, were destroyed by fire, and Arnold was charged in a newspaper with having himself set fire to the building, in order to get the insurance, which was largely beyond the value of the property. He prosecuted the publisher of the paper for a libel, laid the damages at thousands, and recovered, by the verdict of the jury, two and six pence! Such was the estimate formed by a St. John's jury of his probity.

NUMBER FORTY.

LYONS.

Hotel de l'Europe at Lyons—The hill of Fourvières—Description of the Panorama seen from its top—Distant view of Mont Blanc—Pilgrimages to the shrine of our Lady of Fourvières—Resort of beggars and almsgiving on the part of the Pilgrims—Anecdote of a professed Scottish beggar—The bronze tablets containing the speech of the Emperor Cladius—Martyrdom of Saint Irenæus and Blandina—The Persecutions of the early Christians as recorded in ecclesiastical history compared with the cruelties practised at Lyons in the French revolution.—Wholesale massacre in the Brotteaux—Escape and career of Jacquard, the inventor of the celebrated loom that bears his name—saying of Napoleon I. about him—His epitaph.

We passed a few days at Lyons, a city which I have, in the course of my wanderings, visited three times, and ever with undiminished satisfaction. To begin with our lodgings, there is a gloomy grandeur about the *Hotel de l'Europe*, which I do not dislike in an old European city. It resembles a princely palace, and in fact probably was one. Its rooms are of vast height; the ceilings painted, and that not contemptibly, in *fresco;* the walls hung with old family portraits of Louis Quatorze and the Regency; the floors tiled or inlaid with woods once bright and particolored; the chimneys of colossal length, depth, and height; everything, in a word, on a grand scale, not excepting, I must own, the dirt,—which one must take in these old continental hotels, together with the grandeurs. In the fare there was nothing to complain of; nor in 1818 in the bill. All this may have changed since I was last there in 1841.

This first visit to Lyons was made before the halcyon

days of Murray. That trusty guide, after giving with some minuteness, a local description of the city, says with italicized emphasis, "these dry topographical details will be best understood when the traveller has scaled the height of *Fourvières,* which *he should do the first thing after his arrival,* on account of the view it commands." Whether at the instigation of some older Murray or some discreet *valet de place,* or led by our own sagacity, I do not recollect,—but our first care was to ascend the hill of *Fourvières,* which we could perceive from below must command a glorious panorama of Lyons and its environs. The approach would seem artistically contrived to heighten, by contrast, the magnificence of the prospect. It is in the rear of an extensive but confused pile of building, now occupied as an asylum for the insane, and a hospital for incurables of the most wretched description, who are attended, however, with exemplary self-sacrifice, by the brothers and sisters of charity. This sad retreat of suffering humanity, (such are the vicissitudes of human fortune in men and things,) occupies the site of a palace, in which, some seventeen centuries ago, two Roman Emperors, Claudius and Caracalla were born! After emerging from this locality you begin to ascend the hill through steep and narrow lanes, sometimes by steps apparently cut in the native rock, winding through vineyards, and olive gardens, and groves of fig trees,—(such at least was the case forty years ago,) and you reach at last the summit called Fourvières, which is supposed by the antiquaries at Lyons, to be the modern French form of the Latin *Forum vetus,* "ancient Forum." The scene is certainly one of transcendent natural beauty as well as uncommon historical interest. It cannot have escaped the professed tourists; but I do not remember to have seen it particularly described.

Through the defiles of Mount Cindre on the north, you catch a glimpse,—it is but a glimpse,—of the golden slopes of Burgundy. The lofty and serrated ridges of Auvergne, within whose secret laboratories, heated by concealed volcanoes, nature distils some of her most salubrious mineral waters, bound the prospect on the west. The misty hills and genial valleys of Dauphiny and Languedoc stretch far away to the south in dreamy luxuriance. On the east comes in the headlong turbid Rhone, swelled by the tributary floods of the Lake of Geneva, of the Arve, and of the Arveiron; and through them, sharing with the Rhine, the Danube, and the Po, the waters that trickle from hundreds of Alpine Glaciers. You follow the line of the Jura with some distinctness on the north-east, and further in the east, especially with the aid of a glass, the eye, glancing from the Schreckhorn, the Finster Aar Horn, and the Jungfrau, unclimbed by the foot of man till it was ascended by our own Agassiz, rests at length, at the distance of a hundred miles, on imperial Mont Blanc itself, visible in a clear day even to the naked eye. There you behold it swelling grandly to the sky, laden with the piled storms of untold centuries; bright as the ocean of sunshine that bathes its cold, unmelting sides; pure as the deep blue Heavens, which canopy its vestal snows; mysterious as the conscious stars which look down at midnight into its fathomless chasms; a vast eternal mountain of glittering crystal,—indescribable monument of Creative Power!

When you turn at length from this all-glorious panorama and look down upon the confluence of the Saone and Rhone at your feet, the recollections of nearly three thousand years crowd upon the mind. Here in the remotest antiquity sixty Gallic nations assembled to celebrate the annual sacrifices of the primitive Celtic race. What interests, what policies, what controversies, agitated at these gatherings, lie buried in the grave of ages! This was the focal point, from which the power and the policy of Rome, overleaping the Alps, radiated to the west and north, and, turning the flank of the eternal Alps, rushed north-eastwardly upon Germany. Here the great Dictator paused to meditate, as from some lofty watch-tower, with dilating thought, on the mighty career of conquest which was opening before him in Gallia, in Brittania, in Germania, and which is still felt in the language, the laws, the national divisions of modern Europe. This was the central station from which Marcus Vipsanius Agrippa laid out the four great roads, pathways of empire, which traversed and tamed impatient Gaul. Here the subjugated races erected a temple to Agrippa's patron and father-in-law, the Emperor Augustus. Four columns of Egyptian granite, stolen perhaps originally from Memphis or Egyptian Thebes to support the canopy of the altar dedicated to Augustus, now sustain the cross of the Abbey Church of Ainay, beneath whose pavement rest the ashes of some of the earliest martyrs of the Christian faith. In the same quarter Caligula established his *Athenæum*, and instituted his prize declamations; crowning the successful competitor with honors and rewards; chastizing the unsuccessful, and compelling them to wipe their orations from their tablets with their tongues. Happily for modern orators, this operation is now left to the impartial hand of time. Here, in fine, the liberal Trajan erected a splendid edifice for the markets, the fairs, and the courts.

These monuments of ancient power and altars of ancient worship have passed away; mutilated statues, fragmentary inscriptions transferred to the museum, and doubtful substructions buried deep beneath the modern level of the soil, are all that attest their former existence. The Church of our Lady of *Fourvières*, surmounted by a colossal figure of the Virgin in gilded bronze, looks down from the summit of the hill upon the scene and the ruins of all this ancient magnificence. The popular faith ascribes miraculous powers to the consecrated image of the Virgin enshrined within the temple; the walls of which are hung thick with *ex voto* memorials of the dangers escaped and the cures performed by her intercession. The little shops, which line the lower part of the narrow lane by which you ascend the hill, contain articles of this kind, ready prepared to be purchased by the pilgrims who come to pay their devotions and make their acknowledgments at the shrine.

We happened to visit Fourvières on the day of the great annual resort for this purpose, when pilgrims in large numbers and from considerable distances flock to the church. These pilgrimages are the great harvest of the beggars of Lyons and the whole neighboring region, who, in numbers quite equal to that of the devotees, assemble at the same time and place. The two classes, contemplated together, present a curious spectacle. The pilgrims moving in single file, except when some feeble brother or sister requires the support of a friendly arm, occupy the middle of the pathway up the hill. The beggars line the sides, from the bottom to the top; singly for the most part, sometimes in families; standing, sitting, lying; the maimed, the halt, and the blind; the sturdy, business-like, and impudent; the humble, looking up with pitiful deference; some clamorous, some trusting to the mute eloquence of decrepitude and mutilation; of every age and either sex; and suffering under every form of real or pretended distress. Long established usage sanctions the resort, on these particular occasions, and settles the amount of the expected bounty; a *liard*, which is, I believe, about half a farthing, from every pilgrim, sometimes the poorer personage of the two, to every one of the beggars; some of whom are said to amass comparatively large sums of money in the course of years. So much a matter of business is it—so little of delicacy or feeling is there on either side in this conventional wholesale almsgiving, that we continually saw the parties making change with each other. A *sous*, which, if I mistake not, is worth three *liards* in the old French coinage, was handed by the pilgrim to the beggar. The beggar knew that he was to retain only a part of this magnificent sum, and returned two *liards* to the pilgrim, who was thus furnished with small change for those who stood next.

Sir Walter Scott, in his description of the professed beggars of his country, relates an anecdote of one Andrew Gammels, who belonged to that privileged class, which discloses a charitable thrift not unlike that practised at Fourvières. Having asked alms of a gentleman, who regretted that he had no silver, as in that case he would have given Andrew a sixpence, the well-to-do beggar replied, "I can gie ye change for a note, Laird."

What a contrast upon the hill of *Fourvières* on occasion of these pilgrimages, between the charities of man and the charities of Heaven! Man making change with his brother man for half farthings; and the dear God causing his rich big clouds to rain down plenty on the just and the unjust; and his noble rivers to flow from their secret urns in the eternal mountains; and his health-giving waters to sparkle from the secret dispensaries of the earth; and the breezy wings of his mighty winds to fan the languid pulses of creation into cheery vigor; and his wine and his oil to stream from every hill-side; and the finest of his wheat to wave in yellow luxuriance over a thousand fields; and all his imperial heavens, from their opening windows, to pour down every day upon the evil and the good one golden, genial deluge of morning light!

There are a great many very curious relics of antiquity in the Museum at Lyons. One of them, nearly if not quite unique in its way, consists of the bronze tablets, containing a speech made by the Emperor Claudius, in the Roman Senate, while he filled the office of Censor, in the 48 of our era, and recommending that the inhabitants of Transalpine Gaul should be admitted to the privileges of Roman Citizenship. These tablets probably preserve the very words of Claudius, and the engraving is still perfectly distinct and legible. Lady Mary Wortley Montague was so much struck with them, that she took the trouble to transcribe them in a letter to Pope, written from Lyons; probably, however, copying them from some printed description, though she does not say so.

Lyons is celebrated in Ecclesiastical History as the see of Saint Irenæus, the second Bishop of the diocese, one of the most important of the early writers of the Church, who is said to have suffered martyrdom, with eight thousand fellow-Christians, in the reign of Severus. This Emperor is supposed to have treated the Christians of Lyons with especial rigor, in consequence of some affront which he had received while living there; a tradition which strangely corresponds with the anecdote told of Collot d'Herbois,—that his inhuman cruelties toward the inhabitants of this devoted city in the French Revolution, were in revenge for having been hissed by them, when he appeared in their theatre as a fourth-rate actor. A former persecution under Marcus Aurelius is famous as that in which the gentle Blandina, (a name which has acquired a happier and let us hope a not less permanent celebrity in our own country and day, for a noble act of enlightened liberality,)* trod the thorny path of martyrdom.

The skepticism of the last century, under the guidance of Gibbon, was disposed to view with distrust the accounts transmitted to us by the Historians of the Church, of those wholesale butcheries, the famous ten Persecutions. It is not necessary to contend too anxiously for this precise numerical arrangement of the sufferings inflicted upon the confessors of the new faith, under the reign of the predecessors of Constantine. But historical monuments of undoubted authenticity prove that the early Christians were subjected to the most cruel treatment, and often paid with their lives for their rejection of the religion of the State. Whatever doubts may have existed as to the wholesale butcheries in question, as transcending in the number of their victims all credible measures of brutal tyranny, have been but too sadly removed, by the atrocities practised, at this very city of Lyons, after its seige and capture by the army of the Convention in 1793.

* The endowment of the Observatory at Albany, by Mrs. Blandina Dudley.

There is nothing in the ten Persecutions which, either for the number of the sufferers or the diabolical rage and malignity with which they were consigned to their fate, exceeds the records of the revolutionary tribunals at Lyons, under Couthon, Fouché, and Collot d'Herbois. We have but to read the account in the third volume of Alison, or what on this subject may seem a safer authority, though they draw from the same sources, Lamartine's history of the Girondins. I could scarcely believe, in traversing the Brotteaux in 1818, that twenty-five years only had elapsed, since it was the scene of the unimagined horrors practised under those monsters. Finding the guillotine too slow to satiate their thirst for blood, they filled the square with the best citizens of Lyons, their hands tied behind them, to be swept down by grape shot, ranging along a cable to which they were secured, and then bayonetted them at leisure, as they lay mutilated and gasping on the reeking ground. Nothing in the legends of the church need be disbelieved after reading that, in the last decade of the eighteenth century, the ruling power of France decreed that the second city under their government should be razed from the face of the earth; its inhabitants exiled or put to death; its name blotted from the catalogue of cities; and that three and a half millions of dollars should have been expended in tearing down the houses that lined its finest streets and squares!

Among the heroic defenders of Lyons, who happily escaped these sanguinary horrors, and lived to reap in peace the reward of his marvellous ingenuity, was the modest and patient Jacquard. This wonderful man, the inventor of the loom which bears his name, and which has given a new character to the art of weaving in figured and raised patterns, throughout the world, was the son of a common weaver of Lyons. He was reduced so low, even in middle life, but before he had succeeded in bringing his loom into working condition, that he was compelled to support himself by aiding his wife in the preparation of the straw, which she braided for the hats worn by the peasantry. Although, in consequence of his invention, the number of weavers has been increased a hundred, not to say a thousand fold, they were so incensed against him, when his looms were first constructed, that he narrowly escaped being thrown by a mob into the Rhone! Napoleon, by an imperial decree at Berlin in 1806, granted him fifty francs (about ten dollars) on every loom constructed on his pattern. It was all he asked, and Napoleon, astonished at his moderation, exclaimed, as he put his name to the decree: "Here's a man who is content with a little!" If all the Berlin decrees had been as harmless in their purport, the war of 1812, between the United States and Great Britain, would not have been fought. If Napoleon himself had been also "content with a little," Jacquard's epitaph might have been written on his monument, "A man of virtue and genius, he died at home."*

* Homme de bien et de génie, mort à Oullins, *dans sa maison*, 7 Août, 1834.

NUMBER FORTY-ONE.

FROM LYONS TO GENEVA.

Silk fabrics of Lyons—First glimpse of mountain scenery—Nantua—Bellegarde—Ingenious smuggling—Pert du Rhone—Cæsar's description of the defile—Ancient Switzerland compared to Michigan and Wisconsin—First appearance of the Helvetii or ancient Swiss in history—Emigration of the entire people into France—Overtaken and defeated with great loss by Cæsar, and the survivors compelled to return to Switzerland—A muster-roll in Greek characters discovered in their camp which gives their numbers—Cæsar's great career begins with the conquest of the Helvetii—beautiful prospects on the way from Fort l'Ecluse to Geneva.

After a sojourn of three days we left Lyons with regret, for it contains objects which might occupy the time of the observant traveller not unprofitably for weeks and months. The silk fabrics, especially, are well worthy attention; the contrast between the brilliant colors, taseteful figures, and rich materials of the brocades and the dingy and dreary aspect of the rooms, machinery, and I may add, operatives employed in their manufacture, was very striking. They are carried through the loom and come out, without a spot or blemish, from apartments, through which it is not easy to pass without getting your clothes soiled. We were told that some of the richest tissues were destined for the markets of the East. It shows the hopeless inferiority of the Asiatic civilization, that the luxury of those regions, where a species of refinement has existed for at least four thousand years, should be tributary to the Celtic forests,—or what were Celtic forests in the days of Xerxes and Darius,—for their richest adornments. In fabrics wholly wrought by hand, the East, it is true, still maintains her superiority. France has striven in vain to rival the shawls and muslins of India; which is, however, but another proof at how low a price human labor and time can there be commanded,—itself an indication of social and political wretchedness and degradation. The remarkable copies of Stuart's Washington, recently produced in the looms of Lyons, and introduced into this country by Mr. Goodrich, resembling, at a very moderate distance, a fine engraving, show to what perfection the textile arts have been carried in Lyons.

There is nothing of much interest on the road from Lyons to Geneva till you reach the Jura mountains. The Rhone flows through an extensive plain unmarked by any attractive features; but from the time you reach the region where it bursts through the mountains, till you have made the tour of Switzerland and have descended the Alps on the Italian side, all is picturesque beauty and wild sublimity. At Cerdon the road begins to rise, and here most travellers from the Atlantic States of America or from England will get their first impressions of genuine mountain scenery. Though they may have seen greater elevations, they will probably not have seen detached summits ascending so abruptly and boldly and separated by such yawning chasms, or roads winding at such alarming heights along their sides. The landscape as you begin to ascend after passing Cerdon, is beautifully variegated by the winding of the stream, by a tumbling cascade, and several ruined castles. Of these last I did not learn their history if they have any. They belong I suppose, to that period in the annals of mediæval Europe, when every commanding eminence or narrow defile was the site of a fortress, and every robber count and petty baron went to war on his own authority. Europe is full of the ruins of these strongholds, and they form the most striking point of contrast with American scenery.

We passed the night at Nantua, a quiet little place, embosomed in Jura. It is surrounded on three sides by bare cliffs, rising hundreds of feet almost perpendicularly from the plain, and on the fourth side it lies open to a pretty lake, along the shores of which you approach the town. This contrast of the placid surface of the water, as we saw it in the dusk of the evening, with the dark woods and frowning crags that tower above, was remarkably pleasing. The Lake of Nantua and the little streams that feed it, are famous for their trout and fresh water shell-fish, and our well served table at night bore witness that the fame was not unmerited; though it must be owned that young travellers, who have been on the road since daybreak, without stopping to dine, are much more likely to appreciate the quantity than the quality of what is placed before them at supper.

We started early in the morning under a deluge of rain and a truly Egyptian darkness, which gave a sort of ghostly solemnity to our passage through the mountains. Day dawned upon us through jagged chasms as destitute of vegetation as the rocks on which the ocean has beaten since the creation of the world; while far below our feet the Rhone wound its devious way, and little farms, with their cottages, patches of vineyards even, and pastures lined its banks. While the sun was still low in the horizon, and shooting his beams aslant into these awful hillside recesses, which foot of living being never penetrated, some sudden turn of the road would carry us round into what seemed a sort of vast mountain prison, open but to the heavens, and lighted up only by the cold gray dawn.

Bellegarde is the frontier between France and Geneva. The rail roads in Europe have, I am told, forced upon the Custom-house officers a laudable promptitude in examining the baggage of travellers. Unless there is something very suspicious in the appearance of the traveller or his trunks, the search is almost nominal; and when appearances are suspicious, the individual is detained and the train allowed to proceed. We were told of an amusing trick sometimes practised here, as elsewhere on the frontier, to elude the vigilance of the Custom-house. Powerful dogs are trained to cross the frontier by lonely paths through the mountains, little known except to the smugglers. The poor animals are kept rather short of food, till they arrive at their destination, where they are liberally fed; and, what seems the hardest part of the discipline, in order to make them particularly careful to give the *douane* a good berth, they are soundly beaten, from time to time, by persons wearing the uniform of Custom-house officers. Small cases, containing the movements of watches and musical boxes, and some fine Swiss fabrics, are strapped about the bodies of the dogs, and a considerable contraband trade thus carried on. At this frontier, the rigor of the Custom-house, if at all, would be felt on entering, not on leaving, France. At any rate, we were treated with great consideration, and neither there nor elsewhere had any thing to complain of, in the examination of our baggage.

A short distance from the Inn at Bellegarde is the famous *Pert du Rhone*, (Loss of the Rhone,) the place where the river, at a low stage of the water, wholly disappears, and finds an underground passage for more than a hundred yards through the limestone rock, not a very uncommon circumstance in a calcareous formation. The river, when we saw it, was swollen by the heavy rain of the preceding night, and the volume of water was too great to pass entirely through the subterranean conduit. There was consequently nothing remarkable in the external appearance of things. The passage of the Rhone through the Jura is, however, under any circumstances, a striking object. The gorge is narrow, formed by precipitous heights, and the river is contracted to about the tenth part of its width at the outlet of the Lake of Geneva. When swelled by heavy rains or the melting of the Alpine Glaciers, it roars with magnificent violence through the narrow defile. Cæsar describes the road that passes by its side with minute accuracy, although modern engineering has contrived to supersede the "*angustum et difficile inter montem Juram et flumen Rhodanum* [*iter*], *vix qua singuli carri ducerentur*," by a broad railroad track.

Fort Ecluse stands at the extremity of the defile nearest France. The military position is naturally very strong; according to Cæsar *ut facile perpauci prohibere possent*, so that a very few persons could obstruct the passage. In addition to this, it was fortified, I believe, in the reign of Louis XIV., but the fortress in some subsequent war has been destroyed. When we passed, there was said to be an intention to rebuild it.

This passage has, in all time, been one of the main entrances into France on the Italian side, a highway trodden by mighty armies from the dawn of history. It was through this passage that the ancient Swiss (the Helvetii) emerged to the notice of the world. They were unknown to the Greeks in the palmy days of their greatness; and even in the decline of Greece, her writers, to the amazement of M. Simond, "speak of the Rhone and the Lake of Geneva, much as Canadian hunters do of Lake Michigan and the Blue Fox River." "It is curious," he says, "to imagine such a country as Switzerland, in the state in which the interior of America is in our day." M. Simond travelled in Switzerland in the same year (1818) in which I did. At that time Lake Michigan and the Blue Fox River might be said to be in the remote interior of America, and the regions watered by them still comparatively in a state of nature, and occupied by tribes somewhat lower in the scale of civilization than the Helvetii before the time of Cæsar. Forty years only have passed away, and Lake Michigan and the Blue Fox River at the present day (if that mean the Fox River of Wisconsin) water a region many times as populous as Switzerland; containing rapidly multiplying towns and villages; with churches, schools, and colleges; traversed by railroads and electric telegraphs, and affording in their rich wheat fields a bountiful home to the starving thousands who emigrate from Europe,—in due proportion from Switzerland!

The mind is stirred to busy thought on a spot like this. The Swiss, whose neutrality is now consecrated by the law of nations, and who have for centuries been protected by it from being absorbed by their powerful neighbors, are first known by one of the most extraordinary encroachments which history records. Not long after the Romans had reduced the south-eastern corner of Gaul to the condition of a *Province*, (of which a memorial never to be effaced is stamped upon the very language of the country, in the name of *Provence*,) an army of barbarians, of which the Helvetii formed a part, about a little more than a hundred years before our era, defeated the Roman Consul near Marseilles; but in consequence of a diversion effected by another Roman army in their rear, were obliged to return and defend their own country. The two armies met, it is supposed, not far from the spot where the Rhone, descending from the Valais, is about to enter the Lake of Geneva. The trained legions which had overrun Macedonia and all the conquests of "Macedonia's madman" in Greece, in Asia, and in Egypt, were broken by their barbarous enemies. Another and a larger Roman army soon met the same fate; and then the tide of fortune, as so often before in Roman history, was turned. The Helvetii and their confederates were defeated in two great battles at Aix, in Provence, by Marius, and soon after associated with the Cimbri and the Teutones, in their final attempt to force their way into Italy, they experienced a last overwhelming defeat by the same fortunate chieftain. One cannot but feel that there is "nothing new under the sun," when he reflects, that in the year 101, before our Saviour, the Germans of that day fought their battle of Solferino, in that very *quadrilatère*, within which the fortunes of their race, as far as Italy is concerned, are now (23d July) trembling in the balance of a doubtful diplomacy.

These foreign expeditions, however disastrous at the time, did not break the spirit of the Helvetii. That was an achievement reserved for a greater than Marius. They had tasted the figs of Provence and "quaffed the pendent vintage" of Burgundy, and resolved to abandon the shores of the lake of the "four sylvan cantons" and the cold sides of the Alps and the Jura, for a milder region. In a word, they determined to transfer their entire population from Switzerland to Gaul; from which we may infer that in those primitive days, the mystic attachment of the Swiss to his native mountains did not exist. After two years of secret preparations, in which stores were collected for the sustenance of an invading nation, the great movement commenced, according to Cæsar, on the 28th of March, of the year 58 before our Saviour. The aged and infirm, the women and the children, were placed on wagons, drawn by oxen; determined never to return, they burned their twelve Cantonal towns and four hundred villages; and moved forward an invading nation toward the coveted plains of Burgundy. Cæsar, at that time, governed the Province with pro-consular power, but seems to have been taken somewhat by surprise. The single legion, which composed his whole force, could oppose but an ineffectual resistance to the advance of an entire people of hardy adventurers; and leaving Labienus to watch their progress, he hastened to Italy for new levies. The Helvetii, in the mean time, turned the wall, which Cæsar had constructed from Geneva to the mountains, and, guided by the river, broke through Jura, where the Rhone does. There was no one to oppose them on the "lofty mountain," where "a very few could have stopped their way," and they rushed into Gaul.

But they rushed to their fate. Cæsar, who construed the law of nations with great strictness against the "rest of mankind," and deemed it an outrage for anybody but the Romans to encroach upon his neighbors, overtook them with six legions before they had wholly passed the Saône; cut off their rear (one-fourth part consisting of the Zurichers,) while they were passing the river; defeated the main body in a general action; hung upon the retreat of those that escaped; and after having destroyed three-fourths of their entire number, allowed the remainder, crushed and humbled, to return to their native vallies, and rebuild their cabins at the foot of the glaciers. He found among the spoils of their camp a register of their forces, kept in "Greek letters," and no doubt also in the Greek language; though on that point the learned are not agreed. It was unquestionably drawn up by some "Græculus esuriens" (hungry little Greek) an adventurer from Marseilles; for personages of that class,—adventurers if not renegades from civilized regions,—are invariably found in barbarous and semi-civilized States, in offices of trust requiring literary attainments. Italians, Germans, and Polish Jews are found, at the present day, in employments of that kind, at the courts of the Turkish, Persian, and Tartar Emirs and Viziers from Syria to India. By this Greek Register, it appeared that this invading force consisted of 263,000 Swiss and 105,000 of their allies from the Jura, the Lake of Constance, the Grisons, and the Tyrol; amounting together to 368,000 persons, of whom a fourth part, not a large proportion for tribes in that state of civilization, were fighting men. No great reliance is to be placed on the geographical synonyms, by which the Helvetian allies enumerated by Cæsar are referred to modern localities; and numerical *data* are matters of great uncertainty in all ancient authors, owing to their liability to error in the process of transcription. The foregoing numbers, however, do not appear exaggerated. A half a million is a moderate estimate for the entire population of a region whose arms defeated those of Consular Rome at the height of her power.

After being compelled to return to their former homes,

the ancient Swiss remained in subjection to their conquerors, protected for a while from new swarms of invaders, more barbarous than themselves, by the terror of the Roman name. Cæsar, meantime, in conquering them struck the first blow for the conquest of his country and the world. The liberties of Rome fell not so much when he crossed the Rubicon as when he crossed the Arar,* to attack the Swiss. That was the commencement of his unparalleled career.

The road from *Fort L'Ecluse* to Geneva is beautiful; a richer prospect is rarely to be seen. The rain had washed the dust from lawn and grove and thicket, and the verdure of Autumn had sprung up and covered the stubble of harvest. Every thing looked fresh and bright. Jura running off to the north-east bounded the view on the left; the distant Alps in front and on the right; Mont Blanc in the extreme background, glittering in a meridian sun. Before you, as you proceed, a beautiful plain descends gradually to the Lake, and cultivation is pushed up to the roots of Jura. Farm-houses, villas, patches of wood, the Rhone hurrying to its struggle through the mountains, and bearing along with it the sparkling tribute of a hundred silver brooks from the highlands, give life and charm to the landscape. At noon we reached Geneva; it was a fast day; the gates of the city were shut upon all egress, and the streets were still and sad.

* The ancient name of the Saône.

NUMBER FORTY-TWO.

EXCURSION FROM GENEVA TO CHAMOUNI, MONT BLANC.

The various attractions in Geneva—The influence of Calvin—The road to Chamouni up the valley of the Arve—Remarkable scene beyond Bonneville—Nant d'Arpennaz—First view of Mont Blanc—Goitres, whether considered a beauty by the peasantry—Lac de Chède—Servoz—The Upper Arve—Entrance into the valley of Chamouni—The glaciers—Description of a glacier—Their motion—Investigation of the cause by Professor Agassiz—The valley of Chamouni first made known to the travelling world by Pococke and Windham in 1741—Alpine scenery less frequently described by the poets than might have been expected.

FEW places unite in the same degree as Geneva and its vicinity, the attractions of natural beauty, historical association, and great names. Its lake, the deep blue waters and divided current of its river, the confluence of the Rhone and the Arve in the immediate neighborhood, Jura and Mont Blanc,—which may be said to belong to Geneva, or rather Geneva to them; its ancient memories, going back to the time of Cæsar; its curious mediæval annals, and the fortunes of its independent municipality; the great characters which, beginning with the greatest of all, Calvin, have adorned it; the names which it has given to modern letters, Rousseau, Voltaire, Gibbon, de Stäel, which, if not native to the region, have been intimately connected with it; these are sufficient to establish its claims to an equal variety and pre-eminence of interest. In the heraldry of the moral sentiments, the ideas which, through the Pilgrim fathers, the English dissenters and Puritans, and the Scottish covenanters trace their descent from the government and ministry of Calvin, will be found to fill no second place in the spiritual and intellectual aristocracy of the world. I suppose there are more persons, belonging to the reading and thinking classes of society in Europe and America, whose opinions on the most important subjects have been to some extent influenced, if not wholly determined, by the Instructions given in the church of St. Peter in Geneva, three hundred years ago, than by those of any other human teacher. Calvin's grave, without any monument or memorial but the letters J. C., attracts every year the visits of hundreds—perhaps thousands—of pilgrims; and his manuscripts in the public library (of which he was the founder) are examined with greater curiosity than any thing else contained in it. By a somewhat curious coincidence, the same library contains a manuscript on papyrus, of extreme antiquity and unique biographical value, of some of the discourses of St. Augustine,—the still greater Calvin of *his* age, at least as far as doctrine is concerned.

Geneva was rapidly becoming a foreign,—almost an English city,—forty years ago; a process which has, as I understand, been steadily going on ever since, especially since the era of railroads. Its beautiful environs furnish, for the year through, a more comfortable residence than those of the Italian cities, for the Russians and English, who in great numbers seek foreign homes. Many persons are attracted by the charming villa scenery of the Lake; not a few of the younger portion, by the opportunity of acquiring a tolerably good French accent, at a cheaper residence than Paris; a considerable number of families by the schools, at which their children are educated in or near Geneva. The hospitable and highly cultivated social circles of the city often tempt the tourist to prolong his sojourn far beyond its intended duration. My visit was too short to enable me to do much more than to feel the constantly experienced drawback on the gratifications incident to travel, either abroad or at home,—I mean the regret,—often the sorrow,—of forming a brief acquaintance with persons of highly cultivated minds and the most estimable social qualities, whose society you enjoy for a few days, and from whom you part to meet no more on earth.

But Mont Blanc is the object uppermost in the mind of the traveller on arriving at Geneva. After a few days spent in the city, we made our visit to Chamouni. The road, constantly ascending, lies for the greater part of the way along the banks of the Arve or through its valley. I never before felt so strongly the truth of Mr. Jefferson's remark, that it is the rivers which have made the mountains passable and opened their gates to man. The process described in his famous account of the confluence of the Potomac and Shenandoah, at Harper's Ferry, is repeated all over the world. Everywhere the waters have burst or worn their way through the mountains; and thus opened a path not only for themselves but for man and his highways.

Nothing very striking presents itself on the way to Chamouni, till you have passed Bonneville, a small town about half way on the first day's journey. After crossing the Arve, as you leave this place, you enter a stupendous scene. The valley is broad, but surrounded by rocky walls steeper than the goat can climb,—perpendicular in some places, nay, in some actually overhanging the road. They seemed to realize the simple imagery of "touching the sky." In some places as we passed, heavy clouds of mist hung half way upon their sides, gilded by a flood of sunbeams pouring over their tops. As the valley makes several sudden turns, we found ourselves more than once, surrounded on every side by these eternal barriers, whose contorted strata add not a little to the wildness of the scene. A person who should be conveyed while asleep into one of these mountain prisons would perceive no outlet nor inlet, and would think he must of necessity have fallen from the clouds. There is occasionally, however, a considerable space betwen the river and the foot of the precipice, which is clothed in all the beauty of a rich culture. The rays of the sun are condensed, as on a hot wall, and produce an almost tropical climate in the near neighborhood of Mont Blanc. Unmitigated adamantine barrenness and a luxuriant vegetation are thus brought into immediate contact with each other. A little beyond Maglan, you pass the *Nant d'Arpennaz*, a waterfall of great height and surpassing beauty, which, at some seasons of the year, after breaking into dust like the Staubbach, is condensed again into water, in the latter part of its course, and crossing the road under a bridge darts in foaming eddies to the Arve. The contorted stratification to which I have just alluded is very conspicuous in the limestone wall, over which the Nant d'Arpennaz plunges.

We passed the night in a decent inn at St. Martin. Here we caught the first fair full view of Mont Blanc, with all its snows and glaciers gloriously illuminated by the setting sun. What I had seen at the distance of a hundred miles, from Fourvières at Lyons, resembling a heavy white cloud in the horizon, now towered to the heavens, a mountain of purple light. The traveller should, by all means, if possible, arrive at St. Martin in season to enjoy this sunset view of Mont Blanc. In the morning it is seen under a different light, and loses something of its splendor. But whether seen in the morning or the evening, the first distinct near view of Mont Blanc is an era in a man's life. It is twelve or thirteen miles distant from St. Martin, but such is the pure transparence of the mountain air, that you feel as if the next step would bring you to its crystal sides. Great, however, is the deception. The moderate distance which intervenes between you and the summit of the mountain is still sufficient to soften the savage outline, bounding what seems a smooth, glittering, inclined plane,—on which you might, to all appearance, walk gently up to heaven. It is not till you have contemplated the surrounding and nearer objects,—measured the valley of the Arve with your eye, as it ranges up the course of the river, and surveyed the sides of the Col de Forclaz, dark with forests, its top not too high for

Alpine pasturage,—(we fancied that we could hear the tinkling of the cowbells, but the distance was too great,)—and then some of the outer buttresses of Mont Blanc which lie beyond, that the mind corrects the illusion of the sight, and forming a clearer idea of its distance, you more fully appreciate its majestic dimensions.

At St. Martin we left our post-chaise, and took a char-á-banc, the light vehicle of the mountains, for Chamouni. Seated by the side of the driver, I endeavored to learn from him if there was any foundation in truth for the current notion, that the *goitre*, which begins to prevail as you penetrate the lofty Alpine vallies, is deemed a beauty by their inhabitants. Anecdotes built on that supposition are found in books of travels and novelettes in the Periodicals. "What a beauty that Miladi would be, if she only had a *goitre!*" A wretched object in whom this deformity was very conspicuous passed us, as we were toiling up the road before reaching Chède. I repeated to the driver one of the anecdotes of the kind alluded to, and asked him whether the young men and women of that region really thought the *goitre* a beauty. He looked at me somewhat reproachfully, and answered, "*Malheureux ceux qui en ont*," woe to those who have it!

The road is very steep at Chède. Here we turned aside to see a pretty cascade, the *Nant de Chède*, arched by a brilliant rainbow. Farther on we came to the *Lac de Chède*, in which Mont Blanc was reflected as in a mirror. The guide book states that in 1837, it was filled up with stone and black mud, in one of those *debácles*, or mountain freshets, which are continually changing the aspect of the vallies in the upper Alps. The road now passes over what was the *Miroir de Chède*. The road constantly ascending crosses the bed of a torrent,—probably the same which in some former inundation filled up the *Miroir*, and still often changes its track by the chaotic accumulations brought down by every violent storm. The considerable effect sometimes produced, in this way, in a few hours in the narrow vallies interposed between these lofty mountains, teaches a significant lesson as to the vast results of great elemental forces acting for a succession of ages,—of mighty geological periods,—on the earth's surface.

We breakfasted at the little village of Servoz, which lies about half way between St. Martin and Chamouni, and here we got the last view of the summit of Mont Blanc before turning into the valley. Farther on it is hidden by intervening "Domes," as these vaulted mountain heights are expressively called in French. Not far from Servoz, you cross a mountain torrent called the Diosà, and soon reach the Pont Pelissier, where the Arve whose turbid stream first attracted your notice at its junction with the pure blue Rhone below the Lake of Geneva, and which has been coquetting with you all the way from the lake up to Chamouni, rushes out from a mountain gorge, and gives a character to the valley. It still, as you toil onward, keeps you company on the left, bounding from terrace to terrace; raving through the rocks, which it has itself rent from the mountain sides, sometimes plunging into depths, where the eye would seek in vain to follow it, but occasionally spreading out for a few yards into a smooth mountain pool. Mont Blanc now looms upon you in all its grandeur, although its summit is hidden by the Dome du Gouté. You are now in the valley of Chamouni; you cross by another bridge to the right bank of the Arve, which runs parallel with the foot of the Breven and at a short distance from it, while on the opposite banks a succession of glaciers stretch into the valley, at right angles to its course.

A glacier of the largest dimensions is to the thoughtful student of nature one of the most extraordinary phenomena on the surface of the globe, while it is also one of those of which, without ocular inspection, it is most difficult to form an accurate idea. It is a vast mass of ice and melted snow, in some cases seven or eight hundred feet thick, and several miles wide and long, filling the space between two Alpine ridges, or the gorge which cuts deep into the face of a mountain. It is, therefore, a frozen sea, whose shores are composed of wild granatic or calcareous cliffs, open on its lower end to the valley. The glacier is not homogeneous, but its lower strata consists of solid ice, while the upper portion is a mass which has alternately melted and frozen, and is somewhat porous. The surface is rough and undulating, and broken by crevices, some of which are narrow and easily leapt over by the aid of the Alpine staff, shod with iron, which is placed in the traveller's hand; others are wide, deep, and impassable; a yawning, frozen grave to the hapless tourist, who should miss a step upon the brink. A very striking case of a fatal accident of this kind is narrated, in the London Illustrated News for the 27th of August, 1859. From the lower extremity of the glacier a stream of water issues, produced by the action of the sun on the exposed surfaces of the mass, and percolating through the crevices, and the porous substance of the glacier, whose volume thus suffers a diminution in the summer, sometimes equal to its increase in the winter.

But the most extraordinary fact in connection with the glaciers is their motion. It has long been known that the mighty mass, which one would suppose must, independent of its weight, be frozen immovably to the eternal rocks that bound and underlie it, is nevertheless steadily ploughing its way, with irresistible force, down the inclined surface on which it lies, grinding and throwing up vast furrows of granite, limestone and gravel, called *moraines*, from the sides of the gorge. This fact, I say, was noticed by the early observers, but much doubt rested on the cause of the motion. The researches of Professor Agassiz, carried on with unwearied diligence, wonderful acuteness of observation, and sagacity of inference, have established the theory, now generally accepted, that this forward motion is caused by the action upon each other of the particles which compose the somewhat porous mass of the glacier, and which are alternately expanded and contracted by change of temperature. This theory attracted great attention as first brought to general notice by Professor Forbes, (who speaks of the glaciers as " viscous " bodies,) who passed some weeks with Mr. Agassiz on the gigantic glacier of the Aar, where, for several successive seasons, this last-named illustrious Philosopher had been pursuing his investigations.

It is not the least remarkable circumstance in connection with Mont Blanc and Chamouni that they remained so long unknown to the travelling world. The common accounts represent them as having been discovered by Dr. Richard Pococke (afterwards Bishop of Ossory) and his companion Windham, in 1741. Mr. Simond, one of the most intelligent of modern travellers, says, " Incredible as it may seem, this valley of Chamouni, *till then unknown, was discovered* in 1741 by two Englishmen, the celebrated traveller Pococke and a Mr. Windham." This, however, requires explanation. The Priory, which still gives its name to the central village of Chamouni, and to the house of entertainment there, was founded toward the close of the eleventh century ; a visitation of the Bishop of Geneva, in whose diocese it lay, is recorded in the fifteenth ; and St. Francis de Sales visited it in the seventeenth century. I take these facts from Murray's handbook, where others to the same effect may be found ; but the statement also given there, that the Report of the excursion of Messrs. Pococke and Windham to Chamouni " is in the Royal Society's transactions in 1741 " is erroneous. There is nothing of that kind in that volume, nor as far as the index of Reuss can be trusted, any other volume of the Royal Society's transactions, unless it appears under some other name. There is no reason to suppose that the valley of Chamouni was " unknown," in any strict sense of the word, from the earliest antiquity, in any other way than all thinly inhabited and remote mountain regions were unknown, till a comparatively recent period, during which travelling for recreation and pleasure has become so much more frequent than it ever was in former times. There must always have been a road, though not the most direct one, from Geneva, up the valley of the Arve, through Chamouni, by the way of the Col de Balme, to Martigny, where a Roman legion was stationed by Julius Cæsar. It is, however, most true, that the visit of Messrs. Pococke and Windham is the earliest that is known to have been made by modern tourists, and seems to have first turned the attention of the world of travellers in that direction.

It is somewhat noticeable that natural phenomena, so peculiar and extraordinary as the awful peaks and icy seas of the upper Alps, should not more frequently have furnished the poets with appropriate imagery. Even if we assume that the *Mer de Glace* and Mont Blanc were "discovered" in 1741, other portions of the Alpine chain were known from time immemorial. A continual intercourse for the purposes of trade as well as war has been kept up between Italy and the regions west of it, at least from the time of the Roman conquests, and through the middle ages, down to the present day. One might have expected that natural objects of a character so grandly marked and peculiar would, through the reports of intelligent travellers, have been reflected into the literature,—prose and poetry—both of the ancients and moderns. Cicero and Cæsar, Petrarch and Tasso crossed the Alps, as did Milton and Addison, Thomson and Gray. It would be hazardous to say that, in the wide range of ancient and modern poetry, there is no description of the scenery in question, till the last century, but I am inclined to think that, in poets of the first class, it does not go beyond general allusions. Milton speaks of "many a frozen Alp," Thomson describes an Avalanche, Coleridge in a hymn, mainly borrowed, it is said, from the German,* chants the solemn glories of Chamouni before sunrise, and Byron, who wrote his Man-

* De Quincey's Literary Reminiscences, Vol. I., p. 156.

fred within sight of Mont Blanc, consecrates one majestic Quatrain to "the monarch of mountains." But I recollect no master passage (like the descriptions of the Eruption of Ætna by Eschylus and Pindar) of which you would say after reading it, that it was conceived by the side of an Alpine glacier or at the foot of an Alpine peak. Some splendid stanzas in Childe Harold may be deemed an exception to this remark.

NUMBER FORTY-THREE.

THE MONTANVERT, THE SEA OF ICE, AND THE GREEN GARDEN.

Excursion to the Jardin Vert—Ascent to the Montanvert—Prospect from it—Solitary cabin—Beautiful midnight scene—Crossing the Mer de Glace, crevasses—Dangerous pass along the face of the mountain—Reach the Jardin—Sublimity of the scene—Return to the Montanvert—Descent to the lower end of the Mer de Glace and the source of the Arveiron—Geological significance of the recent inquiries into the formation and movement of the Glaciers—Importance of these bodies in the economy of nature.

Desirous of seeing a fair specimen of Alpine scenery, and not having time to multiply excursions, we determined on visiting the *Jardin Vert*, (the Green Garden,) the highest point of vegetation in Europe. This spot can only be reached by ascending the Montanvert,* and crossing the *Mer de Glace*, (Sea of Ice,) which is one of the noblest glaciers in the Alpine range. The excursion requires a day and a half from the valley of Chamouni, is very fatiguing, and at that time, as will presently be seen, was not unattended with danger. It was, therefore, not very frequently undertaken. Some improvement has, I believe, been made in the most difficult passes, by which the danger is diminished; and excursions to the *Jardin Vert* are, in consequence more common than they were forty years ago.

Having laid in a small stock of provisions, we started from the Inn in the valley of Chamouni, at three o'clock in the afternoon. The road for the first part of the way lies

* This name is variously spelt. In the French motto to the highly interesting chapter on Chamouni, in Beattie and Bartlett's Switzerland, Vol I., it is written *Mont Envers*

through the valley of the Arve, but begins to ascend rapidly after you strike into the pine woods that skirt the foot of the mountain. There was in 1818 no beaten pathway through this patch of forest, and we suffered a good deal of fatigue in following our guides, as they led us over fallen trees, projecting roots, scattered boulders from the heights above, and across the bed of torrents, which, after a heavy rain, came foaming down the mountain sides. But the fine views that continually open upon you as you ascend—the opposite summits of the Breven, the range of the valley, and presently the magnificent peak called the *Aiguille de Dru*—amply repay you for the labor. The distance to the Montanvert, as we travelled it, was about three leagues, which took us about half a mile above the level of the valley. There was accordingly, in some of the steeper places, no little need of the long staves, shod with iron, with which our guides had provided us.

We reached the Montanvert about sunset, and there enjoyed a prospect of transcendent grandeur and beauty. The elevation above the level of the sea is about equal to that of Mount Washington, in the White Mountains; it is nearly the highest easily accessible point in the Alps. Light evening clouds were floating on the opposite sides of the Flegere and Breven, touched and gilded by the twilight of a mild September evening. Directly before us and beneath the level of the Montanvert was the Sea of Ice, entering the valley of Chamouni abruptly, nearly on a range with the spot where we stood, and stretching for miles backward and upward to the right. This immense glacier is called the "Sea of Ice" from its magnitude, and because its rough, broken surface looks as we may suppose the sea would look, if it could be suddenly frozen solid at the height of a storm. All was silent on the top of the mountain, except that a cow-boy was singing his *ranz des vaches*, as he drove his four or five animals to their shed, and the Arveiron, in the stillness of the evening, was heard with a hollow murmur, bursting out from beneath the glacier below, and rushing to the Arve.

A tolerably substantial cabin, consisting of one room, but wholly destitute of furniture, except two or three wooden benches, was the only habitation for man on the Montanvert in 1818. A small inn with two or three bed-rooms has since been erected for the accommodation of travellers. A cow-herd and his boy were the only occupants of the lonely spot at that time, and milk and curds the only food to be obtained there. As we were to pass the night on the mountain, we had provided ourselves more substantially, and made a hearty meal on dried goat-mutton. This done, we kindled an immense fire, drew two benches together, and with our feet to the blazing logs, and our knapsacks for pillows, lay down to sleep. At midnight I was wakened by the moon, full or nearly so, pouring upon my face, through the window of the cabin. I did not hesitate to obey the summons, and went out to contemplate a scene at once the most lovely and awful that my eyes ever rested on. The light of the moon at this great elevation, and in consequence of the purity of the air, had a strange metallic intensity. The supreme stillness of Nature on these lofty Alpine summits, unbroken by any thing but the moan of the Arveiron, would have been dreary, had not an occasional tinkle of the cow-bell from the shed near us given a token of life. A sharp crack from the glacier from time to time also told that there was motion there. The mildness and serenity of midnight in these frozen solitudes were as pleasing to me as they were unexpected. I had been anticipating benumbing cold and roaring winds, loaded with blinding particles of drift snow.

We were abroad at the earliest dawn. Below us was the frozen sea, six or seven miles in length, and then branching out into two other glaciers, running further back into the inmost recesses of the Alps. Directly in front of us was the *Aiguille de Dru*, and further in the rear and on the right the

Aiguille du Moine, the mighty granitic steeples of Nature's temple, rearing their ragged pinnacles to the heavens. About midway between the Dru and the Moine is the *Aiguille Verte*, which overtops both, and reaches the height of nearly thirteen thousand feet above the level of the sea; twice the elevation of the Montanvert. The intervals between these peaks, which are miles apart, are filled with numerous other *needles* (Aiguilles), as they are called, of various sizes and heights, which unite to give an inexpressible savageness, if I may so call it, to the scene. If the reader will fancy to himelf an immense mountain gorge, six miles long, branching into two others of about equal length, the whole forming something like a Y, the sides bounded by two or three parallel ridges of bare granite, from which at irregular intervals the above-mentioned pinnacles rise to the clouds; and will then conceive this strange enclosure to be filled with a stormy sea, which, at the moment when it was tossing most wildly, had been frozen to the bottom, so that it should spread out a vast rigid mass, with all its icy billows and deep crystal chasms, and here and there a stray boulder on its surface; he will have as correct an idea of the *Mer de Glace*, as seen from the Montanvert, as can be formed without ocular inspection.

Our day's work was to cross this frozen sea diagonally, and return before night. The distance to be traversed on the glacier might, in a straight line, be about three miles, but it was considerably increased by following a serpentine course. We had screwed sharp iron points into the soles of our boots, and our long poles were armed with iron. With this preparation we started, each following his guide. The *moraines* were first to be crossed, by a toilsome, and frequently difficult, and even dangerous path. The surface of the glacier was in some places extremely rough and uneven, and broken by crevices, some of which appeared, as we looked down, to be forty or fifty feet deep. Woe to the wretch who should fall into one of them! Some of the deepest of these crevices communicate with the currents that flow beneath the mass, and carry off the percolating waters. It is related that in 1787, a shepherd, who was living sixty years afterwards, fell into one of these deep crevices,—*crevasses*, as they are more commonly called by the French name,—which, happily for him, communicated with the vaulted passage worn by the trickling waters, through which he escaped to the light of day with no worse injury than a broken arm.

A little snow had fallen shortly before we crossed the glacier, and it was necessary to use great care, not to step on places where it had, by drifting, formed a frail and treacherous crust over one of these crevices. With all our care to place our feet exactly in the footsteps of our guide, we were sometimes misled by the apparent solidity of the adjacent surface, and slipped into holes three or four feet deep. Besides the smaller crevices which break the surface of the glacier, it is traversed by broader fissures, at right angles to the main direction of the mass, which often make it impossible to advance in a straight line. Occasionally one of the huge boulders just mentioned would afford the means of crossing these fissures; sometimes they were bridged over by broad cakes of ice; and sometimes it was necessary to climb down on one side and up on the other, by the aid of the projecting inequalities in the icy wall. In this way we travelled by estimate about six miles in three hours, and found ourselves landed at the foot of the opposite mountain, called the *Couvercle.* Here we rested for half an hour. The almost perpendicular face of this mountain was next to be climbed, and here the danger seemed to me far greater than at " the Ponts," which Murray's Hand-book calls the most difficult part of the excursion, which " no one who has not a steady head should attempt to cross." It is probable that the constant downward march of the glacier, ploughing its way towards the valley may, in the course of forty years, have produced important changes in the *moraines* (the chaotic ridges) that bound it.

In ascending the side of the mountain, it is necessary in one place to pass along its almost perpendicular face at a height of five or six hundred feet from its base, with no other support for the feet but the cavities, an inch or two deep, some natural, some apparently artificial, by means of which, supporting yourself in the mean time with your hands, you sidle along. One of the guides introduced us to this passage, called the *Egralets*, by the tranquillizing exclamation: "Here take care how you step, gentlemen, or you are lost!"

After this formidable pass we had still to climb the mountain, but by a safer ascent, for an hour and a half, and then, having crossed the head of the glacier, we reached the *Jardin Vert*, a small green spot, in the very heart of the Alps, more than nine thousand feet above the level of the sea. Its size varies with the length of the preceding winter, or the heat of the season. It is sometimes seven or eight acres in extent, but it appeared to me less than two. It is the highest point of vegetation in Europe, and covered with a coarse Alpine grass. No description can do justice to the feelings which one experiences at this great elevation—the joint result of sensation, thought, and emotion. You still see around you the magnificent peaks already described, while other columns and glaciers open upon you from the new point of view. Far away as you are in these terrible mountain fastnesses, from every living being, the mind sinks under the fearful solitude and overwhelming grandeur of the scene. There was not a cloud in the sky; its tint was nearly black; the rays of the sun were condensed as in a vast concave mirror; and the heat so intense that our faces were too much blistered to use a razor with any comfort, for a week afterwards.

After a hearty lunch and a short nap, we started on the return. This we were able to accomplish in rather less time than the ascent, partly because a considerable part of the way was down hill; and in other places because we had our morning's pathway in the snow to guide us. The *Egralets*, however, appeared to me rather more formidable than they did in the morning. The snow that lodged in the excavations above-mentioned had partly melted and coated them with thin ice. I have, in the course of my life, been a few times in what seemed to me dangerous situations, but never in one where the peril appeared so great. We got back to the Montanvert at about four o'clock in the afternoon, having accomplished the difficult expedition, much to our satisfaction, in about ten hours from the time of starting, for nine of which we had been in motion. Our guides told us that the *Jardin* was not often visited; and they knew of but one lady who had made the excursion; a daughter of the celebrated aëronaut Montgolfier.

I took my leave of the Montanvert with a sorrowful feeling, that I should never probably revisit the scene of so much sublime beauty. We descended by a different and steeper path, in order to see the source of the Arveiron. A part of the way the inclination was too great to admit any use of the feet, walking or running; we were obliged to resort to a simpler form of locomotion, which speedily brought us to the foot of the mountain, and to the front of the glacier as it presents itself to the valley. This is what may be called the outlet of one of the three of the largest Alpine glaciers; for among six hundred which Escher estimates to be the entire number, that of Mont Blanc just described, of Monte Rosa, and of the Finster-Aar-Horn in the Bernese Alps, are the largest and most important. The last-named has been explored with the greatest care, and is that on which the observations of Mr. Agassiz were made, which have furnished the basis of the accepted theory of these extraordinary formations.

The arched cavern in the middle of the face of the glacier, from which the Arveiron was pouring forth the entire drainage of the *Mer de Glace*, varies in dimensions in different seasons. It appeared to me, at the outlet, about ninety feet high,—the entrance to a magnificent crystal grotto. In winter it is said wholly to disappear. It begins to be formed in spring, increases in height and width with the advance of summer; and sometimes the upper arch, sometimes the lateral buttresses become so much softened and melted away, that a considerable portion comes down with a mighty crash. Contrary to what might be expected, the water, which issues from these mountains of ice and snow, is not remarkably clear. It is generally turbid, sometimes charged with earthy deposits, the result no doubt of the grinding action of the glacier on its rocky bed and sides.

This is not the place for a disquisition on the important geological inferences, which have been drawn from the more accurate study of the Swiss glaciers of late years. The surface of the globe, wherever it has been explored, presents appearances, which can be best referred to the action of these mighty masses of ice, driven along, in some former condition of our planet, by oceanic currents, like those which at the present day bring down the terrific icebergs of the North to our temperate latitudes.—At the present day, it is justly observed by the able editor of Murray's Hand-book of Switzerland, that "it is highly interesting to consider, how important a service the glaciers perform in the economy of nature. These dead and chilly fields of ice, which prolong the reign of winter throughout the year, are, in reality the source of life and the springs of vegetation. They are the locked up reservoirs, the sealed fountains, from which the vast rivers, traversing the great continents of our globe, are sustained. The summer heat which dries up other sources of water, first opens out their bountiful supplies. When the rivers of the plain begin to shrink and dwindle within their parched beds, the torrents of the Alps, fed by melting snow and glaciers, rush down from the mountains and supply the deficiency; and at that season (July and August) the rivers and lakes of Switzerland are the fullest."

NUMBER FORTY-FOUR.

GENEVA, FERNEY, LAUSANNE.

Rousseau's house—His manuscripts—Partial insanity the best apology for his conduct—Voltaire's Chateau at Ferney—Description of his room and list of portraits in it—Other memorials—Contrast of Ferney as it was during Voltaire's life-time and its present appearance—His life and works an entire failure—Coppet and Madame de Staël—Gouverneur Morris—Lausanne—Gibbon's house—its appearance in 1818—Summer-house in the garden, where he was accustomed to study—Last lines of the Decline and Fall written there—Hume's striking remark in 1767, on the stability and duration of the English language, in consequence of its prevalence in America.

HAVING little time to spare, we made the return to Geneva in one day, which was done with the greater ease, as the road is generally on the descent, and with the greater willingness, as the prospects looking westward are far less magnificent. Our lodgings were at the *Ecu de Genève*, which commanded in the rear a most pleasing view of the River and the Lake. The former is perhaps a finer object than that portion of the Lake which is seen from the terrace. The "arrowy" swiftness of the Rhone, the deep blue tint and purity of the water, as it hurries in its divided current through the city, are renowned in prose and in poetry. Every one has heard of the confluence of the Rhone and the Arve, a short distance below the city, and the stately refusal of the former to mingle its limpid current with the turbid waters of the latter stream. At the *table d'hôte* of the hotel there were persons (as we had the means of knowing) of eight different countries, speaking that number of languages. There might have been still others of different nations and tongues. Among the English was

Mr. Elmsley, whom I had the good fortune to know at Oxford,—one of the best Greek scholars of his time, and then on his way to examine the classical manuscripts in the Ambrosian library at Milan.

The house in which Rousseau was born is on a street which bears his name. Though of three stories in height, it has a mean appearance. Over the door are inscribed in plain letters the words *Jean Jacques Rousseau, né ici xxviii Juin,* 1712, "John James Rousseau was born here on the 28th of June, 1712." A number of the original manuscripts of Rousseau, including that of his "Confessions," were preserved at Geneva, at the time of our visit, in the possession of the son of the friend to whom he bequeathed them. We were promised an opportunity of inspecting them, but were accidentally prevented from availing ourselves of it. Rousseau describes his own mode of writing as extremely laborious, and speaks of his manuscripts as being "full of erasures and blots, and undecipherable." The manuscript of the *Confessions* was represented to us, as being in his own hand, written with great neatness, and entirely free from erasures and blots. It was of course a fair copy, written out by himself. The directions given by him, that his autobiography should be published as written, without alteration or retrenchment, were, it seems, to some extent disobeyed, by the omission of passages too gross to see the light. It would have been well for his good name if these scruples had been carried further. One apology,—a wretched one, it is true—may be made for some of the details of his book, in which the frailties of others are meanly divulged in connection with his own. His intention was that the publication should not take place till 1800, and when he probably thought that all those whose names were introduced by him would have passed away. It appeared, however, the first part in 1781, three years after his death, and the second in 1788. The injurious effects of its disclosures, or what purport to be such, on the characters of others were in a great degree neutralized by the generally prevailing impression that no statement made by him is entitled to belief, which rests merely on his own authority. It has been shown in some cases that the whole truth was not told by him, even in reference to breaches of morality confessed by himself, and where the frankness of the admission might seem to challenge belief.

The best apology to be made for the life as for the writings of Rousseau is, that he was partially insane. Such seems to have been the opinion of the most renowned of his admirers. In Byron's poetical apotheosis of Rousseau, he says :—

> " But he was frenzied,—wherefore who may know?
> Since cause might be which skill could never find;
> But he was frenzied by disease or woe,
> To that worst pitch of all, that wears a reasoning show."

No other theory so well explains his character as a writer and as a man; and this I am aware is only saying in other words that they admit no rational explanation or defence. It is doubtful whether the last century, so fertile in France of publications adapted to deprave the public taste and poison the minds of the young of both sexes, produced any thing worse than the writings of Rousseau. He had too much discernment,—if entitled to be called a rational being, to be unconscious himself that this was the character and tendency of his writings; and yet when Voltaire, not yet his enemy, at the time of the persecutions occasioned by the appearance of *Emile* offered its author an Asylum at Ferney, Rousseau, with affected candor, replied, " I do not love you, you have corrupted my republic in giving it a theatre." Such was the edifying anxiety of the author of the *New Eloise* for the morals of the young men and women of Geneva! On one occasion a person introduced himself in the following manner: " You see before you a father who has educated his son agreeably to the principles in your Emile." Rousseau's reply was "So much the worse for you and your son!"—It seems to have been the design of Providence to furnish in the conduct and in the autobiography of Rousseau, an all-sufficient antidote for the poison of his writings.

Voltaire's residence at Fernex, or Ferney, as it is usually written, is about six miles from Geneva, and just within the limits of France. After his quarrel with Frederic the Great, and a temporary residence at Lausanne and at *Les Délices* (a villa which still bears that name, and which you pass on the way from Geneva to Ferney) he established himself at this last named place, where he lived *en grand seigneur* for twenty years, till his triumphant return to Paris. There is but little natural beauty about it, though it enjoys a distant view of the lake. Whatever must be said unfortunately of Voltaire's political or religious influence, he was a beneficent landlord, and built up Ferney, which before his time was a small poverty-stricken hamlet, into a large and prosperous village. The mansion, *Chateau*, (castle,) as with some latitude of application it is usually called, is a large, and may have been in other times a somewhat imposing, residence; but it had in 1818 a forlorn and dilapidated appearance. There was a small chapel on the left as you enter the enclosure which is said to have borne the inscription *Deo erexit Voltaire*, and sometimes given in French *à Dieu Voltaire*.* This inscription, if it ever existed, has long since disappeared. It is said to have been obliterated during the French Revolution.

We were shown Voltaire's bedroom, and told that we saw it as he left it. In size it may be eleven or twelve feet by fifteen or sixteen; it is on the ground floor, and was scantily and meanly furnished. The chair coverings and curtains were of silk, once blue, much faded, and greatly mutilated by travelling *virtuosi*, for whose benefit no doubt they are from time

* "Erected by Voltaire in honor of God."

to time renewed. The bed is a single one of very ordinary materials and appearance. Directly over the bed inside hangs the portrait of the celebrated actor, Le Kain, the great reformer of the French stage, to whom Voltaire felt under special obligations for having contributed to the success of his plays, by the spirit and naturalness of his acting. On one side of the bed is a likeness in crayon of Frederic the Great, and on the other of Voltaire himself. The indignities which he suffered from his royal patron did not make him wish to have their friendly relations forgotten. On the side of the room, as you enter, is a strange kind of monument erected to him, in a sort of coarse porcelain, by his adopted daughter, Madame de Villette. It contained the heart of Voltaire, with the inscription in French, "His spirit is everywhere, his heart is here." In the French Revolution the heart was removed to the Pantheon at Paris. Nothing can be in worse taste than this memorial. On the same side of the room is a portrait of the Empress Catharine II. of Russia, wrought in needle-work by herself and presented to Voltaire; an engraving of Pope Clement the XIV., and of Voltaire's favorite Savoyard servant. On the opposite side of the room is a portriat of Madame de Châtelet; and on the fourth, on one side of the window, are engravings of the family of the unfortunate Calas, of Delille, under which is written, in Voltaire's hand—

"Nulli flebilior quam tibi, Virgili," *

of Diderot, Newton, and Franklin, (these in one row,) and under them Racine, Milton, WASHINGTON, and Corneille; and on the other side of the window, in one row, Thomas, Leibnitz, Dortons de Maire, and d'Alembert, and under these Helvetius and Marmontel, with an emblematic engraving of the monument of Voltaire, placed there after his death. These paintings and engravings are here enumerated as we

* "Lamented by no one more than by thee, O Virgil."

saw them in 1818. Other lists are given, and it is very likely that changes have been made in the course of the eighty-one years which have elapsed since his death, during which the *Chateau* has been the property of several owners. In the garden was a monument of wood, erected in honor of Voltaire by one of his admirers, covered with votive inscriptions; and in the gardener's house an album was shown us containing the seals of Voltaire's correspondents separated from the letters, with the names of the writers placed under them in Voltaire's hand. The aged gardener, who spoke with great respect of the memory of his illustrious employer, gave us some specimens of the seals and of Voltaire's writing, from this book. As the same favor was extended by a descendant of the gardener a few years ago to one of my children, and has been no doubt to an entire intervening generation of travellers, the album and its contents may be supposed to be endowed with some self-renewing property.

It is, of course, impossible from its present desolate appearance, after moth and rust, and time and tourists, and invading armies and revolutions have done their worst upon the *Chateau* and its belongings, to form an idea of what Ferney may have been in Voltaire's time, when it was the seat of a profuse hospitality; of entertainments at which two hundred sat at table at once; when plays were performed in his private theatre, in which he himself took part; and he, the most popular writer of the day, was the centre of attraction to a throng, in which the most distinguished persons of all countries were eager to mingle. When Mr. Fox saw him, which was a "long time ago," he "lived in great elegance." Voltaire was immensely rich, and though methodical in the management of his property, scattered his income with a free hand. Beyond the circle of his immediate dependants, he was not a favorite in the community. In Geneva, his infidel principles, and the profligacy of some of his poetical writings, combined with the aristocratic state which he kept up, to make him an object of universal dislike. He had succeeded as little as Rousseau, in corrupting the simple manners and depraving the austere morals of the miniature republic. He repaid the aversion of his neighbors with sarcasms upon the limited dimensions of their territory. "When I shake my wig," he was accustomed to say, "I powder the whole republic." The shabby magnificence and tawdry and faded splendors of Ferney are not out of keeping with their master's career; in which you know not which most to wonder at; the astonishing versatility and vigor of the natural endowments, or the miserably inconsequential and ephemeral results. It was the great and avowed aim of Voltaire's life and writings to destroy the popular faith in the Christian Religion. His works, constructed with that main object in view, and with the utmost boldness of direct attack and skill of covert and adroit insinuation, attained a contemporary reputation, which no other writings of the same description perhaps ever possessed. Besides this, his theories and speculations were reduced to practice, and his godless ribaldry turned into ghastly realities, by the only great political movement in the world ever built on the negation of religious responsibility; and yet by the mysterious working together of things, in the disposal of an all-wise Providence, there perhaps never was a time since the primitive conversion of France to Christianity, when it was more generally treated throughout that country with outward respect, than at the present day, and when, as far as we have a right to judge, it was more cordially embraced by the mass of the people, as a system, a rule, a comfort, and a hope.

A short distance from Geneva, on the western side of the Lake, lies Coppet, famous as the residence of M. and Madame Neckar, and their still more celebrated daughter, Madame de Staël. The room in which she is said to have written Corinne, her desk and inkstand, are shown to the traveller. The present generation can hardly form an adequate idea of the celebrity of this lady as a writer and a politician. Her father's reputation as a financier, at the outbreak of the French revolution, the popularity of the daughter's romances, especially Corinne, whose laurel wreath was supposed to have been woven with autobiographical sympathy, her proscription by Napoleon, her European fame as a conversationist, her courage in undertaking, even with the intelligent guidance of August Schlegel, an exhaustive survey of the philosophy and literature of Germany, of which very little was known at that time either in France or England, and the masculine shrewdness and eloquence of her speculations on the French revolution had earned for her a most brilliant name in England and in this country. I had letters to her from persons whom she held in great respect, whose names I record with melancholy satisfaction,—Mr. Gouverneur Morris, Mr. Gallatin, and Mr. Clay; but her illustrious career was closed the year before I went to France. The letters procured me a most amiable reception, from the surviving members of her family, the Baron August de Staël, and from her son-in-law and daughter, the Duke and Duchess de Broglie, whose *salons* were the centre of the most refined and intellectual circles of Paris. Mr. Gouverneur Morris, as the American Minister at Paris in 1792, was on terms of familiar intimacy at M. Neckar's house. Madame de Staël in her Germany calls him "Un Americain fort spirituel," (a very ingenious American,) and quotes with applause his remark that "the French had gone beyond liberty."

It took us the better part of the day to reach Lausanne, starting from Geneva in the morning and passing by Coppet, Niort, Rolle, and Morges. The first thing to be done at Lausanne is, of course, to visit Gibbon's house, where he passed much of his life and wrote his great monumental history. It was with some difficulty that we got a direction to it from our hotel, and from the servant who conducted us through the premises we received the satisfactory intelligence that Mr.

Gibbon formerly lived there, but was now dead. The house stands high on a terrace, commanding a fine view of the Lake, which appears to greater advantage here than at Geneva. The ornamental trees in front of the house have been cut down, and the grounds planted with fruit trees, were in 1818 entirely unpicturesque. The principal rooms on the lower floor of the house had been converted into the counting-rooms of its proprietor, who was a man of business. A long staircase of stone, inside the house, conducts you to the terrace or garden, which is long and narrow. At its extremity, in a grove of dwarf beech trees, is a sort of summer-house occupied by Gibbon as a study. On various places on the walls of this apartment, as on the surrounding trees, were nailed small pieces apparently of tin, painted white, (they may have been canvass,) on which were printed striking passages and mottoes principally from the Latin Poets. Their appearance was far from being tasteful.

It was in this summer-house, as he informs us in his autobiography, that, on the 27th of June, 1787, between the hours of eleven and twelve, he wrote the last lines of the last page of his great work. "After laying down my pen," he adds, "I took several turns in a *berceau* or covered walk of acacias, which commands a prospect of the country, the lake, and the mountains. The air was temperate, the sky was serene, the silver orb of the moon was reflected from the waves, and all nature was silent."

That was indeed one of the great moments in the intellectual history of man, when the foretaste of an immortal name is enjoyed by a master spirit. It breathed a tenderness into the somewhat gross and cynical temperament of Gibbon. There is a curious association of Gibbon's literary career with the diffusion of the English language in this country. He had early in life lived a good deal on the continent, and under the impression that French was to be the universal tongue, wrote his first Essay in that language. He sent a copy of it to David Hume, who wrote him in 1767, in acknowledgment of it, as follows: "Why do you compose in French, and carry 'faggots into the wood,' as Horace says with regard to Romans, who wrote in Greek? I grant that you have a like motive to those Romans, and adopt a language much more generally diffused than your native tongue. But have you not remarked the fate of those two ancient languages in following ages? The Latin, though then less celebrated, and confined to more narrow limits, has in some measure outlived the Greek, and is now more generally understood by men of letters. Let the French, therefore, triumph in the present diffusion of their tongue. *Our solid and increasing establishments in* AMERICA where we need less dread the inundation of barbarians, *promise a superior stability and duration to the English language!*"

What a contrast between these sensible remarks of Hume and the sneers of English tourists and critics on the state of the English language as written and spoken in America!

NUMBER FORTY-FIVE.

FROM LAUSANNE TO FREYBURG.

General Laharpe, the instructor of the Emperor Alexander—Origin of the Holy Alliance—Schools at Lausanne and the neighborhood—Scenery—Road to Vevay—Vineyards—Church of St. Martin at Vevay—General Ludlow's monument—Fate of the regicides—Scenery at Vevay—Clarens—Chillon—Its dungeons—Burke's judgment of Rousseau's writings—Moudon—Payerne—Bertha's saddle—Freyburg—Local description—The ancient Linden—Strange bas-relief at the cathedral—Point of junction of the French and German languages—Suspension bridge.

THE Cathedral at Lausanne is one of the most important buildings of this class in Switzerland. Its interior presents points of architectural interest and singularity which have attracted much attention from the students of mediæval art; but it has suffered by the changes required for the convenience of the simpler forms of Protestant worship. The sepulchral monuments contained in it extend from the reign of Henry the Third of England to the last generation, and cover all the varieties of human fortune from the crown and the tiara to the fireside of private life.

We had the opportunity and satisfaction of becoming acquainted at Lausanne with General Frederic Cæsar Laharpe, the instructor and friend of the Emperor Alexander of Russia. This distinguished gentleman, a native of the Canton de Vaud, found himself in St. Petersburg in early life; and having become known to the Empress Catharine, gained her confidence so completely that she confided to him the education of her grandsons, Alexander and Constantine. After they had outgrown his tutelage, he returned to his native country; but his salary and liberal gratuities from the Emperor were continued to the end of his life. After his return to Switzerland, he took a very active part in public affairs on the liberal side. He retained the friendship of the Emperor Alexander to the last, and is supposed to have exercised an influence with him greatly to the advantage of his country, in the territorial arrangements at Paris and at the Congress of Vienna.

He spoke to us with great warmth of the amiable personal qualities of Alexander, and thought his political principles were liberal and generous. He said, by way of pleasantry, that he feared he had got into bad company at the Congress of Sovereigns at Aix-la-Chapelle; but he was sure that, as far as depended upon him, nothing would be attempted against the gradual extension of liberal ideas in Europe. General Laharpe denied all foundation to the rumors current at that time, that the political course of the Emperor Alexander had been shaped under the influence of the celebrated Madame von Krüdener. He said that the Emperor had ever evinced great susceptibility to religious impressions, and that the wonderful events of 1805–1815, during which period he had passed, as the Emperor of Russia from the lowest point of adversity, for himself and his Empire, to the foremost position in Christendom, had given great warmth and strength to his convictions and feelings on the subject of an overruling Providence. It was these convictions and feelings, in the opinion of General Laharpe, which led the Emperor to undertake, in conjunction with the Emperor of Austria and the King of Prussia, the formation of the Holy Alliance in 1815; but he would not allow that it was in any degree inspired by the religious exhortations of Madame von Krüdener, to which, however, he did not deny that Alexander was fond of listening. The son of this eccentric lady was for several years the respectable minister of Russia at Washington. I enjoyed an intimate acquaintance with him, and I may, without impropriety, add, that his statements on this subject coincided with those of General Laharpe.

Great improvements, I understand, have been made at Lausanne since my visit there in 1818. It has at all times been an attractive residence for foreigners, especially the Russians and English. Many American boys have of late years been sent to the schools of this and of other places in Switzerland, under the mistaken impression, that a better education is to be had abroad than at home. This is not the case, except as far as the acquisition of a foreign language goes. French and German can of course be best learned in countries where they are spoken; and music is more generally taught in the schools of Continental Europe than in those of the United States; but up to the age at which boys are usually sent to college in this country, as good an education can be obtained in America as in Germany, France, or England. I make this remark with some confidence, from personal observation in each of those countries.

The views from the heights above Lausanne are surpassingly beautiful. There is, I think, no part of the shores of the Lake where it is seen to greater advantage; no part of Switzerland, so far as I have seen it, where the prospect on all sides is finer. The distant Alps, glimpses of the valley of the Rhone beyond the Lake, the beautiful expanse of the Lake itself, the nearer views of the Bernese Alps, and Jura, the surrounding country filled with villages and covered with farms and vineyards combine to form a landscape of infinite variety and grace.

From Lausanne to Vevay is about a couple of hours drive. The road is lined with vineyards, which cover the slopes of the hills to the very top; and give an appearance to the country not unlike the banks of the Rhine, with no difference but that between river and lake. The culture of the vine has been established in the neighborhood of Vevay from the time of the Romans. The climate and soil do not admit the growth of the most generous wines; but those which are produced at all are cultivated, I was told, with greater certainty of a crop, than the more delicate vintages of Burgundy and Bordeaux. It was principally from Vevay that the culture of the grape was introduced by Swiss emigrants into this country, where it bids fair to become a very important branch of industry. The banks of the Ohio, in the neighborhood of Cincinnati, bear a striking general resemblance to those of the Rhine, and are probably as favorable to the growth of the grape.

We visited the Church of St. Martin, which stands on the outskirts of Vevay, and is pleasantly sheltered by vines and trees. It is here that General Ludlow and some of his republican associates are buried; others rest in the soil of America; others perished on the scaffold at home. The great regicide of all died in his bed; but his skull, or what is believed to be such, after having been exposed at Temple bar, is exhibited in the Ashmolean Museum at Oxford. He himself has been pronounced, by her most eloquent historian, to be the greatest prince that ever ruled England, and Hume admits in substance, that she is indebted for the preservation of her liberties to the party in Church and State which brought Charles the First to the block!

The situation of Vevay, upon the whole, seemed to me the finest on the Lake. There is nowhere so much variety and composition in the landscape. The country about Geneva subsides into the broad valley of the Rhone; it is pleasing but not picturesque. At Vevay it comes up to the walls of the city, in the shape of luxuriant vineyards on the slopes of the hills, and of elegant villas, while the narrowness of the Lake, without impairing the charm of the water view, enriches the scene with the wild romantic rocks of the opposite shore. Something is added to the liveliness of the landscape by the bustle of a miniature commerce, produced by a little fleet of boats at the quay, rigged with lateen sails and loaded with lime to go down the lake. Vevay and Lausanne are in the Canton de Vaud, first separately organized as such in 1814.

From Vevay is but about a league and a half to the Castle of Chillon, on which Byron has bestowed a portion of his immortality; on the way to it we passed through Clarens, a small but not attractive village, to which Rousseau has imparted a portion of his. His admirers endeavor to identify it with his descriptions, and the Handbook declares that "the spot where the beautiful *bosquet de Julie* (Julia's bower) is sought for, is now a potato field."—I must confess the question whether the topography of a licentious French novel, however celebrated, is accurately described from nature, did not seem to me one that would reward a very laborious inquiry. The position is magnificent;—the view of the Lake, of the valley of the Rhone, and the mountains beyond is fine, but the village itself altogether uninviting. Lord Byron has clothed it with the charm of some of his most exquisite stanzas; and his poetry and Rousseau's prose will no doubt continue to make the fortune of Clarens with all sentimental travellers.

Chillon is an ancient castle, built upon an insulated rock in the Lake, but very near the shore, to which it is joined by a wooden bridge. The water is said to be of great depth beneath the walls of the castle; but M. Simond makes it pretty clear, that the dungeon floor is not, as is generally supposed, beneath the level of the lake. Chillon was used as a State's prison by the Dukes of Savoy. The principal apartment is large and lofty, and not destitute of air and light. There is a ring bolted into one of the pillars, by which Bonnevard is supposed to have been confined from 1530 to 1536, and the floor near it is worn, according to tradition, by his continued pacing up and down. M. Simond thinks the traditions inconsistent with each other; but it does not appear that the chain may not have been long enough to allow the prisoner to walk a moderate distance, backward and forward. The dungeon is frightful to contemplate. Its only entrance was by a trap-door. This being opened, a spiral staircase of three steps presented itself; *there was no fourth step*, and the miserable victim, condemned to perish in this way, was precipitated to a depth of eighty feet and never heard of more. I give this to the reader, as I have it myself, on the faith of the guide. Such dungeons, called *oubliettes*, are not without example in the mediæval prisons. In the ancient palace of the Popes at Avignon. I saw one which had been broken open and its horrid secrets brought to light, in the French Revolution.

The valley of the Rhone begins to open upon you at Chillon, but at first with no attractiveness. The river enters the Lake through a broad alluvial plain, formed by its own deposits. Its waters are turbid, its current sluggish; it is in all respects the reverse of itself as it issues from the Lake. Historically, the spot is remarkable as the scene of the memorable battle, alluded to in the forty-first Number of these papers, in which Divico, the first Helvetian chieftain whose name appears in history, defeated a Roman Consular army, and compelled it to pass under the yoke.

The road from Lausanne westward, is somewhat less picturesque than that which lies along the Lake. Vineyards now disappear, but their place is taken by cornfields, pastures, orchards, and woodlands. There is a continual succession of hill and valley; the farms are divided by hedge-rows and dotted with cottages. There is a more domestic and home-like look about such a country, than in one lined with vineyards; a species of culture which implies a less equal division of property. We breakfasted at Moudon, which stands on the site of a very ancient Roman Colony (Minidunum) of whose name it preserves an abbreviated form. In a niche on the outside of the *Hotel de Ville*, we saw an ancient altar, which was discovered in 1732. Its inscription, with a dedication to Marius Aurelius, sets forth that it was erected in honor of Jupiter and Juno, in commemoration of a large sum of money bequeathed to the city to build a gymnasium.

We made no other stop, till, having passed through a country resembling some of the best parts of New England, we reached Payerne. This is a place of considerable antiquity, having been founded in the sixth century. It was distinguished by the benefactions of Bertha the sovereign of Burgundy; and her saddle, which was shown us, is the great wonder and boast of the place. It certainly puts to shame the saddles of these degenerate days, being equally remarkable for what it is not, and what it is. It is evidently not a *side*-saddle, and it is furnished, in addition to the usual appliances for equitation, with a distaff fixed to the pommel, in order, it would seem, that her Highness might spin as she journeyed. This curious relic of antiquity, if genuine, must date from the tenth century.

We noticed, throughout this day's journey, more than usual civility on the part of persons whom we happened to meet on the road. Not content with a friendly nod or a touch of the hat, it was generally raised from the head with a courteous word of salutation. The costume of the female peasantry of Switzerland, as we saw it, changed on passing the frontier of almost every Canton. Such was the case on entering the Canton of Freyburg, where the broad-brimmed straw hats, with almost no crowns, began for the first time to appear. These Cantonal differences of costume are, I am told, yielding to the more powerful influences of fashion. With their disappearance, Switzerland will lose not a little of its picturesqueness.

We reached the city of Freyburg before night, a place of 7,000 or 8,000 inhabitants; the capital of the Canton of the same name, of which the population is almost exclusively Roman Catholic. There are not less than nine Monasteries and Convents in the little city. It is not to be supposed, however, that their inmates are all furnished by the Canton of Freyburg, of which the population does not exceed 90,000.

They are places of retreat for heart-stricken men and solitary women, from all parts of Switzerland, and the neighboring regions of France and Germany.

The local position of Freyburg is remarkable. It is built on the slope of a steep promontory formed by the windings of the river Saarine. Many houses are built up to the edge of the precipitous bank of the river. In some places, owing to the steepness of the declivity, the street passes over the roofs of houses, excavated in the solid rock below. The ancient walls are for the most part entire, and, following the irregularities of the surface of the hill, present, with their watchtowers and embattled gateways, a remarkable appearance. They are built of the greenish sandstone of the region, not unlike that which is so much in use in Cincinnati. The streets are narrow, the houses upon them ill-built, and in many cases decaying; and the look of the town in this respect singularly uninviting. Such was the state of things in 1818.

Its greatest curiosity was the venerable Linden tree planted on the 22d June, 1476, in commemoration of the famous battle of Morat, in which the Burgundian army, under Charles the Bold, was defeated with tremendous slaughter by the Swiss. The tradition is that a young man, escaping wounded from the battle, ran the whole way to Freyburg to bring the joyous news, and fell down dead, after uttering the word "Victory." His fellow-citizens planted the Linden twig which he carried in his hand. It took root, and has become a tree of twenty feet in circumference. It is unquestionably of very great antiquity, and was in 1818 sustained with props, and otherwise tended with care. A Court for the adjudication of small controversies and called *Linden-Gericht* (Linden-Court) was formerly held under its branches. The Cathedral is one of the finest of the ancient Swiss Churches, and from the summit of its tower you enjoy a prospect which well repays the fatigue of the ascent. There is a most extraordinary bas-relief over the portal of the tower, dating from the fifteenth century, and representing the last judgment by images of the most grotesque description. We visited the College of Jesuits, who, after being reduced to one aged Canon, had just been restored by the majority of the Cantonal Council, against the vehement reclamations of the minority.

Freyburg is remarkable as forming the point of junction between the German and the French languages, the former being spoken in the lower town and the latter in the upper; neither, it may well be supposed, with purity. In the *patois* of the peasantry there is a considerable mixture of the *Romansch* dialect, which in the middle ages was spoken in the region of the western Alps. *Sept heures et demi,* (half past seven,) as spoken by the postilion who drove us into Freyburg, sounded *Shat or et dmi.*

There are two suspension bridges at Freyburg erected since my time, one of which is pronounced by the Hand-book to be the largest bridge of a single curve in the world. It is supported by four cables of 1056 wires each. Its length is 905 feet, and its height above the river 180. The bridge at Menai is 580 feet in length to a height of 130; the breadth being respectively 22 feet at Freyburg and 25 at Menai. The dimensions of the suspension bridge below Niagara Falls are 800 feet length, 230 feet height above the water, and 40 feet width, with a two-fold roadway, one for the railroad above and one for ordinary vehicles below. It is supported by sixteen wire cables of 1100 feet in length and a foot in circumference. The Freyburg bridge was erected in eight years, at the moderate expense of about 120,000 dollars—the suspension bridge below Niagara Falls at a cost of 190,000 dollars.*

* Appleton's Travellers' Guide, p. 214. Edit. of 1853.

NUMBER FORTY-SIX.

BERNE.

From Freyburg to Berne—Change of costume—Appearance of the city—Lofty parapet wall and extraordinary leap from it—Alpine scenery—The Bear the heraldic emblem of Berne, and living bears kept at the public expense—The University—Manufactures of Berne, the Messrs. Schenck—Visit to the establishments of M. Von Fellenberg at Hofwyl—Anecdote of the director Reubel—High School—Industry School—The celebrated assistant teacher Wehrli—Agricultural School—M. Von Fellenberg's establishments, formerly an object of great attention in Europe.

Our next stage was to Berne, a distance of about six leagues. The road was fine, running mostly along the river, and often presenting beautiful views of the distant mountains. For the first part of the way, however, we had a landscape of a different character, but one familiar in some portions of our own country; a dense forest of pine. There is a strongly marked point of difference in the forest scenery of those parts of Europe in which I have travelled and of this country. With us, wherever civilization has penetrated, the primitive forest has been assailed with axe and fire, as the first and greatest obstacle to agricultural improvement. In Europe the conservation of the forests is an object of government regulation, and great care is taken that the trees should not be improvidently cut down. The management of forests forms the subject of regular courses of lectures at the German Universities.

Neueneck is the name of the village, in which you pass from the Canton de Vaud into that of Berne; and here one of those abrupt changes of costume takes place, to which I alluded in the last Number. Instead of the broad straw hats worn in the Canton de Vaud, the female peasantry in the Canton of Berne adorn their heads with a singular structure of black gauze made of horse-hair, standing out all round, in such a manner as to resemble wings, and forming a droll contrast with the red bodice laced in front.

Berne, as you approach it, has the appearance of a large, fortified city. Like Freyburg, it is mainly built of the handsome greenish sandstone already described. The streets are lined with rows of houses constructed with arcades on the lower story, which give them a stately though rather heavy appearance, and furnish an admirable protection against the weather ;—a matter of no small interest in a climate like that of Switzerland. In fact, it is somewhat surprising that an arrangement, possessing such great and obvious advantages, both for summer and winter, has not been generally adopted in the domestic architecture of compactly built places. The position of the city of Berne, on a promontory enclosed on all sides but one by the Aar, is very commanding. The bank is in some places sloping and covered with turf, in others steep, cut into terraces, or supported by almost perpendicular walls. The wall in one place is a hundred and eight feet high, but an inscription upon it sets forth that, in the middle of the seventeenth century, a young student mounted a horse which was grazing on the terrace, and that the animal, having been frightened, leaped to the bottom of the bank. The horse was killed, but the rider escaped with the fracture of some of his ribs, and lived to an advanced age as a village pastor. Two years before our visit to Berne, a woman, employed according to the custom of that time, in laboring in the streets as a punishment, leaped from the terrace and was killed on the spot.

Nothing can exceed the richness and varied magnificence of the views of the neighboring country and the Alpine peaks, as seen from Berne in clear weather. From some points of the terraced banks of the Aar, ten or twelve lofty summits—so well known some of them by their awe-inspiring names, Wetterhorn, Schreckhorn, Finster Aarhorn *—may be distinctly seen; the Jungfrau in the centre. Vast glaciers fill the spaces between these peaks; that which surrounds the Finstor Aarhorn is supposed to be the largest in Europe. Its superficial extent has been estimated at a hundred and twenty-five square miles. The general effect of the prospect varies so much under different lights, that we made it a business to contemplate it early in the morning, at noon, and at evening. The last is by far the most favorable part of the day for this purpose. If the state of the atmosphere is propitious, which it happened to be once during our short stay in Berne, the rays of the setting sun are reflected, with strange beauty, from the snow-crowned peaks and sparkling glaciers. In picturesque variety and a certain mysterious wildness, these views appeared to me to excel those of the Montanvert.

The heraldic emblem of Berne, as its name would import, is taken from the Bear, probably from some primitive legendary association. Two animals of this kind, in coarse sculpture, and of *heroic* size, guard the gateway as you enter from Freyburg, and two living bears are kept in the fosse at one of the other gates. This is in pursuance of a practice which has been kept up for centuries. The animals are supported at the public expense, and are said to be superstitiously regarded by the masses, as in some degree connected with the prosperity of the city. In the year 1798 the bears of that day were transported by the French to Paris, and placed in the *Jardin des Plantes*, where they attracted as much notice from the *gamins* of the city as the bronze horses from St. Mark's, placed on the arch of triumph in the Carousel, did from the *virtuosi*. Berne is copiously supplied with running water and with fountains, some of which are ornamented with

* Storm Peak, Terror Peak, the Dark Peak of Aar.

grotesque sculptures. The *bear* is the prevailing subject. The *Kinderfresser Brunnen* (Fountain of the child-devourer) derives its name from a figure, which the antiquaries suppose to be that of Saturn, represented as crowding a child into his mouth, while others are peeping from the pockets in quiet expectation of their turn.

By the kindness of Professor Schnell, (to whom we had been furnished with letters from Mr. Stapfer, a gentleman of great worth, formerly representing the Helvetic Republic at Paris, and still residing there in 1817,) we had ample opportunity of visiting the University of Berne. Mr. Schnell himself was one of three law professors; and there were fourteen other professors in the different faculties, including three of veterinary practice! a department in which I presume there is not a single professor in all the Colleges and Universities of the United States. The number of students was about a hundred and fifty; the fixed salaries of the professors five or six hundred dollars each, with a small fee paid by those who attend the lectures. The institution served as a place of academical education for Bernese students, but was little frequented from abroad. It was organized on the plan of the German Universities, the instruction being almost wholly given in lectures. The celebrated Wyttenbach of Leyden, well known as the editor of the moral works of Plutarch, was a native of Berne, and probably received his early education there. He was one of the most learned men of the last generation. There is a large public library at Berne, of which Haller, one of the most distinguished names of the last century, was the librarian. The saying of Voltaire, who used to extol his genius and learning, is well known, but will bear repetition. When told that Haller did not return the compliment, but spoke in disparaging terms of him, Voltaire replied, "Very likely we are both wrong."

Berne has been distinguished at times for the prosperity of her manufactures. They were languishing in 1818 in consequence of the prohibitory duties imposed on their introduction into France, and still more on account of the influx of British fabrics. Two persons belonging to the peasantry and whose education was very defective, of the name of Schenck, were much spoken of as practical and scientific machinists, instrument-makers, and engineers. Mr. Schnell informed us that his countryman and friend Hassler, who commenced the coast survey of the United States, and provided himself for that purpose with the best instruments that could be procured in London, after examining those of Messrs. Schenck at Berne, gave the preference to the latter. It is possible that national partiality may have had something to do with this preference.

During our stay at Berne, we devoted a day to visiting Hofwyl and the educational establishments of M. Von Fellenberg. These establishments and M. Von Fellenberg's plans for improving the education both of the wealthier classes and of the peasantry in Switzerland, attracted great notice at that time, and are still spoken of with respect and interest in works on education. They formed the subject of an elaborate and instructive article, contributed by Mr. Simond to the sixty-fourth number of the Edinburgh Review, which was much read at the time of its appearance.

M. Von Fellenberg belonged by birth to the *noblesse*, but partook the liberal ideas which prevailed so extensively throughout Switzerland, during the French Revolution, and which led to a corresponding movement there. He was one of the Commissioners, who represented the Helvetic Republic at Paris. Being in conference with the Director Reubel on the condition of his country, and the suffering state to which the people were reduced, threatening an entire disorganization of society, the Director, in a pause of the conversation, threw up his window, and ordered a servant "to bring Finette." This was a favorite spaniel, which was accordingly brought in with a litter of puppies, in a basket. This levity and indifference so disgusted M. Von Fellenberg, that, despairing of serving his country as a politician, he demanded his passports, and left Paris the next day—resolved to set about the slower work of improving the condition of his fellow-citizens by moral influences, and by introducing a system of education calculated to make better patriots and better men.

His plan comprehended a high school for the aristocracy of Continental Europe; an industrial school for the sons of the peasantry, and a school of agriculture. The first only, if I do not mistake, was self-supporting;—the Industry School was entirely gratuitous. The high school, when I saw it, was attended by about eighty pupils from all parts of the continent—from Russia, Poland, and every portion of Germany. The number of pupils from the South of Europe was small. M. Von Fellenberg had felt the want of such a school for his own children; not thinking the influences which prevail at the *gymnasia* and universities of the Continent favorable to the formation of character on high moral or even patriotic principles. All the branches of a liberal education—not including strictly professional studies—were taught in this school, as far as possible by instructors who had themselves been formed at Hofwyl, and who united the most exemplary personal qualities to skill in their several departments. The young men were all boarded and lodged within the establishment, and M. Von Fellenberg and his amiable family, the professors, and the pupils of the school sat down to their daily meals at one table. In this branch of the establishment, there seemed to be nothing peculiar, as far as the general plan and system of the school were concerned, but its management as far as I could judge, was singularly efficient and successful; and of schools it may be said much more than of governments—that which is "best administered is best."

The Industry School was at that time almost a novelty. This was a school for the practical instruction of the children of the peasantry, not merely in the common branches of a plain education, but in agriculture and the various trades to which they are usually apprenticed. M. Von Fellenberg took pains, as far as possible, in the first years of the institution, to obtain pupils from the democratic Cantons, as furnishing more hopeful materials for his undertaking. Serious prejudices arose against his establishment; the Swiss peasantry was not at that time (is not probably now) predisposed to innovate upon old ways; and as M. Von Fellenberg required that the pupils of his school should come at seven years of age and stay ten years, a considerable sacrifice in the time of the children was required of the parents. M. Von Fellenberg was obliged at times to keep up his numbers by adding vagrants from the streets; some of whom, however, did the best justice to their opportunities. Eight or ten hours in the day were devoted to labor on the farm or in the shops, according to the season, and the rest of the time was given to indoor lessons, meals, and recreation, the children being entirely supported and taught at M. Von F.'s expense; and at an average cost, over and above the product of their labor, of sixteen or seventeen dollars per head annually.

Much of the success of this branch of M. Von Fellenberg's establishment was ascribed to the personal qualities of Wehrli his assistant. This remarkable young man was the son of a schoolmaster in the Canton of Thurgau, who visited Hofwyl in 1809, to learn the modes of teaching pursued there. He was so much pleased with what he saw, that he offered his son as an assistant teacher. He was accepted in that capacity, and proved himself in the sequel admirably adapted to the place. His reputation spread with that of the Industry School at Hofwyl, throughout Europe. He soon, of his own accord, left M. Von Fellenberg's table, to share the meals as well as the labors of the boys of the Industry School. This he did with unflinching assiduity, placing himself in all respects on a level with his pupils. He appears to have been a person of singular versatility and the utmost conscientiousness. He was but eighteen years of age when he came to Hofwyl.

The school of Industry was ruled entirely by persuasion, example, and love; without resort either to punishment or reward. It had been in operation, I think, twenty years when I saw it, and in that time punishment had been inflicted but twice. M. Von Fellenberg's entire system of education assumed the superior efficacy of gentle influences over the coercion and rigor of the old *regime*, and certainly his success was such as to confirm his theory.

An agricultural school with shops for the manufacture of improved implements of husbandry formed a part of M. Von Fellenberg's establishments. He commenced life with experiments for an improved system of cultivation. He wholly changed the character of an extensive patrimonial estate by a system of drainage, by which from being an unprofitable bog, it was converted into arable fields. His attention was next turned to the subject of the implements of husbandry used in Switzerland at that time, which he was convinced could be made not only lighter and more efficient but cheaper, and with these objects in view, he connected an agricultural school with the educational establishments just described.

At the time of our visit Madame Von Fellenberg, sharing the noble zeal of her husband, was, with her daughters, about to found a school for girls, corresponding with the school of Industry for boys. I have never heard whether this project was carried into effect; nor am I acquainted with the present condition of M. Von Fellenberg's establishments, except that the hand-book states them to be under the care of Dr. Edward Müller. Education on philosophical principles has, of late years, made such progress in Europe and in this country, that the preceding recollections of Hofwyl may hardly seem to the reader entitled to the place I have given them. But, at the time of my visit, M. Von Fellenberg's establishments were deemed of the highest European interest. Perhaps at any time a well conceived plan for educational improvement, especially one having in view the benefit of those least favored of fortune—a plan formed and pursued by an intelligent, persevering, earnest, and conscientious man—is as important an object as can engage the attention of the patriot or the moralist. When the Emperor Alexander was in Switzerland, he visited Hofwyl, and in token of his appreciation of M. Von Fellenberg's labors, decorated him with an order of knighthood. In this he honored himself rather than M. Von Fellenberg, who daily enjoyed the more substantial reward of seeing those whom he had rescued from want, ignorance, and unenlightened toil, raised by his means to useful and honorable positions in the community.

NUMBER FORTY-SEVEN.

THE NINETEENTH OF APRIL, 1775.

Materials for the Romance of our history scattered through the country—Events of the 19th April, 1775—Alarm given from Boston to the neighboring towns—Escape of Adams and Hancock from Lexington to Woburn—A salmon left behind and sent for—Second retreat to the woods—Capture of a prisoner by Sylvanus Wood on the 19th of April—After thirty years Wood applies for and obtains a pension—Visits Washington and is introduced to General Jackson—Proposed National monument at Lexington commemorative of the 19th of April.

In times to come, when the novelist and the poet shall seek out the romance of our history, it will be discovered, in rich abundance, in every part of the land. Tracing the annals of the United States, from the first settlements at Jamestown and Plymouth, it will be found, that, in addition to the great events and the great characters, which form the substance of the public narrative, there are incidents of a local and personal kind, not immediately affecting the political fortunes of the country, but often of a most stirring or touching character. There is nothing in ancient or modern history more beautiful than the story of Pocahontas. The captivity of Mrs. Rowlandson is not to be read without tears, after a lapse of nearly two centuries. How wonderful the spectral appearance of one of the Regicide Judges of Charles I., to repel an assault of savages on a New England village in 1675! The life and adventures, the wars and the wanderings of Daniel Boone, in more recent times, will furnish one day the staple of an Iliad and Odyssey of border prowess and fortune; and then the glimpses of pure Indian life, as we catch them on the prairie and in the wigwam, uncontaminated or unrelieved by the contacts of civilization!

The straits and sufferings of our forefathers, who first landed on the continent; the perilous exposures of a wild frontier (and such a frontier, though ever flitting westward as you approach it, there has always been—is now);—the military operations of the colonies in the wars between England and France, from Louisburg to Carolina, from Detroit to the Spanish Main; above all many incidents which occurred in the great struggle for Independence, have filled the country with romantic traditions, many of which have already been turned to good account by ingenious writers of the present day, while others await the future poet and novelist. Even the ancient churchyards have a rich harvest in reserve for our Old Mortalities. Hearts as brave as any that rest under monuments of brass and marble in Westminster Abbey moulder beneath old moss-grown slate stones, in every part of the United States. These reminiscences of bye-gone times are not, however, all of a tragic or even a serious cast; some of them, on the contrary, contain the lighter element, which is required to make up the tragi-comedy of human fortune, though sparingly admitted into the sober pages of history. Some traditions of this latter kind, closely interwoven with events of the greatest gravity, are preserved in the neighborhood, (Burlington, Mass.,) where this paper is written.

Several circumstances led the patriots in Boston in the early spring of 1775, to anticipate that some important movement into the country would be made by the Royal forces, partly for the seizure of military stores, which had been collected in many of the towns in the interior, partly to arrest obnoxious individuals, to overawe the people, and generally to subdue the spirit of disaffection. As early as November, 1774, a secret society had been formed in Boston, composed principally of the mechanics and artisans of that town, but in close concert with the patriotic leaders, for the express purpose of obtaining information in advance of all projected movements of this kind. Among the circumstances which, in the spring of 1775, led to the expectation that some expedition into the country was meditated, was the detachment, by the royal governor of Massachusetts, Gage, of eleven hundred men, who traversed the neighboring villages, about the end of March, throwing down the stone walls by which the fields, in that part of the country, are divided and enclosed. One can scarcely imagine any thing better calculated to cause alarm and indignation, that being the season of the year in which good farmers put their stone walls and fences in order. Officers in civil dress were also sent round the country, to survey the roads and obtain information where military stores were deposited. A party came to Concord in Massachusetts, for this purpose, on the 20th of March, 1775, the very day on which Burke, in the House of Commons, spoke the last word of peace and hope in the inimitable oration "on Conciliation with America."

But the fated hour drew nigh. It had been preparing for centuries. It was too late for prudence to avert; for force to resist; the mighty clock of ages and empires must strike, and the new era begin. On the 15th April the grenadiers and light infantry, the flower of the army, were relieved from daily routine duty, under pretence of learning a new exercise. At twelve o'clock the next night, the boats of the transport ships in the harbor, having been repaired, were launched and moored under the sterns of the men-of-war. Not a step of these movements—the displacement of the troops—the midnight preparation of the boats for service—but was scanned with eagle eyes by the members of the society above mentioned. It had been concerted that, if the royal forces were embarked in boats to cross to Charlestown or Cambridge two lanterns should be lighted in the steeple of the old church on Copp's hill, and one if they marched out by land through Roxbury.

The 19th of April was the day appointed by Governor Gage for an expedition to Concord. All possible means were adopted, by guarding the roads the evening before, to prevent the tidings from spreading through the country. Ah, Governor, the words "Grenadiers, forward, march!" are hardly whispered at dead of night, at the head of the column, before two flaming messengers from the belfry of the old church, are streaming over the graves of the sleepers on Copp's hill. Like the beacon fires which announced in the palaces of Argos that Troy had fallen, these flashing heralds ran through the villages of Middlesex, to proclaim that the sceptre of a mightier than Priam had departed. Not content with lighting the signal in the old church steeple, Paul Revere immediately crossed in a boat to Charlestown, borrowed deacon Larkin's horse, dashed by the royal sentinels who were guarding the road by the gibbet, at the end of Charlestown neck, passed at the top of his speed through Medford and West Cambridge, giving the alarm and setting the bells to ringing on the way; and in a few hours the tocsin was sounding from half the steeples in Middlesex county.

At about midnight, Revere reached Lexington, and delivered to John Hancock and Samuel Adams a message from Dr. Joseph Warren, (the hero of Bunker Hill,) acquainting them that the troops were in movement, as was supposed, for Concord, and that they must provide for their own safety, their seizure no doubt being one of the objects of the Royal governor. These proscribed patriots were passing the night at the house of the Rev. Mr. Clark, the minister of Lexington, between whom and Hancock there was a connection by marriage. It would not be possible within the limits of one of these papers, if indeed this were the place for such a narrative, to relate the events of that eventful morning, as they occurred on Lexington green, nor is it necessary. They have been told in some of the brightest pages of the history of the country. Our business is with what passed under the humble roof of Mr. Clark's dwelling, an old, black, weather-beaten house, the front buried in shade, still standing, and well worth going to Lexington to see.

Besides Hancock and Adams there were at Mr. Clark's house, Mrs. Hancock, the widow of the governor's rich uncle, and Miss Dorothy Quincy, to whom the governor was paying his court, and who afterwards became his wife. Not sorry, it may be presumed, to display his chivalry before her, he passed the night (as she was accustomed to relate) "in cleaning his gun and sword, and putting his accoutrements in order," determined to go out and join the militia on the green. It was with great difficulty he was dissuaded by Mr. Clark and Samuel Adams, the latter of whom, clapping him on the shoulder, said, "That is not our business; we belong to the Cabinet." It was not till daybreak that he yielded, and consented with Samuel Adams to retreat to a place of greater safety. They left the village of Lexington as the bayonets of the grenadiers were seen gleaming in the distance, Samuel Adams exclaiming at the sight, "Oh, what a glorious day is this!"

Hancock and Adams were hastily conducted to the house of the Reverend Mr. Jones, the minister of the north-west precinct of Woburn, now forming the town of Burlington. This house, a respectable rural parsonage, shaded by noble trees, is now occupied by the Rev. Samuel Sewell, one of the successors of Mr. Jones, and is next door to that from which this paper is written. The ladies, whose safety was not supposed to be threatened, had been left behind; but the bullets whizzed about their heads, as they stood at the windows watching the strange scene. At length they were sent for, to come to Mr. Jones' in Mr. Hancock's carriage, and (it must be mentioned as one of the recorded *res gestæ* of the day) they were especially enjoined to bring with them a fine salmon, which had been provided for their dinner; rather earlier, it would seem, in the season than salmon are now brought to market. Had the British officers known that it was left behind, on the flight of the Patriots, they would probably have thought that it was a fair prize, even without a process in a Court of Admiralty. Happily the Royal army passed on, without a suspicion of the dainty treasure within their reach.

The ladies arrived with it in due time, at the Burlington parsonage, but scarcely had the party, who, in the confusion of that wild hour of peril and flight, had not broken their fast, set down to an early country dinner, of which the rescued salmon formed the most important part, when one of the yeomanry from the neighborhood burst into the house, in wild affright, with the information, that the regulars were on the way, adding that " his wife was already in *etarnity*." It was no time to think of dining, even on an early salmon. The carriage was taken into the woods for concealment, and Hancock and Adams were hurried off to a lonely dwelling, lying at the corner of Woburn and the two adjacent towns, not connected by the high road with either of them, or with any other settlement in the civilized world,—a dreary, solitary place, which you approach, you hardly know how, by a private road through the forest. Here the patriots were secreted, and all hope of salmon having vanished, they made a frugal but hearty meal, so says tradition, on cold salt pork and potatoes. In this house they passed the night, not learning till the next morning, that the second alarm was unfounded. That they had yielded to it, however, was no matter of reproach. The danger from which they had just escaped at Lexington was imminent, and no one could tell where the next blow would fall.

One of the incidents of the day was the capture of a British grenadier single-handed by a volunteer from Woburn. This individual, Sylvanus Wood by name, and a shoemaker by trade, of diminutive stature, but with a spirit beyond his inches, when the alarm was given in Woburn early in the morning on the 19th, hastened to Lexington. He paraded with Captain Parker's company on Lexington Green, and after they were dispersed by the overwhelming force of the enemy, he followed toward Concord in the rear of the royal army. At a turn of the road, he came, by surprise, upon a soldier who had loitered behind and was seated by the wayside. Wood sprang toward him, threatening to fire if he resisted. Having taken from him his gun, cutlass, and equipments, Sylvanus marched him back to Lexington, and there surrendered him "to Mr. Welch and another person."

In the year 1826, being then a member of Congress, and representing Wood's district, I received a memorial from him, setting forth the facts above stated, and his service afterwards in the army of the revolution. The application was referred to the Committee on Pensions, and in the course of a few years, what with the prisoner and what with his service afterwards, he obtained a pension of ninety-six dollars a year, with several years back pay, from the time his petition was first presented. It was probably more money than he had ever seen at once before, and he seemed to have but an indifferent opinion of the ordinary places of deposit and modes of investment. He told me that he kept it in his hat by day, and under his pillow by night. My own services in procuring the pension which were diligently rendered for several years, were liberally acknowledged by Sylvanus, by the present of a basket of apples, (Baldwins,) the only reward which ever fell to my lot, for carrying a claim through Congress. Such was the rude simplicity of those days!

The great improvement in his worldly circumstances, effected by his pension, awoke a desire in Sylvanus to see something of the great world. He found his way to Washington, and it naturally devolved on me to do the honors of the metropolis for him. I introduced him to the celebrities; showed him the library of Congress, the Indian Bureau, the Patent-Office, the "East-Room," and in fact made the most of my sturdy little constituent, "who had taken the first prisoner in the Revolutionary war." Having thus made the rounds,

Wood, whose appetite for grandeurs grew with what it fed on, expressed a wish to be introduced to the President of the United States, General Jackson. I hesitated a little, feeling some compunction, though one of "the opposition," to contribute even in this small degree to increase the annoyance of receiving visitors; one of the heaviest burdens of high office in Washington. But the thought of the "first prisoner," perhaps a grenadier eight feet high in his cap, marching down the road in fallen majesty before the sturdy little militia-man, overcame my scruples. I addressed a note to General Jackson, acquainting him with the wish of my constituent to be introduced, and promising if he would receive us to stay but a moment. The President readily appointed a time to see him; Sylvanus promised me faithfully that he would *not* tell him the story of the "first prisoner," (for on that theme he studied fulness of detail more than conciseness of narrative; and we entered the cabinet at the appointed time. It was half full of persons to whom the General was giving audience; but, nothing daunted with the novelty of the scene, Wood walked boldly up toward the President, who took him kindly by the hand. This was rather more than he expected, and disconcerted him for a moment. He immediately recovered himself, however, and evidently tacking together in his own mind, as with a fine waxed thread, the capture of the first prisoner in 1775 and the fighting of the last battle in 1815, with a native oratory not studied in the schools, said, "Mr. President, I'm glad to see you:—since [the battle of] Orleans I've loved your person." As I had promised, I made a movement to withdraw immediately, but the President kindly prolonged the interview for a few moments.

Wood, I think, had not a little reason to be proud of his exploit. As a matter of legal principle, the first thought, I imagine, with many a person at that day—at any day—finding himself in such a position, a private man, not acting under orders from anybody, in the very near neighborhood of a soldier in the service of a government whose authority was still admitted, would be to pass quietly by on the other side. As a matter of prudence, it would have occurred to most men, standing five feet high, that it was somewhat hazardous to undertake the capture of a grenadier. His gun might be out of his reach, but he had "his cutlass and equipments." Wood took no counsel of loyalty or prudence; his blood was up, and he captured his Anakim; little thinking that that day's work and his participation in it would, after thirty years, procure a provision for his old age from a powerful, independent government, and a personal introduction to its chief.

The capture of the first prisoner was the point of central interest in Wood's career; he valued himself upon it. After he obtained his pension, not being needy before, he was in what might be called comfortable circumstances, but not disposed to impair them by waste. Still, whenever a little contribution to a charity or a donation to a public object was desired, a trifle could generally be obtained from Sylvanus, by beginning with an inquiry about "taking the first prisoner." He died a few years ago, in his ninety-third year. There is no harm in thus prolonging for a few years his humble memory.

Before closing this paper, I may observe that a movement has been commenced at Lexington, to erect in that beautiful village near the scene of the battle, an appropriate monument, in commemoration of the first blood shed in the revolutionary war. A simple obelisk was set up in the year 1799 on Lexington green, in memory of the event, and on the 19th of April, 1835, the ashes of those who fell on the momentous day, sixty years before, were removed from the village graveyard, and, with appropriate and affecting ceremonies, placed under the obelisk. It is now proposed to erect in the neighborhood a monument more in keeping with the importance and grandeur of the event, to be surmounted with the statue —not of any one individual, for there is no one entitled to

19

that distinction—but of a "Minute Man," the representative of the class which flew to arms on that eventful morning, and took the first step in the march of the revolution. This is the class to which the honors of the day are due, and the spot is one which will be named in all after time, with Marathon and Thermopylæ;—not for the dimensions of the conflict in a military point of view, but for the importance of the era in the world's history which it inaugurated. The favoring sympathy of the country at large may be anticipated for the movement.

NUMBER FORTY-EIGHT.

FROM BERNE TO SACHSELN.

The Aar and its valley—Thun, its environs and lake—Unterseen—The Lauterbrunnen and Staubbach—A glimpse of the Swiss peasantry—Curious misprint in Goldsmith's Traveller—The Lake of Brienz—The Giesbach—The musical schoolmaster and his family—The pass of the Brünig—Entrance into Unterwalden—Lungern and its lake—Partially drained—Sachseln—St. Nicholas von der Flüe—Legends concerning him.

A DRIVE of four or five hours took us from Berne to Thun; since the construction of the railroad, it is the affair of a short hour. Persons travelling in the opposite direction, from Thun to Berne, frequently take the market boats which descend the Aar. This river is, next to the Rhone and the Rhine, of which it is the most considerable tributary, one of the most important channels, by which the waters of the Swiss ice-mountains find their way to the sea. Its principal sources are in the glaciers of the Schreckhorn and the Grimsel, at no great distance from those of the Rhine. It foams through frightful ravines, and plunges over lofty waterfalls, in the first part of its course, but it is navigable for the greater part of the way from the lake of Thun, and winding by Berne, Soleure, and Aarau, unites its waters with the Rhine, about half-way between Basle and Schaffhausen. Between Berne and Thun, the valley of the Aar is charming. You see but little of the river, but substantial farm-houses line the road, and rich pastures spread rural plenty far away before and around you. The sky was cloudless, and the sparkling summits of the Alps, beyond the sources of the Aar, bounded the prospect. There is, perhaps, no country where the state of the weather is so important to the tourist. It makes all the difference between the dreary uniformity of cold, leaden clouds, which are the same in all countries, and the unmatched glories of the Jungfrau and Mont Blanc.

Thun is a picturesque old town, of three or four thousand inhabitants, and though not among the more celebrated resorts, struck me as one of the most attractive spots for a quiet residence in Switzerland. It is about a mile from the lake, and the Aar, as it dashes out of it, is not inferior in sparkling beauty to the Rhone, as it rushes from the lake of Geneva. An ancient church, a ruined castle, smiling meadows in the environs, modern villas, the river, the lake, and beyond, the glaciers, the wooded heights, and in the background the Sovereign MAIDEN;—no element of loveliness or grandeur is wanting at Thun. But these mountain regions have their perils and disasters, unknown to the lower world. We contributed our mite to the relief of the inhabitants of a valley, which had lately been buried by an avalanche; and our hasty excursion will soon bring us to the melancholy ruins of Goldau.

A little steamer now plies from Thun to Interlachen; we crossed the lake by a more picturesque conveyance, a broad, flat-bottomed boat, rowed by women, with a very inconsiderable draft of water, which enabled us to creep nearer to some beautiful spots along the shores of the lake, which with a greater draft of water would have been inaccessible. We were about three hours on this delightful, secluded little sheet of water. There were but few villas at that time on the shores of the lake—just enough to give assurance that you were not "out of humanity's reach," without changing the rustic simplicity of the scene by the alloy of suburban magnificence. The shores of the lake for some distance from

Thun have changed their character, I believe, in this respect of late years, by the erection of numerous villas.

Unterseen, as its name imports, (between the lakes), lies about half way between the lake of Thun and the lake of Brienz. It is rather a forlorn place; the black, weather-stained houses, which are reported in the hand-book as "being two hundred years old," have grown young since we were there; our guide assured us they were two thousand years old! We took a *char-a-banc* directly at the landing-place for *Lauterbrunnen* and the Staubbach. Lauterbrunnen (clear spring) is a most romantic spot; a narrow vale, almost a ravine, between lofty calcareous walls leading up toward the Jungfrau. The village, of the same name as the valley, containing between a thousand and fifteen hundred houses, is a sombre spot; its houses are far apart; the prodigious rocky walls that overhang it must nearly shut out the sun in the short winter days; vegetation wears a coarse, wiry, Alpine look. The most remarkable feature of the scene consists in the numerous waterfalls, some of them insignificant, and others of some magnitude, which break over the edges of the surrounding mountains. They vary in volume of course with the weather and the temperature; some of them flowing down to the level of the valley; some breaking over the summit, in a considerable torrent; others merely fringing the rocks over which they fall. The Staubbach alone (or *dusty* torrent) has obtained celebrity. The volume of water in this famous cascade was not very considerable as we saw it, but it is at all times a most striking object. American tourists who go to see the Staubbach, with their heads full of the image of Niagara, are disappointed. It is one of the characteristics of Niagara that its oceanic volume defies the seasons. Melting snows and deluging rains do not swell it; the droughts of midsummer do not sensibly affect the mighty flow of its waters. But the Staubbach sometimes steals down the face of the rock in a thin silvery thread; and at other times, when swollen by heavy rains, shoots fiercely out from the rock, boldly arching over the valley, and swept to and fro by the wind. Byron in his journal * compares it to " the tail of a white horse streaming in the wind, such as it might be conceived would be that of the pale horse, on which Death is mounted in the Apocalypse. It is neither mist nor water, but a something between both; its immense height (nine hundred feet) gives it a wave or curve, a spreading here or condensation there, wonderful and indescribable." He has transferred this grand figure of the tail of Death's pale horse to his Manfred, in which other images also are painted from Alpine scenery.

On our way back from this pilgrimage to one of inanimate Nature's most awe-inspiring shrines, we stepped into several cottages, to get a nearer view of human nature, in the life of the Alpine peasantry. I cannot say that it gained on closer inspection. We were generally received with a sort of stolid apathy; the dialect is the harshest I ever heard spoken; there was an entire absence of that delightful feature of humble life, which is so well expressed by *tidiness;* an appearance of want, and of no ambition to smooth it over by ingenious little make-shifts; and at times, I must say, a sinister cast of countenance. M. Von Fellenberg had prepared me for this state of things, the sorrowful contemplation of which gave the first impulse to his educational efforts. Far from regarding Education as a mere intellectual process, designed to impart a certain amount of useful knowledge; he looked upon it as the only agency by which the condition of the masses, physical, social, political, and moral, could be improved. Aware how much America has suffered in the hasty generalizations of tourists, I should be very sorry to do injustice to any part of Switzerland;—but as I had no reason to suppose that what I saw between Unterseen and Lauterbrunnen formed an excep-

* Moore's life of Byron, Vol. II., p. 14. Am. Ed.

tional specimen of life in the higher Alps, I have ventured to record it. There is, to all appearance, a marked discrimination, as might be beforehand expected, between the character of the peasantry in the ungenial regions of the Oberland, and the substantial yeomanry of the middle agricultural region, and the highly cultivated population of the large towns and their neighborhoods. It resembles the contrast between Lapland and Saxony, except that in one case it is produced by difference of latitude; in the other by difference of elevation.

With respect to the Swiss, Goldsmith has pretty fairly presented, in the Traveller, the two phases of their character, without clearly referring them to the different regions to which they pertain. In the beautiful edition of the Traveller, published, with superior illustrations, by the London Art Union in 1851, a curious misprint occurs, in the commencement of the description of the Swiss, not only in the text of the Poem, but in the quotations from it explaining the illustrations. In the following couplet,

> Where the *bleak* Swiss their stormy mansion tread,
> And force a churlish soil for scanty bread,

instead of "bleak" this edition in both places reads "black."

We passed the night at Unterseen. A company of singers, five in number, undertook to regale us with national airs. Their appearance certainly was not prepossessing; their voices were harsh, and their manners destitute of refinement. We encouraged their performance at first, in the hopes of hearing some national ballads; the legend of Tell, or the wild traditions of Lauterbrunnen itself. Their *répertoire*, however, contained nothing but commonplace sentimentalities, which, being destitute of skill or grace in the performance, soon wearied.

Unterseen was alive in the morning with a cattle fair. The scene resembled similar gatherings in our own country, except in the costume of the drovers. We pushed our way through the crowd, on the road to Interlachen, and there embarked for Brienz, which lies at the further extremity of a lake of the same name, greatly resembling that of Thun, but somewhat smaller, and surrounded with ruder scenery. The Aar flows through both. Of the five boat*men* who formed our equipage, four were women. The men seek foreign military service, (which is now forbidden by law,) or drive the flocks and herds to the mountains, leaving the women to do the work at home. The flat-bottomed boats, which we found on these little mountain lakes, have everywhere been banished by steamers. The Alpine echoes are now awakened by the panting engine and screaming whistle. Opposite to Brienz we landed to view the *Giesbach,* (gushing torrent,) an extremely picturesque and beautiful object. There is no one fall as lofty as the Staubbach, but the succession of cascades is higher; the stream pours down a greater volume of water, and is surrounded with a far more pleasing landscape. It bounds from rock to rock, its pure silver water glittering through groves of fir, and lower down oak and beech woods, and after a long winding path down the mountain side, dashes foaming into the lake.

Opposite the falls a schoolmaster of Brienz had established himself in a small cottage, with five motherless children, the oldest of whom was but ten or eleven years of age. He accompanied them and himself on the harpsichord, and as the little ones had wonderful voices for their years, the effect was very pleasing. They executed for us some very pretty *Ranz des Vaches,* with tasteful variations on the native airs of the Oberland. After forty years he is still perched and chirping in his Alpine nest, for it must be the same individual who is described in the hand-book, "whose family and himself are celebrated as the best choristers of native airs in Switzerland. He is now a patriarch of eighty, and most of his children are married, but he is training his grandchildren to the same profession of songsters." Let us hope that they too will not leave the poor old Alpine minstrel.

Brienz is a beautifully situated village at the upper end of the lake; its inhabitants had all gone to the fair at Unterseen. Here the traveller usually takes horses to cross the Brünig mountain to Lungern, but the horses were gone to the fair with the men. We could get but one for ourselves, baggage, and guides. My companion had lamed himself, and was entitled to ride, and I was well pleased to climb the mountain on foot. The road was in some places very steep, and hardly afforded a foothold on the mountain side. The Brünig forms the barrier between Berne and Unterwalden, and after you enter the latter Canton, every thing that deserves the name of a road disappears in this quarter. Nothing remains but to scramble among the rocks, following the footsteps of your guide. But the youthful traveller does not reject this rough contact of mountain life, and the scene as you descend the last hill, repays the fatigue a hundred fold. It was difficult to refrain from cries of delight as we looked down upon the lake and village of Lungern, quietly enfolded by the surrounding hills clothed with woods to their summits, the dark green tint of the meadows at their feet, the peaceful seclusion of the region, traversed by nothing that can be called a highway, and on one side of which there was no approach by wheel carriages; the sound of vespers chimed from the steeple as we drew near the village, the tinkling bells of the returning herds, and the plaintive chant of the cow-boys, and as the evening closed in, the long shadows of the mountains stealing over the lake. Such were the sights, the sounds, as we descended the Brünig to Lungern.

It was probably on his tour to Switzerland, that Sir Walter Scott conceived the idea of making Baillie Jarvie in Rob Roy propose to drain Loch Lomond. The inhabitants of Lungern had labored for years by a tunnel through the Kaiserstuhl, (Emperor's chair,) which forms a natural dam between the lakes of Lungern and Sarnen, to lower the former. The cost of the work, the want of engineering skill, and the political convulsions of the times, had defeated the execution of this deplorable *improvement*, and I saw the sweet lake of Lungern in all its natural beauty, as lovely an object as there is in Europe. But keener land speculators, richer companies, more skilful engineers, have accomplished the work. In 1836 the final perforation of the Kaiserstuhl took place, and in sixteen days the water in the lake of Lungern fell to the level of the tunnel. By this operation a broad strip of poor land has been gained round the margin of the lake. In some places its steep banks, having lost the support derived from the pressure of the water, have crumbled and slid into the lake. The newly acquired soil is divided into small holdings, each with its *châlet*, and is said, on the hand-book, to look like the common "property of a free-hold land society."

On entering Unterwalden, one of the four primitive Cantons, you find yourself literally in the Switzerland of the Swiss. Almost all the great traditions and patriotic legends cluster about this region. We started in the morning from Lungern with a second horse, for which one of our guides had gone round by Meyringen yesterday, while we footed the Brünig. With this reinforcement of the cavalry we entered Sachseln, an ancient Swiss village, held in reverence as the scene of the labors of Saint Nicholas von der Flüe. The parish church dedicated to him is a somewhat stately building; its black marble pillars obtained from quarries in the neighborhood. Saint Nicholas was born in the early part of the fifteenth century, and, after leading an active political and military life, left a large family, and retired heart-stricken with the sins and sorrows of life, to a hermit's cell in the mountains. The fame of his austere penances, of his piety, of his superhuman abstinence, went abroad throughout Unterwalden. He did not live on earthly food. It was rumored that he partook no nourishment but that of the sacred elements received but once a month. The Bishop sent to investigate the fact, and, according to the tradition, it was substantiated. He once averted a civil war, by appearing with a message from Heaven, in a Council of eight Cantons assembled at Sarnen, and thus preventing the brethren from breaking up in wrath. This exploit forms the subject of a coarse fresco, in the portico of the church. The skeleton of the saint himself, a frightful object enough, is set up in a shrine before the altar, and readily exhibited to travellers. It is partly clad in robes richly ornamented with jewels, the gift of devotees, with gilded rays shooting from the head, which give it a dismal resemblance to Death on the pale horse, in Mr. West's picture. A cross set with jewels occupies the place of the heart within the ribs. On a lay figure in a side chapel the garments actually worn by the saint are displayed; and they are borne in procession, on the great festivals of the church, throughout the year. The peasantry of the Canton consider themselves under his especial tutelage, and the feeling toward him seems to be more kindly than one would have anticipated from his ghastly osteological presentment. They call him Brother Claus. When the harvest is abundant, and the flocks and the herds increase and multiply, and the produce of the dairy finds a ready sale, Brother Claus has the credit, and if the reverse of these blessings overtakes them, they are sure Brother Claus has struggled hard with the Evil One, though this time without success.

NUMBER FORTY-NINE.

STANZ, LUCERNE, TELL

Sarnen, proposed drainage of the lake—The Landenberg—Schiller's Wilhelm Tell and birthday—Commotion in Unterwalden in 1818—Type of Swiss houses—Arnold von Winkelreid—Resistance to the French in 1798—Atrocities described by Alison—The attack on Stanzstade commanded by General Foy—His character—Lake of the Four Cantons—Lucerne—General Pfyffer's model of Switzerland—Thorwaldsen's lion—Küssnacht one of Gessler's strongholds—Is the history of Tell authentic?—The story of the Apple said to be found in the Danish sagas—Does this prove Tell a myth?—The hollow way.

SARNEN, on the pretty lake of that name, is the seat of government of Unterwalden. We passed but a few hours here, but long enough to find out that here also the atrocious project of draining the lake to a lower level was in agitation. Whether, as in the case of the lake of Lungern, this project has been carried into execution, I have never heard. It is natural that Americans, with whom the best land in the world sells at a dollar and a quarter the acre, should not be able to sympathize with the Swiss, whose arable territory is so limited, in this eagerness to acquire a few more acres. But to obtain this object by draining their beautiful lakes, seems a most extraordinary blindness to what makes so much of the attraction of the country, and annually fills it with a throng of tourists, whose progress through the cantons may be traced by the golden wake they leave behind them.

There are some objects of interest in and about Sarnen. The Council-house contains the portraits of the Landammen, or local rulers of the canton, for several centuries. That of the Cantonal Saint Nicholas von der Flüe is the best; none of them have any merits as works of art; and the earliest of them cannot be coeval with the persons commemorated. The *Landenberge* rises behind the Council-house. This was the residence of one of the Austrian Bailiffs, whose oppressive rule brought on the Swiss revolt in the fourteenth century. Every trace of the castle itself has disappeared, but the traditions connected with it form a prominent portion of the history of the all-important event, which has given these little Swiss republics their name and their praise among the nations of the earth. I have on my table, as I write these sentences, the copy of *Schiller's Wilhelm Tell* in a pocket edition, which was my travelling companion in Switzerland, and from which, as I sat within sight of the Landenberg, I read the pathetic scenes describing the cruelty of the Bailiff to Hienrich von der Halden. A few days ago the centennial anniversary of this illustrious poet was celebrated in every part of the civilized world, where the noble language in which he wrote is spoken or read. Nowhere could it have been celebrated with more grateful enthusiasm than in these secluded vales and mountain fastnesses of Switzerland, to whose natural beauty and historical interest he has added the attractive charm of some of the finest modern poetry.

This quiet little nook, in the spring of the year in which we visited it, was almost the scene of a less glorious insurrection. In the anticipation of a scarcity, a peasant had, at the instance of the Diet of Unterwalden, imported a considerable quantity of grain from Italy. Before its arrival, the market price of wheat had fallen below that which was agreed upon with the peasant, and the Diet were disposed to recede from their bargain. The old Unterwalden spirit of the Melchthals and Winkelreids was at once kindled, and the yeomanry made common cause with the importer of the grain. The indignation against the Diet became so strong, that troops were called in from the powerful neighboring canton of Berne, to prevent an outbreak. Peace and harmony were at length restored, mainly, as we were assured on the spot, by the intercession of Brother Claus, whose reputation as a peacemaker began in his lifetime, and has been sustained ever since.

From the time you enter Unterwalden, you observe a type, seldom departed from, in the domestic architecture of Switzerland. The little Swiss cottages in our toy shops afford a very good idea of it. The houses are of wood, of one upright story above the basement, galleries running wholly round the house, projecting roofs, low studded, the outsides of the houses frequently covered with small shingles, and the windows composed of small octangular panes of glass, set in leaden frames,—a picturesque style of window, of which specimens were frequently seen in this country at the beginning of this century, and which, as far as my observation goes, has now wholly disappeared in America. The Swiss cottages seem rarely to be painted; they have consequently a dark, weather-beaten, gloomy aspect, which materially detracts from the sprightliness of the landscape. This may have changed with the increase of wealth and the progress of luxury of late years.

From Sarnen we proceeded to Stanz, by a wretched road, passing a part of the way along the bed of a torrent. This is the capital of the lower division of the Canton of Unterwalden, as Sarnen is of the upper. It is a village of perhaps fifteen hundred inhabitants, but had in 1818 a convent of sixty-five nuns, a monastery of twenty-five monks, and a parish church served by seven priests. In front of the hotel was an uncouth statue of Arnold von Winkelreid, one of the heroes of the great Swiss revolt, who, at the memorable battle of Sempach, in order to break the line of the Austrians, gathered as many of their spears as he could clutch in his arms, and received their points in his body, thus making an opening in the hostile ranks, which enabled the patriots to break through, and gain a glorious victory. In the statue just alluded to, he is represented grasping the Austrian spears. A house is shown as that of Winkelreid, and the surrounding fields bear his name. The traces of the military operations of 1798 were still visible. A monumental tablet erected at the church commemorates the massacre of three hundred and eighty-six of the inhabitants, who were destroyed by the French in the campaign of that year. When all the rest of Switzerland had submitted to the French, the inhabitants of these ancient central Cantons, faithful to the principles of their fathers, strove to prevent the imposition of the foreign yoke. The shepherds and farmers of Unterwalden refused to take the oath of fidelity to the new Constitution, and their brethren from Schwytz and Uri, as in days of yore, flew to their assistance. On the 2d of September, eight thousand French crossed the lake of Lucerne, and landing at Stanzstade, attacked the patriots, who, fighting under every disadvantage, and in greatly inferior numbers, sustained the contest for several days. Alison has given a beautiful description of this disastrous struggle.

"Every hedge, every thicket, every cottage was obstinately contested. The dying crawled into the hottest of the fire, the women and children threw themselves upon the enemy's bayonets; the gray-haired raised their feeble hands against the invaders, but what could heroism and devotion achieve against such desperate odds? Slowly but steadily the French columns forced their way through the valley; the flames of the houses, the massacre of the inhabitants, marking their steps. The beautiful village of Stanz, built entirely of wood, was soon consumed; seventy peasants, with their curate at their head, perished in the flames of the church. Two hundred auxiliaries from Schwytz, arriving too late to prevent the massacre, rushed into the thickest of the fight, and after slaying double their own number of the enemy, perished to the last man. Night at length drew her veil over these scenes of horror, but the fires from the burning villages still threw a lurid light over the cliffs of the Engelberg; and long after the rosy tint of evening had ceased to tinge the glaciers of the Titlis, the glare of the conflagration illumined the summit of the mountain." *

* Alison, Vol. IV., p. 470.

In the foregoing account, Alison, following the Annual Register, represents the village of Stanz as having been burned. This is a mistake. There was no appearance in 1818 of its having been so recently destroyed and rebuilt; and Mr. Simond, a very accurate writer, expressly says that it was saved by the humanity of some of the French officers. He states that sixty-three persons who had taken refuge in the church were massacred with their priest, but not that they perished in the flames of the building. The error probably arose by confounding Stanz with its little port on the lake, called Stanzstade, which was wholly destroyed.

One cannot but read with painful emotion that the French troops in the attack on Stanzstade were commanded by General Foy, who not only became, under the restoration in France, one of the most honored of her liberal statesmen, and especially one of the very few of her public men who possessed eminent parliamentary talent, but a citizen whose personal character was marked by every thing generous, benevolent, and amiable. Of all those with whom I became acquainted in Paris in the winter 1817–'18, no one in the same political circle appeared to me to be the object of as much personal good-will as General Foy. He had not yet entered the chamber of deputies, but his rare conversational powers, united with the sterling probity of his character, gave him an almost unlimited social influence. He died in 1825, at the age of fifty; a hundred thousand persons walked in his funeral procession, and a million of francs were raised by subscription throughout France, as a provision for his widow and children. But this was the same person who visited upon the citizens of Unterwalden the direst extremities of war, for striving to throw off the detestable yoke of the French Directory!

The road from Stanz to Stanzstade, the little landing-place from the lake, is beautifully shaded with trees, nearly the whole way. Here we took a boat to cross the lake to Lucerne, the lake of the four Cantons, or to call it by its more expressive German name, the lake of the four sylvan Cantons (*Vierwaldstädtersee.*) Mr. Fox used to say that it was the most beautiful lake in the world, and Sir James Mackintosh describes it with unwonted enthusiasm. Its shape is very irregular, and it consists rather of a group of four lakes joined together by narrow straits, than of one regular expansive sheet. Its shores present every variety of landscape, from broad fertile meadows, dotted with scattered farms and compact villages, to dark, precipitous rocks, which seem to tower perpendicularly from the waters. We were rowed in a small boat from Stanzstade to Lucerne, by two girls and a man. The weather was as fine as a cloudless sky and a mild September breeze, just curling the surface of the beautiful lake, could make it.

I do not know that I can add any thing to the account in the Hand-book of the objects of interest at Lucerne. I must confess that in Switzerland our attention was principally turned to the beauties and sublimities of nature. One tires at length, in Europe, of ancient churches, (except the great mediæval piles, which you survey with ever renewed awe and wonder,) bridges, collections of armor, and galleries of doubtful original paintings, which would hardly be thought valuable, if they were certainly the works of the great masters whose names they bear; but of lakes, and mountains, and glaciers, and cataracts, and precipices like those of Switzerland, no one who has any sense for the beauties and grandeurs of nature, can ever grow weary.

One of the objects which travellers go to see at Lucerne, is General Pfyffer's model in relief of the central portion of Switzerland. General Pfyffer belonged to the ancient aristocracy of Lucerne, but when he was ten years of age went to France to receive a military education there. In due time he entered one of the regiments of Swiss guards, in which his father was a captain, and succeeded to the command of the company on his father's death. Having served with distinction in the several wars waged by France while he was in the army, he returned home to Lucerne after sixty years, to close his life in his native city. As an employment of his leisure, he undertook to construct, from actual measurement and with geometrical accuracy, a model of the central part of Switzerland, on a scale of thirteen and a half inches to the square league. Not only every mountain, lake, river, and glacier, but every cottage is indicated. The model represents a portion of six or seven Cantons, and occupies a space of about twenty-two and a half feet by twelve, corresponding to some hundred and eighty square leagues of territory. The good old general died in 1802, at the age of 86, enjoying to the last his pasteboard mountains. This model is still shown in the house where he lived and died. Thorwaldsen's magnificent monument to the Swiss guard, who sacrificed their lives in defence of the falling monarchy, on the dreadful tenth of September, 1792, is erected in the gardens of General Pfyffer. He was himself, I believe, one of the few who escaped alive from the butchery of that terrible day.

From Lucerne we took a small boat to Küssnacht. These traverses across the lakes of Switzerland are now all made by steamers, but far less agreeably, I should think, than formerly in the row boats. Küssnacht is the site of one of the legendary strongholds of Gessler. I call it "legendary," in consequence of the doubts which, in the last century, were cast upon the authenticity of the history of Tell. The fact that a story somewhat similar to that of the Apple is found in two versions in the legendary history of Denmark, has been generally thought a sufficient proof that the tale as told of Tell must be a myth. Numerous works on the subject appeared in the last century. The Curate Freudenberg of Berne published an essay in 1760, entitled *William Tell a Danish Fable.* The government of the Canton of Uri caused it to be burned by the public executioner. Several answers were written to this work, and in defence of the traditional accounts of Tell.

The eminent historian Johan von Müller regards the exploits of Tell as authentic history, and, with the exception of the Apple, Mr. Simond is of the same opinion. Gibbon, as might be expected, regards them "as a fable, which has not even the merit of originality, William Tell being but a clumsy imitation (imitation assez grossière) of a Danish hero, perhaps as fabulous as himself." * I have not seen the ancient Danish Sagas and legendary histories, where the duplicate story of Tell's apple purports to be found; but it does not appear to me, that such a repetition amounts to a proof of fabrication. In an age before the invention of gunpowder, and when archery flourished, it may not have been an unheard-of display of skill to shoot an apple from the head of a living person. There is an account of a border marksman in our Western country who was allowed by his comrades,—such was their reliance on his skill,—to shoot with his rifle at small objects placed on their heads. Gessler may have commanded of Tell this proof of his skill, of which he had seen examples. Is it certain that the Danish legends are older than the Swiss? Tell's adventure, as the more renowned, may have been the foundation from which the Danish traditions were derived, the old Scandinavian manuscripts being notoriously interpolated. Finally, if we give up the Apple as legendary, it will not follow that the substantial portions of the history are unauthentic. They are supported by widely prevailing and unbroken traditions, records nearly contemporary, public monuments, and national institutions. In fact, they compose a part of the historical treasure of the modern world, of which it will not easily allow itself to be despoiled. There are certain grand events and results, in history, in letters, in politics, and morals, which defy the sceptic, and laugh to scorn a pretentious and half-learned criticism. They find an echo sometimes in the sound common sense, sometimes in the patriotic

* Gibbon's Miscellaneous works. Vol. III., p. 266.

sentiments, sometimes in the natural sympathies; sometimes in the religious instincts of the masses—and the plausible refinements by which they are called in question, after a brief popularity, pass into oblivion.

A small portion of Gessler's stronghold at Küssnacht remains, and a little distance from it you pass through the "hollow way," where the tyrant met his fate. As we entered it, a youth, with a cross-bow, sprang into the road before us, and earned a few pence by showing us just how Tell shot Gessler. A chapel of considerable antiquity marks the spot to which tradition points as the scene of this remarkable occurrence.

NUMBER FIFTY.

GOLDAU, ALOYS REDING, GRUTLI, THE TELLENSPRUNG.

The lake of Zug—The destruction of Goldau—Mr. Buckminster's description of it—Account of it by Dr. Zay of Arth, an eye-witness—Schwytz—Its early history—Events of 1798—Character and conduct of Aloys Reding—Brunnen—Passage to Altorf—Grutli—The three founders of Swiss Independence—The Tellensprung—Enthusiasm of Sir James Mackintosh—The Legends of the Apple-shooting.

From Tell's chapel at the "hollow way," we walked on to Immensee, an inviting little spot on the Lake of Zug. Here we intended to take a boat down the lake to Arth, a thriving village at its lower extremity, but clouds began to gather on the opposite sides of the Righi and the Rossberg; the surface of the lake became rough and black; and we found the boatmen and boatwomen no more disposed than ourselves to take the risk of the threatening squall, which, however, did not burst upon us. Pursuing our way by a footpath along the shores of the lake to Arth, we soon had the counterpart of the scene which had driven us from the water. The wind came round to the pleasant quarter; the stormful clouds retreated sullenly from the Rossberg; a bright sunshine lighted up Righi, and the little lake was soon as smooth and as bright as a mirror.

Tourists who ascend Righi stop at Arth for guides; but the uncertainty of clear weather led us to forego that laborious excursion. Taking a *char-à-banc* at Arth for Schwytz, we pursued our way over the site of Goldau. It was now just twelve years since the shocking event that buried that and the neighboring villages in ruins. Goldau (*the golden meadow*) was the name of the fertile and picturesque vale between the Rossberg and the Righi, through which lay the road from Arth to Schwytz, passing through a succession of four or five prosperous villages. The account of Dr. Zay, a resident at Arth, and an eye-witness of the scene, is the source from which subsequent tourists have derived their descriptions. I must, however, except from this remark the Rev. Mr. Buckminster, who being in Switzerland about the time the disaster happened, passed over the ruins a week afterwards, while those who escaped were still seeking to recover their friends that had been buried, some of whom were believed to be still alive. His account must have been written before Dr. Zay's was published.

"Birds of prey," says he, "attracted by the smell of dead bodies, were hovering all about the valley. The general impression made upon us by the sight of such an extent of desolation, connected too with the idea, that hundreds of wretched creatures were at that moment alive, buried under a mass of earth, and inaccessible to the cries and labors of their friends, was too horrible to be described or understood." *

Mr. Buckminster's graphic account of this most disastrous event concludes with the following striking remark :

"I cannot but reflect upon my weakness in complaining of our long delay at Strasburg. If we had not been detained there ten days, waiting for our passports, we should have been in Switzerland the 3d of September, probably in the vicinity of the lake of Lowertz—perhaps under the ruins of Goldau."

The destruction of Goldau and the neighboring villages was caused by a slide from the side of the overhanging mountain, the Rossberg. The summer of 1806 had been unusu-

* Mr. Buckminster's interesting account of the destruction of Goldau is contained in a letter to his friend, Arthur M. Walter, Esq., written on the 26th Sept., 1806, from Geneva, and printed in the notes to Mr. Thacher's memoir of him in the first volume of his sermons.

ally wet, and on the 1st and 2d of September it rained incessantly. The deposits of clay, deep below the surface of the mountain, became softened and swelled, and the superincumbent mass, lying at a considerable angle to the horizon, began to move. Crevices were seen to open on the surface; a cracking noise was heard from within; stones started from the ground; rocks rolled down the mountain. At two o'clock in the afternoon of the 2d September, a large rock became loose, and in falling raised a cloud of black dust. Toward the lower part of the mountain the ground seemed as pressed downward by the weight above. When a stick or spade was driven in, it moved of itself with the ground in which it was placed. A man who had been digging in his garden ran away with fright at these extraordinary appearances. Soon a fissure larger than all the others was observed; insensibly it increased; springs of water ceased all at once to flow; the pine trees of the forest absolutely reeled; the birds flew away screaming. A few minutes before five o'clock, the symptoms of some mighty catastrophe became still stronger; the whole surface of the mountain seemed to slide down, but so slowly, as to afford time to some of the inhabitants to escape. This, however, was but very partially the case. Over a hundred houses were buried in the ruins or crushed to atoms by the furious avalanche of earth and rocks, and between four and five hundred human beings perished. In one case an old man, who had often predicted some such disaster, was quietly smoking his pipe when told by a young person running by, that the mountain was in the act of falling, He rose and looked out, but came into his house again, saying he had time to fill another pipe. The young man, continuing to fly, was thrown down several times by the rush of the driving fragments, but finally escaped. Looking back, he saw the house in which the old man had loitered to fill his pipe, dashed off to destruction.

A party of eleven travellers from Berne, belonging to the

most distinguished families there, arrived at Arth on the fatal 2d of September, and started on foot for the Righi, a few minutes before the catastrophe. Seven of the party preceded the others and had just entered the village of Goldau. The other four were a little behind, and were looking through a telescope at the summit of the Rossberg—four miles off in a straight line; where some strange commotion seemed to be taking place. All at once a flight of stones like cannon balls shot through the air above their heads; a cloud of dust obscured the valley; a frightful noise was heard; they fled! As soon as the dust and darkness had cleared up so that they could see, they sought their friends who had preceded them; but the village of Goldau had disappeared under a heap of stones and rubbish, one hundred feet in height, and the whole valley was a chaos! Of the four survivors one lost a bride to whom he was just married, one a son, a third two pupils under his care. All efforts and researches to recover their remains proved unavailing. Nothing was left of Goldau but the bell which hung in its steeple, and which was found at the distance of about a mile.

These, and other striking and pathetic anecdotes of the destruction of Goldau are given by Dr. Zay, from whom they are copied by Mr. Simond and the "Hand-book." As we traversed the spot twelve years afterward, it was still a dismal ruin. No attempt had been made to rebuild the villages; instead of the "golden valley," the road from Arth to Schwytz now passed over a continuous ridge of barren rocks and gravel, bare or covered with a rank growth of weeds and coarse grasses. A chapel and an inn were the only buildings which, in 1818, marked the spot where Goldau had been.

Lalande, in the first volume of his travels in Italy, p. 47, mentions some examples of catastrophes of this kind still more shocking. The most remarkable of these is that which befell the village of Pleurs, in the Grisons, in 1618, when two thousand persons perished in the ruins. There are traces in the vale of Goldau of former slides of the Rossberg, as the streets of Herculaneum are paved with lavas from older and otherwise forgotten eruptions.

After emerging from the desolation of the ruined villages, we pursued our way through a delightful vale, that of Schwytz, the counterpart, no doubt, of what Goldau was. Schwytz, or, as it might more properly be written, Schweiz, is the very central point of Switzerland, which is, in their own language, called *Die Schweiz.* Why one of the smallest of the Cantons, with a moderate-sized village for its capital, should give its name to the entire Helvetic Confederacy, it may not be easy to say. Popular tradition assigns as a reason for this preference, that the patriots from this Canton took the lead, and distinguished themselves for their bravery at the great battle of Morgarten, in 1315.

The picturesque mountain, called the Myten, rises directly behind Schwytz, and seems to threaten it one day with the fate of Goldau. In front you catch a fine view of the Lake of the four Cantons, at a distance of about three miles, between the lofty summits which recede from each other, as if to open the prospect.

The citizens of Schwytz are justly proud of the place which it holds in the history of their country. They exhibit in the public armory the standards taken from the Austrians at Morgarten, in 1315, with the banners borne by their fathers at the other great battle-fields of the fourteenth and fifteenth centuries. I own I looked with respectful emotion at these tattered and dusty memorials of conflicts, which will be remembered in history with those of Marathon and Platæa, of Bunker Hill and King's Mountain.

But Schwytz is not obliged to go back to the middle ages for her patriotic recollections. The great leader of the heroic resistance made to the French in 1798, Aloys Reding, the master spirit of the patriotic movement of that day, was a citizen of Schwytz, and died but a few months before our visit to the Canton. This distinguished patriot, in his youth served in the armies of Spain, and if I mistake not was at one time with his regiment in the Island of Cuba. Retiring with honor from the Spanish service in 1788, he was elected chief magistrate of his native Canton. When the French Directory sent their armies into Switzerland ten years afterwards, to force the new constitution upon that devoted country, Aloys Reding organized the resistance of the democratic Cantons, and led their armies.

I gained great favor with our guide, on the way to Schwytz, by questioning him about Aloys Reding. When I asked him if it was true, that some of the women fought with their infants on their left arms, he exchanged a smile with his young wife, who was walking by his side with a market basket, and said, "If she had been old enough at the time to know what was passing, she could vouch for the fact."

From Schwytz we proceeded to "the charming village" of Brunnen, a distance of about three miles. This place is the port of Schwytz, and lies upon the lake of the Four Cantons, at the mouth of the little river Muotta. You would not think it possible that a village in this secluded spot, nestled at the foot of Alpine crags, and on the shore of the central lake of Switzerland, walled in on almost every side by some of the highest mountains of Europe, could be a place of active business. Such, however, is the fact; the cattle from the Northern Swiss Cantons are driven down to Brunnen, there embarked in flat-bottomed boats to cross the lake to Altorf, and being landed there, are driven up the valley of the Reuss, and by the pass of St. Gothard into Italy. In the course of the year immense droves take this route, and at certain seasons fill Brunnen with the noise and movement of trade. Quite a flotilla of boats was collected to convey some droves across the lake, which were expected the next day, *en route* for a fair at Lugano. The *Angelus* was sounding from the steeple of the parish church at Schwytz as we left it at six o'clock in the morning, and the neighboring peasantry were flocking to early mass. Brunnen, like Schwytz, is honorably associated with the annals of Switzerland. It was here that the confederation between the three pioneer Cantons (Unterwalden, Uri, and Schwytz) was formed after the battle of Morgarten in 1315; and here that Aloys Reding established the short-lived league between the same Cantons in 1798, when they rose against the armies of the Directory.

We were compelled, when on the point of embarking for Altorf, to enter into much such a discussion about the weather, as that which is contained in the first act of Schiller's *Wilhelm Tell*, where Baumgarten is urging the boatmen to carry him across the lake from the opposite shore. It is well known that while engaged upon this beautiful drama, Schiller explored the localities with great care; and for a short time the splendid passage, to which I have alluded, might have been taken for a description of that which was passing before our eyes. But, after waiting about an hour, the wind shifted, and our boatmen ventured out with their not very stanch-looking craft.

The shores of this part of the lake are in strong contrast with those along which we coasted from Stanzstade to Lucerne; there every thing was soft and placid; here dreary perpendicular walls, towering up from the lake, frowned over the dark surface of the waters.

We stood over the lake to the shores of Uri, and landed at Grütli or Rütli. This is the spot, where the ever memorable founders of Helvetic liberty met by night—Werner Stauffacher of Schwytz, Arnold Melchthal of Unterwalden, and Walther of Attinghausen of Uri—and took the solemn oath "to be faithful to each other, but to do no wrong to the Count of Hapsburg." Sir James Mackintosh thinks "these poor mountaineers in the fourteenth century furnish perhaps the only example of insurgents, who, at the moment of revolt, bind themselves as sacredly to be just and merciful to their oppressors as faithful to each other." * But the obligation strongly resembles in spirit the sentiments of the Petition of the Congress of 1774 to the King, in which the statement of the grievances, which had brought the colonies to the verge of revolution, is accompanied by the warmest professions of loyalty to the person and government of *their* Count of Habsburg, George III. Our guide, who said that he and his associates had bought the spot of the Canton, vouched for the authenticity of the tradition of the three springs, which is more than I can venture to do. The separation from one fountain wears every appearance of being artificial. The guide asked if we would like to hear some poetry. I was in hopes he was going to treat us to an ancient national ballad, but it turned out to be some well-meant, but indifferent lines denouncing the French invasion of 1798.

From Grütli we crossed to the other side of the lake, which is here quite narrow, and came to *Tell's Chapel*, on the rock upon which, according to the tradition, he leaped from the boat in which Gessler was conveying him to Küssnacht. There is nothing in the localities which makes the fact improbable, or very difficult. Although it is frequently remarked that the contemporary records are silent, not only with respect to the Apple, but the other traditions of Tell, Mr. Simond states, as a matter of history, that eighty-one years after the event took place (which is two years less than the interval which has elapsed since the Declaration of Independence), a chapel was constructed on this rock, and that one hundred and fourteen individuals who had known Tell were then living.

The present chapel is of later date, and covered on the interior with coarse frescoes, representing the principal events in Tell's life. That of his leaping on the rock has been lately renewed, and in a style much superior to the rest. A sermon

* Life of Sir James Mackintosh by his Son. Vol. II. p. 307.

is annually preached from the Tellensprung (*Tell's Leap,*) commemorative of the event, and the hearers assembling from the neighboring Cantons, gather round the rock in their boats.

Sir James Mackintosh says:

> "The combination of what is grandest in Nature with whatever is pure and sublime in human conduct, affected me in this passage, more powerfully than any scene I had ever seen. Perhaps neither Greece nor Rome would have had such power over me. * * * Grütli and Tell's Chapel are as much reverenced by the Alpine peasants as Mecca by a devout Musulman."

I reserve a few remarks, in addition to those made in my last Number, on the alleged plurality of Apple-shooting legends, till we make our visit to Altorf next week, and stand on the spot consecrated by Switzerland as the scene of the event.

NUMBER FIFTY-ONE.

ALTORF, THE VALLEY OF THE REUSS, THE VALAIS.

The Canton of Uri—The traditions of Tell—Valley of the Reuss—Wildness of the scene—The Devil's bridge—The army of Suwarrow in 1799—Andermatt—Head waters of the Ticino—Short Alpine summer—Passage of the Furca—Glacier of the Rhone—The Valais—the Brieg—The Simplon road—Farewell to Switzerland.

A SHORT sail from *Tell's Leap* brings you to Fluelen, the little port of Altorf. The lake is here narrow, a sort of arm of the lake of the Four Sylvan Cantons, pushing its way up into the heart of Uri, the smallest and the feeblest member of the Swiss Confederacy, not supposed in 1818 to contain more than eleven or twelve thousand inhabitants. Among them, however, are said to be the finest specimens of Swiss muscle and blood, after the type of the men of the fourteenth century. The weather became fine as we pushed off from the *Tellensprung*, and we made the rest of the way under the dark shadow of the perpendicular rocks, which in some places rise to the height of eight hundred feet on the eastern shore of the lake, while the opposite coast was kindling in sunshine. Nowhere are the contrasts of Nature so sharply defined as in the Swiss mountains.

Fluelen is the counterpart of Brunnen, a little landing-place from the lake, and it is here that the Reuss finds its outlet. The whole character of the scene, which wore the aspect of almost oppressive seclusion, when I passed through it, is doubtless changed by the arrival and departure two or three times a day of the steamer from Lucerne. We committed our baggage to the stout shoulders of Helvetian porters, and walked up to Altorf, a distance of two miles. This is a place of no great account, its population, thirteen or fourteen hundred, with visible traces of a fire which had, about twenty years before, laid it in ruins. But this is ALTORF; the point of central interest in the early history of Switzerland; for here, according to the tradition, is the scene of that immortal mountain epic, which is interwoven with the fibres of her nationality. Criticism, as we have already seen, is at fault, as to the true historical foundation of the legend, but it bears and will bear to the end of time the same relation to Switzerland, that the "tale of Troy divine" bore to Hellas; and there is, to say the least, as much reason to question the authenticity of the one as of the other. It has recently been stated that this feat of shooting the apple from the head of a living person is not only found in the legendary Danish history of Saxo Grammaticus, but in five or six other Northern legends; nay, that it is common among "the Turks and Mongolian Tartars," and that it is found, chapter and verse, among "the wild Samoyeds." But this seems to me to be proving too much. That the "wild Samoyeds," "the Hottentots of the North," as they are called by Malte Brun, can produce chapter and verse for this or any other legend of the middle ages, is a thing much more easily said than proved; and that the mountaineers of Uri had, either in the fourteenth or fifteenth century (when this legend certainly existed in Switzerland) pushed their antiquarian researches into the Scandinavian Sagas and the chronicles of Saxo Grammaticus, which were not published till the sixteenth century, or the legends of the Mongolian Tartars, is equally questionable. We must, however, pay that respect to honest Saxo, which Tell would not pay Gessler's cap, and respectfully bow to the monkish chronicler, from whom Shakespeare borrowed the outlines of HAMLET! Mythical or historical, Altorf is not the place to question the traditions of Tell. One might as well deny the story of King John at Runnymede, or maintain that Miles Standish is a myth at Plymouth.

A fountain in the market-place of Altorf marks the spot where Tell stood when he shot the apple from his son's head, and it is stated that the linden against which the lad was placed, existed, in a decayed state, till the middle of the seventeenth century. Another fountain has been placed upon the spot where it grew. And now if all this humble prose shall induce the readers of the LEDGER to turn to the third scene of the third act of Schiller's William Tell, in the original if possible, if not in Mr. Brooks' translation, they will not regret the time we have devoted to the topic.

At Altorf we took horses to pass up the valley of the Reuss. The rate of speed promised us may be judged from the fact that our guide accompanied us on foot. Schiller's exquisite drama—a better guide—minutely describes the road. We turned a little out of our way to pass through Bürglen, the village where Tell lived. A chapel occupies the spot on which his house is believed to have stood. A lineal descendant, John Martin Tell, died as late as 1684, and the family became extinct, by the death of a female descendant in 1720. These facts give an air of authenticity to his personal history, which, after all, does not go back beyond the reach of the parish Registers of every part of Europe. Opposite to Bürglen is Attinghausen, the domain of Tell's father-in-law, one of the immortal conspirators of Grütli.

The valley of the Reuss is far more romantic and picturesque than that of the Arve, which is described in the forty-second number of these papers. The chasms through which it passes are narrower, and the precipices along which you wind, at considerable elevation, are of an alarming declivity. At times you enter a chill ravine, with a roaring torrent at the bottom, that fills the air with a powdery spray; while a cold wind drawing down the narrow road-way seems to repel the intruder. In some places the path on the mountain side is shaded by noble fir trees. Where this is the case you see at intervals the furrow of the avalanche, which has ploughed up the growth of centuries. In several places you cross bridges of a single arch, suspended aloft above the torrent. Such is the scene as far as Gœschenen. Here it assumes a wilder character. You are approaching the dividing point of the Alpine waters; those behind you pass off to the Rhine, and you are not far from the Glacier of the Rhone; one system of waters bound to the Mediterranean, the other to the German Ocean! You soon reach the limit of fertility, and rapidly ascending, as you proceed, find yourself in a chasm between two mountain walls of bare, iron-bound rock. The path lies upon the declivity on one side of the chasm. The sun had already sunk behind the summits that surrounded us;—it was bleak and gusty; our guide had stopped to gossip with some *Freyschützen*, at the last village, and left us to find our way alone, through these silent and desolate defiles. Our faithful animals, to whom we gave the reins, found it for us. The only sound heard was the raving torrent and the tramp of the horses on the rock, like that of the Commander's marble foot in *Don Giovanni*. At lengh we reached a gallery of considerable length, in the perpendicular rock, and terminating at the famous *Devil's Bridge*. This was a bridge of a single arch, thrown across the Reuss from wall to wall, at the height of sixty feet from the water. At this ill-named spot, and in the middle of the bridge, we encountered a flock of mountain sheep on their way down the valley. They were alarmed at our horses, which, in their turn, were somewhat startled at the violent rush of the sheep, urged by reckless shepherds and fierce mountain dogs. A good deal of earnestness was manifested, I must confess, on both sides, not to be detruded over the low parapet into the torrent. We passed the bridge in safety, and immediately entered another gallery cut in the solid rock.

The traveller of the present day knows nothing but by tradition of the passage of the ancient *Devil's Bridge* over the Reuss. The modern structure is solid, fenced in by lofty parapets, and approached by a convenient terraced pathway on each side. It is nearer the plunging cataract of the Reuss than the old bridge, but this last is (or was, for I know not if it is still standing) so narrow, its pathway so exposed, and its whole appearance so insecure, that it really seemed unsafe to cross; particularly if you had to force your way on horseback, through a flock of wild sheep, driven forward by clamorous shepherds and their dogs. Our guide informed us that when the army of Suwarrow was pursuing the French in this gorge in 1799, finding the bridge blown up, the Russians made a temporary bridge, over which they crossed, by tying small timbers together with the silken sashes of the officers. The Hand-book says it was not the *Devil's Bridge* that was thus blown up, but a smaller arch over one of the lateral torrents, which is more probable. Alison, however, who rather affects the graphic, represents the *Devil's Bridge* as being blown up, and says that the Russians in their march, "found an impassable gulf two hundred feet deep, surmounted by precipices above a thousand feet high," and swept by a murderous fire from the enemy's artillery.* There is no more frightful chapter in the history of modern warfare than the Campaigns of 1798 and 1799 in Switzerland.

Passing through the gallery I have just mentioned, called the *Hole of Uri* (Urner Loch,) you leave the terrors of the Reuss vale behind. You now enter a smooth, green plateau; encircled, it is true, by rocky walls of great elevation, but placed at a considerable distance, and enclosing, as it were, a secluded garden in these Alpine solitudes. The elevation is about four thousand five hundred feet above the level of the sea; the air was shrewd and piercing;—the aspect wintry.

* Alison, Vol. V. p. 130.

It is traversed by the Reuss and its little tributary the Matt, and lies at the foot of St. Gothard. Thousands of travellers annually pass by this defile into and from Italy, although (in 1818) the road was not carriageable, and mules or litters for the timid furnished the only conveyance. Pursuing this road, (which we did not,) you soon meet a dividing ridge, which sends its waters to the Ticino, and by that channel to the Adriatic. The Head Springs, accordingly, are not very remote, not merely from those of the Rhine and the Rhone, but of the Inn and other tributaries of the Danube; fountains of the waters which that noble river, traversing Würtemberg, Bavaria, Austria, Hungary, Temesvar, and Wallachia, pours into the Black Sea!

At "The Three Kings" of Andermatt, we found as good fare as is to be met in hotels of much higher pretensions, and much nearer the level of the ocean. The mountain trout, fresh from the crystal waters of the Matt, formed the staple of the evening repast; and a genial fire, civil attendance, and clean beds, seemed, in the opinion of the weary travellers, to entitle the quiet Alpine nook to the name which Schiller gives it, "the Vale of Joy."

We started early in the morning for the Valais. It was the day before Michaelmas, which closes the short Alpine summer. June, July, August, and September, the flocks and herds pass on the mountains; at Michaelmas they come down to the meadows and vales. The paths were filled with the animals descending to their long winter quarters; but where they could find pasturage in the wild region above us is a mystery. The vale of Andermatt, otherwise called Urseren, is celebrated for the manufacture of the cheese which bears that name, and is of the quality otherwise called *Zapzeiger*, that is, cheese made from the milk of sheep and goats. At Andermatt travellers who come from Altorf on horses exchange them for mules, as being surer of foot for the somewhat difficult pass of the Furca.

The Furca is a ridge which forms the boundary between the southern extremity of Uri and the Valais. The path is steep and difficult in portions of the way along the very precipitous side of the mountain, in which in some places holes are cut for the feet of the mules. This seems to me the most dangerous pass I had ever crossed in the saddle, and indeed many travellers dismount. I must confess there were many places where I preferred trusting the mule's feet to my own. Our guide cautioned us not to strike our mules, when they halted, before setting their feet in critical places. "They know what they are about," said he, "and do not like to be hurried."

Shortly after turning the summit we came in full view of the glacier of the Rhone, and at length began to pass along its front. It is one of the grandest masses of ice in the Alps. Having seen this noble stream at Lyons and at Geneva, it was with no little interest that we beheld its headwaters bursting from the glacier. We had already stood by the sources of the Arve and Arveiron, and could now claim some acquaintance with the magnificent river which springs from them. Scarcely has it become a currrent from the glacier, when a hundred torrents begin to bound from the mountains, on either side, and it soon swells to a considerable stream, foaming over rocks which obstruct its course, eddying round projecting cliffs, roaring and flashing onward, as if rejoicing to run its race to the ocean.

A distance of six leagues separates the last builidng in Uri from the first in the Valais; the last we left was a chapel, the first we met was even the same; the altar has moved further upward than the *chälet*, into the recesses of these Alpine regions.

We passed through the villages of Oberwald, Obergesteln, Münster, and Viesch, all lying on the Rhone. Before entering the former, the river plunges into a deep, gloomy gorge, not inferior to those on the banks of the Reuss. At Obergesteln, towards the beginning of the last century, eighty persons were overwhelmed at once by an avalanche, and lie buried side by side. The German language, as the names of the villages indicate, still prevails in the upper Valais. It is to this region, that some writers have referred the ridiculous notion that the Goitre is deemed an ornament. We saw some shocking specimens of it in the course of the day. M. Lalande, who had travelled in the Valais, and knew that no such feeling existed there, transplants it to the Tyrol. We passed the night comfortably at Laax.

Resuming our journey in the morning, the Valais opening, and the Rhone increasing in volume as we proceeded, we passed through several villages of which I have retained nothing but the names, and in two or three hours arrived at Brieg. This is the starting point for travellers bound for Italy, who descend as we did from the North, and those from the South, who have occasion to pass the night at the foot of the Simplon, stop at Brieg. The great Simplon road, however, commences not at Brieg, but at a little place called Glys, a few miles below. At Brieg we found our carriage and courier, who had come directly from Geneva, and awaited our arrival from our circuit round the central Alps.

Brieg is a quiet place of less than a thousand inhabitants, lying on a little tributary of the Rhone, which here makes a sudden bend. It is built of a sparkling gneiss, which gives it a bright metallic appearance. It is only, I believe, since the opening of the Simplon road, that it has acquired any notoriety. This magnificent avenue into Italy was constructed by Napoleon the First, in the early years of his accession to power. The expense was divided between France and the Kingdom of Italy. The distance, by the road, from Glys to Domo d'Ossola on the Italian side, is given at fourteen French leagues, and the road was constructed at an expense of twenty-five thousand dollars per mile. This seems to me a very low estimate for a road through such localities. The average inclination of the road is an inch in three feet; its width twenty-six feet, and the height above the sea, at the greatest elevation about six thousand feet. It maintains its moderate and equable grade, by pursuing a very circuitous path, winding round heights, which it could not possibly scale in any other way, and sometimes taking a seemingly retrograde course. It is furnished with culverts, tunnels, bridges, and houses of refuge in great numbers; the engineering is at once audacious and solid; and when I travelled it in 1818, though the mighty genius which had called it into being had passed away, and the two governments immediately connected by it (Switzerland and Sardinia) were not among the wealthy powers, it was in good repair. There are perhaps no monuments of the elder Napoleon which will carry down his name to the grateful recollections of posterity, so effectually as the magnificent roads of Mt. Cenis and the Simplon.

The reader who has done me the favor to accompany me in these rapid and simple sketches, will think I linger in Switzerland. I confess that I quit it with reluctance; it has ever had a peculiar influence for me. The unequalled magnificence and beauty of the scenery in its range from the quietest to the most terrific aspects of nature; the network of lakes; the inaccessible peaks; the travelling mountains of ice; the historic traditions and patriotic memories; the simple manners, free institutions, and peculiar political position of these little republics, furnish much food for contemplation and thought. The glaciers are the central fountains which, through four of her great rivers, refresh half Europe; the mountain fastnesses of Switzerland have, in all ages, been the strong holds of Freedom, and the barrier against Universal monarchy;—and if the Fear of God should ever flee before the corruption of city and plain, it will surely find a temple and an altar in the glorious Alps.

NUMBER FIFTY-TWO.

DANIEL BOON.

The "West" suggestive of important subjects of thought—Progress of settlement in South and North America—Conditions of life on the gradually receding frontier—Sergeant Plympton's fate in 1677—Daniel Boon the great Pioneer—His life by Mr. W. H. Bogart—Account of his family, parentage, and birth—Removal to North Carolina and settlement on the Yadkin—Marries Rebecca Bryan—Mission of the Anglo-Saxon race in America—Boon with five companions starts in quest of Kentucky in 1769—First sight of—Captured by the Indians—Escape—Meets his brother Squire—Squire Boon's return to the settlement for supplies—They both go back to North Carolina, and Daniel determines on a permanent removal to Kentucky.

It has ever seemed to me that "the West" furnishes to the American citizen some of the highest subjects for thought which can engage his attention. They multiply and increase in importance as we reflect upon it. The earth which we inhabit was destined by the Creator to be the abode of rational beings; and the manner in which the family of Man has become possessed of its heritage is one of the most curious and instructive topics of historical inquiry. As it respects what we call the *Old World*—the united continents of Europe, Asia, and Africa—the gradual steps of this process are lost in the remoteness of Antiquity. The concurrent testimony of Scripture, Tradition, and Language point to Asia as the cradle of the race, but they throw scarce a ray of light on the dispersion of mankind to the four quarters of the globe.

On this continent the case is different. It is true that of the original peopling of America History teaches nothing; but the disclosure of the Western Continent to the Eastern world, and the steps by which the civilized races of Europe have established themselves in the new-found hemisphere, are of comparatively recent occurrence, and within the domain of authentic history. Some of the most important steps in the great movement have been taken within the lifetime of men now in existence.

After the discovery of America by Columbus, the occupation of the portion claimed by Spain and Portugal commenced almost immediately, and was permanently completed by the end of the sixteenth century. Besides the political influence upon the European system of these vast transatlantic colonies, and the new direction given by them to the commerce of the world, the influx of gold and silver revolutionized the monetary relations of Europe.—Meantime, the American Continent North of Mexico lay neglected. With the early years of the seventeenth century, the foundation of the Anglo-American colonies was laid; but barren as they were of the tropical fruits and the precious metals, their progress was not hastened by those keener stimulants. It advanced in the slower march of Agriculture, and under the influence of the moral sentiments, which sent the Cavaliers to Virginia, the Puritans to New England, and the Quakers to Pennsylvania. In addition to this, their progress was obstructed by the conflicting claims of France and England, combined with the geographical features of the country—a ridge of mountains rising in the rear of the Anglo-American settlements, and beyond them a chain of noble rivers and lakes—the mighty entrenchments—Nature's gigantic fosse and mound—which seemed to confine the English settlements to a strip along the coast. By these causes, and mainly by the political relations of France and England, the advance of civilization beyond the Appalachian mountains was retarded for a century. With every rupture between the leading powers of Europe the flames of savage warfare were kindled by the French along the frontier—from Canada to the farthest English settlements in the South.

This frontier receded slowly to the westward, as the settlements were pushed onward; but the Connecticut River was infested by parties of French and Indians as late as 1755; powerful tribes of savages existed in the State of New York in the American Revolution; the first white settler entered Kentucky ninety years ago; the power of the Aborigines in Ohio was not finally broken till the year 1794; nor in the States farther West till the war of 1812. The western part of Georgia and the States of Alabama and Mississippi were opened to civilization by the campaign of General Jackson in 1818; and the warlike races on the upper Mississippi occupied that region till Black Hawk's war in 1833.

In this way that conflict has taken place, in part within our own time and beneath our own eyes, between a civilized and a barbarous race, which took place in the west of Europe in the days of Julius Cæsar. Its recurrence whenever the two are brought into contact, is one of the saddest mysteries of our Nature.

In the progress of this conflict, commencing with the first settlement of the country, many most interesting and romantic occurrences, as I have observed in a former Number of these papers, have taken place, and many original and strongly-marked characters have been formed. The conditions of life on the frontier, and in the territory beyond the frontier, whether in peace (if peace ever existed on the frontier) or in the warfare with the native tribes, are so utterly remote from those of civilized life, that in the older settlements we probably form a very faint idea of the new influences, under which men live and act who lead the advancing column into the wilderness. We everywhere find, however, that there was a spirit of adventure, an endurance, an alertness, a fertility of resource, a courage, in a word a heroism, on the part of men and women, equal to the circumstances in which they were placed. The fields were tilled as industriously, when the farmer had to carry his musket along with the implements of husbandry, as they are now in the safe neighborhood of our great cities. Men went to the log-church on the frontier, whose crannies admitted the drifting snow, though they were obliged to go armed, as regularly as they now roll in luxurious chariots to carpeted temples in fashionable squares. The wave of settlement swelled steadily up to the frontier, though the pioneer was subject to the risk of Indian captivity, and death in its direst forms. From a narrative, recently reprinted by the Bradford Society at New York, of the surprise of a party working in the fields at Hatfield, in 1677, it appears that one of the poor creatures captured was, for no visible cause but that of savage caprice, burned alive in the neighborhood of Chambly. Horrors like this were perpetrated in Ohio, as late, if I mistake not, as 1789.

Of all the pioneers of civilization in this country, no one name stands out so prominently and distinctly as that of Daniel Boon. The contemporary records of his adventures are imperfect, and his autobiographical recollections are strangely travestied in the inflated style of Filson, to whom he narrated them. Still the tale of his wanderings has upon the whole been well preserved; and satisfactory accounts of his remarkable career have been given to the public. The most recent of these is Mr. W. H. Bogart's interesting work, entitled, "Daniel Boon and the Hunters of Kentucky." He modestly calls it a compilation, and makes ample acknowledgment of the aid derived from his predecessors. But the materials drawn from them are skilfully combined by Mr. Bogart with his own reflections, and the whole wrought into a volume, which when once commenced, will not willingly be laid down by the reader, till it is finished.

Daniel Boon's grandfather, George, emigrated from Devonshire in 1717, with nine sons and ten daughters, and settled in Berks County, Pennsylvania. He felt, no doubt, that the almost boundless colonial territory of England was the true place to bring forward a family of nineteen children. He took up wild lands not only in the neighborhood of his settlement in Pennsylvania, but in Maryland and Virginia. One of his sons bore the absurd but common name of Squire, and *his* son, Daniel, the pioneer, the fourth of a large family, was born in Bristol, on the Delaware, about twenty miles from Philadelphia, on the 11th of February, 1735. Three years afterwards his father removed to Reading (Pa.,) then a frontier settlement, and there Daniel grew up amidst the scenes of border life and the traditions of Indian warfare. Whether the family were of the Episcopal church or the Society of Friends, has been so skilfully contested, that Mr. Bogart pronounces it "most difficult to decide" the question. Daniel, at any rate, belonged to the austere communion of those who love to worship in the solemn aisles of cathedral woods and at the trickling fountains of mighty streams. In boyhood he left his father's home, and built him a hunting cabin in the forest.

One would have thought that there was room enough in Pennsylvania, at that time, even for families whose sons and daughters were counted by the score. But it was the "Mission" of the age to push onward to the West. Sydney Smith says that it is the calling of the Anglo-Saxon race to spin and weave cotton. It may be so in the crowded lanes of Manchester and Birmingham. On this side of the ocean, its vocation is to subdue the wilderness and found States; to draw out the living threads of civilization across the boundless prairie, and in the mystic words of Goëthe, to weave the fortunes of Empires yet to be, in the sounding loom of the Ages.

Squire Boon, the father of Daniel, emigrated in 1753 to the mountain region of North Carolina. This was the memorable year in which George Washington, by three years the senior of Daniel Boon, made his commencement of active public life, in the arduous journey to the French fort of Venango.

The Boons settled on the Yadkin, in the immediate neighborhood of one of the most powerful tribes of Indians, the Cherokees, on the borders of the primeval forest. Here Daniel married Rebecca Bryan. The legend tells that, mistaking her bright eyes for those of a deer, he had nearly shot her in the thicket. Historical accuracy repudiates the romance; there were no shots exchanged between them but those which darted from Rebecca's eyes, and which healed their own wounds. The first place of settlement on the Yadkin did not satisfy the instinct which was driving Daniel westward, and he moved with his bride further up the valley.

Here, to all appearance, Boon passed about sixteen years in the rough, healthful, and somewhat perilous life of the frontier. Nine of them were years of war, for two years of conflict on the American frontier were added to the Seven years war of Europe. Of this part of his life little seems to be known, but passed as it was in the immediate neighborhood of the Cherokees, it must have been, especially during the war, a period of exposure as well as hardship. But both were wanted as a preparation for the great career of his life.

John Findlay or Finley—first of civilized men—had, as early as 1764, with a small party, penetrated through the Northeastern portion of Tennessee to the banks of the Kentucky river, and brought back glowing accounts of the beauty of the country and the abundance of the game. This touched a sympathetic chord in Boon's bosom, and with five companions, of whom Finley was one, on the 1st May, 1769, "I resigned," says Boon, in the language of Filson, "my domestic happiness for a time, and left my family and peaceable habitation on the Yadkin river, in North Carolina, to wander through the wilderness of America, in quest of the country of Kentucky." Daniel Boon started *in quest of the country of Kentucky*, in the year in which Humboldt, Napoleon, and Wellington were born. Humboldt died last year, and Kentucky, with a population of 1,200,000, is now sending ten members to the Congress of United States, and boasts her statesmen, orators, and jurists among the brightest names of America!

There are no more delightful pages of modern history, than those in which Mr. Bancroft has described this first expedition of Daniel Boon and his companions.* On May-day morning, 1769, they started, these six bold men,—and one of them a hero,—to find Kentucky. They had not far to seek; it lay before them, but the Cumberland mountain rose between; and it was not till the 7th of June that they reached the summit of an eminence on the Red River, and looked down "with pleasure on the beautiful level of Kentucky." John Finley knew the spot; he had traded there with the Indians, years before. Here they encamped and "made a shelter to defend them from the elements." From this they reconnoitred the country and followed the chase. "Everywhere," (says Boon, though unfortunately it is John Filson who holds the pen,) "we found abundance of wild beasts of all sorts, through this vast forest. The buffaloes were more frequent than I have seen cattle in the settlements, browsing on the leaves of the cane or cropping the herbage on those extensive plains, fearless, because ignorant, of the violence of man. Sometimes we saw hundreds in a drove, and the numbers about the Salt Springs was amazing."

And so they roved and hunted through a long Kentucky summer and autumn, till the 22d of December, an eventful day, in all coming time, for the descendants of the Pilgrim Fathers, and in that particular year for Daniel Boon and his companions. On the 22d of December, 1769, "John Stewart and I had a pleasing ramble, but fortune changed the scene, in the close of it." Here John Filson sews on a patch of rather unseasonable rhetoric upon the homely frieze of Boon's narrative. He will have it that they "passed through a great forest, in which stood myriads of

* Bancroft's United States. Vol. VI., p. 298.

trees, some gay with blossoms, [22d December,] others rich with fruits. Nature was here a series of wonders and a fund of delights. Here she displayed her ingenuity and industry in a variety of flowers and fruits beautifully colored, elegantly shaped, and charmingly flavored, [oh! John, you know they found nothing richer than a frost-bitten persimmon,] and we were diverted with innumerable animals presenting themselves perpetually to our view." And now for the catastrophe so artistically preluded: "In the decline of the day, near Kentucky River, as we ascended the brow of a small hill, a number of Indians rushed out of a thick canebrake upon us and made us prisoners. The time of our sorrow was now arrived, and the scene fully opened. The Indians plundered us of what we had, and kept us in confinement seven days, treating us with common savage usage."

Boon and his companions with infinite tact and discretion, resigned themselves in appearance to their fate, and made no attempt to escape. Their captors were thrown off their guard by their seeming indifference. At length, in the night, and while the Indians slept, they slipped the cords which bound them; regained their muskets, and crept undiscovered away. They returned to their old encampment; it was broken up, and their four companions gone;—never to be heard of more on earth. Thus left alone in the wilderness, hundreds of miles from kindred and friends, their hearts were soon gladdened by the arrival of Squire Boon, Daniel's brother, and a nameless companion, who had come to join company with the pioneers. They replaced for a while the missing four; but "John Stewart was soon killed by the savages," and the man who came with Squire Boon went home to the pleasant banks of the Yadkin. Daniel and his brother were left alone, "not a white man in Kentucky but themselves." Thus situated," says Boon, "many hundred miles from our families, in the howling wilderness, I believe few would have equally enjoyed the happiness we experienced. I often observed to my brother, you see how little Nature requires to be satisfied ! "

The season wore on ; " they hunted every day, and prepared a little cottage to defend them from the wintry storms." They remained undisturbed till the Spring ; and then, when the buds of the hickory swelled to the size of a mouse's ear ; when the blue grass carpeted the native lawns ; when the cane shot up like mammoth asparagus ; and the brooks let loose from their icy chains, and swelled by April showers, began to prattle through the meadows ; and the flowering dog-wood whitened the thickets ; and the chattering magpie, the robin, and the red-bird, filled them with life and music, Daniel's brother returned to North Carolina for supplies, and the Pioneer remained alone in Kentucky, " without bread, salt, or sugar, without company of my fellow-creatures, without even a horse or a dog : "—all alone, but in the best of company—a good conscience, a bold heart, and the Blessing of Heaven.

In three months brother Squire returned with supplies ; they hunted together another Autumn and another Winter, and in the Spring of 1771 went back to their families on the Yadkin, determined, as soon as possible, to leave the older settlements, and make a final remove to Kentucky " which," says Boon, " I esteemed a second paradise."

And here, though at the threshold of his adventures, his perils, his toils, and his achievements, we must part from the noble Pioneer. The tale of his subsequent migrations ;—of his establishment, rather say his encampment in Kentucky ; —his block-house warfare ;—his captivity among the savages ; —his escape ;—the fierce Indian wars ;—the growth of the settlements, and the crowding of the population ;—the trials and troubles of advancing age ;—his removal to Missouri ;— and the closing scene ;—these all related with accuracy and spirit from authentic resources, may be found in the volume of Mr. Bogart.

NUMBER FIFTY-THREE,

AND THE LAST OF THE SERIES.

THE NEW YORK LEDGER.

Description of the Ledger establishment—Common printing—The power press—The Electrotype process—Press work—Distribution of the paper—Eighty thousand by mail—Ross & Tousey's news agency—"Ledger day" described—Immense amount of Printing annually done in the "Ledger" office—Convention for international copyright—Mode in which the establishment has been built up and general character and objects—The "Unknown Public"—Conclusion of the Mount Vernon Papers.

Having occasion lately to pass a few days in New York, I availed myself of the polite invitation of the Proprietor and Editor of "the Ledger" to visit his establishment. As I had kept close company with "the Ledger" for the last twelve months, during which, with a party of about a million of readers, we have, besides shorter excursions in the neigborhood, performed together three hundred and sixty-five journeys of twenty-four thousand miles each, and, at the same time, one of five hundred millions of miles in circuit, I felt a natural curiosity to examine a little more particularly the extent and organization of the concern.

Most of my readers, I suppose, have some knowledge of the art of printing as commonly practised. They understand that the letters of the alphabet, at the end of small pieces of metal called types, are arranged for use in little square boxes, on a slanting desk, and that a workman called a "Compositor," having before him the writing which is to be printed, picks up these types, letter by letter, and places them in a frame, called a composing-stick, till he has got a line. A second line is formed the same way, and so on till he has set up enough for a page of a book, or a column of a newspaper. When pages enough to form a sheet, or columns enough to form two sides of a newspaper, have been thus set up, and secured in their places by an iron frame, they are put on a broad stone, and are ready to pass through the press to be printed on paper, moistened and applied to the face of the types for that purpose. Some attempts have been made to set up types by machinery, contrived like the keys of a piano-forte, but nothing of this kind, as far as I am aware, has been introduced into newspaper offices. As far as we have now gone, and in this part of the work, there is nothing particular in the " Ledger " printing office. As one paper only a week is printed, the force employed in this department is, of course, less than in offices where a paper is to be published every day. It may be remarked, however, that in addition to the persons employed in setting up the types, a considerable number find constant occupation in designing and engraving the illustrations; an entirely separate branch of the art, for which in the daily journals there is no occasion.

Thus far, then, every thing is done by hand. At this stage of the work a piece of machinery contrived about thirty years ago, and a chemical process of still more recent invention are introduced to accelerate the printing of papers of extensive circulation. The machinery to which I allude, is the power press; the chemical operation is the process of electrotyping. Till about thirty years ago, printing presses were wrought exclusively by hand, and the operation was one requiring great endurance and strength, on the part of an able-bodied man. Presses of this kind have been superseded, except in small establishments, by presses moved by steam, heated air, or water power. These presses are of various construction and efficiency; the most celebrated being those of our countryman Hoe at New York, of which also there are different kinds; some called the "lightning presses," used in the offices of the great daily journals, where the utmost speed is necessary, and others of which the execution is less rapid, and which for that reason admit of greater precision and finish in the work. The "Ledger" is printed on presses of this description, of which ten are kept constantly at work twenty-three hours out of the twenty-four, in printing each number of the "Ledger." In other words, so large is the number of the weekly issue, that it becomes necessary to print at the same time five editions of the paper.

And how are these five editions got ready for the press? Are the types set up that number of times? Such would have been the case some years ago, if papers of such vast circulation had existed, but by the process of electrotyping this labor is saved. This is a process, by which an exact copy of the page of types can be taken in copper, that being the metal used by printers; though silver and gold are electrotyped in the fine arts, for expensive works of taste and luxury. In electrotyping for the printing office, an impression in wax is taken of the page of types, which is to be multiplied. This waxen plate is immersed for twelve hours in a solution of copper in a galvanic trough. At the end of this time, the face of the waxen page is covered with a thin coating of copper. The wax is then removed by hot water, and melted type metal poured upon the copper net work. The back of the type metal is then smoothed off, and the electrotype plate is ready for use. This operation is repeated as many times as is required to furnish plates for all the presses; and as many persons are employed in electrotyping as in setting the types. From this statement the reader perceives, that every page of "the Ledger," to which he looks for his weekly comfort and delight, has, between the pen of the writer and the eye of the reader, passed through four states, and existed in four different forms and substances, viz.: the first setting in type, the waxen impression, the electrotyped copper and the printed paper. How much science, art, and mechanical dexterity are developed in these several operations!

Now, gentle reader, if you will take your Ledger, before it is cut, and unfold it, you will find that it is printed on one large sheet, and that pages 1, 4, 5, and 8 are on one side of the sheet, and pages 2, 3, 6, and 7 on the other. This you will think an odd arrangement; but when the sheet is folded you see it comes right, and the pages follow in proper order. These eight pages are made up for the Press in two "forms," of four pages each, which are separately printed, so that each sheet has to pass through the press twice. Great care is required in printing the second side of the paper, to lay the sheet in the right place, so that the two sides of the paper shall exactly match. In the "lightning presses," in consequence of the rapidity with which they are worked, this point, which is of great importance, if the papers are to be bound in a volume, is apt to be neglected. But I never saw "bad register," as this defect is called, in a sheet of the "Ledger." When the electrotype plates are ready, those of pages 1, 4, 5, and 8 are placed together ("locked up") in one form, and pages 2, 3, 6, and 7 in another, and they are now ready to be put to press.

It would be in vain to attempt to describe a power press. In order to understand its construction and operation, you must go and see it. According to their construction, they throw off from 500 to 20,000 sheets in one hour. Mr. Bonner has eight power presses constantly at work, and about forty-five persons are employed in his press-room, whose aggregate wages are four hundred dollars per week. Besides this, he pays about two hundred dollars per week for printing, which he is unable to do on his own presses. A good deal of this outside work is in printing back numbers of the "Ledger;"

for it is perhaps peculiar to this journal that there is a large and steady demand for back numbers.

When both sides of the paper have passed through the press, that Number of the "Ledger" is printed. To bring about this result, it has required from eight to nine hundred reams of paper every week, at a cost probably of six and a half dollars per ream, for you observe "the Ledger" is printed on very handsome paper. If six and a half dollars a ream be assumed as the average cost of the paper, the amount for eight hundred and fifty reams per week will not fall much short of three hundred thousand dollars per annum.

The journal thus printed, to the number of about Four Hundred Thousand copies, is to be distributed about the Union. How is this effected? The main supply of the country is through the medium of news-agents, and large dealers, in all the principal cities, towns, and considerable villages of the United States. These receive the paper from New York in large packages, as will presently be stated, and furnish it in detail to their customers. But beyond the reach of the news-agents, there are a multitude of persons, readers of the "Ledger," scattered over the country; who, not having any wholesale dealer in their neighbourhood, address themselves by letter to the proprietor in New York, and receive their papers by mail. About twenty-five clerks and folders are employed in the office in Ann Street in folding and mailing papers for this class of subscribers, to the number of Eighty thousand!

But the principal distribution of the paper takes place at the news agency of Messrs. Ross & Tousey in Nassau Street, who purchase weekly of the Proprietor above Three Hundred Thousand of the paper, which they furnish to all parts of the country in large parcels, by Express and Mail, to the wholesale dealers in the city of New York, and in every part of the Union, and to the news-venders for the retail circulation of the city and neighborhood. Messrs. Ross & Tousey deal extensively in Periodicals and weekly journals. They distribute from their office eight hundred thousand papers weekly, the "Ledger" forming nearly one-half of their business, which within four or five years has risen from one hundred and twenty-five thousand dollars to one million dollars' worth annually, principally of periodicals and literary Papers.

Their office and the streets on which it stands, Nassau street in the front and Theatre alley in the rear, exhibit on "Ledger-day,"—Monday of each week,—a most extraordinary scene. Every square foot of open space in the office has been filled up with piles of the "Ledger,"—fifty copies in a pile. Large bundles, some of them containing a couple of hundred, have been put up in wrapping paper, addressed to wholesale dealers, and to be despatched by Mail and Express all over the country. These are placed for momentary deposit, in a basement room in the rear of Messrs. Ross & Tousey's premises. The rest of the mighty edition, laid in piles, fills the counters and shelves in the central and front portions of the office, the counting-room, and the basement, wherever there is room for a pile of the paper.

Twelve o'clock on Monday is the appointed hour. As it approaches, carts and drays assemble in Nassau street and Theatre alley to receive the larger parcels; the front of the office is filled with clamorous newsboys, crowding the space around the counter three deep, eager to get their supply for the streets, the Railway Stations, and the Steamers, while the draymen and porters, in quest of the larger parcels, gather in the rear. The entire force of Messrs. Ross & Tousey is put in requisition to wait upon the newsboys. In the rear the clerks, porters, and draymen are allowed to come in and help themselves. At the last stroke of twelve upon the clock, the rush begins and the scene is, for a short time, one of great activity and bustle. These hundreds of thousands of Ledgers are seen moving off on the shoulders of porters, and in the hands of newsboys, in drays and carts, in every direction;

but twenty minutes is enough for the work, and by that time the throng is dispersed, and the ubiquitous journal is on its way to the remotest corners of the land.

This strange scene is not confined to the premises of Messrs. Ross & Tousey. The persons mentioned as assembling in the rear of their warehouse are the clerks and salesmen of other wholesale news-agents who come to get a supply for their customers; often a very large one. The House of Dexter & Company take thirty-three thousand, and that of Hendrickson & Co., nineteen thousand. The larger part of this supply is for country custom, the residue for the city. There are seven or eight of these large dealers in the city of New York, and in their offices on "Ledger-day," the same crowd of newsboys takes place, a half an hour later, as that which we have just witnessed in the front part of Messrs. Ross & Tousey's establishment.

Perhaps, reader, you were not before aware of the extent of the system to which you are indebted for the punctual and nearly simultaneous supply of the "Ledger" throughout the country, and to which you owe so much of your weekly amusement and instruction. You have not probably reflected, that hundreds, perhaps it would not be an exaggeration to say thousands, of persons are directly or indirectly employed and supported, in order to bring you the welcome sheet, at the appointed hour, to your door. There are, on the lowest calculation, above three thousand shops, *depôts*, and news-stands, in the United States for the sale of newspapers and periodicals. As each copy of "the Ledger" for one year forms a folio volume of four hundred and sixteen pages, the quantity of printing annually executed on Mr. Bonner's presses, (without taking the reprint of back numbers into the account,) is of course four hundred thousand folio volumes of that thickness; being about four times, I suppose, the number of the volumes in that noble library, which forms such an imperishable monument to the name of Astor. If, as is probably the case, not more than a fourth part of the volumes in that magnificent collection are folios, and the other three-fourths volumes of a smaller size,—quartos, octavos, and duodecimos,—then the quantity of printing done in the "Ledger," office in the course of a single year, being equivalent to sixteen hundred thousand octavo volumes, will exceed ten or twelve times the amount of printing contained in the books of the Astor Library. As very many of the papers are taken by reading clubs, consisting of several persons, and the "Ledger," is eminently a paper for Family use, it does not seem extravagant to assume, that each paper is on an average habitually read by four individuals; and consequently, that the whole issue is read by twelve or fifteen hundred thousand persons!

When a convention for international copyright between this country and Great Britain was negotiated a few years ago, while I was in the Department of State, a great alarm was raised against it, as if it was going almost to put an end to the printing business in the United States. Petitions against its confirmation poured into the Senate, signed not merely by publishers engaged in reprinting English works, but by type-founders, paper makers, and every other class of persons however remotely connected with the art of printing. Now not to mention that the Convention did not apply to the great mass of Standard English literature, but only to a few modern copyrighted works, I satisfied myself that any one of the great New York *Dailies*,—and as we have seen the same is true of the New York "Ledger,"—gives a greater amount of employment to all the trades and handicrafts connected with printing, (with the exception of book-binding,) than is given by the entire reprint of English copy-righted publications; for no one, I presume, would think of rating it as high as sixteen hundred thousand octavo volumes annually.

But to return to the New York "Ledger," this vast concern has been built up, within a very few years, by the untiring industry, tact, energy, and good sense of one self-made man, entering upon the business with no advantages of education but those of a common school, without capital, without powerful friends, and without resorting to the ordinary means of gaining public favor and securing lucrative patronage. The "Ledger," has not been the mouth-piece of any party, religious, political, or sectional; it has not been a *news*-paper, nor a commercial paper; it has not inserted advertisements, nor reported Buncombe speeches; it has retained no "correspondent," in other cities to transmit to New York libels, that would be rejected with scorn by all decent journals in the places where they are written; and has admitted no police reports, personal scandal, or pungent criticisms, as they are called, on the literature of the day. It has simply aimed to be an entertaining and instructive Family newspaper, designed, in the first instance, to meet the wants of what is called, in a very sensible and striking paper in Dickens' Household Words, for the 21st of August, 1858, the "Unknown Public." The New York "Ledger," is the first attempt in this country, on a large scale, to address *that* public; and the brilliant success, which has attended it thus far, is a strong confirmation of the truth of the closing observation in the remarkable article alluded to, that the time is coming when "the readers, who rank by millions, will be the readers who give the widest reputations, who return the richest rewards, and who will therefore command the services of the best writers of the time." The author of the article in question, probably Mr. Dickens himself, adds, "to the penny journals of the present times belongs the credit of having discovered '*a new Public.*'" To that credit in this country, the Editor and Proprietor of the New York "Ledger" is richly entitled. Not only so, but he has taken a step—and that a very important one—beyond the papers published for the "Unknown Public" in

England. Without at all neglecting the claims of the masses of the community, he is steadily adapting the "Ledger" to the tastes of a more critical and fastidious class of readers. It may be mentioned as the most extraordinary, the most creditable, and as an example to others, the most salutary feature of Mr. Bonner's course, that in the entire progress of this great enterprize and in its present management, he has never signed nor endorsed a note of hand, nor borrowed a dollar; and that in every part of his immense establishment SUNDAY IS A DAY OF REST. I think it due to him, in closing this account of his operations, to say, that it has not been drawn up by me at his request or suggestion; and that his first knowledge that I had any thought of preparing it was derived from my letter of inquiry, asking information as to some facts known only to himself.

In bringing the series of the "Mount Vernon Papers" to a close, as I do with the present Number, I beg leave to return my thanks to the readers of the "Ledger," for the favor with which they have been received. I cannot deny that I entered into the engagement to write them, with great misgivings. I recoiled from the task of furnishing a weekly paper (to be read by a million of my countrymen), amidst incessant interruptions of every kind, under the pressure of other onerous duties, of a heavy correspondence, of public engagements requiring frequent journeys, a part of the time with indifferent health, and in other circumstances, which wholly unfit the mind for cheerful exertion. But I could not resist the temptation to add the great sum of Ten Thousand Dollars, so liberally offered by Mr. Bonner, to the Mount Vernon Fund; and the favor of the multitudinous readers of the "Ledger," of which I have received the most gratifying assurances from all parts of the country, has long since relieved my anxiety, and turned the task into a relaxation and a pleasure. Though not sorry to be released from the responsibility of a weekly contribution, I cannot say that I terminate the series of the "Mount Vernon Papers" without regret, and I shall gladly avail myself of the opportunity, which Mr. Bonner's invitation affords me, of occasionally renewing my communications with the readers of the "Ledger."

EXITUS ACTA PROBAT.

APPENDIX TO PAGE 10.

In pursuance of the suggestion at the close of the first Number of the foregoing series, many contributions to the fund for the purchase of Mount Vernon were remitted to the subscriber, to the amount in the whole of THREE THOUSAND NINE HUNDRED AND ONE DOLLARS. Of this amount, five hundred and twenty-five dollars were in sums of one dollar, and less; the residue in larger amounts, among which was the generous donation of five hundred dollars, from Messrs. Pettengill & Co., of New York. The first subscription received was one of ten dollars, from Mr. N. D. Sawin, of Cambridge (Mass.), which was sent in a few moments after the NEW YORK LEDGER, containing the first Number of the Mount Vernon Papers, was published in Boston. Very liberal donations were received from several Military Companies, Masonic and Odd Fellows' Lodges, Engine and Hook and Ladder Companies, and Schools. To each person, whose name was transmitted as a contributor, a receipt, handsomely engraved, and signed by the President and Treasurer of the Auxiliary Mount Vernon Fund, was returned. A complete list of all the donations of one dollar and upward, with the names of each contributor, is in preparation, to be furnished for publication in the Mount Vernon Record; every person contributing to the fund not less than a dollar, being constitutionally a member of the "Ladies' Mount Vernon Association for the Union."

The subscriber will still be happy to receive contributions to the Mount Vernon Fund. Although the amount necessary to effect the purchase of the estate has been raised, a large sum is still needed for repairs, and for the restoration of the house and grounds, as far as practicable, to their condition in 1800, as well as to form a fund for their future preservation and care.

EDWARD EVERETT.

BOSTON, *May*, 1860.

www.ingramcontent.com/pod-product-compliance
Lightning Source LLC
LaVergne TN
LVHW021317110826
845150LV00003B/599